INDUSTRIAL
ORGANIZATION
AND
ANTITRUST POLICY

INDUSTRIAL ORGANIZATION AND ANTITRUST POLICY

Revised Edition

PETER ASCH

JOHN WILEY & SONS
New York   Chichester   Brisbane   Toronto   Singapore

Library of Congress Cataloging in Publication Data:

Asch, Peter.
   Industrial organization and antitrust policy.

   Rev. ed. of: Economic theory and the antitrust
dilemma. 1970.
   Includes bibliographical references and indexes.
   1. Trusts, Industrial—United States. 2. Industry and
state—United States. 3. Industrial concentration—United
States. 4. Industrial organization (Economic theory)
I. Title.
HD2795.A82   1983   338.8′0973   82-20012
ISBN 0-471-09762-4
Printed in the United States of America

10   9   8   7   6   5   4   3   2   1

For My Mother and Father

Preface

Since this book was first published, as *Economic Theory and the Antitrust Dilemma* in 1970, some substantial changes in pertinent areas of both economics and law have occurred. During the past decade there has been a significant expansion of the empirical evidence bearing on the organization, conduct, and performance of firms and markets. Not only the quantity of this evidence but also its quality have enabled economists to understand better a number of relationships that carry important public policy implications.

Legal developments in antitrust during the same period have been uneven, but their cumulative effect is substantial and suggests that business managers are subject to somewhat different "rules of the game" than they were just a few years ago. During the decade of the 1970s there have occurred also some changes in government enforcement activities and apparently in national opinion about the proper role of public regulatory programs.

This edition reflects these changes, primarily through a revised and somewhat expanded discussion of empirical evidence, and a thorough updating of legal case doctrine. In revising this book, all of my old debts remain intact, and new ones have been incurred. I have benefited from the comments of Roger D. Blair, Robert J. Carbaugh, Robert M. Feinberg, Albert N. Link, James W. McKie, David Sappington, Edward L. Sattler, Lawrence J. White, and many students past and present. In addition, I owe a special debt to Malcolm R. Burns for a painstaking and perceptive critique of the entire manuscript and to Rosalind S. Seneca for pointing out to me numerous ways of improving both the substance and exposition of the original version. The usual disclaimer, however, applies most emphatically. All the shortcomings of this edition are my own doing, and have emerged in most instances over the strenuous objections of the persons named.

Peter Asch

October 1982

Preface to the First Edition

Economists are sometimes a critical, even cantankerous, lot. We are especially prone to complain about public policies formulated in ignorance of the lessons of economic analysis or, worse yet, based in ''bad'' economics. Antitrust policy has thus been forced to compete with other areas for its share of criticism, but, all things considered, it has more than held its own.

The main purpose of this book, of course, is not to complain. Instead, it is to survey and analyze the important issues in American antitrust from an economic viewpoint. Antitrust decisions invariably affect the structure and behavior of firms and industries, and rational decision processes must take account of these influences. It is here that economic analysis can prove most useful.

The precise role of economics in antitrust is often misunderstood. Consider the case of huge corporations in the United States. These firms, by their very existence, enrage some and enchant others. There is no objective way to determine who is right or wrong—if, indeed, these words have meaning here. Yet there is a good deal of pertinent information to be had. The enraged should know, for example, that big companies may contribute significantly to our national output and living standards; and the enchanted should know, for example, that there is a sense in which large and powerful concerns may adversely affect society's welfare. Both costs and benefits are associated with large firms (or with the absence of such firms). Economics, as such, *cannot* define the socially appropriate level of firm size, because it cannot tell us what we *ought* to desire. It *can,* however, help to define the costs and benefits associated with policy decisions that affect size. What we, collectively, do with this information depends on the results we want. But the information itself is vitally important. Without it, neither the enraged nor the enchanted can hope to reach judgments that are rational from their own point of view.

The purpose of this book, then, is not merely to ''cover'' antitrust materials, but to indicate something about the potential and actual contribution of economic analysis to policy formulation. The organization of the book reflects my own biases. I do not believe that any sensible discussion of antitrust can proceed without some knowledge of relevant economic theory and measurement. These topics thus receive substantial attention, although in retrospect it appears that they might have been pursued even further. I hope that this book will be useful not only to students in courses dealing with antitrust but also to those individuals (policymakers included) who have a general interest in the area. The theoretical and empirical sections assume relatively little background on the part of the reader. Although some previous exposure to microeconomic theory is helpful, it is not absolutely necessary.

Like most writers, I owe a very large debt to others. I have benefited immeasurably from a critique of an earlier draft by Franklin M. Fisher, and from many acute criticisms by Burton G. Malkiel, Matityahu Marcus, Jesse W. Markham, David McFarland, R. W. Pfouts, Richard E. Quandt, and Joseph J. Seneca. And also I have been greatly helped on a number of specific points by the comments of Gary W. Bowman, John F. Graybeal, and Stanley H. Masters. Any weaknesses in the book remain despite the best efforts of these individuals. Sometimes an author just cannot be saved from himself.

I am most grateful to Mrs. Geraldine Dructor, who typed successive drafts of the manuscript with care and skill, and to the Rutgers University Research Council for generous financial support.

Finally, I owe a real debt to my family. My wife Rita not only provided the necessary moral support but helped with the thankless tasks of reading and editing the final manuscript. My children, Eric and David, are also to be thanked and congratulated for tolerating the past months cheerfully, if not silently.

Rutgers College   P. A.
1970

Contents

INTRODUCTION

The antitrust laws of the United States encompass a large, and sometimes bewildering, group of provisions designed to encourage competition. The rationale for these laws is complex, involving social and political as well as economic motives. But it is clear from the written record that the presumption in favor of competition—both within economics and without—is deeply ingrained in American life. A free society tends to distrust concentrations of power, whether private or public; and competition, although subject to varying definitions, often is associated with the absence of dominance by one or a few interests.

Anyone taking even a superficial glance at our modern economy may be struck by an apparent gap between the competitiveness that we advocate and the centralization of power that we tolerate. Most corporate wealth and income is accounted for by the 200 largest firms. Many of our major markets are dominated by a few large companies,[1] and the growth of major conglomerate enterprises whose activities span many industries has been dramatic.

No reasonable observer, however, could term the American economy "monopolistic." With a very few exceptions,[2] markets are characterized by some meaningful competition. Virtually no corporation seeking to sell its goods has the luxury of ignoring rivals, actual and potential. Our largest firms are indeed powerful in traditional economic terms, but whether they are **secure** in their power is quite a different question.

Such observations raise the fundamental questions about our economic system and the priorities of society. How strong is our commitment to competition? Does the existing concentration of economic power imply that the antitrust laws have failed in their stated purpose? Is the absence of "true" monopoly an indicator of success? Or is the notion of competition itself ambiguous, defined by individuals in different ways? These are some of the general questions to which this book is addressed.

---

[1] This is especially true in the manufacturing sector. In such important markets as automobiles, computers, cigarettes, detergents, and most primary and fabricated metal products, the four largest firms account for more than 50 percent of total production and sales.

[2] The main exceptions are found in the publicly regulated industries, for example, electricity, gas, and water.

COMPETITION: THE ECONOMIC RATIONALE

If one accepts the writings of Congress and the courts at face value, an important motivation for antitrust legislation and enforcement has been economic.[3] Here the antitrust rationale rests on a number of familiar propositions: that producers and sellers put forth their best efforts when threatened by effective rivals; that the economic desires of society are fulfilled when no individuals or groups within the marketplace possess the power to exploit; in short, that competition as a market force compels the best economic results.

The intuitive sense of these propositions can be illustrated simply. Consider, for example, an individual stranded in an automobile, out of gas on a country road. If a second motorist should come along and offer to supply him with enough gas to reach the next town, we may expect that some transaction will occur. But what will be the terms of this transaction? If the second motorist happens to be a Good Samaritan, the gas may be offered free of charge or at cost; but suppose instead that he behaves as a ''rational'' business manager, seeking to extract the maximum possible profit. The price that he can obtain for his gasoline cannot be specified without more information: for example, how anxious the stranded driver is to get going, how repugnant to him is the idea of walking to the next town. It is quite likely, however, that the price paid for the gas will be, in some sense, abnormally high. Why? In simplest terms, because the stranded driver has no alternative except to forego the gasoline. The seller has no competitors and is thus under no compulsion to offer a particularly attractive bargain; indeed, the price he can obtain is limited only by the buyer's desires and ability to pay.

It may be objected that there is a missing element here, that the abnormal price paid for the gasoline may be due not simply to the presence of a monopolistic seller but also to the unusual circumstances in which a gallon of gasoline may be valued more highly by the buyer than it ordinarily would be. This is a valid observation; yet the fact remains that the transaction might have been quite different if, for example, four motorists had appeared simultaneously, each offering to sell the required gasoline and each willing to compete for the sale, or if the motorist had run out of gas near an intersection containing several service stations. The seller's power, deriving from the absence of competitors, does influence the terms of the exchange.

Examples of monopolistic exploitation are commonplace. Prices charged at a ''24-hour'' general store, located some distance from shopping centers, are likely to be relatively high because the store enjoys a partial monopoly in both location and time. The price of a soft drink at a theater intermission or a glass of beer at a ballpark may similarly reflect a degree of monopoly power. This is not to imply, incidentally, that the entire differential between these and more ''ordinary'' prices is attributable to monopolistic control. The general store, for example, may well incur higher unit costs than a supermarket, and its best (profit-maximizing) price may thus tend to be higher for reasons of cost as well as because of its monopoly position.

---

[3]The distinction between ''economic'' and ''noneconomic'' motivations is not always clear-cut, and is discussed shortly.

Freedom from competition, however, does make a difference. The ability of the store, or the ballpark or theater vendor, to charge more depends upon the difficulty customers encounter in going elsewhere.

It should be made clear at this point that the economic argument in favor of competition does not rest simply on intuition or homey examples of exploitation. As we shall see, economic analysis demonstrates in a formal and rigorous fashion the inevitable superiority of competitive market results. It concludes, in other words, that there is some sense in which competition always benefits society more than partial or complete monopoly.

Despite the clarity of this conclusion,[4] our competition-promoting antitrust policies reside today in a state of some disarray. What is confused in part is the legal status of complex and somewhat ambiguous provisions. But the more basic confusion—and a major source of policy dilemmas—concerns the relationship between what the law does, on the one hand, and what economic analysis might suggest, on the other.

This is not to imply that antitrust legislation generally has run contrary to the lessons of economics. Much, and perhaps most, public competition policy possesses a cogent economic rationale, and antitrust policy very likely has had a positive effect on the competitiveness of the American economy. The problem is rather that some apparently straightforward theoretical conclusions have not provided a clear basis for policy action. We have a highly developed economic theory of competition but an ambiguous policy for its maintenance and encouragement. A primary task of this book is to explore the reasons that it has proved difficult to move from a theory of competition to a policy toward competition. Once these reasons are recognized, it may be possible both to define limitations to the relevance of theory to policy and to suggest ways in which policy might be brought into closer accord with economic analysis and its implications.

COMPETITION: ECONOMIC DESIRABILITY AND NONECONOMIC OBJECTIVES

Economists have long recognized the benefits of competitive markets; yet public policies toward competition are not motivated solely—perhaps not even primarily—by economic objectives. Social and political factors also are important, and although these are not our direct concern here, it would be myopic to pretend that they do not exist. Interestingly, the presumption in favor of competition that is made on noneconomic grounds is closely related in some ways to economic arguments.

As we discuss in Chapter 1, the economic "case" for competition is in effect an argument that competitive markets are the most efficient form of industrial organization. Efficiency, however, is defined in a rather specific way: The competitive market is said to be efficient because it most accurately reflects and executes the desires

---

[4]The conclusion of competitive superiority is at this point nothing more than an assertion. Its validity is discussed in Chapter 1.

of individuals as consumers, that is, the desires of the community as a whole. In a free society, a premium is placed on democratic decision making. If competitive markets make economic decisions efficiently in the above sense, then such decisions are made in an essentially democratic fashion. That is, the decisions reflect the desires of the community without the distortions that powerful interest groups can impose.

The competitive market may thus appeal to us in two rather different ways. Economically, it provides efficient **results.** Socially (or politically), it gives us a democratic **process** under which our economizing decisions can be made. There are, however, some important reasons for not carrying the economic optimality argument too far into the noneconomic or social realm.

It is true that competitive markets do an efficient job of allocating resources and that the allocations may be democratic in the sense that the "dollar votes" of consumers are accurately translated into the desired output decisions. It may be, however, that the "dollar votes" are themselves distributed among consumers in a pattern that one would regard as "unfair," "unjust," or even "undemocratic." Most societies, ours included, are characterized by highly unequal distributions of income and wealth. Simply stated, some consumers have many more "votes" than others.

Even if such a situation is itself considered undesirable, resources may still be allocated efficiently by a competitive market system; but the desirability of the resulting allocations would be subject to question in light of the initially poor distribution of spending power.[5]

COMPETITION: THE GAP BETWEEN THEORY AND POLICY

Whether or not one considers economic objectives to be paramount, there can be no question that they provide a relevant motivation for antitrust action. It therefore follows that the general formulation of antitrust policies must take account of economic implications, even though these implications may not always be the controlling factor in policy decisions. Much of the economics literature of the past 30 years has attributed policy failure and confusion to a gap between theory and action. Some observers have contended that policymakers frequently ignore or fail to understand the economic implications of what they are doing. It has long been argued specifically that there is a legal–economic dichotomy in approaches to antitrust problems and that policymakers sometimes act in an economically illiterate fashion.

Some of these statements are accurate; but if we ask why there is a gap between economic theory and public policy, there is a large variety of possible answers, each with some claim to truth. Many of the arguments familiar to students of industrial organization rest on a common point: For one reason or another, it appears that we

---

[5]One might suggest (as many have) that efficiency and equity (''fairness'') are separate considerations that ought to be pursued independently. Thus, if efficiency is a worthwhile objective, it remains so whether or not society also contains elements of unfairness. This position has some logical appeal; yet in practice the two considerations can be very difficult to keep apart.

cannot decide whether theoretical conclusions about competition are fully **relevant** to policy formulation.

This ambivalence is not too surprising. There often is a question in economics as to whether theoretical conclusions apply directly to problems of the "real world." In the area of competition policies, this question is acute because the conclusion of competitive superiority is derived under a number of rather restrictive assumptions. If the abandonment of some restrictive assumptions could alter the conclusions, then there would be no firm a priori basis for determining an appropriate public policy.

A second source of ambivalence lies in the imperfect nature of real markets. The conclusion of competitive optimality rests on a comparison between the economist's strict definition of a purely or perfectly competitive market and other market forms. Policy decisions, however, do not involve choices between perfection and imperfection but, rather, between various kinds of imperfection. Theoretical bases for such choices are relatively weak, and even if we could decide as a rule to opt for "more competitive" markets, there is serious difficulty in defining and measuring what this means.

Although theoretical conclusions may be quite meaningful, there are some real difficulties in moving from theory to policy. To the extent that objective analysis falls short of providing full prescriptions for policy, it becomes necessary to look at empirical evidence: that is, to examine what actually happens in different kinds of markets. As we shall see, a good deal of information on market behavior has been gathered. The data yield a number of useful clues about the ways in which performance patterns vary with the structure of industry. It is not clear, however, that this evidence brings us much closer to unequivocal statements about the kinds of policies that will yield particular ends.

If both theory and evidence are inconclusive, we cannot accurately predict the effect of policy changes. It is not appropriate to be too pessimistic at this point, however. We may be able to say a good deal about the likely effects of alternative policies, even if such statements cannot be made with complete precision or confidence. Moreover, improved predictions in the future, based especially on new empirical clues, may occur quite rapidly.

It must be pointed out that, whatever the current status of economic theory and measurement, even perfect predictions of policy effects might not be conclusive. The question of what public competition policies ought to be adopted obviously depends upon the effects of the alternatives; but it depends as well on **society's evaluation** of these effects. This statement appears self-evident, but it is not trivial. Society has numerous objectives. We would be pleased to have, for instance, an equitable distribution of income, efficient resource allocation, rapid innovation, and wise resource conservation. But even assuming that we could agree on the meaning of these noble aims, the appropriate policy for their implementation might be unclear.

The objectives conflict, because a policy that emphasizes one (or more) must also deemphasize one (or more). The question then becomes: how does society assign priorities, that is, decide which goals are more important than others? This kind of question cannot be answered on the basis of economic analysis or empirical evidence. Such information is helpful in delineating society's alternatives, but it cannot tell us what sorts of policies are desirable or undesirable.

ORGANIZATION OF THE BOOK

This book is divided into three main sections. The first part, Theoretical Underpinnings, examines competititon, monopoly, and—most important—intermediate markets, in which elements of competition and monopoly coexist. We consider here the economic argument for competitive markets that justifies a public antitrust program.

Part Two, Empirical Problems and Evidence, reviews what we are able to observe about firm and market structure and behavior. Does the evidence support the theoretical expectations developed in Part One? Can it provide clearer guides to policymaking than analytical constructs alone? In discussing these questions, we attempt to define what policy officials should know as they make decisions that affect the nature of competition in markets.

In the third part, Antitrust Policy, we look in detail at our public treatment of market competition. We examine the legal rules that have been developed with regard to conspiracy, monopoly power, mergers, price discrimination, and a variety of potentially restrictive business practices. In addition, we consider the regulatory approaches employed in those sectors in which competition may be impractical. Part Three ends with some evaluations of public policy. By that point, however, it is hoped that most readers will be prepared to render their own judgments.

PART ONE

THE THEORETICAL UNDERPINNINGS

This section sets forth the economic theory that contains the pure economic justification for American antitrust poilcy. The economic rationale of antitrust policy rests in the traditional body of price theory and, specifically, in the theory of market behavior. Although it is rather easy to argue intuitively that "competition" may benefit consumers more than "monopoly," the casual demonstration leaves a number of questions unanswered. It does not tell us, for example, whether a competitive market **inevitably** yields superior results or whether economic problems at times may be better resolved under "imperfect" or "monopolistic" conditions; nor does the casual, common-sense approach tell us whether **all** economic problems are best solved by competition.

Therefore, it is useful to examine in a more precise fashion the analytical basis of statements about competition, monopoly, and intermediate market forms. This investigation will clarify the meaning of our presumption in favor of competition and will make it easier to evaluate actual policies in light of their economic implications. The first task in this examination of market theories is to define the exact nature of competitive market results. We shall see that competition yields an **optimal** solution of the fundamental economic problem; that is, a solution that is not only preferable to a "monopoly" result but is, in some sense, the **best possible** outcome. It is necessary, however, to append a number of significant qualifications; for the conclusion of competitive optimality rests upon certain assumptions that, although perfectly legitimate from a theoretical standpoint, may cast doubt on a policy that single-mindedly pursues "more competitive" markets.

It is also useful to analyze in some detail the working of "imperfectly competitive" and "oligopolistic" markets, which contain elements of both competition and monopoly. Policy decisions dealt most frequently with these intermediate markets, and they are therefore of considerable practical interest. It is also in this area, however, that theories of market behavior have proved at least satisfactory, and some of the reasons for fundamental policy difficulties should become quickly evident.

CHAPTER 1

The Welfare Implications of Competition and Monopoly

It is a basic and familiar conclusion of microeconomic theory that differently structured markets behave in fundamentally different ways. A convenient starting point in the analysis of market behavior is the comparison between the extremes of pure, or perfect, competition and pure monopoly. These market forms, although they are infrequently (if ever) encountered in the modern American economy, yield much insight into the processes by which prices and output levels are determined.

COMPETITION

The economist's benchmark in discussions of market behavior is pure, or perfect, competition. A perfectly competitive market is one that is characterized by:

1. **Many Firms.** The number of firms is sufficiently large, and each individual firm is sufficiently small, that none can perceptibly affect market price by varying its output.
2. **Homogeneous products.** The products offered by firms are identical, not only in physical characteristics but also in the minds of consumers. That is, consumers have no preference whatever for the product of one seller over that of any other.
3. **Free Entry and Exit.** There are no unusual or artificial barriers that might deter firms from entering or leaving the market in the long run.
4. **Perfect Knowledge.** No participants in the market can be exploited because of ignorance.
5. **Independence.** Firms make decisions individually, that is, without collusion.

A number of consequences relevant to market behavior that can be inferred immediately from these characteristics are shown in Figure 1.1. Part a of the figure depicts the competitive market supply S and demand D curves, which determine equilibrium price P_E, and quantity, Q_E.

We see in part b that the individual firm in the competitive market faces a perfectly elastic demand curve, d, at market price, P_E. This follows from the fact that the firm is insignificantly small in a homogeneous-product market, and thus cannot affect market price by changing its output. The horizontal demand curve indicates

9

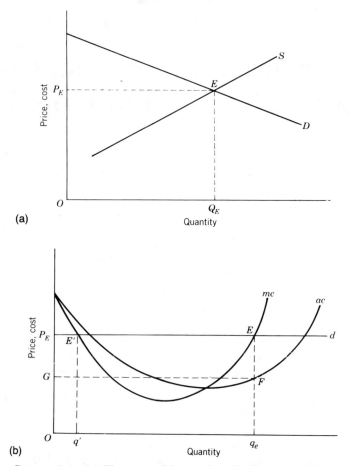

Figure 1.1 (a) The competitive market. (b) The competitive firm.

that the firm can sell any amount it produces at P_E. There is no meaningful pricing decision for the firm in a purely competitive market. If it were to charge more than the market price, it would sell nothing. Yet if the firm seeks maximum profits, there is no incentive to charge less than the market price, because its entire output can be sold at the prevailing rate.

If we now specify that the firm confronts marginal-cost and average-cost curves *mc* and *ac*, respectively, in Figure 1.1*b*, the short-run equilibrium position of the firm occurs at point E.[1] The firm's profit-maximizing output is q_e, because at this output marginal cost, *mc*, equals marginal revenue (given by demand curve *d*).[2] At

---

[1] The short run is an unspecified period within which certain inputs such as the firm's scale or plant size, cannot be varied. Over the long run all inputs are variable.

[2] A horizontal demand curve is also a marginal-revenue curve (and an average-revenue curve as well). That is so because as successive units are sold, the price of the last unit—and of all previous units—remains unchanged. Thus the net addition to revenue, or the **marginal revenue of the last unit,** is simply its price.

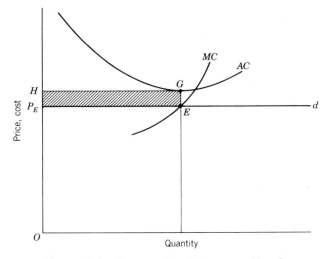

Figure 1.2 Short-run loss by a competitive firm.

any output less than q_e, the firm is foregoing profits on additional units for which marginal revenue exceeds marginal cost; whereas at any greater output, the firm is producing some units whose marginal cost exceeds marginal revenue and are therefore unprofitable.[3]

In Figure 1.1b the price obtained for each unit, P_E, exceeds the average cost of production, OG. In other words, the firm is earning profit P_EG on each unit it sells, and its total profit is represented by rectangle P_EGFE. Referring back to the characteristics of the competitive market, however, it can be seen that these excess profits will not persist. If entry and exit are free, the existence of net profits should induce other profit-seeking firms to enter the market. The new entrants increase the supply of goods to the market—shifting S to the right in Figure 1.1a—and tend to drive down the market price. From the firm's point of view, demand curve d will fall.[4] Entry will continue until profits are entirely competed away and the inducement for more new firms to enter disappears.

Conversely, suppose that the short-run situation had been the case portrayed in Figure 1.2. Here the price received by the firm, P_E, fails to cover its average cost OH.[5] The firm loses P_EH (or EG) on every unit sold, and its total loss is rectangle HP_EEG. Once again, this short-run situation cannot persist indefinitely. Some firms

---

[3]Note, however, that point E' in Figure 1.1b (output q') is **not** a profit-maximizing point, even though marginal cost and marginal revenue are equated. (It is actually a profit-minimizing position, since marginal cost exceeds marginal revenue for every unit sold.) Although profit maximization requires the marginal-cost–marginal-revenue equality, not all such equalities imply maximization. It is necessary to add a second maximization condition, namely, that the marginal-cost curve cut the marginal-revenue curve **from below.**

[4]Entry of new firms may or may not shift the firms' cost curves as well; the possibility that costs will be altered is ignored here.

[5]Notice that there is **no** point at which this firm could cover all its costs; average cost is everywhere higher than the price, P_E, at which the firm can sell. Point E remains an equilibrium position, but the firm, even when doing as well as possible, loses money.

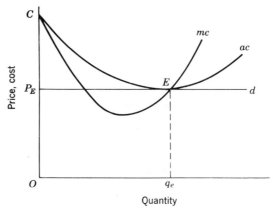

Figure 1.3 Long-run equilibrium for the competitive firm.

will be forced to leave the market as losses continue, market supply will fall as the industry supply curve shifts left, and price will be forced up until all losses are eliminated. From the viewpoint of the remaining firms, demand curve d will shift upward.

We see, then, that net profits and net losses in a competitive market are a short-run condition. Where profits exist, entry is stimulated and continues until those profits disappear. If losses occur, some firms must exit, and these exits will again continue until the losses vanish. This adjustment mechanism brings us to the long-run equilibrium position of the competitive firm, depicted in Figure 1.3.

Equilibrium again occurs at a point E involving an output level q_e at which marginal cost and marginal revenue are equated. In the long-run, however, this equilibrium occurs also at a point for which price and average cost are the same. At equilibrium, then, the firm's average revenue from sales just covers its average cost. Total revenue just covers total cost, and the firm is said to be in a "zero profit" position. This is an important element of the long-run competitive equilibrium.

"Zero profit" is more accurately termed "zero **excess** profit." The firm must earn some return with which it retains its investors and management. This return, or "normal" profit, can be treated as an economic cost—the cost of attracting funds and hiring the entrepreneurial factor of production. Thus, "zero profit" means that the firm earns no profit **beyond** that which can be defined as an economic cost.

Diagrammatically, the firm's long-run equilibrium occurs at a point of tangency between average-cost curve ac and demand curve d, which also coincides with the intersection of d and mc. This may seem quite a coincidence, but it simply reflects the process just described. In the long run, the firm's best (or equilibrium) position ($mc = d$) implies neither net profits nor net losses (price $P_E = ac$). Notice that equilibrium occurs at the minimum point on ac.[6] This is a clear hint of the efficiency of the competitive market.

---

[6]The marginal-cost curve must intersect the average-cost curve at the minimum point on ac. But this minimum must also be the point of tangency to a **horizontal** demand curve.

Some brief observations about firm and industry supply are now in order. Notice that in each of our previous diagrams, the amount that any firm supplies in the short run can be read directly from its marginal-cost curve; *mc* **is** in effect the firm's short-run supply curve. The amount that the industry will supply at any price in the short run is the sum of what each firm will supply at that price. The short-run industry supply curve may therefore be defined as the sum of the individual firms' marginal-cost curves, but with one important qualification. As industry output expands, the prices of some factors of production may well be pushed up. If so, the industry demand curve is not the simple summation of the firms' *mc* curves, for the *mc* curves themselves will be shifting in response to factor price changes.

The definition of the long-run industry supply curve is somewhat more complicated. Industry supply remains anchored to the supply responses of constituent firms. But in addition to the fact that firms enjoy greater flexibility in their long-run decisions, the **number of firms** in the industry is no longer given. Entry and exit may occur, and we cannot define the supply terms of various quantities without knowing how individual cost curves may shift as the industry undergoes expansion and contraction.

For firms in the industry, price must (at least) cover long-run average costs, and equilibrium will tend to occur at a zero-profit point. It, therefore, follows that price and average cost will be closely related in the long run. To define precisely the long-run industry supply curve, however, requires that we answer questions of the following sort: If industry output expands (contracts), firms enter (exit), factor prices change, and all firms adjust optimally, how will the average cost of supply be affected?

PURE MONOPOLY

In pure monopoly, a single firm is the sole supplier of a commodity for which no close substitutes exist. The firm and the industry are the same. The monopolist thus faces a conventional, downward-sloping demand curve, such as D in Figure 1.4, and maximizes profits at that output level for which marginal cost equals marginal revenue. In Figure 1.4, the monopolist will produce output Q_M and will charge price P_M, the price that the market will pay for that quantity. The portrayal of equilibrium for monopoly is essentially the same in both the short and long run.

A number of interesting observations may be made with respect to monopoly equilibrium. First of all, it is obvious that the monopolist succeeds in doing something that competitive firms cannot do: charging a price in excess of marginal cost and perhaps in excess of long-run average cost. The reason again is that competitive firms have no power over price and are assumed to act independently. If the competitive firms were to conspire, they too could take advantage of the downward-sloping industry demand curve, and presumably they could arrive at a price-quantity solution similar to that of the monopolist. It is worth noting that the monopolist's ability to ''exploit'' the market, in the sense that it charges a price in excess of marginal cost, does not imply any unusual motivation such as extreme greed (nor is the competitive firm more altruistic). Under the assumptions of traditional price theory, all

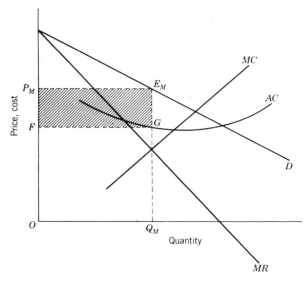

Figure 1.4 Monopoly equilibrium.

firms seek maximum profits. If the monopolist succeeds better than most, it is only because the market is less effective in restraining that firm's actions.

A further observation of interest is that there are some constraints on the monopolist. It cannot pursue maximum profits "without regard to supply and demand forces," as some naive statements might imply. Quite the contrary. Its maximizing calculations must take account of the demand and cost curves, precisely as the competitive firm takes account of these factors.

Notice that in Figure 1.4, the monopolist earns profit $E_M G$, the excess of price over average cost, on each unit sold.[7] Total profits are shown by the shaded rectangle, $P_M F G E_M$. When such net profits appear in monopoly, they will not tend to be eroded over the long run by entry of firms, as occurred under competition; for our definition of monopoly does not embrace competitors, actual or potential. Entry is, in effect, ruled out.

Finally, it may be observed that there is really no such thing as a monopoly supply curve. The monopolist sets price according to the position of the demand, marginal-revenue, and marginal-cost curves. But we cannot read off the output that will be forthcoming at various prices by referring to any single curve. It is, in fact, quite easy to see that, for a given MC curve, the equilibrium price–quantity combination may occur at various points on the diagram, depending on the position of D and MR. Given appropriate shifts in demand, a particular output level may be priced differently, and a given price may be associated with different outputs.

---

[7] The existence of net profits in monopoly, although quite likely, is not logically inevitable. Conceivably, one may monopolize a product that consumers are not willing to purchase at prices above average cost.

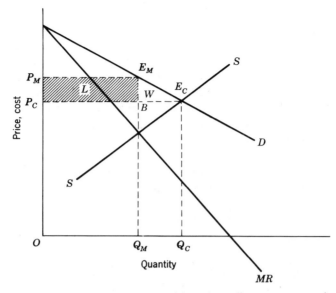

Figure 1.5 Monopoly and competition: the rudimentary comparison.

MONOPOLY AND COMPETITION: THE INITIAL COMPARISON

The usual comparison of market results under pure competition and pure monopoly may be examined in terms of Figure 1.5. In the short-run, competitive equilibrium occurs at point E_C, the intersection of the industry supply and demand curves. Monopoly equilibrium occurs at E_M, reflecting output Q_M (the level at which marginal cost and marginal revenue are equal) and price P_M (the highest price at which industry demand will accept quantity Q_M).

This extremely simple comparison constitutes one standard demonstration of the superiority of competition to monopoly. The competitive industry produces more and charges a lower price for its output, a result that most would agree is preferred.[8] There are several problems and qualifications to this comparison, but setting these aside for the moment, it may be noted that this conclusion is not in itself a terribly strong or surprising one. It states only that pure competition provides goods to the market on somewhat more generous terms (from the consumer's point of view) than does pure monopoly. But it does not tell us directly whether the competitive solution is an extraordinarily "good" one or the monopoly solution an extraordinarily "bad" one; nor whether the difference between the two is significant.

---

[8] This is something of an oversimplification. Even if it is agreed that more goods generally are preferred to fewer, it does not necessarily follow that raising the output of a particular industry is always desirable. If the economy is at full employment, for example, increased production in one area implies decreased production elsewhere; and there is a question of whether the **allocation of resources** is improved or worsened by such a change.

The simple comparison, then, does not provide very extensive information, but it does lay the basis for more ambitious analysis. In Figure 1.5, for example, shaded rectangle L ($P_M P_C B E_M$) represents monopoly profit, a transfer of income from consumers who must pay P_M rather than competitive price P_C for the good in question. This transfer traditionally is not viewed as a net social cost of monopoly, since both consumers (who lose income) and sellers (who gain) are members of society. As we shall see later, however, there is much to debate on this point.

Triangle W in Figure 1.5, usually called the "deadweight" or "welfare loss" triangle, does represent a social cost of monopoly. It is, in effect, a measure of the benefits sacrificed by those who are "priced out" of the market at P_M—consumers who would have bought the good at P_C but will not buy at the higher monopoly price. Notice that there is no compensating gain for the monopolistic seller. W does not show up in the monopoly profits area. It is thus a net cost to society, and economists have made considerable efforts to estimate the magnitude of this effect of monopoly.

COMPETITIVE OPTIMALITY

The intuitive argument for competition may be strengthened a bit by noting that competitive output occurs precisely at the intersection of the market supply and demand curves (Q_E in Figure 1.1a). As we have seen, the competitive supply curve reflects the cost to society of producing any output level. But similarly, the demand curve measures the **value or benefit** that consumers attach to any output at the margin. If, for example, consumers demand 10,000 loaves of bread at a price of 90 cents, the last (marginal) loaf **is worth** (at least) 90 cents. We are simply observing that the **value** of a product is defined by the willingness of consumers—that is, the market—to **pay** for it.

Consider the implications of this observation. If output were at some point below Q_E in Figure 1.1a, its marginal value, or demand price, would exceed its marginal cost, or supply price. Society would therefore gain on balance from an expansion of output (we place a higher value on the additional units than they cost to produce); and this is precisely what the competitive market will do as it moves toward equilibrium Q_E. Conversely, if output were above Q_E, its marginal cost would exceed its marginal benefit; and society would therfore gain from a reduction in output, eliminating those units that cost more than they are worth. Once again, the competitive market will act correctly, pushing production down toward Q_E. Only at Q_E, where marginal benefits and marginal costs are equated, can society not gain from a change in output; and this is just where the competitive market will place us.

The economic case for competition can be stated more rigorously. Generally it can be shown that the competitive outcome is not merely better than that of pure monopoly but is also in some sense the **best possible** from society's viewpoint. To demonstrate this proposition, it is necessary to say something about the meaning of "best possible" situations and then to indicate how competitive markets yield such situations.

Welfare economists have devoted much effort to the definition of **optimal** and **efficient** positions for society. The first question that arises here is: **who** is to judge the goodness or badness of alternatives? The usual approach to this question assumes that choices among alternatives can be made only by the individuals affected. If we wish to know, for example, whether a change improves or damages the welfare of individuals, we must ask them or examine that part of their behavior which reveals the answer. No one else can tell us what is best for those persons.[9]

Once it is accepted that individuals are to judge their own welfare, the pertinent task is to define the welfare of that **collection** of individuals who comprise **society.** The definition of social welfare is complicated by the fact that different persons are likely to regard alternatives differently. Let us suppose that society has two production choices: A, which involves the production of more national defense goods (''guns'') and fewer consumer goods (''butter''); and B, which increases the output of butter at the expense of guns. It is virtually inevitable that some members of society will perfer A while others will prefer B. How are we then to say which alternative is **socially** preferable?

This question is a very old one, but it has never been resolved in an entirely satisfactory way. There are, of course, some practical methods of solution.[10] If the choice is between more guns and more butter, we might vote in order to determine which alternative the majority prefers. It has been shown, however, that simple voting procedures generally violate one or more reasonable conditions for democratic choice.[11] In addition, the principle of majority (or plurality) rule itself may be subject to question. If opinion on the guns-or-butter issue is quite evenly divided, but one group is passionately concerned while the other is close to indifferent, should we not take account of this information as well? Perhaps we should, but there are great difficulties in measuring objectively the intensity of individuals' feelings.[12]

The difficulty in making interpersonal comparisons is such that we often seek to finesse the problem (although never with total success). It is extremely useful, albeit

[9]The alternative to this approach is to assume that an individual's welfare can be meaningfully defined by an external arbiter (e.g., the government). Although such an assumption will be repugnant to many, it is interesting to note that even a democratic society adopts this principle at certain times. Consider, for example, automobile seat-belt requirements, the ban on cyclamates in foods, and laws against ''victimless'' crimes. All these governmental provisions require behavior that consumers would not undertake voluntarily.

[10]After all, we continually make decisions in which conflicting preferences must somehow be weighed. Whether to adopt a government spending program, and, if so, how to finance it, are obvious political examples. At a more local level, the choice of an evening's entertainment by a family or group of friends is likely to present precisely the same sort of issue.

[11]The pioneering proof of such propositions is found in Kenneth J. Arrow, *Social Choice and Individual Values,* Cowles Commission Monograph No. 12 (New York: Wiley, 1951).

[12]One possibility is for intensity to be measured by willingness to pay. We might, for example, ask the probutter and proguns groups how much they would pay to have the decision in their favor (this is, after all, the way in which market decisions are made). The trouble here is that we are measuring not only intensity of feelings but the distribution of spending power as well. The decision is likely to go to the group with the most funds, and this is not necessarily a desirable outcome unless we are convinced that the distribution of funds is ethically ''correct.''

somewhat confining, to analyze situations in which conflicts of preference do not arise. This leads us to the Pareto criterion,[13] a cornerstone of welfare economics, that states:

any change is a social improvement if it makes one or more members of society better off while making no one worse off.

A change that helps some and hurts others cannot be termed "bad"—it is simply **not capable of evaluation** under this approach. Extending the criterion, it follows that we have an optimal situation in Pareto terms when no further Pareto improvements are possible. The **Pareto optimum** is thus a situation in which the well-being of one or more members of society can be improved **only by harming** the position of some other(s).[14]

We have said thus far that the definition of a social welfare optimum encounters the, perhaps insoluble, problem of conflicting preferences among individuals. In order to avoid this, while retaining the ability to make some useful judgments, we turn to the Paretian notion of optimality. It now remains for us to see what specific conditions are implied by Pareto optimality and to define the role of competition in relation to this concept of an economic welfare optimum.

Pareto Optimality Conditions

Our definition of a Pareto welfare optimum states, in effect, that we cannot rearrange goods or resources in such a way that we help someone without hurting someone else. It will be useful to note without elaborate derivation the conditions under which this type of optimum exists. Suppose for simplicity an economy in which two goods (X and Y) are produced, two factor inputs (i and j) are used in the production of each good, and there are two consumers (A and B). The optimality conditions in this simplifed case would apply equally to more realistic (larger number) situations.

Optimal Distribution of Goods Among Consumers   This requires that each consumer have **the same marginal rate of substitution** between the goods, that is

$$\frac{MU_{XA}}{MU_{YA}} = \frac{MU_{XB}}{MU_{YB}}$$

where MU_{XA} is the marginal utility of good X to consumer A, MU_{YA} is the marginal utility of good Y to consumer A, and so forth. This condition means simply that goods are distributed in such a way that each consumer places the same relative valuations on them.

If this were not the case, both consumers could improve their position by exchanging goods. The consumer who valued X highly relative to Y could trade

---

[13] Vilfredo Pareto, *Manual d'Economie Politique,* (2nd ed. Paris: Girard, 1927).

[14] Consider what this means. At a Pareto optimum, all the "free" or "easy" improvements—those that harm no one—have already been made. Further efforts to improve anyone's lot must hurt someone else and, therefore, cannot pass the Pareto-improvement test, even if society considers them reasonable. The Pareto criterion may appear noncontroversial, but it is **not** an "objective" or "value-free" approach to social welfare.

some of his Y to the consumer who valued Y highly relative to X (and receive some X in return). Only where the marginal utility ratios are the same is a mutually beneficial trade, which would be a Pareto improvement, impossible.[15]

Optimal Allocation of Inputs to Productive Uses   This requires a closely analogous condition, namely, that

$$\frac{MP_{iX}}{MP_{jX}} = \frac{MP_{iY}}{MP_{jY}}$$

where MP_{iX} is the marginal product of input i in the production of good X, MP_{jX} is the marginal product of input j in the production of good X, and so forth. If this equality in the **marginal rates of transformation** is not satisfied, one input is relatively more efficient in the production of one output (and the other relatively less efficient in producing the same output). If each input were reallocated to some extent into its more efficient use, society could expand total production at the same level of input use—a move that would permit the welfare of some to be improved without harming the welfare of others.[16]

Optimal Amounts of Outputs.   Assuming efficient production and distribution of goods, optimal output levels require that the goods be produced in quantities such that

$$\frac{MU_X}{MC_X} = \frac{MU_Y}{MC_Y}$$

where the MU is marginal utility and MC is marginal cost. The condition thus states that the ratio of marginal utility to marginal cost must be the same for each good produced. Were the ratios unequal, society could plainly benefit by producing more of the good that yields the higher utility per unit cost at the margin.

Summary   The three conditions outlined above define an optimal situation in the Pareto sense. In fact, these are nothing more (or less) than efficiency requirements denoting the particular configurations—of output distribution, input allocation, and output production levels—under which "free" improvements in welfare cannot be made.

---

[15] The argument is not entirely obvious, and a simple example may help. Suppose that we have:

$$\frac{MU_{XA}}{MU_{YA}} = \frac{30}{10} \text{ and } \frac{MU_{XB}}{MU_{YB}} = \frac{10}{5}$$

That is, consumer A's marginal rate of substitution betwen X and Y exceeds that of consumer B. Now suppose that consumer B trades 3 units of good X to consumer A in exchange for 7 units of good Y. This trade will increase B's total utility by 5 units and A's total utility by 20 units (check the numbers). A Pareto improvement has occurred, implying that the situation initially was not Pareto optimal.

[16] If this point is unclear, try the same sort of numerical example as that used in footnote 15. In fact, the same numbers may be used.

The Role of Competition

It now remains to be noted that competition will yield a Pareto optimal economic result. This proposition can be demonstrated specifically with reference to the three marginal conditions.

It is easily seen that equal marginal rates of substitituion will occur under any pricing system that sets commodity prices at the same levels for all consumers. A utility-maximizing consumer equates (in equilibrium) the ratio of marginal utility to price for each item consumed.[17] If all consumers pay the same price for commodities X and Y, each must act so that his marginal utility ratio, MU_X/MU_Y, is equal to **the same** price ratio, P_X/P_Y. Therefore, every consumer's marginal utility ratio (or marginal rate of substitution) is the same. Since a competitive market offers goods to all at the same prices, it satisfies the condition; and it is interesting to note that this condition will be satisfied for any arbitrary set of prices, so long as those prices are fixed at the same levels for all consumers.

The condition for optimal input allocation is similarly satisfied by competition (or by any system that fixes all input and output prices at the same levels for all producers and consumers). This condition provides that the ratio of the marginal products of two inputs in the production of one good must be the same as their ratio in the production of another good. We know that a profit-maximizing firm whose input and output prices are fixed must hire each input to the point at which its price is equal to the value of its marginal product.[18] If input and output prices are fixed at the same levels for all firms, each firm will pay the same amount for any given nput, and the value of any given input's marginal product must be the same in all uses.

This implies that for any input i,

$$P_X \cdot MP_{iX} = P_Y \cdot MP_{iY}^{19}$$

and for any other input j,

$$P_X \cdot MP_{jX} = P_Y \cdot MP_{jY}$$

It then follows directly that

$$\frac{MP_{iX}}{MP_{jX}} = \frac{MP_{iY}}{MP_{jY}}$$

The assumption that all input and output prices are fixed at the same levels for all firms and consumers thus implies satisfaction of the condition, and such an assumption is again embodied in the model of a competitive market.

---

[17] That is, he must act so that, for commodities X and Y, $MU_X/P_X = MU_Y/P_Y$. If this were not the case, more utility could be gained by switching some purchases to the commodity yielding the higher utility per unit spent at the margin.

[18] If the value of the marginal product exceeds the input price, the firm is foregoing profitable units of the input; if input price exceeds the value of the marginal product, the firm has hired some unprofitable input units.

[19] We have already said that the **value** of the marginal product of any input must be the same in all uses. With fixed output prices, however, the value of the marginal product of an input is simply its marginal **physical** product times output price; and the marginal physical product is the value of the marginal product divided by output price.

The final Pareto condition states that the marginal rate of substitution between goods X and Y (MU_X/MU_Y) must equal the marginal rate of transformation between the two goods (MC_X/MC_Y). We know that utility-maximizing consumers will equate the marginal rate of substitution between any pair of goods with the price ratio of the goods: $MU_X/MU_Y = P_X/P_Y$. But as we also have seen, firms **in pure competition** will produce any product to the point at which its marginal cost equals its price. Thus, $MC_X = P_X$, $MC_Y = P_Y$, and $MC_X/MC_Y = P_X/P_Y$.

At this point we have said that the marginal rate of substitution between X and Y and the marginal rate of transformation between X and Y will, under competitive conditions, be equal to the ratio of the prices of X and Y. Assuming once again that P_X and P_Y are fixed uniformly, this means that the marginal rate of substitution is equal to the marginal rate of transformation, that is,

$$\frac{MU_X}{MU_Y} = \frac{MC_X}{MC_Y} \quad \text{and} \quad \frac{MU_X}{MC_X} = \frac{MU_Y}{MC_Y}$$

The final condition is thus satisfied.

Summary

The arguments outlined above indicate that the Pareto optimality conditions are satisfied by an economic system in which the following holds true.

1. The prices of all inputs and outputs are fixed at the same levels for all producers and consumers.
2. Producers seek maximum profits and consumers seek maximum utility.
3. Firms produce to the point at which the price of any product is equal to its marginal cost.
4. All markets are cleared.

Since circumstances 1 through 4 hold for competitive markets, we may conclude that the result of a competitive system is a Pareto optimum.[20]

It must be pointed out, however, that there can exist many Pareto **optima**. Suppose, for example, that I am a pauper and you are affluent. There will be some distribution of goods between us that is efficient in the Pareto sense that we cannot both benefit from trade. If, however, we now specify that I am the affluent one while you are consigned to poverty, we shall again be able to find a Pareto efficient division of society's outputs.

The notion of Pareto optimality must therefore be treated with caution. Some economists in fact believe that we ought not to speak of **optimality** but only of **efficiency** in the Pareto sense. The marginal conditions define a particularly efficient result, but many efficient points exist. Some efficient points would undoubtedly be considered by society to be superior to others; and some Pareto optima might be judged **worse** than some nonoptima.

---

[20] Notice that conditions 1, 2, and 4 might hold in other kinds of markets also.

The crux of the difficulty should be apparent. The Pareto criterion stands largely mute on the question of an appropriate income distribution. It simply defines the efficient set of arrangements for any given distribution. What may be the best distribution of income for society is not a question that has a ready, objective answer. But society does care about this issue, and the inability of the Pareto criterion to shed much light here is a significant limitation.

IMPLICIT ASSUMPTIONS IN THE DEMONSTRATION OF COMPETITIVE OPTIMALITY

The conclusion of competitive optimality rests upon a number of assumptions, some of which have not yet been stated explicitly. It is possible that certain of these assumptions may restrict the analysis in an important way, and they thus bear brief discussion.

No Externalities in Consumption

It has been assumed implicitly in the above analysis that any individual's enjoyment of consumption is independent of the consumption patterns of others. That is, we assume that the individual consumer's satisfaction depends purely on his or her own consumption; neither pleasure nor displeasure is derived from what others consume.

The necessity for this assumption is quite obvious. Suppose, for example, that consumers are envious of one another. A rearrangement of society's output that apparently increases the satisfaction of some, while leaving others as well off as before, could **not** be said to be Pareto desirable. Why? Most simply, this is because those who are left "as well off as before" in terms of their own consumption patterns are now envious of those who have more.

The more general difficulty is that if satisfaction is influenced by the consumption of others, there is no way to define optimal (equilibrium) positions for consumers in terms of their own experience. Accordingly, we could not move from statements about individual preferences among combinations of goods to statements about the preferences of all individuals—that is, of society. We might be forced to say, for example, that although every individual is as well off as possible (given relevant constraints), the community as a whole is **not** as well off as possible. It is this kind of complication that we seek to avoid by assuming that an individual's satisfaction in consumption is determined solely by his or her own experience.

No Externalities in Production

A very similar assumption about the absence of externalities underlies the production side of the analysis. Recall the condition for optimal output levels: equation of consumers' marginal rates of substitution with producers' marginal rates of transformation—that is, the marginal cost ratios of goods X and Y. If $MU_X/MC_X = MU_Y/MC_Y$, we concluded, outputs are at their best possible levels for the community as a whole.

Clearly, however, this equation "works" only if the marginal costs to which suppliers respond are a good measure of marginal **social** costs. We are implicitly supposing that the marginal rate of transformation (MC_X/MC_Y) is the same for private producers as for the community or, in perhaps slightly more familiar language, that marginal private costs equal marginal social costs.

In practice, however, we know that production externalities—divergences between private and social costs—are hardly uncommon. Where they exist, the private market equilibrium will **not** coincide with the social optimum. Suppose, for example, that a steel company pollutes the atmosphere in the process of producing its goods. Such pollution creates real and important costs for society, including damage to human health. Yet the steel company is unlikely to consider such costs in its own output and pricing decisions. The effects of pollution fall largely on people who are neither producers of steel nor customers of the producer; they are simply "third parties," in effect, innocent bystanders **external** to the market.

Pollution costs are thus not fully counted by the market (they do not show up in either cost or revenue functions of the polluting firms). There is an external diseconomy in the production of steel, with the probable result that too much steel (and pollution) is produced from a social standpoint.[21] The market thus fails to do a correct allocation job, and a case for government intervention is apparent.

Examples of externalities in production are familiar. An educational system, for example, likely benefits society above and beyond those benefits that accrue directly to the educated individuals. The willingness of individuals to pay for education is based on the private benefits they expect to receive; but it cannot very well reflect social benefits (e.g., the political stability of an educated nation). The important aspect of such externalities is that the competitive market mechanism breaks down as the servant of society. If the measurement of benefits and costs by firms differs from that of society, the equilibrium toward which the firms tend need not correspond to society's best interests.

Competitive optimality, then, requires the absence of external effects; however, external effects are quite common in reality. The direct implication is that even if all the requisites of pure competition are met, there may be instances in which it is not a socially appropriate form of market organization. Or, alternatively, it may be that society can superimpose a system of rewards or penalties in order to render the competitive market socially appropriate. This qualification is of practical importance because it implies that even in areas in which a market can function, competition may not lead to socially optimal results.

Increasing Costs

A basic assumption in the analysis of competition is that the costs of producing output turn up fairly quickly. Or, to state the point in reverse, it is assumed that scale

---

[21] An external economy exists when the private benefit or profit that may be gained through economic activity is **exceeded** by the social gain; **too little** of the relevant good or service will be forthcoming from society's standpoint.

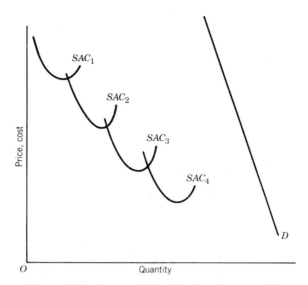

Figure 1.6 A case of significant scale economies.

economies are not so important that firms must grow large relative to the market in order to operate efficiently.

As we have seen, firms in pure competition reach an equilibrium level of output at a relatively small size, so small, in fact, that the market hardly takes notice of what each is doing. Suppose, however, that production is characterized by significant economies of scale. Every firm finds that it can lower unit output costs by increasing its scale of operation.

The position of such companies is illustrated in Figure 1.6. Each short-run average-cost (*SAC*) curve represents a different plant size or scale of operation; and it is apparent that larger plant size tends to be more efficient, at least to some point (*SAC*$_4$ implies much lower production costs per unit than *SAC*$_1$, for example). Whereas each firm in the short run is "stuck" with whatever plant size it previously chose, we should expect that over the long run companies will seek efficient scales.

Notice the implication. If firms tend to choose the plant size represented by *SAC*$_4$ and market demand is *D*, the market simply will not support a large number of firms. Each company, seeking to produce efficiently, will take over a substantial portion of the market.[22] This need not represent an excessive or illegitimate attempt to monopolize the market. Quite the contrary, it is the underlying cost conditions that impel the growth of firms.

In this type of industry, small, "competitive-sized" firms cannot survive. The case of significant economies of scale, therefore, is one in which pure competition becomes technically impossible and, under an efficiency criterion, undesirable. Our

---

[22] In the extreme case known as **natural monopoly,** a single efficient-sized firm would take over the entire market. Such situations, discussed later, suggest that the competitive market mechanism may have to be abandoned.

earlier demonstrations of competitive optimality have implicitly assumed away this sort of complication. Where economies of scale are important, we shall not necessarily lose faith in the competitive process; but neither are we likely to argue for a market of many very small firms.

Community Preferences Independent of the Form of Market Organization

A further assumption implicit in the earlier analysis is that the preference patterns of individuals are not altered by changes in market organization. In other words, society's evaluation of alternative output combinations is assumed to have nothing to do with the shape of the markets in which those outputs are produced. Should a previously competitive industry become monopolized, this will not affect consumer preferences.

The need for this assumption should be clear. For instance, if the advent of monopoly were to change consumer likes and dislikes, there would be no way to compare, even hypothetically, the goodness of allocation at competitive and monopolistic points. The problem would be akin to that of trying to compare the well-being of two individuals (or groups) with different tastes.

The role of the assumption may be clear, but once again it is subject to some question. Characteristically, many industries whose firms possess some market power do exert considerable effort to affect demand conditions—that is, to alter consumer preferences. Advertising and product differentiation through other promotional means are familiar examples of this effort. It is quite possible that the community's evaluation of a commodity is **not** independent of the type of market in which the commodity is produced. This possibility, however, is not easily verifiable, and in any case it cannot be taken account of within the standard analytical framework.

Society's Production Possibilities Independent of the Form of Industrial Organization

One of the most controversial assumptions relevant to the conclusion of competitive optimality is that utilization of resources is equally efficient, in a technical sense, under competition and monopoly. The conclusion that competition is the best allocator of resources **for a given technology** fails to take account of the possibility that a monopolistic industry may employ quite different productive techniques than its competitive counterpart.

One of the most important advocates of this possibility was Joseph A. Schumpeter, who argued that the invention and introduction of new products and processes is centered in the large, typically monopolistic or semimonopolistic firm.[23] To the extent that this is the case, new innovations and technology will be more likely to occur in monopolistic than in competitive industry. Accordingly, a

---

[23] J. A. Schumpeter, *Capitalism, Social and Democracy* (New York: Harper, 1950).

comparison of monopoly with competition at a fixed technological position, systematically understates the social contribution of the former. The Schumpeterian contention may be illustrated diagrammatically as follows. The competitive market produces at a point such as E_C in Figure 1.7, where short-run marginal cost equals price. If this industry were monopolized, the ordinary expectation would be a price increase and output decrease to point E_M. However, if the monopolist in such an industry introduces cost-saving innovations, the entire marginal-cost curve may fall to some level MC'. If the curve falls far enough, the monopolist may actually produce more at a lower price (point E'_M) than the original competitive industry, even though the monopolist fully exploits its market power!

The assumption that society's production possibilities do not respond to changes in the form of industrial organization is not strictly necessary to the analysis described above. Competition is Pareto optimal regardless of whether this assumption holds. The Schumpeterian contention is, rather, that society may achieve **more desirable** levels of production under monopoly than under competition, even though such points might turn out to be nonoptimal in the Pareto sense.[24]

It is, of course, possible that society will remain worse off under monopoly even though the monopoly innovates. The benefits of innovation may not outweigh the costs of monopolistic exploitation, and as long as they do not, the community's position will deteriorate when monopolization occurs. The Schumpeterian hypothesis thus need not be interpreted as postulating the **inevitable** superiority of monopoly, although Schumpeter himself may have intended to suggest this conclusion. The

[24]This point may be illustrated with reference to transformation and indifference curves, as in the figure below. Suppose a consumer is initially at point E, a tangency between indifference curve I and transformation function TT. This is the standard utility-maximizing position. If the transformation curve shifts outward to $T'T'$—which is what might happen under the Schumpeterian contention about monopoly—the consumer might find himself at a point such as n. It is true that the consumer now suffers from monopolistic distortion and cannot reach the best possible position on $T'T'$. Yet his welfare has improved; indifference curve I' is surperior to I.

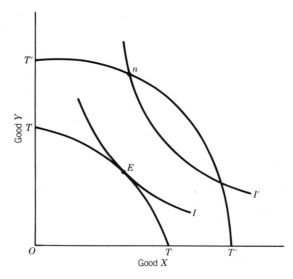

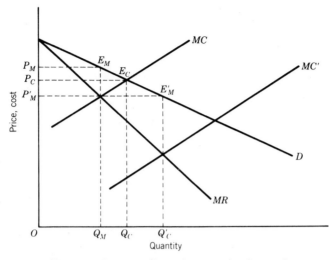

Figure 1.7   The effect of cost-saving innovation.

troublesome implication may be, rather, that the standard comparison of competition with monopoly is **irrelevant** for many problems posed by a dynamic world in which productive techniques are subject to continual change.

The "Static" Comparison and "Dynamic" Considerations

Many of the difficulties that arise in attempting to compare competitive and monopolistic results can be discussed in terms of a **static** versus a **dynamic** approach. Although the definition of these terms suffers from a degree of ambiguity,[25] they are helpful in discussing a very basic problem of economic analysis. The problem arises because, in complex economic systems, many things are changing at once. It thus becomes extremely difficult to isolate the effects of changes in a single variable. If we wish to examine the influence of a factor X_1 on some other factor Y, we can, of course, look at the way in which Y changes as X_1 changes. But if the behavior of Y also is influenced by factors $X_2, X_3, \cdots , X_n$, account must somehow be taken of these.

This kind of problem may be circumvented conceptually by confining the analysis of some problems to a moment in time. Various influential elements that are known to change over time are thus "frozen," and the consequences of a change in a single factor may be analyzed in a sense before the others have a chance to "catch up." This is, in effect, a "static" approach and is quite familiar in the form of *ceteris paribus* assumptions in economics. (In drawing a demand curve, for exam-

[25]For an early but useful discussion of alternative interpretations, see Fitz Machlup, "Statics and Dynamics: Kaledioscopic Words," *Southern Economic Journal,* **26** (October 1959), 91–110. .

ple, we examine the effect of price changes on quantity demanded at a moment in time, assuming that all other factors that might affect demand are constant.)

The comparison between purely competitive and non-purely competitive market results utilizes such a static approach. If we were simply to compare the results of different markets, we would observe discrepancies that are due to a variety of factors. The question in which we are interested, however, is: What difference in market solutions is attributable entirely to the **difference in the organization of the markets?** To abstract from other influential factors, it is assumed that these elements—for instance, distribution of income, the tastes of the community, and technology—are fixed. If these factors were allowed to vary, we could no longer observe the "pure" distinction in which we are interested.

It is the assumption of constant or fixed technology that presents the most difficulty. For not only is it likely that technology will vary over time—a likelihood also associated with the other factors assumed constant—but there is an argument that changes in the organization of the market will cause technology to change in a consistent way. Suppose for the moment that the Schumpeterian contention were correct in its extreme form; that is, large monopolistic firms so expand the frontiers of technology that a community is in some sense better off when competitive industries are monopolized. This fact does not challenge the logical validity of the static conclusion that competition is superior. But it suggests that the fixed-technology assumption of the static approach so restricts the analysis as to render its conclusions uninteresting. One might argue, for example, that the static result, although it is correct in its own terms, is less relevant to certain of the policy problems in which we are ultimately interested than a dynamic approach, which allows for change in elements such as technology.

A word of caution is in order at this point. The Schumpeterian hypothesis **is** a hypothesis rather than a proven fact of life. (As we see in Chapter 9, attempts to verify the Schumpeterian arguments empirically have not been very successful.) Efficient resource allocation in the static sense is not society's sole economic objective, but neither is it a trivial objective. The possibility that static misallocation costs would be outweighed by other, dynamic gains should be borne in mind. But it is precisely that: a possibility.

COMPETITIVE OPTIMALITY RECONSIDERED

The conclusion that competitive markets allocate resources efficiently is sometimes challenged on the ground that is it "unrealistic." If "unrealistic" is taken to mean that pure competition is not likely to exist in the real world, then the challenge, although descriptively accurate is a relatively empty one. Competition serves as a standard because of its relationship to optimally efficient allocation. It takes on **normative** significance, which is simply to say that it has something to do with the way things **ought** to be. Whether competitive markets are frequently found "in reality" is thus largely irrelevant.

A more pertinent challenge, also couched at times in terms of "realism," concerns the qualifications that are placed on the analysis by some of the assumptions discussed above. Once again, realism itself is not the issue. Some assumptions employed in the analysis of competition are, to be sure, inaccurate descriptions of the world as it is. It would, of course, be desirable to discard all inaccuracy and pursue wholly realistic theories; yet if this were easily accomplished, the very need for the theories would be called into question. The kinds of analytical constructs or models that we work with are useful precisely because they simplify situations of enormous complexity. Realism is necessarily lost in the process, but this is, in effect, the price that must be paid to reduce some problems to manageable proportions.

If realism is not the issue, however, we are still left with a meaningful question: Do the assumptions of the analysis so restrict its applicability that the conclusions that emerge are of little practical interest? A reasonable answer is **no,** though the point is in principle debatable. The implication of competitive efficiency is a real and important one, again partly in a normative sense.

Let us turn the coin over for a moment and ask about the evils of monopoly rather than the virtues of competition. Should the arguments above convince us that monopoly is invariably a bad thing for society?

We have already examined the most obvious cost of monopoly: distortion in the allocation of resources. By limiting output and raising price above (marginal and perhaps average) cost, the monopolist induces consumers to make inefficient choices. We demand less of the monopolist's goods because we receive an incorrect signal in the form of a price that is greater than the true cost of supplying those goods. Society would benefit from an expansion of output, but the monopolist will not provide it.

Another important effect of monopoly concerns the distribution of society's income. The monopolist is likely to earn excess profits (see Figure 1.4). These profits do not materialize out of thin air; they come from consumers who pay prices in excess of supply costs. It seems doubtful that such income shifts from buyers to sellers are socially desirable;[26] and we may, therefore, want to know more about the magnitude of these redistributions to judge the cost of monopoly.

Does monopoly provide any counterbalancing benefits? We have looked at one circumstance, significant scale economies, in which efficiency may dictate that only a few firms can survive in a market. In addition, we have noted the Schumpeterian contention that large companies with some market power may be the primary contributors to the economy's stream of new products and techniques over time. There are, then, some situations in which markets populated by only a few large firms may be economically desirable. Such markets do not really constitute "monopoly" in the sense we have used the term, but they are obviously a far cry from the purely competitive model.

The economic argument for competition is a powerful one. Whereas there are some important qualifications to the analysis of competitive optimality, these should not obscure the central point. Freely functioning markets tend to allocate society's resources in a particularly effective way.

---

[26]What is desirable, however, is at least in part a matter of judgment, and we are unlikely to find unanimous agreement here.

CHAPTER 2

"Monopolistic" Competition: The Chamberlin Contribution

For many years economic theory centered on the exclusive and opposite cases of pure competition and pure monopoly—the market extremes. Some analysis in the nineteenth century had focused on the theory of duopoly but had not been widely pursued, perhaps because of the highly simplified and somewhat naive nature of the models proposed. In 1932, however, a book appeared that has redirected the attention of economists to this day. This was the work of E. H. Chamberlin expounding the theory of "monopolistic" competition.[1]

The term **monopolistic competition** is quite accurate in describing the thrust of the Chamberlin innovation. Monopolistic competition refers to a form of industrial organization in which elements of competition and monopoly coexist. Put differently, it designates a form of competition subject to market imperfections. These imperfections alter the nature of the equilibrium solution so that it is distinct from both the purely competitive and the purely monopolistic equilibriums. The end result is a kind of in-between outcome, which should engender interest if only because imperfect markets seem to be the rule in the modern economy. The polar extremes of pure competition and pure monopoly are rarely, if ever, visible in the real world. It is true that some agricultural and financial markets seem to approximate pure competition, whereas a narrow definition of a market or industry may disclose some cases that are similar to pure monopoly.[2] Relatively few markets, however, fall within these categories.

The notion of monopolistic competition may be seen to follow from the observation that one particular market imperfection is almost universal: **product differentiation.** There are almost no markets in which consumers fail to make some distinction among different sellers. All aspirins, for example, may be the same physically, but

---

[1] Edward H. Chamberlin, *The Theory of Monopolistic Competition* (Cambridge, Mass.: Harvard University Press, 1932). Page references in the footnotes below are to the 7th ed., 1956. A distinct but related work by Joan Robinson appeared at about the same time: *The Economics of Imperfect Competition* (New York: Macmillan, 1933).

[2] If the market is defined narrowly enough, any firm may be said to have a "monopoly" of its own product. (General Motors, for example, has a monopoly on new Chevrolets.) Very few instances of monopoly under broader definitions are seen, however. Exceptions include public utilities and perhaps patented inventions.

consumers nevertheless seem to believe that differences exist, and the aspirins are thus differentiated within the economic meaning of the term. Similarly, at the retail level the same products often are sold in different stores. If consumers have a preference for some stores over others—whether this preference arises by virtue of the services offered by the stores, the availability of parking, the personalities of the salespeople, the different locations that make some stores more convenient, or anything else—then such products are differentiated. In Chamberlin's words:

A general class of product is differentiated if any significant basis exists for distinguishing the goods (or services) of one seller from those of another. **Such a basis may be real or fancied,** *so long as it is of any importance whatever to buyers, and leads to a preference for one variety of the product over another.*[3]

If true homogeneity is rare, it also is difficult to find cases that meet the pure monopoly condition of "no close substitutes" for the product in question. Without quibbling over the meaning of closeness in substitution, we know that consumers generally have some alternatives to any good or service. One product may be preferred to another, but the seller of the preferred commodity rarely has the kind of leeway commonly attributed to the pure monopolist. If he attempts to raise his price much above that of an acceptable substitute, a large number of customers may well desert him. This means that the firm that has some power over price may still face relatively high price sensitivity (elasticity) of demand for its product. An increase in price, **the prices of other goods remaining constant,** may well induce a disproportionate decrease in purchases.

THE SIMPLE ANALYSIS: THE FIRM IN THE SHORT RUN

Consider the Chamberlinian case in which a relatively large number of firms sells slightly differentiated products. Again, the precise degree of difference or closeness should not be a stumbling block in the initial analysis. The products are ordinarily assumed to be consumer substitutes, that is, capable of performing the same function; yet they are distinct in consumers' minds. Since the goods are distinct, each firm faces a downward-sloping demand curve, such as d in Figure 2.1a. It is likely that the presence of close substitutes will cause this curve to be relatively elastic. That is, a small price increase may drive away a relatively large number of customers, while a small decrease will substantially increase sales, assuming in both cases that the prices of substitute goods remain unchanged. This elasticity may be reflected in a rather flat or shallow slope, although it is dangerous to guess about elasticity values by inspecting the slope of a curve.

The short-run analysis of the firm in monopolistic competition is precisely the same as that of the pure monopolist. The firm will produce at the point at which marginal cost equals marginal revenue, and it will charge the price that the demand curve accepts for such a quantity (quantity Q and price P in Figure 2.1a). This is, in

---

[3] See footnote 1 above at p. 66; emphasis added.

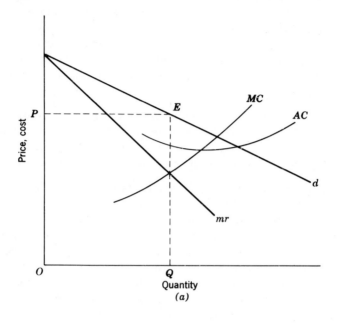

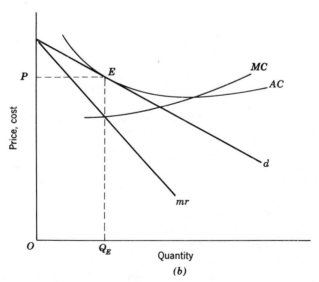

Figure 2.1 The firm in monopolistic competition.
(*a*) Short-run equilibrium. (*b*) Long-run equilibrium.

effect, a monopoly price, which likely enables the firm to earn an "excess," or above normal, profit.

THE SIMPLE ANALYSIS: THE FIRM IN THE LONG RUN

The long-run situation of the firm is altered by the possibility that new firms will enter the market. Assuming free entry, as Chamberlin does, the existence of above-normal profits cannot persist beyond the short run. New firms will be induced to enter and will produce differentiated products that are closely substitutable with those already marketed. As in the case of pure competition, this will have the effect of depressing the demand curves faced by established firms. The curves will retain their negative slope since product differentiation continues; but the firms, which had been earning profits, will now find that they are unable to sell as much at any price.

The process of entry will continue as long as excess profits exist, and firms will ultimately reach a long-run equilibrium at a point such as *E* in Figure 2.1*b*; that is, as long as price exceeds average cost, profits exist and entry continues. Entry ceases only when price is driven down to the level of average cost; that is, when a zero-profit position has been reached. In Figure 2.1*b*, the firm continues to produce at a level of marginal-cost–marginal-revenue equality. However, the demand curve has been sufficiently depressed that the price that the firm can obtain for this optimal output no longer exceeds its average cost of production. Price equals average cost, and total revenue just covers total cost.[4]

This zero-profit equilibrium of the monopolistic competitor is obviously similar to the long-run equilibrium condition for the firm in pure competition. There is, however, one important difference. Production under monopolistic competition does not occur at a point of minimum average cost. Diagrammatically, as long as there is **any** negative slope in the firm's demand curve, zero-profit equilibrium can be attained only at some point to the left of minimum *AC*. It is for this reason that monopolistic competition is sometimes referred to as an inefficient form of industrial organization, one that implies a persistent excess capacity for firms.

Indeed, the welfare implications of monopolistically competitive markets may be viewed quite negatively. Production costs are higher than under pure competition, and consumers pay higher prices (price exceeds marginal cost and in the long run corresponds to a higher level of average cost). Yet sellers still earn zero profits in the long run, so no one is better off! Monopolistic competition does, however, imply a wider variety of goods than the purely competitive market. This may suggest some welfare gain for consumers.

EQUILIBRIUM OF THE FIRM AND GROUP

A point of interest in monopolistic competition analysis is the nature of the demand curve confronting the firm. Since each firm has rivals that produce closely substitutable commodities, demand for the firm's product will depend partly on the

---

[4]Once again, we assume that some "normal" profit is included in the firm's cost curve.

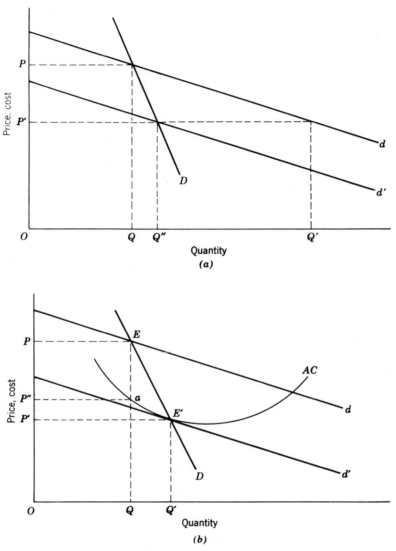

Figure 2.2 Price adjustments in monopolistic competition.

prices charged by rivals. Accordingly, the firm's demand curve must embody some assumption about the way in which its rivals' prices behave. In the usual analysis, the assumption attributed to the firm is that prices of other goods remain constant at their original level. The firm in monopolistic competition expects, in other words, that if it alters its price there will be no price reaction on the part of rival sellers. This is a plausible supposition as long as each firm individually is small relative to the market, for a price change by a single firm may then not be an event of great impor-

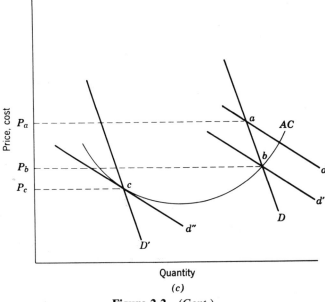

Quantity

(c)

Figure 2.2   (*Cont.*)

tance to the others. As we have noted, the firm's demand curve under this assumption will be an elastic, probably flat curve, such as *d* in Figure 2.2*a*.

Given an elastic curve such as *d*, however, it is quite conceivable that other firms may be induced to attempt price cuts, their reasoning being: "If I cut my price a little I may greatly increase my sales."[5] But if **all** or many firms should actually cut prices, *d* is no longer the relevant demand curve for any individual firm. This curve was drawn on the assumption that the prices of substitute goods remain constant. With the prices of substitutes falling, no single firm will gain as much in sales by cutting its own price. The pertinent demand curve now becomes a curve such as *D* in Figure 2.2*a*, reflecting the less elastic demand conditions facing each firm when the prices of all firms move together. The individual firm under this condition will neither gain as much when it cuts prices, nor lose as much when it raises prices, as it would with rivals' prices constant.

As the juxtaposition of the *d* and *D* curves in Figure 2.2*a* indicates, the nature of rivals' behavior makes a substantial difference to the firm in an imperfectly competitive market. The firm facing demand curve *d* may decide to lower its price from *P*, the prevailing market price, to some level such as *P'*. The firm's expectation is that its sales quantity will increase from *Q* to *Q'*, but if other firms also lower their prices to *P'* the actual sales increase for the single firm will be only from *Q* to *Q''*. If, after moving from (*Q,P*) to (*Q'',P'*), the firm maintains its expectation of constant rivals' prices, it will now confront an anticipated demand curve such as *d'*. That is, the

[5]Note, however, that an elastic demand curve need not indicate that a price reduction is profitable; the firm must still look to its cost of production.

firm's d curve **shifts** down. The firm is disappointed in its original estimate of the sales increase that would follow a price cut, but it still believes that rivals' prices will not respond to its own future price changes. It thus continues to anticipate a relatively elastic demand curve at the lower price level, P'.

The d and D curves also provide an apparatus for distinguishing two types of adjustment in monopolistic competition. Suppose that an "optimal" or "appropriate" number of firms exists initially. Individual firms may be charging a price such as P in Figure 2.2b. At P each firm is earning a net profit of Ea per unit ($PP''aE$ in toto). Under the assumption that rivals' prices will remain fixed, each firm may experiment with a price reduction. But when all firms reduce price, the d curve confronting each firm individually shifts down along D, the relevant demand curve when prices move together. Ultimately an equilibrium price such as P' is established. At this price, d' is tangent to AC at the point at which D intersects AC. Equilibrium is thus achieved by a given group of firms, and it is seen that some tendency toward equilibrium may exist in monopolistic competition apart from entry or exit.

It must be emphasized, however, that as long as the group is not optimal in number, entry and exit remain the crucial, long-run adjustment mechanism. Consider the case in which the size of the group is initially nonoptimal. There will be no common price that would establish a stable zero-profit equilibrium. Such an instance is illustrated in Figure 2.2c, in which d and D are the original demand curves and P_a is original price. A zero-profit position might be reached at point b (price P_b), as firms attempting price cuts find that their d curves shift down along D. But b is not an equilibrium, for each firm will calculate that it would be better off **raising** its price and moving back along d' to a profitable (price in excess of average cost) position. The attainment of an equilibrium in this case requires a change in the size of the group, specifically entry of new firms that will shift D to the left.[6] Eventually, D must shift to some position such as D', at which equilibrium for the firm and group is possible at a point such as c (with associated price P_c).

SOME DIFFICULTIES WITH THE ANALYSIS

Monopolistic competition analysis encounters a number of complications that have not yet been mentioned. One of these stems from a remarkable coincidence that may have been noticed in the preceding discussion. This is the fact that we apparently are able to let d and D represent the relevant demand curves for **any** firm; and we are similarly able to let AC represent the average-cost curve for **any** firm. This striking fact simply reflects the assumption—which Chamberlin himself terms "heroic"— that each firm in the group faces identical cost and demand curves. This means, in effect, that every firm is precisely the same size (it produces similar amounts at similar prices) and that the demand for commodities produced by the group is somehow "evenly" distributed among the differentiated sellers.

---

[6]Entry of new firms will serve to depress, or shift to the left, both the D and d curves; this simply reflects the fact that the demand curve facing each firm under either pricing assumption will fall as more firms enter the market.

It may appear that these uniformity assumptions are quite extreme. Once again, however, the relevant question is not whether the assumptions seem to be "realistic" in some subjective sense, but rather whether we learn anything of importance under the specified conditions. An examination of monopolistic competition theory under more realistic assumptions is beyond the scope of this discussion. It is worth considering, however, one important objection to the uniformity assumptions that has been raised by Stigler. He states:

How can different products have uniform costs and demands? The quantity axes of the various product diagrams are simply not the same: one measures (for example) three-room apartments, another four-room houses, and perhaps still another restaurant meals (an excellent substitute for a kitchen).[7]

In other words, how can it be stated that the demands for, and costs of, "different" products are "the same?" A demand for x units of a three-room apartment is not the same thing as a demand for x units of a four-room house, even if an identical number of units of each is demanded at the same price. What Stigler is pointing out is that the uniformity assumption **is not meaningful** when applied to a group of nonhomogeneous products. Accordingly, the precise meaning of the analysis based on that assumption is open to question.

A further difficulty with monopolistic competition analysis is the very vague character of the Chamberlinian "group." Strictly speaking, the analysis can proceed without a careful definition of the group. That is, the reasoning and conclusions of monopolistic competition theory can be explained almost entirely in terms of the firm, without delineating specifically the group of which it is a part. It is nevertheless helpful to specify a meaningful definition of the group or, at least, to determine whether such a definition is possible. At this point, however, a number of common market-definition problems arise.

All that we know about the Chamberlin group is that it consists of a large number of uniform firms producing differentiated, but substitutable, products. This would present no great difficulty if the line between substitutes and nonsubstitutes were a clear one, but such is rarely the case. What is especially troublesome is that for any defined product group, some "outside" products are likely to exist that are substitutes for some, but not all, of the products within. What, then, is the appropriate definition of "group"? If it is broadly defined so as to encompass some outside products, the group will contain some products that are not substitutes for each other. But if narrowly defined, it will exclude products that may be very close substitutes for some of its constituent items. It is easy to conceive of a spectrum of products, $X_1, X_2, X_3, \cdots X_n$, such that any given item is a close substitute for those lying near it on the spectrum, but is not a good substitute for items lying farther away. For example, X_5 may be an excellent substitute for X_4 and X_6, a fairly good substitute for X_3 and X_7, but a rather poor substitute for X_1 and X_9. An exam-

[7] George J. Stigler, "Monopolistic Competition in Retrospect," in *Five Lectures on Economic Problems* (New York: Macmillan, 1949), pp. 12–24.

ple might be a market in which sellers of physically identical products are differentiated by location. If the sellers are, say, spaced at equal intervals, consumers located in various parts of the market will prefer the sellers closest to them. Each seller will provide a good "substitute product" for those sold by the nearest rivals but a less satisfactory substitute for the products of more remote rivals. There is no obvious cutoff point that would define the group in this setting. The group might be considered to consist of firms 1 through 5, 1 through 10, 6 through 20, 1 through n, or any other segment of the spectrum; each definition would appear equally appropriate or inappropriate.

This kind of market-definition problem is extremely common. The decision as to what product lines should be included or excluded from a grouping is rarely an easy one, and the practical compromises that are reached are often unsatisfactory. In the case of monopolistic competition, the difficulty is at least potentially significant. For although the analysis focuses on the firm, it also presupposes a meaningful idea of the group. As Chamberlin defines it, the group possesses characteristics that are comprehensible; its meaningfulness, however, is compromised by the inherent, and perhaps insoluble, difficulty of market definition.

EVALUATING THE CONTRIBUTION

The nature of the Chamberlin contribution has been a topic of continuing discussion among economists.[8] Although the applicability of specific aspects of the theory is quite limited, the significance of the theory is widely recognized. Monopolistic competition theory is important not so much as a prototype of actual markets but, rather, for the approaches to market analysis that it has helped to stimulate.[9]

Competition and monopoly are no longer viewed as mutually exclusive, "either–or" characteristics. It is recognized not only that most markets combine elements of the two extremes but also that **the analysis of the extremes may be a wholly inadequate tool** for dealing with the combined cases. The attention that economists in recent decades have devoted to oligopoly is in no small part due to the theory of monopolistic competition. Ultimately, it is the opening of such new avenues that may be judged the most important contribution of Chamberlin.

---

[8] For a range of interesting evaluations, see Robert E. Kuenne, Ed., *Monopolistic Competition Theory* (New York: Wiley, 1967).

[9] Notice, however, that Chamberlin's large-group model bears a striking resemblance to many retail markets (e.g., food stores, restaurants, and gasoline stations). Sellers are numerous, products are closely substitutable, and entry is easy. The excess capacity predicted by the model seems to occur in such markets quite regularly.

CHAPTER 3

Oligopoly

The term **oligopoly** is applied to markets in which a few relatively large firms sell similar or identical products. Many industries in the United States are dominated by a few sellers and fall within this category. Numerous smaller firms may exist in the oligopolistic market, and the dividing line between oligopoly and other market forms may be difficult to determine. Most frequently, however, a market is termed oligopolistic when the bulk of its output and sales is accounted for by a small group of sellers.

The primary characteristic associated with this condition of "fewness" in the market is known as mutual or conjectural interdependence among firms.[1] In simplest terms, this means that any oligopolist is influenced by the behavior of its rivals and that its own behavior, in turn, influences those rivals. The firm, then, must consider not only what its rivals happen to be doing at the moment but also how they may respond to its own actions.

Mutual interdependence introduces a severe complication into the analysis of firm and industry behavior. In any market setting, a firm must have some notion of cost and demand in order to determine its most profitable policies. Such knowledge presupposes information about the prices that other firms charge. The oligopolistic seller, therefore, is not unique in its dependence upon the actions of other firms. Many firms face this dependence in the sense that their own demand curves are affected by the prices of rivals. What is unique to the oligopolist is that the actions of rival firms both affect and are affected by it. The situation is thus circular. The optimal pricing policy for an oligopolistic firm A cannot be defined until it is known (or some reasonable assumption can be made about) what rival oligopolist B will do. A's best policy depends upon B. But by precisely the same token, B's best moves cannot be defined without knowledge of A's policy.

The analytical difficulty of this situation is manifest. To determine its best price, A must calculate what B's price is likely to be. But B's price depends upon its calculation of what A is likely to do. To make some estimate of B's behavior, then, A must figure out what B expects it to do. B's position, however, is precisely the same. Its estimate of A's behavior must encompass some kind of a guess about the way in which A expects it to act!

---

[1] The significance of this element is such that some economists prefer to define oligopoly as the condition of interdependence rather than in terms of the number and relative size of firms.

The oligopoly situation is thus akin to a guessing game in which ''I know that you know that I know that you know . . . .'' Presumably there is a reward to out-guessing one's opponents. A particular policy adopted by an oligopolist may be extremely profitable if it surprises rivals, but unprofitable if it is anticipated. This type of ''game,'' however, may be ''played'' in many ways, and for this reason the outcome is most difficult to predict.

Oligopoly, then, contains a far greater element of uncertainty than do any of the markets we have discussed previously. Unlike the pure monopolist, the oligopolist does have rivals to worry about; and unlike the competitive firm, the oligopolist's optimal policy is not dictated unambiguously by the workings of an impersonal market. There is a similarity between oligopoly and monopolistic competition in that the firm in both markets has meaningful rivals. But the oligopolist may not be able to assume, as does its counterpart in the Chamberlin model, that rivals are indifferent to its policies.

In order to maximize profits, the oligopolist must do what any other firm would do: produce to the point of marginal-cost–marginal-revenue equality and charge the appropriate price. The complication, however, is that the oligopolist's demand curve **cannot be specified** without knowledge of rivals' behavior. The amount that the firm can sell at any price will depend upon variables such as the prices that rival firms are charging for their products. And the demand curve confronting the firm may assume quite different positions and shapes under alternative assumptions about competitors' policies.

Oligopoly-type situations frequently are encountered outside the realm of economics and business. In a football game, for example, the best offensive play may depend upon what the defense anticipates and vice versa. A pass may be the best play if the defense expects a run, but if the pass is anticipated, it may turn out to be the worst offensive ''policy.''[2] Military situations in which limited resources must be employed to defend and attack targets are quite similar in nature. The defender's chances are enhanced if he can figure out which targets are likely to be attacked; whereas the attacker's chances improve if he can calculate which targets will be defended. It is not necessary, however, to look beyond the market system for examples of oligopolistic conflict.

Although any yardstick used to classify an industry as an ''oligopoly'' is necessarily arbitrary, it is easy to cite numerous manufacturing industries—for instance, steel, aluminum, automobiles, and cigarettes—in which a few firms account for a large proportion of output. Our interest in explaining the behavior of oligopolistic industries and the firms that operate therein is very strong if only because so much of our national output is produced and sold under these conditions. Unless it is possible to specify the likely behavior of these industries, we may be unable to evaluate their economic performance and to design appropriate public policies toward them.

---

[2]Of course, the outcome of a football game may turn largely on the ability of the players, just as the outcome of a market contest may depend on who produces the best goods. In both instances, however, we could say that strategic considerations may make a difference for any given level of performance.

It may appear at first glance that the oligopoly problem is unmanageable, that is, beyond analysis. Optimal behavior for the firm depends upon rivals' behavior or, perhaps more accurately, the firm's estimate of rivals' behavior. Yet because this is true for every firm, the process seems to lead nowhere. A cannot act without knowing or guessing what B will do; but B cannot act without knowing or guessing what A will do. Obviously, the range of possible actions that the firms might view as optimal may be very wide, and this is the crux of the oligopoly problem.

Although few economists are likely to argue that the present state of oligopoly theory is satisfactory, the problem can be reduced to at least semimanageable proportions. It is possible to specify a number of simple behavioral reaction or response patterns and to trace their implications. This yields some initial notion of the range of possible oligopoly outcomes. As will be seen, however, the range is so broad as to be of little use by itself. What is required is some definition of those behavior patterns that, if not universal, may seem sufficiently reasonable to point in the direction of the most probable market solutions. The task is difficult and involves consideration of several basically distinct approaches. It is worth remembering throughout that no single approach, or specific version of an approach, can be offered as an explanation of the way all oligopolists behave at all times.

THE CLASSICAL DUOPOLY APPROACH

The oldest approach to oligopoly analysis is that embodied in the classical models of duopoly. The duopoly model—involving a two-firm rather than a several-firm market—can be regarded primarily as a simplifying device. The results of the models need not depend upon the existence of precisely two firms, but rather they may hold in a general way for all markets in which the number of firms is small. The process of generalizing from the two-firm to n-firm case, however, may involve some qualification of the market outcome.

Characteristically, classical duopoly models depend on assumptions of extremely simple, perhaps naive, behavior on the part of market rivals. The duopolists are generally assumed to act as profit maximizers, but their expectations of how their opponent will respond to their own policies tend to be both simplistic and persistent.

A Naive Example: The "Macy's–Gimbels" Model

It is quite conceivable that oligopolists, at least over relatively short periods, will price according to rules of thumb. One of the possibilities that could follow from the adoption of shortsighted rules is illustrated by a simple construct called the Macy's–Gimbels model. Without treating the two firms' costs or demands explicitly, suppose that duopolists Macy's and Gimbels adhere to the following pricing rules.

Macy's: will match Gimbels' price.
Gimbels: will undercut Macy's price by 10 percent.

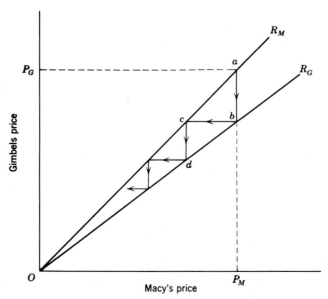

Figure 3.1   The Macy's–Gimbels duopoly model.

The implication of these policies may be traced by constructing reaction patterns or curves for both firms, as in Figure 3.1. On the Macy's reaction curve, R_M, we can read for any price set by Gimbels the price with which Macy's reacts; similarly, the Gimbels reaction curve, R_G, tells us the price with which that company reacts to any price set by Macy's. In Figure 3.1, R_M is a 45-degree line from the origin, indicating that for any Gimbels price, P_G, Macy's responds with the same price, P_M (the scale on the Macy's and Gimbels price axes being identical). The Gimbels reaction curve, R_G, is also a straight line through the origin, but it lies (10 percent) beneath R_M at all nonzero points. This indicates that for any positive price set by Macy's, Gimbels responds with a price that is 10 percent lower.

Suppose that the companies initially are at a point such as a in Figure 3.1. Here Macy's and Gimbels are charging identical prices, P_M and P_G, respectively. Gimbels, following its pricing rule, will not remain at P_G but will cut price by 10 percent, moving the duopolists to point b. But now Macy's, following its pricing rule, will match Gimbels' lower price, with the resulting combination at point c. The pricing path is now clear. Macy's price always will be undercut by Gimbels, Macy's will match the Gimbels price cut, and Gimbels will cut again. If each company ahdreres to its pricing rule—that is, remains on the specified reaction pattern— the ultimate result is that both firms charge a price of zero! No matter how low Macy's price falls, Gimbels will undercut; but no matter how far Gimbels undercuts, Macy's will match.

This strange result can only be explained by the failure of the duopolists to realize what is happening to them. Each firm is reacting to the other, but it is apparently proceeding as if it does not expect the other to react to its own pricing initiatives.

Either firm would do better if it were to select a best (most profitable) price that it could maintain **after the predicted reaction** of the other. Gimbels could reason: "Macy's always will match our price; **given** that they will do so, what price will yield us the highest profit?" Or, similarly, Macy's could determine its best price, **given** that Gimbels will be 10 percent lower. For either firm to act in this fashion means that it has abandoned its reaction curve of Figure 3.1 and adopted a different policy. In fact, each company's reaction pattern, as drawn in Figure 3.1, is **absurd in light of the other's policy.**[3]

The duopolists in this case come to disaster by effectively ignoring part of the mutual interdependence problem. Each rival recognizes his dependence on the price of the other and therefore reacts; but each fails to realize that the other is also re-acting to him.[4] Obviously the firms are making very poor use of their experience, and it is reasonable to ask whether intelligent business managers could be expected to act in this fashion. In general, they probably do not; yet there are cases of price warfare that may reflect a process quite similar to that of the Macy's–Gimbels model. Such contests tend to be short-lived; nevertheless the model does provide some insight into the possibilities for instability in oligopolistic markets.

The Cournot Model

The best known of the classical duopoly models was formulated by the French econ-omist Augustin Cournot in 1938.[5] The Cournot model, originally couched in an example of two adjacent mineral springs owners, employs the following assump-tions:

1. There are two sellers of a homogeneous product.
2. Each seller has identical marginal costs, which for simplicity are assumed to be zero.
3. The market demand curve is fully known to both sellers and for simplicity is assumed to be linear.
4. The sellers are output adjustors rather than price adjustors.
5. Each seller believes that the other will continue to supply to the market whatever amount of the product he is currently supplying.

The final assumption is crucial to the workings of the model and is identical to the naive beliefs of Macy's and Gimbels above. Each duopolist, in effect, concludes that the other is insensitive to his policies, that is: "I will react to your policies but assume that you do not react to mine."

---

[3] Suppose that both firms had utilized a policy of matching the other's price. Here the two reaction curves would coin-cide, since each would be a 45-degree line through the origin, and **any** market price, however established, would tend to persist.

[4] This failure, a common assumption of the classical models, is sometimes termed "zero conjectural variation." The firm, in other words, forms a conjecture (guess) that its rival will have **no** response to its own policies.

[5] *Researches into Mathematical Principles of the Theory of Wealth* (1838), trans. N. T. Bacon, 2nd ed. (New York: Macmillan, 1927).

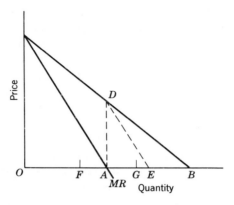

Figure 3.2   The Cournot duopoly outcome.

A common presentation of the Cournot model is shown in Figure 3.2. Suppose that seller A enters the market first. Its most profitable output level will be OA (which is equal to $\frac{1}{2}OB$), that quantity which equates marginal cost (here zero) with marginal revenue. This is the ordinary monopoly result, although the zero marginal-cost assumption is a bit unusual. When seller B enters the market, however, it expects A to continue suppling OA regardless of what B itself may do. Given this expectation, B sees as its relevant demand curve segment DB, that portion of the total market demand not served by A. Accordingly, B will produce quantity AE (equal to $\frac{1}{2}AB$ or $\frac{1}{4}OB$), a point of marginal-cost–marginal-revenue equality for its defined demand curve. Seller A must now reassess its position because quantity AE ($\frac{1}{4}OB$) is being supplied by seller B. Proceeding under the assumption that B's output will be maintained at this level, A will offer its new optimal (profit-maximizing) quantity, in this case $\frac{1}{2}$ $(OB - AE)$ or $\frac{1}{2}$ ($\frac{3}{4}$ OB).

The adjustment process is wholly repetitive. Each seller, assuming the others output to be fixed, will produce that amount which maximizes its own gain. This amount will always equal one half of **OB minus the rival's current output.**[6] Thus, in the first stage, A supplies $\frac{1}{2}OB$. In stage two, B supplies $\frac{1}{2}$ $(OB - \frac{1}{2}OB)$, or $\frac{1}{4}OB$. Similarly in stage three, A supplies $\frac{1}{2}$ $(OB - \frac{1}{2}OB)$, or $\frac{3}{8}$ OB. Continuing the process, total output eventually will approach $\frac{2}{3}$ OB (OG in Figure 3.2), with each seller supplying an equal amount, $\frac{1}{3}$ OB (OF in Figure 3.2)[7] Such a result

[6]This follows from the fact that the marginal-revenue curve associated with any linear demand curve bisects horizontal lines drawn from the price axis to the demand curve. (See Joan Robinson, *The Economics of Imperfect Competition*, (London: Macmillan, 1933); pp. 29–30 in 1959 reprinting.) For the zero marginal-cost situation of the Cournot model, the marginal-revenue curve will intersect the horizontal axis, and become equal to marginal cost, at a point halfway between the origin of the firm's **relevant** demand curve and the point at which that demand curve cuts the horizontal axis. That is, each firm's profit-maximizing output always occurs at the midpoint of its demand curve, where its demand curve is defined as that portion of the market demand curve not served by the opponent. It may be noted that the optimal position is also, in the zero marginal-cost case, a revenue-maximizing position.

[7]Total output will be: $OB(1 - \frac{1}{2} + \frac{1}{4} - \frac{1}{8} + \frac{1}{16} + \ldots) = \frac{2}{3}$ OB ($= OG$ in Figure 3.2). Output of seller A will be: $OB(1 - \frac{1}{2} - \frac{1}{8} - \frac{1}{32} + \ldots) = \frac{1}{3}$ OB ($\frac{1}{2}$ OG). Output of seller B will be: $OB(\frac{1}{4} + \frac{1}{16} + \frac{1}{64} + \ldots) = \frac{1}{3}$ OB ($\frac{1}{2}$ OG) ($= OF$ in Figure 3.2).

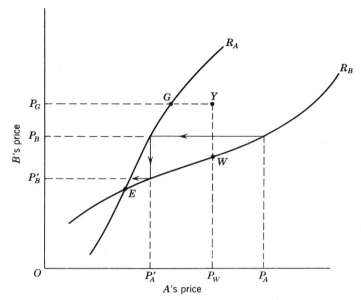

Figure 3.3 A Cournot price-reaction model.

stands in obvious contrast to both the monopoly (quantity *OA*) and competitive (quantity *OB*) outcomes.[8]

A Cournot-type result also can be portrayed in terms of price reaction curves, as shown in Figure 3.3. If sellers A and B are price adjusters,[9] all other assumptions remaining the same, each can calculate his optimal price response to any price set by the other. Should A set price P_A in Figure 3.3, for example, B may set its price at P_B as the response that yields it the highest profits compatible with P_A. A will now react with price P_A', and B will respond with P_B', as the duopolists grope toward point *E*. The reaction curves[10] of A and B, R_A and R_B, respectively, intersect at *E*, a Cournot equilibrium. At such a point, there is no tendency to change, for each seller is already charging the price that maximizes its profits given the price of its rival.

This equilibrium, however, still depends upon myopic behavior by both duopolists. It is a satisfactory solution only as long as each firm believes that the

[8]The Cournot result may be generalized as follows. Equilibrium output is $(n/n + 1)$ (OB), where *n* is the number of rivals in the market. Notice that for $n = 1$, output is simply *OA*, the pure monopoly result. As *n* becomes very large, output approaches *OB*, the purely competitive result.

[9]There is a difficulty in portraying Cournot duopolists as price adjustors since, with homogeneous products, the market should shift entirely to the low-price seller. Strictly speaking, this paragraph does not describe price **adjustments,** but rather the price **behavior** implied by the quantity adjustments of Cournot duopolists.

[10]The reaction patterns are derived by examining each firm's profit-indifference curves—that is, the price combinations charged by the two firms that yield the same profits. The optimal response to any price charged by the rival firm is that price which places the duopolist on the highest profit-indifference curve attainable. See William J. Baumol, *Business Behavior Value and Growth,* rev. ed. (New York: Harcourt, Brace and World, 1967), pp. 17–18.

price charged by the other will persist no matter what it does. Should either duopolist awaken to the fact that its rival is responsive, it can do better than point E. Instead of reacting to B's price as if it were fixed, A may, for example, react to B's entire reaction curve. That is, A may choose that price which yields it the highest profit **after B responds** according to the pattern of R_B. A may choose the most profitable point for it on R_B and price in such a way that B responds by going to that point. In Figure 3.3, A's most profitable position on R_B might be a point such as W; if so, A would set its price at P_W, since B's reaction, now anticipated by A, will place the firms at W. Of course, duopolist B may be the one to awaken. It may choose some price such as P_G, causing A to respond in such a way that duopolists wind up at B's preferred position, for example, a point such as G.

If either one of the duopolists becomes sophisticated in this fashion, the market solution moves to G or W. But suppose that both become sophisticated. If A charges price P_W and B charges P_G, the effective price combination becomes a point such as Y. This point lies off both reaction curves. Each duopolist has indeed abandoned its original response pattern, which was based on the assumption that the opponent's price is fixed. It is possible that each firm will be better off at point Y than it was before. However, there is no reason to expect that Y will be an equilibrium position. To determine whether the price it now charges is optimal, each duopolist must again calculate the response pattern of the other. The Cournot solution thus breaks down under sophisticated behavior, and it is not possible to show where an alternative equilibrium lies or even if one exists. This sort of complication is endemic to oligopoly analysis. Solutions are attainable under simplistic assumptions,[11] but a more "realistic" assumption may do little to facilitate more "believable" conclusions.

The Bertrand Model

A variant of duopoly analysis was suggested by Joseph Bertrand in what was apparently a mistaken and confused criticism of Cournot.[12] Bertrand's notion of duopoly is similar to Cournot's but postulates price-adjusting, rather than output-adjusting, rivals. In the Bertrand model, each duopolist, acting on the assumption that its rival will maintain its present **price,** cuts its own price to a lower level. Since products are again assumed to be homogeneous, the low-price seller takes the entire market; but each seller is in turn undercut by the other. This price-cutting continues and ends only when price is reduced to the level of marginal cost—that is, only when a **competitive** market outcome is established!

It is sometimes asserted that the varying results of the Cournot and Bertrand models lie simply in the difference between price- and output-adjusting rivals. This is correct; yet it may not be obvious why merely changing the decision variable should

---

[11] Some sophisticated observers of business behavior, however, might argue that the simple assumption here is less outlandish than it may seem. Baumol, for example, states: "in practice, management is often not deeply concerned with . . . elements of interdependence in its day-to-day decision-making." Ibid., p. 13.

[12] Joseph Bertrand, "Theorie Mathe-matique de la Richesse Sociale," *Journal des Savants* (Paris: September 1883), pp. 499–508; and *Bulletin des Sciences Mathematiques et Astronomiques,* 2d series, **7** (Paris, November 1883).

produce different market results. The reason is that the Cournot duopolist, in supplying some given quantity for any period, is inherently limiting the portion of the market that it can capture. The Bertrand duopolist, on the other hand, offers a (low) price that can capture the entire market—that is, all consumers will want to switch to the firm at that price, eliminating whatever sales its rival had previously enjoyed. It should be evident that in these contrasting cases, The Bertrand price adjustment will be a quite different and more volatile process. It involves larger swings within the market and a continuing inducement for volatile behavior to continue. The process is limited only by its ultimate unprofitability, a condition that occurs when price has been reduced to the level of marginal cost.

The Edgeworth Model

The Edgeworth duopoly model differs from those of Cournot and Bertrand in introducing a relevant limitation on the productive capacity of the rivals.[13] Like Bertrand's duopolists, Edgeworth's firms are price adjusters, each of whom believes the other's price will be maintained. Cost conditions for the two competitors are assumed to be similar (zero marginal cost is assumed for simplicity), and the products sold may be considered homogeneous.[14] As illustrated in Figure 3.4, the Edgeworth process is initially similar to that of Bertrand. Price is measured vertically on axis OD; DD represents the demand curve for seller A; and DD' the demand curve for seller B. The production constraints (i.e., the maximum outputs that can be produced) here are assumed to be OQ and OQ' for A and B, respectively. Initially, A may enter the market and set monopoly price P_M, at which OM units are sold. On entering the market, seller B could simply match A's price, making equivalent sales of OM'. But B has a more profitable course of action under the belief that A's price will not change: It can undercut A by a relatively small amount, taking away most or all of A's sales—a small price reduction is thus expected to yield a large sales increase. Whether B gets all of A's customers at a lower price, such as P_N, will depend on whether it runs into the production constraint. If not, B can supply his maximum output at P_N, with seller A getting the residual (those customers whom B cannot supply).

Once B sets a price, however, A's calculation is precisely the same: A can now take a substantial portion (if not all) of B's sales by cutting price a bit. This process continues, much as it does in the Bertrand case. Each seller cuts price on the assumption that its rival's price will not change, each price cut carrying with it the expectation of a substantial sales increase. This process ends, however, and is, in fact, reversed by the output limitation. As price falls via the successive undercuts, sales by the two rivals are enlarged (as the demand curves indicate, more can be

---

[13]F. Y. Edgeworth, "Le teoria pura del monopolio," *Giornale degli Economist, XV* (1897). The original article was reprinted in English as "The Pure Theory of Monopoly," in Edgeworth's *Papers Relating to Political Economy* (London: Macmillan, 1925), vol. 1, pp. 111–142.

[14]The products could be treated as similar but nonhomogeneous. This would necessitate an additional assumption about the distribution of demand among the sellers.

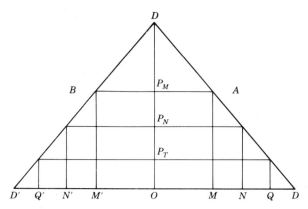

Figure 3.4 The Edgeworth duopoly model.

sold by each at lower prices). At some price, however, the output constraint is such that a further price cut cannot lead to increased sales. Suppose that at price P_T in Figure 3.4 seller A is supplying its maximum output, OQ. It is evident that at this point, seller B has no reason to cut price further. Seller B, too, could dispose of its maximum output, OQ', at price P_T, and cannot benefit by offering the same quantity at a lower price. But there is another option. Rather than being content to sell its entire output at P_T, seller B may rationally calculate that it would earn higher profits by **raising its price** to the monopoly level, P_M, and selling a smaller quantity, OM'. Seller A has, after all, disposed of its entire output at P_T and, assuming that A's policy will not change, B's best stratagem is to behave as a monopolist in the "remaining" portion of the market.

Actually, as long as each rival believes that the other will maintain its price, this price increase may well occur before the maximum output constraint is reached. At any price, each rival must ask: "Am I better off undercutting and receiving an increased sales volume, or would it be more profitable to raise price and accept smaller sales?" As price becomes lower and output larger, each rival's potential sales gain from a further price cut is reduced. Thus, as price falls, the option of a price **increase** becomes progressively more attractive. Undercutting is profitable as long as a modest price reduction causes large sales gains; but when the output constraint intervenes, so that a price cut no longer is expected to produce large sales increases, the cutting policy becomes relatively unattractive.

Reflection should indicate that the diagrammatic presentation of the Edgeworth model is not satisfactory and, indeed, that there may exist some ambiguity in the model itself. Each duopolist is at some points making decisions on the basis of "its own" demand curve (*DD* for A and *DD'* for B in Figure 3.4). Yet when each considers how much in sales can be taken away from the other, the decisions seem to be based on **both** demand curves, that is, on the combined market demand. At best, it appears that the precise meaning of each duopolist's "own" demand curve is unclear; at worst, it may be that the results of the model depend on an inconsistency in behavior whereby the duopolists view the market as segmented at certain times but not at others.[15]

The Edgeworth duopoly model implies no determinate equilibrium. All we can conclude is that there will be a perpetual oscillation: Prices fall through successive undercuts, rise to the monopoly level, and once again begin to fall.

The Hotelling Model

The development of duopoly theory along the Bertrand–Edgeworth line suggested an element of inherent instability in markets populated by few sellers. A model developed by Harold Hotelling challenged the idea that instability is a general characteristic of duopoly.[16] The Hotelling model is less interesting in its specifics than in its general approach and conclusions about stability. The following assumptions are employed.

1. Sellers A and B offer a physically identical product that is differentiated only by the location of the sellers.
2. Specifically, A and B are located, as in Figure 3.5, along a linear market of length L. The market consists of four segments: x and y lie between sellers A and B; seller A is located between seller B and segment a; and seller B is located between A and segment b.
3. Consumers are uniformly distributed along the market, and each consumer makes a given purchase per time period. Demand is thus perfectly inelastic, the quantity sold being assumed invariant to price.
4. Each buyer must transport his or her purchase home at a cost of c per unit distance.

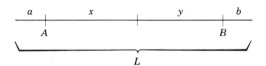

Figure 3.5 The Hotelling model.

The Hotelling duopolists have price discretion, but if either is to make any sales, its price must not exceed the rival's price by more than the cost of transportation from the rival's location to its own. This means, for example, that A's price, P_1, cannot exceed B's price, P_2, *by more than* $c(x + y)$; similarly, P_2 cannot exceed P_1 by

---

[15] Note also that the assumption of a maximum attainable output by each duopolist is really not acceptable in the long run. There is no reason that the duopolists could not ultimately expand their scales of operation so as to produce larger quantities.

[16] Harold Hotelling, "Stability in Competition," *Economic Journal*, **39** (1929), 41–57.

more than $c(x + y)$. Given this constraint, A and B will price in such a fashion that A serves market segment a and B serves b. The portion of the market that lies between A and B is then divided into segments x and y, such that A serves x and B serves y. The actual lengths of these intermediate segments will depend upon the prices P_1 and P_2 that A and B adopt. At the point of division between x and y, however, purchasing from A or B is a matter of indifference to the consumer. Since their commodities are differentiated only by location, it follows that at the dividing point delivered prices are identical. A's price plus transportation cost equals B's price plus transportation cost. That is

$$P_1 + cx - P_2 + cy$$

Moreover

$$L \text{ (the length of the market) } x + a + y + b.$$

Hotelling shows that these equations always yield a determinate and stable solution. What is of major interest is the reasons that led Hotelling to a conclusion so different from those of Edgeworth and Bertrand. The basis of Hotelling's position is that large, sudden switches by consumers from one seller to another, as predicted by Bertrand and Edgeworth, are not characteristic of oligopolistic markets. Hotelling would expect a price cut to attract a few consumers to the price-cutter, but not to greatly increase the price-cutter's sales or to eliminate those of its rival. As long as the consumer switching is gradual, as in the Hotelling model, market stability is likely. Only when it is assumed that all consumers move instantaneously to the low-price seller does the market take on an element of severe instability and possibly an indeterminate solution. This argument is also of interest in explaining differences between the Cournot result, on the one hand, and the Bertrand and Edgeworth results, on the other. The Cournot model, by assuming quantity rather than price to be the rivals' adjustment variable, inadvertently imposes some stability on the market. One rival, by varying output, could not take most or all sales from the other. The quantity-adjustment process in a sense concedes a portion of the market to the rival, and it therefore precludes attempts to capture the entire potential sales.

A further point of interest in the Hotelling model is its long-run implication for seller location. In the short run, with location fixed, price is the strategic variable in the search for maximum profits. In the long run, however, location is variable, and the tendency of sellers to adjust location may be socially undesirable. The socially optimal location of A and B would occur at the quartile points of market L. Transportation costs would here be minimized, with no consumer more than $\frac{1}{4}L$ away from a seller. The tendencies of the sellers, however, will be quite different. Both A and B may be expected to move toward the midpoint of L in an attempt to expand their sheltered markets (a, lying to the left of A, and b, lying to the right of B).[17] If followed, these tendencies may imply a highly inefficient location pattern from society's point of view.

---

[17] Notice, however, that if there are three or more sellers, the location incentives become somewhat more complex.

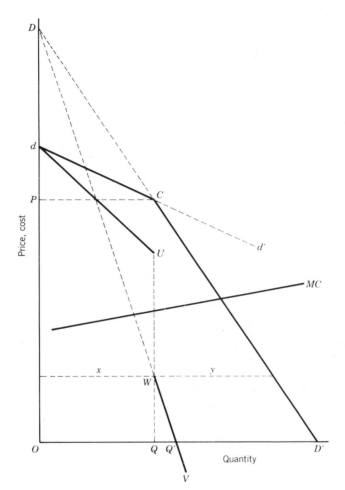

Figure 3.6 The kinked demand curve.

The Kinked Demand Curve

An alternative explanation of stability in oligopoly is provided by the familiar kinked demand curve shown in Figure 3.6.[18] Curve *dd'* represents the firm's demand assuming that rivals do not respond to its price changes. *DD'* is the firm's demand if rivals respond fully—that is, they match any price change initiated by the company in question.

---

[18]For the original presentations see Robert L. Hall and Charles J. Hitch, "Price Theory and Business Behavior," *Oxford Economic Papers*, 2 (May 1939), 12–45; and Paul M. Sweezy, "Demand Under Conditions of Oligopoly," *Journal of Political Economy*, XLVII (August 1939), 568–573.

The kinked demand curve results from the assumption that oligopolists hold different expectations about rivals' responses to their price increases and decreases. The oligopolists believe that other firms will match decreases from the existing market price, P; thus curve DD' is relevant for all prices below P. But they also believe that rivals will not respond to price increases; hence dd' is the pertinent demand curve for prices above P.

Each oligopolist, then, expects that if it cuts price below the existing level, others will follow and the resulting sales gain will be relatively small. If, however, it raises price, competing firms will refrain from raising theirs, and the sales loss will be relatively great. Under the circumstances, neither a price increase nor a price decrease presents an especially attractive prospect to the seller. A market price, once established, thus tends to perpetuate itself, and oligopoly prices may generally prove to be "sticky."

Diagrammatically, the demand curve is kinked at point C in Figure 3.6, so that declines below price P result in relatively small quantity increases, while rises above P lead to large quantity decreases. The demand curve as "actually" envisioned is dCD'. Above C, it reflects the nonmatching expectation; below C, the matching. The firm's marginal-revenue curve, $dUWV$, acquires a discontinuity at output level Q (the point at which demand is kinked). Thus, even if the firm's marginal-cost curve MC shifts, a new equilibrium price may not be established. The curve may shift within the discontinuous portion of the marginal-revenue curve, implying that price P remains optimal. Moreover, if demand should shift, it is not clear where the kink will arise. Conceivably it may be at the same price.

The kinked demand curve explains why a price, once established, may persist. It does not, however, tell us anything about how the price was initially established. We know why and how the kink occurs, but we cannot predict where it will occur (to state that it occurs "at the market price" begs the real question—how was this price determined?). Accordingly, the kinked demand curve is not a full explanation of oligopoly price behavior, and its usefulness is rather limited.

THE GAME THEORY APPROACH

The second major approach is the theory of games, introduced by a mathematician, John von Neumann, and an economist, Oskar Morgenstern.[19] Game theory attempts to define the nature of "rational" (optimizing) strategy in situations of conflict among mutually dependent rivals. Its relevance for oligopoly analysis is thus evident, for it is precisely the problem of oligopoly analysis that the outcome depends on the (uncontrollable) behavior of others. If an optimal strategy could be specified for such situations, it might be possible to say a great deal about oligopolistic market processes.

---

[19] John von Neumann and Oskar Morgenstern, *The Theory of Games and Economic Behavior* (Princeton: Princeton University Press, 1944).

The theory of games is not restricted to examination of the marketplace; some of its most useful applications have, in fact, been in the area of military strategy. A "game" is a situation in which two or more individuals ("players") compete, the outcome being influenced by the actions that each adopts. The setting could be a child's game, an oligopoly market, a poker game, or a war. Each game may be characterized in several ways, for example, according to the number of players and the way in which the outcome responds to alternative modes of behavior; and each player has a set of possible actions corresponding to all circumstances, known as a "strategy." It is usually assumed in analyzing the game that all strategies are known by the players. That is, the players know all possible courses of action open not only to them but to their rivals as well. Given these circumstances, it is possible to explore strategic procedures in simplified cases.

The Two-Person, Zero-Sum Game

The simplest category of game is described as the two-person, zero-sum game. There are two rivals, and the outcome of the game is such that "my gain is your loss." In a poker game, for example, the winnings of one player equal the losings of the other, and the combined winnings and losings under all circumstances **sum to zero.** Another way of describing such games is as "strictly adversary." The players will rank alternative outcomes in precisely reverse order ("my best outcome is your worst," etc.), and each may do as well as possible only by assuring that its rival fares as poorly as possible.

In an economic context, the two-person, zero-sum game may be illustrated by duopolists competing for shares of a market.[20] The strictly adversary nature of the game is obvious. Every percentage addition to the market share of duopolist A implies an equal subtraction from B's share and vice versa. The best outcome for one player (100 percent of the market) is the worst (0 percent) for the other, and the optimizing process for each implies minimization of the opponent's gain. Suppose now that each player has three possible strategy moves. These may involve altering price, advertising, or any other relevant market variable. Every pair of strategies chosen by the two duopolists will determine a particular division of the market between the two. The nine possible outcomes are shown in terms of A's market share in Table 3.1. This table, A's payoff matrix, shows the outcome for A under any pair of strategy moves employed by A and B. If, for example, A selects strategy a_3, and B chooses strategy b_2, A's resulting market share (or payoff) is 5 percent.[21] Given this information, each duopolist knows the alternative payoffs to any strategy selected. A sees, for example, that strategy a_2 will yield 50 percent, 75 percent, or 10 percent of the market, depending on what B does.

---

[20]In this case, the game should actually be defined as "constant" rather than "zero" sum, since the combined payoff of the players always equals 100 percent. The analysis, however, is essentially the same.

[21]The information summarized in the matrix could as easily have been portrayed in terms of B's payoff, and B's payoff matrix can be constructed by subtracting A's payoff under each strategy pair from 100 percent.

Table 3.1   A's Payoff Matrix

	B's Strategy			Row
	b_1	b_2	b_3	Minimum
a_1	45	30	20	20'
A's a_2	50	75	10	10
Strategy a_3	85	5	15	5
Column maximum	85	75	20*	

The Maximum—Minimax Strategy

How might the players in this game proceed? One possibility suggested by von Neumann and Morgenstern is that each will be exceedingly pessimistic in estimating the ultimate market division. Each duopolist may reason that whatever strategy it adopts, its rival will react optimally—that is, will always choose that strategy that "maximizes its share of the market and minimizes mine." If duopolist A proceeds under this assumption, which strategy should it select? Referring to A's payoff matrix, we see that if A pursues strategy a_1, the worst outcome is a 20 percent market share (if B selects strategy b_3). If A chooses a_2, the worst outcome is a 10 percent share (under B's strategy b_3); and if A plays strategy a_3, the worst result is a 5 percent share (under b_2). These worst outcomes are represented by the minimum value in each row of A's payoff matrix, the **row minima**.

Choosing under the assumption that rival B will react optimally—so as to inflict the worst outcome on A—duopolist A should seek the "best" among the three "worst" results. A should choose strategy a_1 on the ground that after B retaliates optimally, A will be better off than it would be otherwise. By choosing a_1, A assures itself a 20 percent market share, rather than the expected 10 percent under strategy a_2 or the 5 percent under a_3. A, in other words, selects the maximum of the minimum values under each strategy, the highest of the row minima. This maximization of the minimum payoffs is called A's **maximin** strategy.

Duopolist B can proceed in precisely the same fashion, assuming that A will retaliate optimally in response to any move—that is, in the best way for A but the worst way for B. Examining the payoff matrix again, we can define B's worst outcome under each of its three strategies as the **highest** market share obtainable by A. B's worst outcome, then, is the highest number in each of its three strategy columns. For strategy b_1, the worst result is an 85 percent share for A; for strategy b_2, the worst outcome is 75 percent for A; and for b_3, the worst is a 20 percent share for A. That is, the worst that B can do under any strategy is represented by the maximum payoff to A in that strategy column. Since B expects A to do its best, thus inflicting the worst result on B, B should select strategy b_3. This limits A's market share to 20 percent at most, whereas A could obtain 75 percent if B plays strategy b_2 or 85 percent if B adopts b_1. B, in other words, chooses the **lowest** among A's **maximum** payoffs, the **minimum** of the **column maxima**. In choosing the best of

its worst outcomes, B plays what is called a **minimax** strategy—one that minimizes A's maximum payoff.

The maximin-minimax strategy combination thus leads to (a_1, b_3). The outcome under this strategy pair, as shown in Table 3.1, is a 20 percent market share for A (and an 80 percent share for B). At first glance, it might appear that this division of the market would be unsatisfactory, especially for A. In fact, however, each duopolist has done as well as it possibly could! **Given A's strategy a_1,** B's strategy b_3 is optimal. It grants A the lowest market share (and B the highest share) consistent with a_1. Had B chosen any other strategy, it would be worse off. But precisely the same is true for A! If B follows strategy b_3, A's optimal response is a_1, yielding a 20 percent, rather than a 10 percent or 5 percent, share of the market. Each duopolist has succeeded in optimizing its payoff, given the strategy adopted by the rival. Neither can do better, and the game finds an equilibrium solution in that neither will now tend to readjust its strategy.

The equilibrium solution of the game emphasizes important qualities of the maximin–minimax strategies. The maximin (minimax) is the best possible course of action against an opponent who pursues the minimax (maximin). In the example above, the maximin strategy employed by A assures it a market share of no less than 20 percent. At the same time, B's minimax has assured it that A will obtain no **more** than 20 percent. Each rival is protected from the possibility of less desirable outcomes, and the maximin–minimax approach serves as an effective sheltering device. Despite the degree of safety offered by the maximin (minimax), however, it may be a decidely inferior strategy against an opponent who does **not** employ a minimax (maximin). [22]

Mixed Strategies

The type of equilibrium solution described above is not found in all games. In fact, the payoff matrix will have an equilibrium only if the maximum of the row minima happens to be the same as the minimum of the column maxima, an entirely fortuitous circumstance. Table 3.2 illustrates a case in which no equilibrium exists. A's payoff matrix again shows the share of the market that A will obtain under alternative strategy pairs. Here A's maximin strategy is a_2, which guarantees it at least 50 percent of the market. B's minimax is strategy b_1, which ensures that A will capture no more than 70 percent. If both duopolists pursue such policies, they will end up at strategy combination (a_2, b_1), where each has 50 percent of the market. Although this will please B (who was acting to prevent A from obtaining more than 70 percent), it is obviously a less pleasing result for A. Had A **not** played the maximin and pursued strategy a_1 instead, it would have taken 70 percent rather than 50 percent;

[22] Suppose that duopolist B had rashly pursued strategy b_2 above. A, playing maximin a_1, would obtain 30 percent of the market; yet if A had played a_2 instead, it would have captured 75 percent. Given that B does **not** minimax, A's maximin may no longer be an optimal strategy. In fact, as this example suggests, it can turn out to be an exceedingly poor course of action.

Table 3.2 A's Payoff Matrix

| | B's Strategy | | Row |
	b_1	b_2	Minimum
A's strategy a_1	70	20	20
a_2	50	90	50'
Column maximum	70*	90	

that is, the maximin is no longer an unambiguously ideal strategy. The choice of strategies is no longer a simple matter.

In such a nonequilibrium situation, it is clearly important for each duopolist to prevent the rival from guessing in advance what its strategy will be.[23] One way the duopolist may do so, ingenious in its simplicity, is to choose its own strategy in a random fashion. The duopolist may reason that its rival is a clever firm that has a good chance of outguessing it in the "I know that you know that I know . . . " situation. Such cleverness may be effectively neutralized by making the strategy decision a matter of chance. Duopolist A, for example, might choose between a_1 and a_2 by tossing a coin, a procedure that assigns a 50 percent probability to each strategy, or by "loading" the odds in some other fashion. This method of selection is known as a **mixed strategy,** since the player, in effect, chooses a combination of alternatives weighted by some probabilities.[24]

The importance of the mixed strategy is that it provides a more favorable expected outcome than could be obtained via the pure maximin. Although we shall not demonstrate this result,[25] it should make intuitive sense. Duopolist A gives up the security of the maximin in return for the higher expected gain of the mixed strategy. A is now vulnerable to the worst outcome [(a_1, b_2) in Table 3.2], but it has improved its expectation of what the actual outcome will be.

Certain aspects of mixed strategies are beyond the scope of this discussion. We shall not, for example, examine the theory of **optimal** mixed strategies or the fundamental theorem of two-person, zero-sum game theory, which states that an equilibrium is determined by mixed-strategy combinations even if none is implied by the pure-strategy combinations.[26] The point of the present discussion is more limited: It is simply that in certain cases, it may pay players to abandon the extremely conservative maximin–minimax strategy for a far bolder approach.

[23] If, for example, A chooses a_1 in Table 3.2, it will do quite poorly if B, anticipating correctly, selects b_2. By the same token, B can expect to fare poorly if A predicts what strategy choice it will make.

[24] In contrast, the simple maximin or minimax is called a **pure** strategy.

[25] The expected value of a game is the sum of each outcome multiplied by the probability that it occurs. Suppose that in the game shown in Table 3.2, A adopts a mixed strategy that gives it a 0.75 probability of playing a_2 and a 0.25 probability of a_1. It is easily verified, using these probabilities and the payoffs in the table, that the expected payoff for A, regardless of what B does, is now greater than if A had pursued a pure maximin. (A's expected payoff under the mixed strategy is 55.0 if B pursues b_1, and 72.5 if B follows b_2. Both exceed the expected and secure value of 50 that A could have assured itself with minimax strategy a_2.)

[26] Several lucid discussions are available, such as Baumol, see footnote 10 above; and R. Duncan Luce and Howard Raiffa, *Games and Decisions* (New York: Wiley, 1957). For excellent and accessible discussions of many strategy issues, see Thomas C. Schelling, *The Strategy of Conflict* (Cambridge, Mass.: Harvard University Press, 1960).

More Complex Games

The two-person, zero-sum game, which has received very extensive analysis, is the simplest of situations. Matters become more complicated if the combined payoff to all players is not constant. In duopoly, for example, the market shares always sum to 100 percent, but it is quite likely that the strategies adopted may alter the size of market sales and accompanying profits. If we consider profit or sales-maximizing rivals in such a situation, the game payoff is a nonconstant sum, and here the variety of outcomes may be considerably enlarged. Possibly it will pay rivals to cooperate, say, to adopt strategies that result in increased total sales regardless of how the larger fund is now divided. If cooperation does not pay, the strategic calculations of the duopolists are likely to become far more complex, and they may not imply a determinate result.

One interesting and important possibility, known as the **prisoners' dilemma,** is that rivals may act to their mutual **dis**advantage. In the well-known original version, two prisoners are questioned separately about their involvement in a crime. The prisoners cannot communicate with each other, and each is told the following.

1. If you both confess, you will receive an appropriate penalty.
2. If neither of you confesses, you will go free.
3. If you confess and the other prisoner does not you will go free and receive an added reward.
4. If the other prisoner confesses and you do not, you will receive a particularly severe penalty, while the other goes free.

These "rules" may be translated into the payoff matrix for A and B, as shown in Table 3.3. A's indicated strategy is to confess, since this will leave him better off regardless of what B does. But B's preferred strategy is also to confess, for the same reason. Both prisoners may thus confess and suffer the consequences, even though it would have been mutually desired for neither to do so! This sort of dilemma may seem more appropriate to grade-D gangster movies than to economics. Its relevance for the analysis of certain oligopoly situations is quite direct, however, and will be seen in later disucssions of collusive behavior.

Equally serious complexities occur in games that contain more than two players. Such situations, called *n*-person games, encounter a wide range of outcomes, some of them quite unwieldy. In addition to some of the earlier alternatives, *n*-person games may result in coalitions, that is, the cooperation of one or more groups of

Table 3.3 A Prisoner's Dilemma: Payoff Matrix for (A, B)

		B's Strategy	
		Confess	Don't Confess
	Confess	$(-1, -1)$	$(+2, -2)$
A's Strategy	Don't Confess	$(-2, +2)$	$(+1, +1)$

players against other groups or individuals. Formal analysis of *n*-person situations is not as well developed as that of the simpler cases. Moreover, the analysis of two-person games cannot be generalized to the more complex situations, which are in some instances far less stable.

Game Theory and Oligopoly Analysis

The application of game theory to oligopoly analysis encounters several difficulties, even in the simplest cases such as two-person, zero-sum games. An initial problem is the assumption, common to many games, that players have very good information about the available strategies and payoffs. Although the theory deals also with games in which information is imperfect, the nature of optimal strategies is altered somewhat; and where ignorance is a serious problem—not an unusual oligopoly case—the suggestions of game theory may lose some force.[27]

Further objections to game theory as a tool of market analysis have to do with the kind of "psychology" required by the prescribed strategies. It has been argued that business managers are simply too optimistic to adopt the conservative, play-it-safe outlook of the maximin–minimax procedure. At the same time, it is suggested, few managers are so amenable to risk-taking that they would actually be willing to allow their own decisions to rest on a random choice, as required by the mixed-strategies cases.[28] These criticisms do not challenge the "logic" or "rationality" of the strategies suggested by the theory of games. They argue instead that these approaches to decision making assume a disposition that business managers are unlikely to possess.

A final problem with game theory is that the minimax–maximin strategy approach is rational only under certain conditions. As we have noted, the strategy may be quite undesirable against an opponent who is pursuing some other strategy. Accordingly, there may be no good reason for any firm to adopt such a course unless it is certain that all rivals do the same. And should anyone experiment with a deviation from the minimax–maximin, there may be no rational incentive ever to return to it.

Even without such possible shortcomings, game theory has not succeeded in defining specific outcomes for all situations of conflict. It has thus far proved impossible to suggest determinate solutions for many of the more complex cases. Thus game theory has failed to define a rational strategy that is directly applicable to the wide variety of oligopolistic markets.[29] Those aspects of oligopoly behavior that

---

[27] A separate but closely related branch of analysis known as **decision theory** suggests criteria that might be adopted where knowledge is severely limited. See Luce and Raiffa, ibid., Chapter 13.

[28] It is difficult to envision a corporation executive calling for "the spinner" when an important policy decision is at hand, and then spinning it to reach the decision. This whimsical example, however, misses the main point: The executive may have neither the knowledge nor the disposition to rely upon any random-choice procedure, no matter how dignified it may be.

[29] Some observers contend that game theory is essentially normative, that is, a statement of how strategies ought to be designed by rivals who wish to act "rationally." As such, the theory might have only limited application to what actually occurs in oligopolylike situations. See Anatol Rapoport, *Two-Person Game Theory* (Ann Arbor: University of Michigan Press, 1966).

puzzled economists prior to the appearance of *Theory of Games and Economic Behavior*, in general, remain puzzling today. But if game theory has failed to provide **the** solution to the oligopoly problem, it has nonetheless laid the foundation for novel approaches to strategy under mutual interdependence, and it has therefore expanded the horizons of oligopoly analysis. Its major impact in economics ultimately may turn out to be that it has led analysts to think in somewhat new terms about the interdependence problem.

THE COLLUSION APPROACH

In 1933, Edward H. Chamberlin[30] suggested that Cournot duopolists, recognizing their interdependence, would adjust output levels so that total market supply reached only the monopoly level (*0A*, or ½*OB*, in Figure 3.2). The duopolists would share equally in the monopoly reward, each doing better than under the conventional Cournot process in which interdependence is never fully recognized. This suggestion illustrates a third group of oligopoly theories that may be broadly termed **collusive.**[31] This approach assumes that mutually dependent firms are aware of their situation and reasons that they may rationally agree to avoid the competitive rivalries that might otherwise develop in small-group markets. Certainly many of these competitive tactics can produce highly undesirable results for the firms involved. This is especially true of any type of price warfare, as in the Macy's–Gimbels and Bertrand and Edgeworth models; yet even in cases that do not involve such obviously damaging consequences, the likely outcome of unrestricted competition may fall short of that which concerned firms would consider optimal. In such circumstances, concerted or cooperative action by firms may be far more profitable than unlimited rivalry.

The collusive approach to oligopoly is in many ways an appealing one to analysts. It is clearly desirable for participating firms who avoid potentially unprofitable competitive tactics. Moreover, "collusion" in the broad sense need not imply a formal or explicit conspiracy that would probably violate the antitrust laws. Rather, it may take the form of a purely tacit "understanding" among competitors, such as an unspoken "gentlemen's agreement" to avoid mutually disadvantageous actions such as price-cutting. In addition to its inherent plausibility, causal observation of American industries suggests that collusion, both tacit and overt, is rather common. Government prosecution of price-fixing conspiracies is frequent and unsurprising, except perhaps to the prosecuted companies. Pricing patterns among competing products are often so uniform as to create suspicion (although not proof) that some kind of tacit agreement exists. Indeed, active price competition may be the exception rather than the rule in oligopoly today. Thus, collusion in the broad

---

[30] Edward H. Chamberlin, *The Theory of Monopolistic Competition*, 7th ed. (Cambridge, Mass.: Harvard University Press, 1958).

[31] The theoretical categories are not entirely exclusive. Game theoretic models, for example, may yield collusive results; and models that begin by assuming collusion may degenerate in such a way that the outcome is not effectively "collusive."

sense is not only a reasonable approach to oligopoly on a priori grounds, but is also an apparent fact of life.

Finally, the theory of collusion offers an extremely simple means of analyzing oligopoly behavior. Analysis of collusive behavior is almost bound to be more straightforward than that of competing firms within an industry. In the collusive case, a group may, in effect, behave as a single enterprise. If this is the case, the problem of oligopolistic interdependence as such no longer exists. Firms need not take account of their opponents' likely response to strategic moves, because both the allowable moves and the countermeasures are defined by the general understanding among them. However, before concluding that this approach is ideal in its plausibility, realism, and simplicity, it is necessary to spell out in greater detail precisely what forms "collusive" oligopoly may take.

Outright Conspiracy

Consider a small group of firms (oligopolists) whose managers are fully aware of their mutual interdependence. These managers will almost certainly recognize that vigorous and unrestrained price competition will not be in their individual business interest. Even if the oligopoly can avoid a truly disastrous course of behavior, it is quite possible that the market outcome will prove unsatisfactory to the firms, in that nonprofit-maximizing prices and quantities will result. In the absence of obstacles such as the antitrust laws, an explicit pricing agreement may appear to be the logical course of action. If the firms agree to fix prices, they should be able to proceed much as if they were a single-firm monopolist. That is, they can choose the price that maximizes total profits of the group and adhere to it as long as it remains appropriate.

In the simplest possible case, we may assume that the cost curves of all firms are identical, as are their anticipated demand curves, under both collusive and competitive behavior. The setting of price by colluding firms, sometimes called a **cartel,** then proceeds in the manner of a monopolist, as shown in Figure 3.7. Group output is determined at quantity Q', the level corresponding to intersection of the industry marginal-cost and marginal-revenue curves, MC and MR, respectively. The resulting price is P'. Recall that the competitive market result in contrast would be at (P, Q). Since we have assumed identical cost and demand curves for all firms, the cartel price–quantity combination should prove satisfactory to each. Group profits, the shaded rectangle $P'E'GF$, will be divided evenly among the conspirators.

This simplified example represents the ideal collusive situation; yet even here conditions may exist that threaten the stability of the result. It is true that under collusion each firm is better off than it would be with unrestrained competition, and, in this sense, every firm has a stake in making the collusive agreement work. In other words, if unrestricted competition is the alternative to collusion, each and every participating firm will be motivated to adhere to the agreement. There is, however, a third alternative that creates complications: the possibility that an individual firm may violate the agreement by secretly "cheating," that is, cutting its own price.

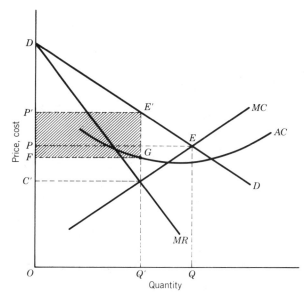

Figure 3.7 A monopolistic cartel.

From the viewpoint of any given firm, this may well be the most profitable of the alternatives; but as we shall see, widespread cheating will destroy the cartel.

Cheating is depicted in Figure 3.8. In part *a* of the Figure, curve *D* is the firm's demand curve drawn on the assumption that all firms in the group charge the same price (it is precisely analogous to the "big *D*" demand curve of the Chamberlin and kinked demand curve models). *MR* is the associated marginal-revenue curve, *MC* is the marginal-cost curve, and point *E* is the equilibrium price–output combination. Under our assumptions, *E* is the solution that will be established by the collusive group.

Curve *d,* however, represents the firm's demand if all other firms **charge the agreed-on price *P*** (it is analogous to "little *d*" in the Chamberlin and kinked demand curve models). Should the firm "cheat" while all others adhere to the pricing agreement, it can expand sales from *Q* to *Q'* by lowering price from *P* to *P'*. This is likely to be an extremely tempting course of action, since the firm can gain a large increase in sales with a relatively small price cut—that is, the "cheating" demand curve, *d,* is relatively elastic. Cheating therefore appears to be a profitable strategy, **assuming** that other conspirators remain faithful to the agreement.

Suppose, however, the firm assumes that others will cheat on the agreement. Diagrammatically, the others will charge price *P'* rather than *P* in part *b* of Figure 3.8. Curve *d* now shows the firm's demand on the assumption that all others charge *P'*—that they cheat. Notice that if the firm were to remain faithful to the agreement by charging price *P* while all others cheat, it would seek nothing at all! This is an

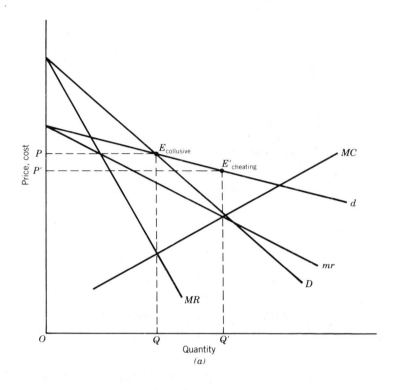

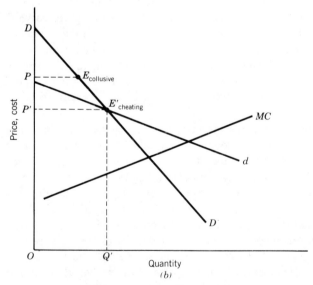

Figure 3.8 Cartel cheating.

extreme example, but the broad lesson is clear. If one expects others to cheat, one cannot likely afford to remain faithful.

We see, then, a basic problem in the maintenance of collusive agreements. Once the agreement is established, cheating may appear to be a profitable course of action for any firm **whether or not** the firm expects others to cheat. If many firms give in to this temptation, however, the immediate effect is to reduce cartel profits, perhaps dramatically.

In Figure 3.9, part *a* depicts the profits (shaded rectangle *PEGF*) of a smoothly running cartel, in which the agreed-on price *P* is charged. Part b is drawn to the same scale, and it shows the diminution of profits (shaded rectangle *P'E'HJ*) when cheating drives price down to *P'*. If cheating is pervasive and prolonged, the cartel

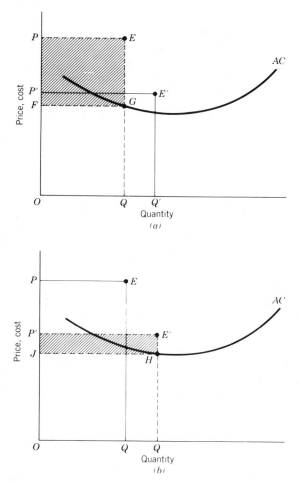

Figure 3.9 Cartel profits.
(*a*) A smoothly running cartel. (*b*) A cartel plagued by cheating.

may break down completely, and market behavior may accordingly return to a noncollusive pattern.

Notice that the cheating problem facing a cartel is precisely akin to the prisoner's dilemma discussed above. The cartel members, like the prisoners, have a mutually profitable course of action: loyalty to their agreement. Yet, again like the prisoners, each member faces a strong incentive to depart from that course—to cheat. If all cheat, however, the profitable agreement breaks down, and all suffer.

Cheating is a potentially serious problem in most collusive agreements, but it should not be assumed that collusion will inevitably break down as a result. If cheating is easily detected by loyal cartel members, its attractiveness may quickly vanish; as noted, the high payoffs assume that one member cheats **and** "gets away with it" undiscovered. Cartels that recognize the destabilizing effects of secret price-cutting may devise procedures to detect it and force compliance to the agreed-on price.[32]

The probability of unstable or ineffective collusion is increased when we drop the simplifying assumption of uniform costs. It is intuitively obvious that a group of firms operating under substantially different cost conditions is unlikely to view a single price as ideal. Given similar demand curves, high-cost firms will prefer higher prices. The question, then, is whether the price that maximizes group profits will prove acceptable to all firms. Actually this question may be appropriately posed in a slightly different form: Granted that all firms agree on the price that maximizes joint profits, will such a price lead to a satisfactory allocation of **sales and profits** among the firms?

Figure 3.10a shows an optimal cartel price, P. This is a pure monopoly price, for it is the price that consumers are willing to pay for output Q, the quantity at which cartel marginal cost equals marginal revenue.[33]

The cartel has determined that it will maximize its profits at (P, Q). But how are the member firms to share the output and receipts? In order to produce total output Q efficiently, each firm must produce the amount for which its marginal cost equals the value of cartel marginal-cost–marginal-revenue equality, or E in Figure 3.10. Part b illustrates a division of sales in a three-firm cartel. Firms A, B, and C are assumed to have marginal-cost curves MC_A, MC_B, and MC_C, respectively; if they produce until marginal cost equals E, the firms will turn out quantities PA, PB, and PC, which sum to PD' or $0Q$, the optimal cartel output. The difficulty with this arrangement is that a high-cost firm such as A will supply a relatively small amount, while lower-cost members enjoy the bulk of market sales and profits. High-cost firms may regard their **share of the market** under the cartel price, rather than the price itself, as unsatisfactory; and it is not surprising that one of the major problems in cartel-type agreements has, in fact, been allocation of the market.[34] Various

---

[32] For pertinent discussions, see Paul W. MacAvoy, *The Economic Effects of Regulation* (Boston: MIT Press, 1965), especially pp. 13–24 and 205–18; and George J. Stigler, "A Theory of Oligopoly," *Journal of Political Economy*, **72** (February 1964), 44–61.

[33] The marginal-cost curve for the cartel is derived from the marginal-cost curves of the member firms; if they obtain inputs in perfectly competitive markets, the cartel marginal-cost curve will be the simple summation of the individual member MC curves. The marginal-revenue curve is associated with the market demand curve.

[34] Note that the members would share the market equally if their marginal costs were identical.

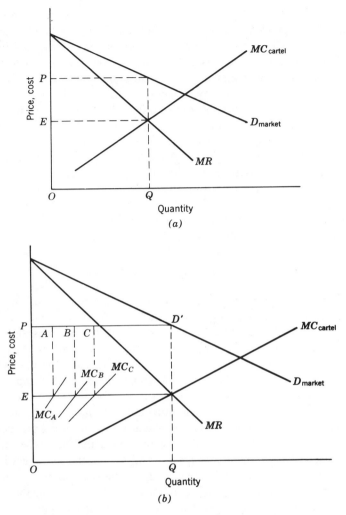

Figure 3.10 Output allocation by a cartel.

market-dividing schemes have been devised to allocate sales and profits among cartel members, but providing each firm with satisfactory shares over an extended period of time often proves difficult.

A further difficulty that may confront the cartel is the threat posed by potential entrants. If new rivals are poised to enter the market, the cartel must decide how to react. It might, for example, adopt price and output policies designed to scare off such firms by making entry appear unprofitable. Alternatively, it could behave so as to "admit" the newcomers, giving up some share of market sales and profits. The complexities posed by the threat of entry are discussed in more detail in Chapter 4.

The administrative problems associated with outright conspiracy are significant. Even if a price acceptable to all firms is established, the temptation to cheat may be strong. However, the establishment of satisfactory price/quantity combinations for all firms may itself be far from easy. When we add the realistic qualification that outright conspiracy among competitors is illegal in the United States, it is not hard to understand why "perfect collusion" may be a rare event, if it occurs at all. This does not mean that the collusion theories of oligopoly should be dismissed. It must be recognized, however, that collusion is not a simple and unambiguous event. We cannot assume that oligopolists band together and behave precisely as a joint monopolist, thus reducing the oligopoly problem to that of monopoly. Something like this may occur at times, but the dangers of oversimplification in most instances should be manifest. If outright conspiracy and cartels are "facts of life," as indeed they are, then so too are the instability and breakdown that may typify many such arrangements. The fundamental difficulty is that the price and output that maximize cartel profits are not invariably optimal for each member firm.

Price Leadership

Rather than resorting to outright collusion, oligopolists may choose to follow informally the policies set by a single firm, the "price leader." Under price leadership, a price changed by the leader becomes a signal for other firms to follow. This type of arrangement has at least two advantages for oligopolists. First, it is extremely simple, mitigating the need for formal and perhaps elaborate agreements that require extensive negotiations. Second and perhaps equally important, price leadership is far more likely to be legal than is any form of overt conspiracy. Although legal rules change over time, antitrust policy in the United States has consistently treated formal collusion more stringently than informal practices.

Analytically, price leadership has the same appeal that any type of collusion model possesses. It is simple and is again "realistic" in the sense that it seems to exist widely. Rather than attempting to explain oligopoly behavior by analyzing the complex interrelationships among firms, price leadership focuses on the behavior of a single firm. All rivals are assumed to have the same simple response pattern: They match whatever price is set by the leader. The plausibility of price leadership is unquestioned; yet the fact that a group of firms adopts this **pricing mechanism** does not by itself tell us much about the **nature of the price** that will be established. The actual price will depend not merely on the existence of the leadership practice, but also on **which firm** emerges as the leader and what pricing rules it follows. Three possible leadership patterns that might emerge deserve some attention.[35]

---

[35] Most of the basic ideas discussed below first appeared in Kenneth E. Boulding, *Economic Analysis*, rev. ed. (New York Harper: 1948), pp. 582ff.; Jesse W. Markham, "The Nature and Significance of Price Leadership," *American Economic Review*, **41** (December 1951), 891–905; and George J. Stigler, "The Kinky Oligopoly Demand Curve and Rigid Prices," *Journal of Political Economy*, **55** (October 1947), 432–449. For some pertinent criticism, see Robert F. Lanzillotti, "Competitive Price Leadership—A Critique of Price Leadership Models," *Review of Economics and Statistics*, **39** (February 1957), 55–64.

Dominant-Firm Leadership. One possibility is that the leadership function will be assumed by the "dominant" firm in the market—one that holds, say, a 50 percent or larger share. This seems likely if there exists a firm so powerful that smaller rivals are reluctant to compete with it. Whatever price the dominant firm sets is accepted by the remainder of the industry, and the firm becomes a leader by default. In this situation, the smaller firms accept the price of the leader as "given" in precisely the same way that perfectly competitive firms accept a market-determined price. That is, the smaller firms do not attempt to find a more desirable price, but simply proceed to produce and sell as much as is profitable at the given level. The immediate question then is: Where will be dominant firm set price?

It may be that the firm will pursue a "live and let live" policy, acting benevolently in the hope that its (partial) monopoly power will not attract the attention of antitrust authorities. If it does so, the dominant firm will price (and produce) in such a way that the smaller group of rivals can sell all that they wish at that price. Such a policy is illustrated in Figure 3.11. Here DD' is the market demand curve, MC_h is the marginal-cost curve of the dominant firm, and S is the supply curve of the smaller firms (the summation of their marginal-cost curves). Since it will allow rivals to sell as much as they wish, the dominant firm can derive its own demand curve by subtracting the output that smaller rivals will produce at any price from the quantity demanded by the market at that price. For example, at price P_1 smaller firms will supply quantity P_1A, the entire amount that the market demands; there-

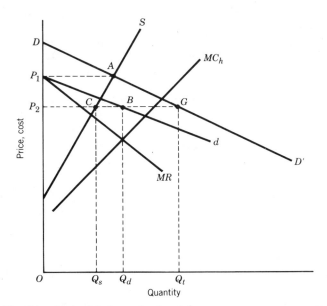

Figure 3.11 Price leadership by a dominant firm.
Market demand is DD'. The dominant firm derives its own ("residual") demand curve by subtracting from DD' the amount that smaller firms wish to supply (S) at any given price. The dominant firm then maximizes profits with respect to its own demand curve, P_1d.

fore, the dominant firm's "residual" demand is zero at this price. At price P_2, small firms will supply quantity P_2C, but the market demands quantity P_2G; the dominant firm's own demand at this price is CG $(= P_2B)$, defining a second point on its residual demand curve., The dominant firm derives its demand curve, P_1d, as the quantity demanded by the market at any price **less** the quantity that the smaller firms will supply at that price. The marginal revenue curve associated with this demand curve is P_1MR.

In Figure 3.11 the dominant firm will produce where MR and MC_h intersect (output level Q_d) and charge its profit-maximizing price, P_2. Smaller firms will supply P_2C (or $0Q_S$) $= BG$ (or Q_dQ_t). Thus the market price–quantity solution is determined at point G, involving price P_2 and output Q_t.

This outcome assumes that the dominant firm is a passive or benevolent monopolist. The firm maximizes profits only after imposing on itself the condition that its smaller competitors must do relatively well. The likelihood of this scenario may appear doubtful, especially in view of the fact that the solution of Figure 3.11 is unstable. The smaller firms have a strong incentive to grow larger, with unpalatable consequences for their dominant rival.

Low-Cost Firm Leadership.   A slightly different version of leadership models suggests that the price leader may be the lowest-cost firm in the industry. There is, incidentally, no reason why the low-cost producer might not also be the dominant firm. Since its optimal price is lower than that of any rival, the low-cost firm may be in a position to impose its preferred policy on the industry.

At this point, the question again becomes: What pricing policy will it follow? The leader may behave as a conventional maximizer of its own profits, forcing a suboptimal price on the other firms; or it may adopt a communal attitude, seeking a price that is more acceptable to other firms. Where price actually is set thus depends upon the leader's preferences, but also upon the leeway that rival firms permit it.

Barometric Firm Leadership.   A third possibility is that the price leadership function will be assumed by a firm that acts as a good "barometer" of market conditions. A company known for its ability to "read" the market, for instance, may become the de facto leader simply because rivals respect its pricing decisions and choose to follow them. Barometric leadership is thus a distinctly noncollusive phenomenon.

There is again no reason why the barometric firm also might not be a dominant or low-cost producer. The barometric firm will remain the industry's price leader only as long as its decisions prove satisfactory to rivals. Such a firm may pursue group-oriented policies, or it may act purely as an unconstrained profit maximizer, in which case the leadership function could shift among firms. Indeed, price leadership does not necessarily imply that the same firm remains the leader indefinitely. Particularly in the barometric case, it is possible that different firms will assume leadership as alternative pricing policies are tried out by the industry.

Summary.   These examples of price leadership may characterize the actual pricing mechanisms of numerous oligopolies (for example, automobiles, cigarettes, and steel). At times the price leader may be caught in a conflict between maximizing its own profits and acting as a maximizer on behalf of the industry.[36] Presumably the market outcome will depend on which course is chosen, or which firm leads, and here an obvious weakness in the price leadership analysis becomes evident. For all its apparent realism, price leadership as a view of "what really goes on" in oligopoly does not yield conclusions that are more specific than those following from the general view that oligopoly is collusive.

It is **not** price leadership that **creates** collusive conditions in oligopoly. Rather, leadership is a **symptom** of noncompetitive behavior, the result but not the cause of monopoly power. As such, the significance of price leadership should not be overstated. It is a device that may explain the conduct of many industries. If we wish to know how, in a purely mechanical sense, oligopoly pricing decisions are made, leadership may be as good an answer as we now have. But if we ask about the quality of market performance that arises from this mechanism, the answer is far less satisfactory. Virtually any result possible under collusive oligopoly could be reached via price leadership.

Informal and Spontaneous Collusion

Collusion in oligopoly may occur without anything so formal or overt as an explicit agreement or recognition of a price leader. Consider, for example, a market in which all firms consider price competition to be potentially dangerous. There is no need for such firms to "agree" to refrain from competing in price. They may simply refrain "independently," as a matter of self-interest. Such conduct patterns are sometimes referred to as "quasi-agreements" or "agreements to agree."[37]

Spontaneous collusion is likely to develop as the result of a trial-and-error process. In a Cournot-type market, for example, rivals may begin by assuming that each other's policies are fixed. After some experience with quantity adjustments, however, the oligopolists are quite likely to recognize that the policies of rivals are not fixed but respond to their own behavior. The rivals may then experiment with different quantities, discarding those that are mutually unprofitable, and groping toward the monopoly result. Similarly, price-adjusting oligopolists may experiment with alternative prices separately but interdependently. If their products are homogeneous, prices will tend to converge to a single value. As individual firms try out new levels (and prices converge at each), they are likely to discard those which prove to be unprofitable, and they will move toward increasingly profitable levels and perhaps a monopoly result.

Purely informal collusion, like other collusive conduct, may lead to alternative market results and will be subject to the same kinds of imperfections and variations

---

[36]The latter course of action does not necessarily mean that we must abandon the traditional view of the firm as a profit maximizer. Rather than concluding that the firm no longer seeks maximum profits, we might argue that it seeks the maximum **subject to certain constraints or limitations,** for example, that it cannot price so as to eliminate all competitors.

[37]See William Fellner, *Competition Among the Few* (New York: Alfred A. Knopf, 1949), especially Chapters 1 and 3.

in effectiveness. Indeed, in a market characterized by relatively many firms and free entry, informal procedures that lack means for discipline may be rather impotent. There is also likely to be some limit to the scope of such arrangements. Spontaneous collusion presupposes objectives that are obvious to all participating firms. Any coordinated policies involving nonobvious restraints on competition, or requiring subtle and precisely coordinated moves, would be difficult to effect without a more highly structured arrangement. This is not to say, however, that informal procedures cannot work well in relatively simple situations. Where firms are very few and where the objective of cooperation is evident, such arrangements may be quite effective.

The pertinent question remains what market results are likely to occur under informal collusion. Company managers would no doubt wish to move market prices toward the pure monopoly level, and some such result is certainly possible. Whether this actually occurs will depend largely upon the ease with which firms can identify appropriate policies. If market conditions permit the companies to see readily which adjustments are mutually beneficial, the chances that the market will approach a monopoly performance pattern are high.[38] If the benefits of adjustments are less obvious (without overt communication or negotiation), firms may still succeed in preventing vigorous price competition, but the market result is less likely to resemble true monopoly.

Summary

The collusion approach to oligopoly may be the most realistic in terms of market conduct; but as a predictor of market performance, it produces less than it seems to promise. Collusive conduct allows oligopolists to take advantage of their joint market power. It may therefore move market performance closer to the monopoly solution than it would otherwise be. Fellner, for one, speaks of "tendencies" in this direction[39]; but the crux of the problem remains that neither the strength nor the consistency of such tendencies is easily characterized.

None of the specific collusive procedures—outright conspiracy, price leadership, or informal collusion—really mitigates the problem of indeterminate solutions in oligopoly, for both the goals of agreements and their effectiveness need to be specified. Sophisticated oligopolists often do act collusively in the sense that they take full account of mutual dependence and seek to avoid the worst outcomes. But the precise implications of this conduct for market solutions are not at all clear. Neither the nature of the price that is determined, nor the stability of adopted arrangements, can be confidently predicted simply by invoking the term "collusion."

---

[38] "Simple" market conditions—such as few firms, a physically standardized product, and stable demand—will clearly facilitate informal or tacit collusion. For the most pertinent discussion, see Stigler, footnote 32 above.

[39] See footnote 37 above.

CONCLUSIONS

The state of oligopoly theory, as this very brief survey should indicate, is quite unsettled. Mutual interdependence permits a wide variety of solutions, none with any particular claim to universality. The fundamental difficulty of oligopoly analysis is that the meaning of optimization for the firm, is obscure. There is no such thing as a "best" course of action unless the actions of rivals are specified; but the specification of rivals' behavior is similarly impossible until **their** rivals are known to act in specific ways. Oligopoly models have proliferated, and there are at least as many market solutions as there are assumptions about firms' response patterns.

The difficulty, however, is not simply that there are many possible solutions. In a real sense, it might be argued that there can exist **no** solution to the basic oligopoly problem. **Any** solution that can be proposed has the property that it is rational for one rival if it is also rational for the other(s); and any deviation or experimentation on the part of rivals may lead them away from the "solution" with no tendency to return.

Efforts to "solve" the oligopoly problem have produced some impressive intellectual achievements; the problem, however, remains. A number of writers have suggested that at least in some specific cases, the reality of oligopoly is simpler than the theory. Firms may eliminate or neutralize some problems of mutual interdependence by adopting a collusive framework. Many uncertainties of price response and counterresponse then evaporate, because they are ruled out by the collusive group. As we have noted, however, the realistic simplicity of collusion may extend only to the conduct of oligopolistic firms without doing much to "pin down" the resulting market performance. The collusive approach does contribute the valuable suggestion that oligopoly behavior may "rationally" tend towards joint profit maximization, but we are left with the need to ascertain how strong or weak such tendencies may be. We have not yet found **the** answer to oligopoly behavior. As William Baumol has put it:

Perhaps the most remarkable failure of modern value theory is its inability to explain the pricing, output and other related decisions of the large, not quite monoplistic firms which account for so large a proportion of our output.[40]

Although the analytical problems are formidable, however, we should not end on too pessimistic a note. It is true that under oligopolistic interdependence, just about any conceivable market result is logically possible. Realistically, however, we can rule out a large range of outcomes as improbable. Even more important, the theory of oligopoly is rich with empirical promise.[41] If the theory itself does not define precisely what patterns of market behavior will occur, it does provide ample suggestions for observation and testing—a topic we discuss in Part 2.

---

[40] See footnote 10 above.

[41] See, for example, Roger Sherman, *Oligopoly: An Empirical Approach* (Lexington, Mass.: Lexington Books, 1972).

CHAPTER 4

The Theory of the Firm: Some Qualifications

The orthodox theories that we have discussed thus far rest on a highly simplified conception of the firm. Typically, the firm is seen as a single-minded pursuer of short-run profits. It operates in a single market, pays little attention to the possibility that current conditions may change, and is extremely well informed about the consequences of any action it takes.

This is a patently unrealistic picture, although realism (once again) is not itself the central issue. Many important conclusions emerge from "artificial" models. The pertinent question is whether we can **improve** our explanations of firm behavior by dropping or modifying any of our simplifications. The answer in some cases is, unsurprisingly, yes.

PROFITS AND CORPORATE MOTIVATION

If it could be shown that company managers frequently try to do something very different from maximizing their profits, the conclusions of much traditional market theory would need to be reexamined. Initially, it is important to understand just what is and is not meant by the profit maximization assumption.

The assumption does **not** mean, for example, that all firms are at all times producing precisely to the point at which marginal cost equals marginal revenue and are charging precisely the maximum price that the market will bear. It does not even mean that the pursuit of short-run profits is so single-minded that all other considerations become irrelevant to the firm. What the profit maximization assumption does mean is that:

First, business managers desire to earn as large a profit as possible, given the constraints under which they operate.

Second, pursuit of this largest possible profit is the dominant objective of the firm; and, accordingly, the most meaningful way of characterizing the firm's behavior is "profit-maximizing."

Viewed in these terms, profit maximization may not be quite the rigid statement that some students of economics would believe it to be. All companies operate under a variety of limitations or constraints that affect the nature of their behavior; yet it may be plausible and useful to analyze such firms as profit maximizers **subject** to whatever constraints impinge on them. We noted in Chapter 3 the example of a dominant company that sets a price at which rivals remain in the market. Such a firm is, indeed, maximizing profits subject to the constraints imposed by the presence of its competitiors.

Although the maximization assumption is typically interpreted as a short-run statement, it may be adapted to different time horizons. The company that introduces a new product, for example, is unlikely to focus solely on its short-term profits; and it may well be that the price that would maximize profits immediately is inconsistent with a longer perspective. Frequently such companies set ''low'' prices designed to broaden consumer exposure to their product; the obvious rationale is that future demand and profits will be expanded by such exposure, even though there may be some immediate sacrifice.

At the outset, then, some of the more nàive challenges to the assumption that firms are profit maximizers can be readily dismissed. The assumption cannot be rejected merely because company policies are constrained by other considerations or even because the outside analyst may have trouble identifying both the constraints and the resulting nature of maximizing policies. Similarly, the maximization assumption cannot be invalidated by observing that firms may not actually attain maximizing positions at any given moment.

A serious challenge to profit maximization, rather, must demonstrate that firms consistently pursue policies that **conflict** with maximum profits, given relevant uncertainties and constraints. It must, in other words, argue that there is **some other goal** or goals that systematically prevent firms from moving in the directions that the traditional models imply. This sort of argument is considerably more difficult to construct than one that simply cites the ways in which firms may fail to **achieve** a maximum profits objective.

It is worth noting again that in purely competitive markets the question of a firm's motiviation does not really arise. The market itself enforces a zero-profit condition that **is** profit maximization under existing circumstances. The motivation of firms becomes a meaningful issue only when there exists some discretion in behavior. Accordingly, the profit-maximization discussion is applicable in a strict sense only when firms exert some degree of market control.

Company Profits and Mangerial Utility

Some objections to the idea of profit maximization have been based in observations of the ''psychology'' of business managers, who determine the policies of firms. A common argument begins by noting that at a time when these managers, or entrepreneurs, were also the owners of their companies, profit maximization **was** a plausible goal. However, the argument continues, in a modern economy owners and managers tend to be different individuals; the managers are salaried employees whose task it is to determine the policies of companies owned by someome else.[1] This well-documented observation poses an obvious problem. Since managers no longer directly receive the profits earned by their companies, perhaps their interest in maximizing those profits will wane. Profits may be pursued with diminished enthusiasm, and the personal motives of managers may actually be substituted for the profit motive. This may, of course, displease the stockholders who own the firms in question, but stockholder control over the policies of management is often weak and may be exercised only in extreme situations.

This argument states in effect that business managers have the **discretion** to pursue goals other than maximum profits for their firms. But will they in fact do so? And if so, how can we tell? Even if we accept the contention that individual psychology has a bearing on business decisions, this does not necessarily imply that nonmaximizing behavior will result. Human traits such as vanity and the desire for power cannot readily be shown to be incompatible with the search for profits. Indeed, to the extent that a company's profits measure the success of its managers—and to the extent that personal motives are satisfied by attaining professional success—the profit-maximization assumption remains plausible.

Economists frequently approach the issue of discretionary behavior by treating the firm as a maximizer of **utility** rather than profits alone. Managers, in other words, are assumed to run companies so as to maximize their own satisfactions. Company profits are likely one element of such satisfactions, but other things may enter in as well. The immediate question is obvious: What factors other than profits contribute to managerial utility?

One interesting and plausible suggestion, by Williamson,[2] is that managers will seek to expand their emoluments and the staff that they supervise. If correct, we should expect that managers with discretion will enjoy higher levels of compensation (both salary and other executive perquisites) and will supervise larger (and perhaps more highly qualified) staffs. Although managerial discretion cannot be measured directly, there is some evidence that where conditions favor discretion, company expenditures on staff and executive "perks" are relatively high.[3]

There is also evidence, however, that executive compensation is itself related to company profitability.[4] Stock option plans, for example, are fairly common in large

---

[1]The pioneering work in bringing to light the "divorce" of ownership and management is Adolph A. Berle, Jr., and Gardiner C. Means, *The Modern Corporation and Private Property* (New York: Macmillan, 1932).

[2]Oliver E. Williamson, "Managerial Discretion and Business Behavior," *American Economic Review,* **53** (December 1963), 1032–1057.

[3]See Franklin R. Edwards, "Managerial Objectives in Regulated Industries: Expense-Preference Behavior in Banking," *Journal of Political Economy,* **85,** (February 1977), 147–162; and Timothy H. Hannan and Ferdinand Mavinga, "Expense Preference and Managerial Control: The Case of the Banking Firm," Bell *Journal of Economics,* **11** (Autumn 1980), 671–682.

[4]For interesting empirical studies, see Robert T. Masson, "Executive Motivations, Earnings, and Consequent Equity Performance," *Journal of Political Economy,* **79** (November/December 1971), 1278–1292; and Geoffrey Meeks and Geoffrey Whittington, "Directors' Pay, Growth and Profitability," *Journal of Industrial Economics,* **24** (September 1975), 1–14. W. Mark Crain, Thomas Deaton, and Robert Tollison have found that the tenure (length of service) of corporation presidents is also related to their companies' profit record. "On the Survival of Corporate Executives," *Southern Economic Journal,* **43** (January 1977), 1372–1375.

corporations. Since stock values depend upon profits, the executive's supplementary compensation may be quite sensitive to the company's profitability. In addition, corporate officers who fail to produce high profits may incur outside risks. Suboptimal performance may induce a takeover bid by a corporate "raider" who sees unexploited profit potential in the firm.[5] If so, the managers responsible for nonmaximizing policies might find themselves out of a job.

Acceptable Profit Levels: "Satisficing" and "Target" Returns

One group of alternatives, consistent with managerial utility maximization, is the possibility that firms may aim for a satisfactory or acceptable, rather than a maximum, level of profits. The goal of firms is assumed to be not maximization of profits, but "satisficing." At least two distinct reasons have been offered in support of a satisficing assumption. Herbert A. Simon has argued that the requirements of maximization in a complex and uncertain world are so immensely difficult that the goal is abandoned in favor of a more definable target.[6] That is, faced with an "impossibly" difficult problem—the maximization of some quantity such as profit—business firms may attempt **not** to "solve" the problem (fo r it is really insoluble), but to **substitute** another, more solvable task, the attainment of a **satisfactory** outcome.

A second kind of argument for the satisficing assumption, discussed by Richard M. Cyert and James G. March,[7] is that there may be factors in the firm as an **organization** that work against maximization as a goal. There is no single **organization theory** of the firm, as such, but the important general principle put forth is that the firm as an organization is distinct from those individuals within it who are charged with responsibility for setting policy. The behavior of the organization reflects the coordination of efforts by individuals and groups of individuals within it, but the transition may not be simple. Moreover, the policies adopted by organizations reflect not only the interaction among individuals, but also the influence of the organization itself upon those individuals.

Simon and Cyert and March criticize the traditional **normative** theory of the firm that bases predictions upon statements of what the firm **ought** to do under an assumption of "rationality," that is, profit maximization. They propose, instead, a **behavioral** theory that would specify what firms **actually** do. In order to achieve this, they argue, we must discover a great deal more about the processes by which organizational goals are adopted and modified, and about the ways in which organizations go about measuring relevant magnitudes. The claims of the satisficing school are not only argued logically but are buttressed by some empirical evidence

---

[5] This was suggested originally by Robin Marris in "A Model of the 'Managerial' Enterprise," *Quarterly Journal of Economics,* **77** (May 1963). See also Henry G. Manne, "Mergers and the Market for Corporate Control," *Journal of Political Economy,* **73** (April 1965), 110–120.

[6] See Herbert A. Simon, "Theories of Decision-Making in Economics and Behavioral Science," *American Economic Review,* **49** (June 1959), 253–283.

[7] See Ricahad M. Cyert, and James G. March, "Organizational Factors in the Theory of Oligopoly," *Quarterly Journal of Economics,* **70** (February 1956), 44–64; and *A Behavioral Theory of the Firm* (Englewood Cliffs, N.J. Prentice-Hall, 1963).

as well. Cyert and March have shown, for example, that rather good predictions of some business decisions follow from their framework.

The behavioral theorists have unquestionably raised serious and troublesome questions about the traditional analysis of the firm. It is less clear, however, that the hypothesis of a satisfactory profits goal provides a much superior foundation. It we postulate that firms seek not maximum profits but other "targets," the question immediately becomes: What is the nature of these targets? Company decision makers may think in terms of "acceptable" or "fair" returns, but what does "acceptable" or "fair" mean?

Firms may even follow procedures, for instance, adding a standard markup to costs in order to determine price, that do not appear to resemble the marginalist maximizing calculations. Yet is it easily to show that such rough rules of thumb can approximate profit maximization closely.[8] An acceptable profit objective may well be defined differently by different persons, and we are left with the question whether such goals in general diverge much from maximum profits.[9] Models assuming satisficing or target-return pricing, then, may not imply a single specific alternative to profit maximization. And it is not inevitable that market results of satisficing differ significantly or at all from profit maximizing, although the calculus of the firm's decisions may be changed.

The empirical status of maximizing and satisficing is rather ambiguous. It is extremely difficult, on the one hand, to deduce much about the policy principles of firms purely from objective data such as prices, outputs, and profit rates. On the other hand, however, there are pitfalls in attempting to ascertain decision rules by questioning business executives. Even if questions are answered with complete honesty, the information obtained is likely to be both subjective and imprecise. It may tell us more about executive attitudes than about actual corporate policy.

Sales Revenue Maximization

William J. Baumol has proposed that firms seek not maximum profits, but maximum sales revenues subject to some minimum profit constraint.[10] That is, the goal of the firm is defined as attainment of the largest possible sales revenue, subject to the limitation that profits not fall below a specified level.

Baumol's hypothesis, associated with the large oligopolistic enterprise, was drawn from his experience as a consultant to business firms. His evidence was admittedly subjective and "impressionistic," but a cogent case was presented. Baumol notes that trends in sales and profits are not entirely independent, but his

---

[8] One can, in other words, choose a profit-maximizing markup or margin over costs. Such a markup will vary inversely with the elasticity of demand for the firm's product; for example, where elasticity is high, perhaps because there are close substitutes, price will be marked up by only a small amount over costs.

[9] For some pertinent suggestions, see Richard H. Day, "Profits, Learning, and the Convergence of Satisficing to Marginalism," *Quarterly Journal of Economics*, **81** (May 1967), 302–311.

[10] W. J. Baumol, *Business Behavior, Value and Growth* (New York: Macmillan, 1959; rev. ed., Harcourt, Brace & World, 1967).

argument is more than a statement that higher sales may be the means to higher profits.[11] Specifically, he points out that managers seem to evaluate the state of their businesses in terms of sales trends, with profits mentioned as an ''afterthought,'' and notes that executive salaries are more closely related to the size of the enterprise than to its profitability.[12] Baumol argues further that the pricing rules of thumb and policy deliberations he has observed are fundamentally consistent with sales revenue maximization. Managements, he believes, are primarily concerned with expanding sales once they are reasonably confident about achieving their ''usual'' rate of return on investment.

The revenue maximization hypothesis requires an explanation of the minimum profit constraint. What profit level is ''acceptable'' or ''usual''? Unless we can specify it, the meaning of revenue maximization subject to this constraint will be, at best, unclear. Here Baumol refers for an answer to the capital markets. Firms that may hope to sell securities in the future must consider that the marketability of future shares depends upon the profits of the enterprises. As Baumol puts it:

Its [the firm's] minimum earnings must supply funds sufficient to pay dividends, and to reinvest in such amounts that the combination of dividend receipts and stock price rises can remunerate stockholders adequately.[13]

In other words, the minimum acceptable profit is that level which permits the firm to remain ''competitive'' in marketing its own securities. And the firm is competitive when its ''payments'' to stockholders—both directly through dividends, and indirectly through stock price appreciation—are sufficient to keep its securities salable in contest with the securities of other corporations.

The behavior of the sales revenue maximizer may be viewed in straightforward fashion once it is noted that Baumol also assumes that oligopolistic interdependence is ignored in day-to-day decisions. That is, the construction of the firm's revenue functions is not complicated by considerations of how rival firms will react. Given that the firm confronts a defined demand (average revenue) curve, its sales-maximizing policy will be as follows: It may produce to the point at which elasticity of demand is unity, that is, the point at which marginal revenue equals zero. This point, S in Figure 4.1, yields an unconstrained maximization of revenues (since any less production would forego positive marginal revenue, while any more would imply negative marginal revenue, thus substraction from total revenue.) If the firm at this point is earning an acceptable profit it has achieved equilibrium. Should this

---

[11] Franklin M. Fisher suggested that most of Baumol's evidence is consistent with the alternative hypothesis that firms maximize short-run profits subject to a minimum-sales or market-share constraint. The idea here is that the relationship between short-run and long-run maximization is somewhat obscure, and that firms pursue short-run profits unless they have some indication that this will cause a deterioration in their long-run position. See his Review of Baumol, *Journal of Political Economy*, **68** (June 1960), 314–315.

[12] The latter observation remains a fair but arguable characterization of the evidence; as we have noted, profits also appear to play an important role. Some writers such as Masson (see footnote 4) argue that the case for revenue maximization on executive compensation grounds is a weak one. The better argument for revenue maximization may be simply that managers prefer to preside over larger ''empires.''

[13] See footnote 10, 1 ed., p. 51.

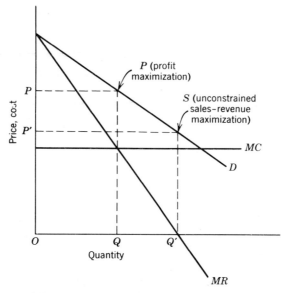

Figure 4.1 Revenue maximization and profit maximization.

sales-maximizing point, however, carry with it an unacceptable rate of return, the output level must be altered so that an acceptable profit is achieved. The firm will then come to a constrained equilibrium at some point on *D* between *S* and *P* in Figure 4.1: It will not be maximizing revenue in an absolute sense, but it will be obtaining the largest possible revenue consistent with its minimum profit requirements.[14]

Sales revenue maximization implies a number of interesting predictions for firm behavior. Generally, the output of a revenue maximizer will exceed that of the profit maximizer, and the associated price will tend to be lower. This point is easily seen once it is noted that the profit-maximizing output must occur within the elastic portion of the firm's demand curve. This is so because the profit maximizer equates marginal cost and marginal revenue at some positive value, and positive marginal revenue implies demand elasticity greater than unity.[15] The unconstrained revenue maximizer, by producing at the point of unitary demand elasticity, will necessarily supply a larger output. In Figure 4.1, profit-maximizing output occurs at an output level such as *OQ*, and revenue maximizing at a level such as *OQ'* (*MR* = 0). Invariably the unconstrained revenue maximizer produces to the right of the profit maximizer. If the revenue maximizer is constrained, however, it will most likely

---

[14]Dynamic versions of the revenue-maximizing hypothesis, also suggested by Baumol, have attracted some attention. Here it is the **growth** rate of sales over time, rather than its level at a given moment, that is seen as the fundamental consideration of business managers.

[15]If demand is elastic, a price decrease of *X* percent will call forth a quantity increase greater than *X* percent. Accordingly, total revenue, *PQ*, will rise, and marginal revenue—defined as the increment to the total—is positive.

produce at some point between OQ and OQ'. Only if the minimum profit acceptable to the firm is identical to the firm's maximum profit will the revenue maximizer prove to be as restrictive a producer as the profit-maximizing firm. By similar token, any increase in the acceptable profit level itself would be expected to result in a restriction of output relative to that which had been produced before.

A further important implication of sales revenue maximization is that prices (and outputs) will respond to changes in fixed overhead. Under the traditional profit-maximizing assumption, changes in fixed cost would not lead to price revisions, since no marginal factors are affected in the short run. That is, the marginal-cost and marginal-revenue curves remain intact, and the most profitable point of production therefore is not altered. If a firm maximizes sales revenue, however, a change in such costs, which alters actual profits, could lead to some price response. If, for example, the firm that is earning precisely its minimum acceptable profit experiences an increase in overhead, it will need to respond with a restricted output and higher price in order to "get back to" an acceptable profit position. It will, in other words, act to recoup some of the profit previously foregone in the quest for higher revenues. Similarly, a tax imposed on the firm may lead to short-run price and output changes even though the tax is not of such a nature as to affect the maximum-profit position. These particular implications of sales revenue maximization would explain a group of phenomena thought to be quite common that cannot be readily accounted for by the more orthodox profits assumption.

Profits in the Long Run

As noted earlier, it seems reasonable to believe that some firms pursue profits over a time horizon that is longer than the "short run." Such companies might even act as long-run profit maximizers or maximizers of the **present value** of the firm.[16] This orientation opens the clear possibility of nonmaximizing behavior in the short run, for the policies that maximize values over long and short time periods may diverge frequently and significantly.

The notion of managers as long-term optimizers is a plausible one that may explain some instances of what appears to be suboptimal behavior. Sacrificing profits today may not only increase profits tomorrow, but increase them by so much that the far-sighted executive will choose to forego immediate gains. There is, however, some ambiguity present.

In Figure 4.2 three profit streams over time are shown. Stream A involves initial high profits that then decline; B offers low but increasing profits; while C is an intermediate case. A company may be able to choose among policies that generate each of these profit streams, but which one will the long-run optimizer select? There is no

---

[16] A detailed discussion of discounting and present value calculations is beyond the scope of our discussion, but can be found in any good introductory or intermediate economic theory textbook. The underlying idea is that the value of any receipt (or payment) depends upon when it occurs. A dollar to be received far in the future is worth less than a dollar received today, if only because today's dollar could earn interest and would thus be worth more than a dollar at the future time; more distant receipts or profits thus have relatively low **present** values.

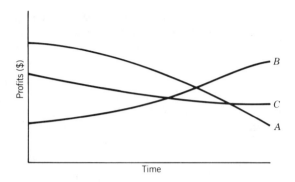

Figure 4.2   Alternative profit streams over time.

clear answer! Which stream maximizes the present value of the company in question depends upon: (1) the decision maker's time horizon—that is, **how far** in the future he looks; and (2) how heavily the decision maker discounts the future—that is, the extent to which distant profits lose present value simply because they **are** distant.

Conceivably, **any** of the profit streams is consistent with optimization under some time horizon and some rate of discount. The nature of the ambiguity is thus apparent. Managers may act as "long-run maximizers," but long-run maximization appears consistent with a **variety** of short-run behavior. If this consistency embraces a very wide range of behavior, that is, if "anything" firms do in the short run can be rationalized as "long-run maximization," then the long-run notion loses its usefulness.

Further Suggestions on Managerial Motivation

Numerous hypotheses have been advanced about the objectives of business managers. Among the possibilities are managerial leisure time, the "good life," security, and a desire to advance the welfare of society.[17] It is not possible to do justice here to these and other suggestions. Many of the suggestions, in fact, turn out not to be readily testable. But one further point deserves our attention.

The debate about corporate motivation and policy is in a sense part of a broader controversy over marginal analysis in economics. This controversy reached its height in the late 1940s when Richard A. Lester presented evidence showing that marginalism does a poor job of explaining some economic behavior in labor markets.[18] Lester presented examples that seemed to indicate that relationships between wage rates and employment patterns do not follow the expectations of marginal analysis. Among the responses to Lester's argument, perhaps the most

[17] For relevant discussions, see Oliver E. Williamson, *The Economics of Discretionary Behavior: Managerial Objectives in a Theory of the Firm* (Markham, 1967); Marris, footnote 5; Tibor Scitovsky, "A Note on Profit Maximization and Its Implications," *Review of Economic Studies,* **11** (1943), 57–60.

[18] "Shortcomings of Marginal Analysis for Wage-Employment Problems," *American Economic Review,* **36** (March 1946), 63–82.

emphatic was that of Fritz Machlup.[19] Machlup, describing the many potential pitfalls in empirical tests of marginal analysis, noted that such elements as marginal revenue and costs of production are "subjective." That is, business firms act on **what they perceive** as the relevant quantities, and not on what is perceived objectively by the calculations of disinterested observers.

The distinction between subjective and objective perception is an important one to bear in mind when assessing empirical evidence. From time to time, for example, it has been found that particular firms appear to produce at a point of negative marginal revenue. Such behavior is, of course, not profit maximizing, but does this sort of evidence justify a rejection of the maximization hypothesis? Quite possibly it does not. The firm's selection of an output level depends on its own view of market conditions. Conceivably this view encompasses constraints of which the empirical analyst is unaware and that are therefore omitted from the firm's revenue and cost functions. If this be the case, the firm may indeed be maximizing by its own lights even though it appears to the analyst to be acting suboptimally.[20]

Suppose, for example, that a company fears an antitrust prosecution it if grows too large. It may rationally price and produce so as to keep its market share below what it regards as the critical level; yet such behavior may appear irrational to an outside observer who is unaware of the antitrust constraint. The troublesome point is that if subjective and objective measures of relevant economic magnitudes are generally very different, the implications of the marginal analysis and the testability of propositions that flow from it will be extremely limited.

The Machlup argument need not be interpreted too strongly. In essence, he concludes only that empirical findings apparently inconsistent with theoretical hypotheses should not lead directly to the scrapping of the analysis. To the contrary, the difficulties and subtleties inherent in formulating hypotheses and their tests are so great that such inconsistencies might well be viewed with suspicion. At the very least, outright rejection of marginalism should not be undertaken lightly; and at least some of those who reject it may have lacked a thorough understanding of the theory and its implications.

Summary

Although there is no general consensus among students of business behavior regarding challenges to profit maximization, the following points would probably find fairly broad acceptance:

1. Challenges to the "simple" profit-maximizing hypothesis raise some troublesome questions and dictate caution in approaching the behavior of the firm.
2. There is no single alternative hypothesis that provides a clearly more useful approach. One reason is that there is a trade-off between the descriptive realism

---

[19]"Marginal Analysis and Empirical Research," *American Economic Review,* **36** (September 1946), 519–554.

[20]Alternatively, the observation of negative marginal revenue could reflect a temporary disequilibrium position for the firm. This would again be consistent with the assumption that the firm is a rational optimizer.

and the analytical manageability of any theory; some theories that seem descriptively more realistic than profit-maximization models become unwieldy and do not yield clear predictions.

3. Alternative models employ the same analytical methods as profit-maximizing models, and at times yield similar predictions. In the latter cases especially, they may not add much to our understanding of firm behavior.

As additional evidence is marshaled, the outlook may change. Possibly some alternative motivational assumption will be found to support verifiable implications about business behavior. It may be, however, that profit maximization is a more satisfactory characterization than some would think, once pertinent constraints are taken into account. That is, it may be that when limitations on the actions of firms are "drawn into" their cost and demand curves, their behavior will appear consistent with maximization of profits.[21]

ENTRY AND LIMIT PRICING

As we have seen previously, the condition of entry into a market determines the possibilities for long-run profits. If entry is easy or "free," as in the cases of pure and monopolistic competition, net profits cannot exist except as a transient phenomenon. By the same token, the persistence of net profits in oligopoly or monopoly depends upon some barrier to entry. Without any obstacles, new rivals would be attracted into the market, and profits would thus tend to dissipate.

The notion of **limit pricing** rests on the premise that established companies recognize the threat that prospective entry poses to them. Rather than passively accepting this threat, they react by adopting policies that **limit** or deter that entry. This type of strategy, introduced widely to the literature by Joe S. Bain,[22] has become a familiar facet of oligopoly analysis. It is of interest here as a further qualification to profit maximization because entry may place a significant constraint on firm behavior.

In broad outline, the implications of limit pricing are straightforward. Consider a market containing a dominant firm, in effect a monopolist, whose ordinary demand, marginal revenue, and cost curves are shown in Figure 4.3. P_m is the familiar monopoly price, but will the firm locate there? If entry for new firms is difficult—so difficult that the potential rivals can see no profitable opportunities at price P_m—the answer is presumably yes. The monopoly price will not induce entry (perhaps because entrants would have still higher costs), thus the predicted behavior of the firm is given by the simple monopoly model.

Suppose, however, that some prospective entrants view P_m as profitable; entry barriers exist but are "moderate" rather than "high." The existing firm might now

[21] For a cogent argument along these lines, see William Lee Baldwin, "The Motives of Managers, Environmental Restraints, and the Theory of Managerial Enterprise," *Quarterly Journal of Economics*, **78** (May 1964), 238–256. An excellent discussion of issues is provided by Fritz Machlup, "Theories of the Firm: Marginalist, Behavioral, and Managerial," *American Economic Review*, **57** (March 1967), 1–33.

[22] *Barriers to New Competition* (Cambridge, Mass.: Harvard University Press, 1956).

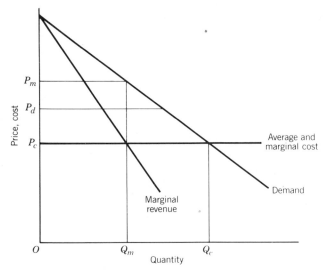

Figure 4.3 Entry-limiting prices.
P_m: the pure monopoly price and the limit price if entry barriers are "high"—entrants' average costs exceed P_m at all output quantities. P_d: The limit price if entry barriers are "moderate." P_c: The competitive price and the limit price if entry is "free"—barriers are "very low" or nonexistent.

have to cut price to P_d to deter entry. Thus P_d becomes the "limit price." Should entry be "easy," the entry-limiting price will be still lower. In the extreme case ("free" entry) it may be at or slightly above P_c, the competitive market price. The price that deters entry is in each instance determined by the entrants' average cost function; so long as average cost lies everywhere above the prevailing price, entry cannot pay.

Note the general implication. The pricing behavior of an established firm can no longer be predicted solely on the basis of its short-run revenue and cost functions; entry also must be examined.

We may examine the argument in a slightly more complicated way. In Figure 4.4 the established dominant firm faces similar demand, D, marginal revenue, MR, and cost, $AC = MC$, conditions. Curve S represents the supply curve of some relatively small, would-be entrants. At any price above P_d these firms will supply positive amounts to the market; that is, entry will occur, and the entering firms will supply more, the higher is the market price. What will the dominant firm do?

If it were to set the conventional monopoly price P_m, rivals would enter and supply q_s. When added to the dominant firm's output, q_m, the market will be faced with excess supply, and price will thus fall. To take account of this possibility, the dominant firm could look to its residual demand curve in Figure 4.4 (derived by subtracting quantity S from quantity D at each price; the firm's residual demand is simply its initial demand at any price **minus** the amount others will supply at that price). By profit maximizing with respect to the residual demand curve—price p'

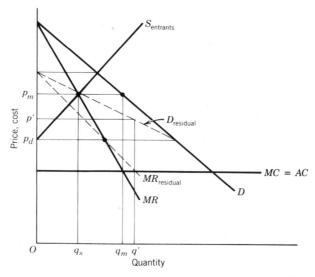

Figure 4.4 Limit pricing with a dominant established firm and a small fringe of entrants.

and output q'—the firm does as well as possible while **permitting** entry to occur. (This result should look familiar; it is the same as that of the dominant firm leadership model discussed in Chapter 3.)

Long-run considerations, however, suggest that the established company may not be willing to act so benevolently. Once new firms enter, they may take over increasing shares of the market. If so, the dominant firm's dominance will erode, with unpalatable profit implications. The company's managers may therefore act to forestall entry. At price P_d prospective rivals will supply nothing. Thus P_d is the limit price, which the firm may choose although it involves a sacrifice of short-run profits. Once again, the threat of entry may force an apparently powerful firm to behave differently than the simple monopoly model predicts.

The implications of limit pricing become considerably more complex under different market circumstances. Suppose, for example, that the established dominant firm faces an entry threat not from a group of small rivals as above, but from a major competitor whose entry would occur on a relatively large scale.[23] Should the new firm come into the market, it is likely that market output will rise substantially, with consequent downward pressure on price—not a happy prospect for the established company. This situation suggests that:

1. The established firm not only has an incentive to discourage entry, but must also consider what strategy will effectively convince the would-be rival to stay out.
2. The prospective entrant, recognizing this incentive, must form some expectation of how the established firm actually would react to its entry.

---

[23] The prospective entrant no longer has anything resembling a supply curve. This simply reflects the fact that its entry and output decisions are not a simple function of a "given" market price.

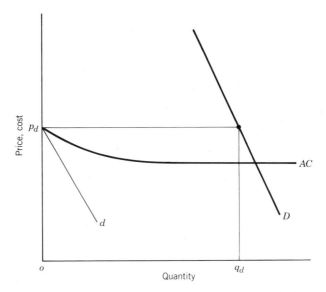

Figure 4.5   The prospect of entry by a major rival.

Consider the situation shown in Figure 4.5, in which both the established firm and the potential entrant have average costs AC, and **market** demand is D.[24] How can the existing firm discourage its rival from entering the market? One possibility is to produce output q_d at price p_d. For the potential entrant's residual demand curve d, defined simply as market demand minus the established firm's output, now carries no hope of a profitable outcome.

This is a straightforward solution, but it rests on a critical assumption: namely, that the prospective entrant expects the established firm to continue producing output q_d if entry occurs (and, further, that the established firm recognizes this expectation). This Cournot-like assumption, known as the Sylos postulate,[25] yields our limit pricing result; but the result is only as plausible as the assumption itself.

The plausibility of the assumption, moreover, is questionable. If the new firm should enter the market at a relatively small scale while the established seller maintains the "limit" output, both may experience losses—but the established firm, with a larger market share, will lose more. It may therefore be severely tempted to cut output and restore the industry's profitability. Such temptation, however, may be visible to the prospective entrant, and if so the Sylos postulate will not hold.[26]

---

[24] Notice that the diagram assumes some scale economies in supply, but no absolute cost disadvantage for the potential entrant. Modification of either or both assumptions would lead to somewhat different results.

[25] It was suggested by Paolo Sylos-Labini, *Oligopoly and Technical Progress*, (Cambridge, Mass.: Harvard University Press, 1962). See also Franco Modigliani, "New Developments on the Oligopoly Front," *Journal of Political Economy*, **66** (June 1958), 215–232; and Douglas Needham, "Entry Barriers and Non-Price Aspects of Firms' Behavior," *Journal of Industrial Economics*, **25** (September 1976), 29–43.

[26] For a demonstration that the Sylos postulate is unreasonable in some other circumstances, see John T. Wenders, "Excess Capacity as a Barrier to Entry," *Journal of Industrial Economics*, **20** (November 1971), 14–19.

The importance of the limit price should be apparent. It suggests that we shall at times observe policies in oligopolistic and even apparently monopolistic makets that are "rational," yet look little like conventional short-term profit maximization. Further, it raises the possibility (though not the inevitability) that, as Shepherd puts it, **"potential competition can substitute for actual competition."**[27] A credible entry threat, in other words, may constrain the behavior of "powerful" firms in very substantial ways.

Despite the clear importance of potential entry, limit price analysis does not yield a single, well-defined market solution.[28] Indeed, the large-scale case serves to remind us that we are still dealing with oligopolistic uncertainties: What is optimal for a company seeking to enter a market depends on how it believes the established firm will behave; yet the best policy for the established firm depends upon its assumptions about the entrant's behavior.[29] The condition of entry is a major consideration for market behavior, but the oligopoly guessing game will not disappear.

RISK AND UNCERTAINTY

The traditional theoretical models discussed above usually have assumed that the firm acts with "certainty" in the following sense: alternative policies will lead to different outcomes, but **given** its policy, there is no real question of what the outcome will be. When the firm chooses a strategy, it is in effect choosing a result.[30]

In practice, of course, this is seldom the case. A company that changes its price launches a new advertising campaign, or introduces a new product, will very likely have made a "best guess" about the result—indeed, it may spend considerable resources to obtain this guess. But the firm's managers will realize that the guess may be wrong, perhaps painfully so (many corporate policies fail; very few are undertaken in the expectation of failure). This difficulty is discussed in terms of risk or uncertainty.[31]

---

[27]William G. Shepherd, *The Economics of Industrial Organization* (Englewood Cliffs, N.J.: Prentice-Hall, 1979), p. 291. Emphasis in the original. As we shall see in Part 3, this possibility carries important implications for antitrust policy.

[28]One reason is that the long-run profitability of a limit pricing strategy is unclear. If the strategy leads to sharply reduced short-run profits, it may pay an established firm to ignore entry, act as a monopolist, and allow its monopoly position to erode over time.

[29]The interdependence problem can become even more involved than it is in our examples above. Suppose that the market is populated not by a single dominant firm but by a small group of rivals (hardly a wild assumption). In order to limit entry effectively, the existing group must not only identify the appropriate price (and output) policy, but must find a way of colluding to implement it.

[30]There are some exceptions. The game theory mixed strategist, for example, formulates only an "average" expectation; while results may approximate this expectation over time, the outcome of each playing of the game is unknown in advance. And Cournot duopolists, while **believing** that the results of their decisions are certain, are invariably **wrong** in their belief until an equilibrium is attained.

[31]The distinction between the two terms was drawn by Frank H. Knight in 1921. Risk is a situation in which the probabilities of alternative outcomes can be measured or estimated; under uncertainty, even the probabilities are unknown. Knight referred to risk as "measurable uncertainty." *Risk, Uncertainty and Profit* (Chicago: University of Chicago Press, 1921).

Table 4.1   Product Introduction: A Risky Choice

Product	Probability of Success	Successful Outcome	Probability of Failure	Failing Outcome
A	$P(a)$	+$1 million	$[1 - P(a)]$	−$0.5 million
B	$P(b)$	+$5 million	$[1 - P(b)]$	−$2 million

Let us suppose, in a obvious oversimplfication, that any corporate policy has only two possible outcomes, success (high profit) or failure (large loss); and that the company's decision makers know the probabilities of all alternatives. This brings us to the central question: in the absence of certainty, what is the **meaning** of "optimal" behavior for the firm? If it differs from what is optimal in a certain world, we shall be forced further to qualify the predictions of models that assume certainty. The issue is a complex one, that we explore only in a limited way.

Consider a company that can introduce either of two new products, A or B, as shown in Table 4.1. Product B offers the higher gain if it succeeds but also the larger loss if it fails. Which product should the company introduce? Quite clearly, it will be difficult to decide without knowing the probabilities of success and failure in both cases. Assume, therefore, that the pertinent probabilities are as follows:

$$P(a) = .5 \quad 1 - P(a) = .5$$
$$P(b) = .5 \quad 1 - P(b) = .5$$

That is, each new product has an even chance of success or failure in the market.

With the probabilities known, the firm could choose to introduce the product offering the higher **expected** outcome or profit. That is, it could respond to risk simply by maximizing expected rather than known profits. The calculations would be as follows:

Expected profit of A = $P(a)$ (Successful outcome) + $[1 - P(a)]$ (Failing outcome)
  = .5 (+$1 million) + (.5)(−$0.5 million)
  = +$250,000
Expected profit of B = $P(b)$ (Successful outcome) + $[1 - P(b)]$(Failing outcome)
  = .5(+$5 million) + (.5)(−$2 million)
  = +$1,500,000

Product B has the higher expected profit by a wide margin. But whereas B offers the higher expected reward, it is also riskier. Failure means the loss of $2 million with B, but only half a million with A. It may thus be that a "rational" decision maker will choose A. (What if the loss of $2 million threatens the survival of the firm?) The key is the decision maker's attitude toward risk. Without more information about this, the decision is unpredictable.

Discussions of risky choices typically observe that managers may not maximize profits even in an expected sense. Rather, they may act as **utility** maximizers, where utility depends upon both profits **and** risk.[32] Given "equally risky" choices, those

[32] For a classic discussion of the issues, see Milton Friedman and L. J. Savage, "The Utility Analysis of Choices Involving Risk," *Journal of Political Economy,* **56** (August 1948), 279–304.

carrying the higher profit expectation will be chosen. But where, as above, one alternative offers higher profits and higher risk—the more typical case—the decision rests upon the strength or weight of each factor in the managerial utility function.

The introduction of risk therefore provides an additional qualification to the traditional maximization-based models. How important is this qualification? One might be willing to treat it simply as another constraint on the orthodox analysis: Profits are maximized **subject** to the holding of risk to an "acceptable" level. Alternatively, it can be argued that risk disturbs the search for profits in a more fundamental sense. Perhaps, for example, minimization of risk itself becomes a goal of the firm (subject to an "acceptable" level of profit).

However one chooses to view it, risk does imply an ambiguity in the behavior of a firm. Given choices A and B in the example above, the risk-averse firm may choose A while the venturesome company goes with B. Yet both choices are consistent with utility maximization, and are therefore "rational."[33]

THE MULTIPRODUCT FIRM

Traditional market theories typically assume that the firm sells "a product." In fact, however, even relatively small companies usually market several goods or services. Should this consideration change our expectations of their behavior?

Suppose that a diversified firm—one that sells goods in several markets—pursues a policy of maximizing total or overall profits. Will this company act as a conventional profit maximizer in each of its markets individually? At first glance, it might seem so. After all, total profit is simply the sum or profits in each market; how could the firm gain by failing to maximize any component of the whole?

Profit maximization for each individual product cannot be ruled out, but there are some cases in which the route to overall maximization is more complex. We shall discuss briefly two of the more important instances. Consider first the case in which the firm's products are interrelated, in either supply or demand.[34]

A simple example is the company that sells both a "premium" and a "regular" brand of beer. The products are substitutes in demand; that is, a significant number of consumers will switch from one to the other in response to a change in relative prices. The first point to notice is that the firm's demand curve for premium cannot be specified unless the price of regular is known and vice versa. This is illustrated in Figure 4.6. The higher the price of one beer, the greater the demand for the other. Raise (or lower) the price of premium, and the demand curve for regular shifts up (or down).

Where should the profit-seeking firm set the prices of premium (P_p) and regular (P_r) beer? A specific answer would require extensive information on the response of

---

[33] The analogy to rational consumer behavior is very close. We typically assume that consumers maximize their utilities, yet we do not suggest that they all buy similar groups of products.

[34] A supply interrelationship implies that the cost of producing one product depends upon the output level of another (or others). Interrelated demands similarly mean that the price and quantity sold of one product depends upon sales of another (or others.)

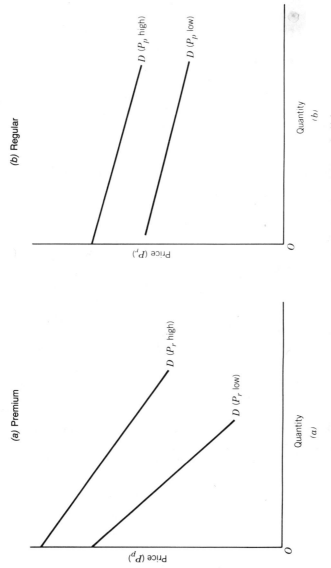

Figure 4.6 A seller of two products: "premium" and "regular" beer.

profits in each product to the set of prices (P_p, P_r). We can, however, make some general observations. First, the (P_p, P_r) combination that maximizes profits for premium **cannot** as a rule maximize profits for regular. This is intuitively obvious. To encourage premium profits, the price of regular must be set "very high," while the premium price is at some relatively low level dictated by marginal revenue and marginal cost. Yet maximization of regular profits requires a "very high" price for premium relative to the (lower) price of regular. There is thus a sense in which maximization of profits in both products cannot occur simultaneously.

By similar token, if we ask what set of prices (P_p, P_r) maximizes overall profits (premium **plus** regular), the answer must be that there is no reason to expect this optimal price set to coincide with the profit-maximizing set in either the premium or the regular market.

This simple example suggests the more general argument. When a firm sells interdependent products, profit maximization for the firm may require apparent **non**maximizing behavior in one or more submarkets. This argument will be extended a bit further in Chapter 16. Even where products are not "naturally" related, it may pay the firm to force a relationship by imposing a tie-in condition on customers.

A second major example in which "nonmaximizing" behavior can prove desirable for the diversified firm, concerns so-called subsidization. A multiproduct firm might choose to take subnormal profits in one market (or even losses, in the extreme)[35] that are "subsidized" by profits elsewhere. The goal is presumably to discomfort, or perhaps drive out, some rivals in the subsidized market—at which point that market becomes **more** profitable for the form in question. Once again we see the possibility of policies that look far from optimal being "rationally" selected by the firm. Notice, however, that subsidization is effectively an example of long-run profit seeking. The firm in question is not a conventional short-run maximizer in the first place.

We see, then, that the multiproduct firm may act in ways different from those predicted by much of the simple orthodox theory. Indeed, one might suspect that diversification across products and markets is itself the **result** of strategies designed to reduce risk rather than to ehance profits.

SUMMARY

The profit-maximizing firm that sells a single product under conditions of certainty is plainly something of an artifact. All the qualifications discussed above suggest possibilities for behavior that are in some ways divergent from what is predicted by our rudimentary models. The qualifications are unquestionably significant.

One should not rush to conclude, however, that the traditional analytical underpinnings are irrelevant. The principles of rational firm behavior do not disintegrate merely because the environment in which the firm operates is recognized to be complex. Some of the complexities, as noted, can reasonably be treated as constraints

---

[35] Such behavior may be interpreted as "predatory," in which case it is a prosecutable offense under the antitrust laws.

appended to the basic models. Other complexities, while potentially important in one sense, fail to suggest well-defined, alternative forms of analysis. These factors must be taken into account by any theory that would explain the world as it is. But it is modification, rather than abandonment of the simple traditional frameworks, that is usually necessitated.

CHAPTER 5

Further Views of "Monopolistic" Markets and the Competitive Norm

As we have seen, traditional economic analysis demonstrates the unique efficiency of competitive market arrangements. Departures from competitive conditions take various forms, but all are associated with nonoptimality of resource allocation. This central conclusion has produced wide acceptance of the competitive system as a norm, or standard, of "the way things ought to be."

A competitive standard obviously carries direct implications for public policy. If competitive markets are desirable, then there is much that government can do, primarily through the antitrust laws, to encourage the appropriate conditions. Even a cursory examination of American markets, however, will disclose that we are a long way from this form of industrial organization. The apparent concentration of power in some important markets is high, and numerous sectors are characterized by the structural conditions of oligopoly—a situation in which a few firms account for the bulk of market activity.

If we take the competitive norm both literally and seriously, it might be expected that current market conditions would provoke a major effort by government to implement more competitive configurations. Some people suggest that this should be done. And it is true that both federal and state governments claim to follow broad policies of promoting competition. Yet it is clear that there has been no serious effort to establish a "strictly" competitive market system.

Why should this be true? Consider some possibilities:

1. the competitive norm, while it receives generous vocal support, is not accepted by society as a basis for public policy. Many persons believe that the economic results of American markets, imperfections and all, have been quite satisfactory and even outstanding. Anyone holding such a view will not likely wish to tamper with success.
2. Competition in the strict sense of the pure model in economics is generally unattainable. Although the desirability of the competitive standard may remain intact, policymakers must focus their attention on achievable goals.

3. The U.S. market system is more competitive than many believe. Those who profess to see pervasive monopoly are looking at the wrong indicators and may tend to compare what exists with irrelevant theoretical notions of competition.

These points raise a number of fundamental issues. Is competition in the strict "theoretical" sense desirable? Is it possible? If not, are we better off seeking the maximum possible "amount" of competition, or might such a policy objective lead to a deterioration in economic welfare? What we now approach is the problem of translating theoretical conclusions into meaningful statements for policy. As will become evident, the translation is neither simple nor straightforward.

THE EXTENT AND COSTS OF MONOPOLY

How competitive or monopolistic is the U.S. economy, and with what effects? Although we postpone a detailed discussion of measurement questions to Chapters 7 through 9, some observations at this point are clearly in order.

The measurement of monopoly, or of "deviations" from competition, is no simple matter, and the ideal index has yet to be devised. Many investigators use some type of **concentration** variable as a proxy for monopoly power; for instance, the share of the market held jointly by a specified "small" number of the largest firms. If, for example, the four top firms have only 9 percent of market sales (as they do in women's dresses), market power is unconcentrated and there is some presumption of active competition. If the top four have 90 percent of the market (as in breakfast cereals), the presumption tilts in the opposite direction.[1]

The shortcomings of concentration measures, however, are apparent. Clair Wilcox, for example, argued some years ago that the conclusions resulting from superficial inspection of industry and product concentration data, are often erroneous.[2] Existing industry and product classifications, according to Wilcox, may give a poor picture of the actual alternatives open to consumers. If these alternatives are understated, the extent of competition within and among markets will be similarly distorted. Moreover, Wilcox contended, the distribution of consumer expenditures as of 1950 indicated that numerous quantitatively important areas—notably housing, food, and clothing—were competitive, or at least unconcentrated.[3]

Such warnings notwithstanding, attempts to derive quantitative estimates of the extent of monopoly in American markets have a long history. Nutter, for example, concluded that the percentage of national income originating in "effectively monop-

---

[1] A presumption, however, is not a certainty. Competition may be active where a few firms dominate and ineffective even though there are many small firms.

[2] Clair Wilcox, "On the Alleged Ubiquity of Oligopoly," *American Economic Review,* **40** (May 1950), 67–73.

[3] The Wilcox argument was directed not only at statements citing specific-industry concentration, but also at assertions based on the concentration of wealth within the economy as a whole. The best known exposition of the general phenomenon is: Adolph A. Berle and Gardiner C. Means, *The Modern Corporation and Private Property* (New York: Macmillan, 1932). Berle and Means found that 49 percent of nonbanking corporate wealth was held by the largest 200 (among a total of 300,000) corporations in 1929.

olized'' industries in 1937 was between 12.9 and 21.1, as contrasted with a figure of 17.4 percent for 1899.[4] Stigler estimated that slightly more than 24 percent of income originated under "monopoly" in 1939.[5] Data for recent years, however, suggest that whether existing degrees of concentration are considered "high" or "low," there has been no discernible upward trend over time.[6] As we see below, a substantial concentration of economic resources does exist, both for the American economy as a whole and within some important markets. Precisely what this implies about the competitiveness of the system is a hotly debated issue.

Some other investigators have attempted to quantify the **effects** rather than the **existence** of monopoly in the United States. Before taking note of their conclusions, it may be useful to look at precisely what the "cost of monopoly" means. We have seen that such cost is traditionally defined in terms of resource misallocation. The monopolist, by raising price and restricting output, devotes "too few" resources to his prod uctive activity; this is fine for the monopolist who maximizes profits, but society would benefit from larger outputs. The question now becomes: How large is this cost of monopolistic misallocation?

Consider Figure 5.1, which shows industry demand and unit cost functions. The competitive result E_c implies price P_c (equal to marginal and average cost) and output Q_c; but if the industry is monopolized, equilibrium occurs at E_m with a higher price, P_m, and lower output, Q_m. The question is thus: What does it "cost" society to be at E_m rather than E_c? The answer is diagrammatically simple, although it may be intuitively surprising.

A move from E_c to E_m damages the welfare of consumers by providing fewer goods at higher prices. This loss is conventionally measured by the reduction in **consumer's surplus**; diagrammatically it is the trapezoid $P_m P_c$ $E_c E_m$.[7] The consumer's surplus loss, however, is not usually viewed as a net loss to society. Monopolistic sellers—who are also members of society—gain in Figure 5.1 the "excess profits" rectangle $P_m P_c A E_m$.

The **net loss** to all of society is thus the "deadweight" triangle $E_m A E_c$. It is the amount by which the loss to consumers **exceeds** the gain for sellers when we move from the competitive to the monopoly result. This is the area that some investigators of monopoly misallocation costs seek to measure.

[4]G. Warren Nutter,*The Extent of Enterprise Monopoly in the United States, 1899-1939* (Chicago: University of Chicago Press, 1951).

[5]Adapted from George J. Stigler, *Five Lectures on Economic Problems,* (London: Macmillan, 1950). Cited in Richard B. Heflebower, "Monopoly and Competition in the United States of America," in E. H. Chamberlin, Ed., *Monopoly and Competition and their Regulation* (London: Macmillan, 1954), pp. 110–140.

[6]See Morris A. Adelman,"The Measurement of Industrial Concentration," *Review of Economics and Statistics,* **33** (November 1951), 269–296; Willard F. Mueller and Larry G. Hamm, "Trends In Industrial Market Concentration, 1947 to 1970," *Review of Economics and Statistics,* **56** (October 1974), 511–520.

[7]Readers unfamiliar with the term *consumer's surplus* might consult Alfred Marshall, *Principles of Economics,* 8th ed. (New York: MacMillan, 1948), pp. 124–133. Briefly, the surplus refers to the **difference** between what consumers would be willing to pay for something at a maximum and what they actually do pay. (Marshall's fundamental observation was that we are seldom forced to pay that maximum amount.) Diagrammatically, the surplus is demand price minus market price; for all units sold, the surplus is therefore the triangular area between the demand curve and the line representing market price.

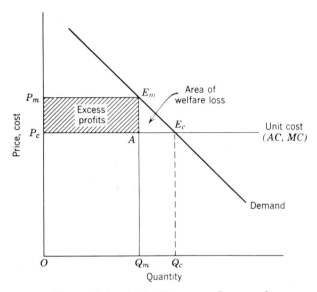

Figure 5.1   The welfare cost of monopoly.

The first major study, published by Harberger in 1954, concluded that monopoly misallocation was smaller than might be thought—about $225 million, or less than $1.50 per capita at the time.[8] Harberger examined rates of return in manufacturing industries. Reasoning that above-average returns reflect monopoly misallocation, that is, the devotion of too few resources to the industry in question, he proceeded to measure the price and output adjustments that would be necessary to remove such distortions. Assuming unitary elasticity of demand in all cases, Harberger found that the "welfare losses" indicated were surprisingly small.

Harberger's methodology has been subject to criticism. As Stigler has noted, the assumption of unitary demand elasticity is "objectionable" in that it suggests that monopolists produce to the point at which marginal revenue is zero.[9] If elasticity were assumed to be higher, the measured welfare loss would increase. Furthermore, Harberger effectively assumed that only deviations from the **average** profit rate in manufacturing signal the existence of monopoly. In fact, the average return may well **include** some monopoly profit; if so, then Harberger's procedure would again understate the true misallocation cost. Despite these and other criticisms, quite a few economists have been inclined to accept the general implication of Harberger's study: monopolistic misallocation—taken alone and defined narrowly— does not seem to impose a major burden on the national economy.[10]

[8] Arnold C. Harberger,"Monopoly and Resource Allocation," *American Economic Review,* **44** (May 1954), 77–87. Similar conclusions have been drawn in a study comparing Canadian industries with their American counterparts; see D. Schwartzman, "The Burden of Monopoly," *Journal of Political Economy,* **68** (December 1960), 727–729.

[9] George J. Stigler,"The Statistics of Monopoly and Merger," *Journal of Political Economy,* **44** (February 1956), 33–40.

[10] For a criticism of such conclusions, however, see Abram Bergson, "On Monopoly Welfare Losses," *American Economic Review,* **63** (December 1973), 853–870.

Some recent estimates of monopoly cost have been substantially higher, however, in part because they are based on more inclusive definitions of cost.[11] It is widely recognized, for example, that one cost to society of monopoly is the resources used to **obtain** (and maintain) the monopoly position.[12] Suppose, for example, that monopoly in a particular market has a present value of $1 million. It is likely that entrepreneurs will spend some money in efforts to achieve that monopoly; under certain circumstances close to the full $1 million might be used up in this fashion. But the resources represented by such spending have real opportunity costs. From society's point of view, these resources are squandered, and much of the monopoly profit may therefore be converted to a net social loss.

Diagrammatically, we are in effect stating that the cost of monopoly consists not only of the traditional deadweight triangle in Figure 5.1, but also of (much or all of) the excess profits rectangle. Measurement efforts that focus solely on deadweight losses are thus likely to understate substantially the full burden of monopoly.

Still a further potential cost of monopoly is suggested by Adam Smith's observation that "Monopoly, besides, is a great enemy to good management."[13] Leibenstein has coined the term "X" inefficiency to denote tendencies within the firm to stray from strict cost-minimizing behavior. Companies with some market power may indulge themselves in a bit of organizational slack, a tendency to take things easy rather than to press for maximum efficiency at all times.[14] This possibility is illustrated in Figure 5.2, where D is market demand and C_c is the industry (marginal and average) cost curve under competition. If the industry is monopolized, X inefficiencies raise costs to C_m. The competitive and monopoly equilibrium positions are, as usual, E_c and E_m, respectively.

The cost of monopoly now includes a new element, area X in Figure 5.2. This is the X inefficiency, the difference between the cost of output Q_m provided by the monopolist, and the lower cost that would have been incurred by the competitive market in supplying Q_m. Estimating the likely size of X inefficiencies is exceptionally difficulty. Some observers believe that this cost of monopoly probably outweighs standard misallocation costs, but no specific figure can be cited with much confidence.

Does the available evidence suggest that monopoly costs should be a matter of serious public policy concern? Despite some disagreement among economists,[15]

---

[11] See especially David R. Kamerschen,"An Estimation of the 'Welfare Losses' from Monopoly in the American Economy," *Western Economic Journal,* 4 (Summer 1966); Keith Cowling and Dennis C. Mueller, "The Social Costs of Monopoly Power," *Economic Journal,* **88** (December 1978), 727–748.

[12] See Richard A. Posner,"The Social Costs of Monopoly and Regulation," *Journal of Political Economy,* **83** (August 1975), 807–827; Gordon Tullock, "The Welfare Costs of Tariffs, Monopolies, and Theft," *Western Economic Journal,* **5** (June 1967), 224–232.

[13] Adam Smith,*The Wealth of Nations* (New York: Modern Library, 1937), p. 147.

[14] Harvey Leibenstein,"Allocative Efficiency vs. 'X' Efficiency," *American Economic Review,* **56** (June 1966), 392–415.

[15] Consider Stigler's remarkable and oft-quoted comment that "economists might serve a more useful purpose if they fought fires or termites instead of monopoly." See footnote 9, p. 34. More recently, S. C. Littlechild has argued that the high monopoly cost estimate of Cowling and Mueller (see footnote 11) is based on methodological flaws that seriously overstate true costs. "Misleading Calculations of the Social Costs of Monopoly Power," *Economic Journal,* **91** (June 1981), 348–363.

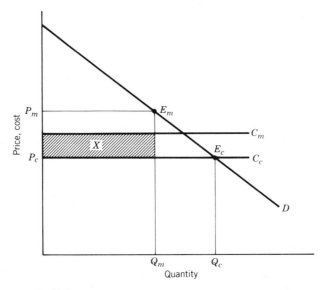

Figure 5.2 "*X*" inefficiency.
The costs of an internally inefficient monopolist, C_m, exceed those of efficient competitors, C_c. Area X represents the sum total of this inefficiency.

the answer surely is yes. All estimates to date have ignored some potentially important monopoly costs, usually on the reasonable basis that they are not measurable.[16] In spite of this bias, however, some estimates of measurable cost have turned out to be quite substantial. Furthermore, as Siegfried and Tiemann have shown, misallocation costs may themselves be highly concentrated within a small number of industries.[17] If this is in fact the case, then appropriate public policies directed toward those industries may be very useful even if misallocation costs in the aggregate are a tiny proportion of our gross national product.

This is not to suggest that we prejudge what **is** an appropriate public policy toward monopoly, but only that the issue deserves attention. Our evidence may not be sufficient to conclude that the economy is extensively monopolistic. In fact, as we shall see in Part Two, the measurement of monopoly in specific industries, as well as for the economy as a whole, presents some subtle problems. There is no doubt that most American markets currently deviate from the competitive ideal, but the extent and implication of these deviations are not entirely clear.

THE THEORY OF SECOND BEST

It is known that the technology of many industries requires relatively large plants for efficient operation and that, consequently, efforts to impose a regime of many small

[16]The most obvious omission has been effects on the distribution of income, a matter that economists are now beginning to address empirically. This is discussed further in Chapter 9.

[17]John J. Siegfried and Thomas K. Tiemann, "The Welfare Cost of Monopoly: An Inter-Industry Analysis," *Economic Inquiry*, **12** (June 1974), 190–202.

firms would be self-defeating. Pure competition, then, is an unrealistic objective at best.

Given this limitation, consider an intuitively plausible statement: If we cannot attain the ideal state of competition, the next best alternative is to approximate it as closely as possible. Public policy ought to work to achieve the maximum possible "amount" of competition in all markets, even though the results are sure to fall short of perfection. This position is an obviously appealing one: If we cannot have the whole loaf, let us at least take what we can. It is true that our best efforts often are stimulated by the pursuit of "impossible" goals. Why worry that the goal is unattainable if it drives us to do more than we otherwise would?

As is sometimes the case in economics, however, the obvious statement has been shown to contain a logical flaw. The difficulty is usually described in terms of the "theory of second best," a group of closely related ideas whose central points are as follows:

. . . if one or more of the marginal conditions for a Pareto optimum cannot be fulfilled, the rest of the conditions are, in general, no longer desirable . . . [therefore] . . . a situation in which more but not all of the optimum conditions are fulfilled, may **not** *be superior to a situation in which fewer are fulfilled; indeed, we cannot state a priori which case is likely to be superior.*[18]

In other words, if **all** the conditions for Pareto optimality cannot be met, there may be no point in attempting to meet as many as possible. Indeed, the **second best** solution to full attainment of the conditions **may** turn out to be **abandonment of the other conditions**. As we have seen, perfect competition in all markets satisfies the marginal conditions for a Pareto optimum. What the theory of second best implies, then, is that if some monopoly element in the economy is inevitable—that is, if it is impossible to satisfy fully all of the marginal conditions—an attempt to foster "as much competition as possible" may actually be detrimental to economic welfare. Indeed, the **second best** solution might be attained by allowing **more monopoly** rather than more competition.

The exposition of the theory of second best is largely mathematical, and its central conclusion is not intuitively obvious.[19] We may attempt to illustrate the idea of the theory in the following way, however. The problem of monopoly is one of resource misallocation: too little in the way of resources flows to monopolized sectors, and too little is produced. But in a universe or world or country, whatever the relevant dimension, that contains both competitive and monopolistic sectors, it also follows that for society to reallocate and arrive at a better welfare position resources must be **taken away** from competitive sectors. In other words, the resource-allocation problem that we traditionally describe as "too few resources in the monopoly sector" can also be described meaningfully as "too many resources in the competitive sector."

[18] See R. G. Lipsey and Kelvin Lancaster,"The General Theory of Second Best," *Review of Economic Studies,* **24** (1956), 11–32; P. Bohm, "On the Theory of Second Best," *Review of Economic Studies, b34* (July 1967), 301–314.

[19] For the mathematical exposition, see Lipsey and Lancaster, ibid.; and Paul A. Samuelson, *Foundations of Economic Analysis* (Cambridge: Harvard University Press, 1947).

Suppose that in a particular economic system all industries are monopolies. There is an argument that, under these circumstances, **no misallocation** will exist! The misallocation of resources is a relative problem. Monopolistic sectors of an economy cannot demand "too little" unless other, nonmonopoly, sectors demand "too much." As Baumol puts it:

If each of a number of runners slow down, none of them need come in ahead of the others, and if each industry is weak in its bidding for resources, no lopsided allocation of these resources need result.[20]

Viewed in these terms, more competition is not necessarily desirable. The misallocation that we have habitually referred to as a "monopoly problem" could be called a "competition problem." And if universal competition is the best of all worlds, universal monopoly may be the next best. Indeed, a world of much competition and little monopoly may represent an unsatisfactory situation that would be worsened by increasing the extent of competition, as long as universally competitive markets are not possible.

This essential conclusion of the theory of second best implies that policies that **partially remedy** monopolistic conditions may be worse than no policies at all. Although this implication has received serious attention,[21] it has not led economists generally to advocate the abandonment of procompetitive public policies. One reason for this is that the theory represents a general equilibrium approach that may not be appropriate to many policy problems. According to the theory a change that is "good" for one segment of the economy may prove to be "bad" in its ramifications throughout the system.

Public policy, however, most often follows a "piecemeal" approach in which direct effects on the immediate segment are considered paramount.[22] This approach makes sense if changes in one part of the economy are thought to hold negligible implications for most others. In a sense, the question becomes one of defining the relevant system or universe. If various sectors of the economy are independent of each other, there is a strong case for treating each as a separate system, that is, as an isolated problem. Although a general Pareto optimum embracing all systems is unattainable, there may be gains in meeting the Pareto conditions in some systems. Even if the sectors in which competition can be effectively induced are related to other, monopolistic areas, the gains may outweigh the losses. As one study notes, if we desire efficient postal services, we are not as a matter of practical procedure

---

[20]William J. Baumol, *Economic Theory and Operations Research*, 2nd ed. Englewood Cliffs, N.J.: Prentice-Hall, (1965), p. 366.

[21]This attention is attested to by an extensive literature. For discussions, see E. J. Mishan, "Second Thoughts on Second Best," *Oxford Economic Papers* (New Series), **14** (October 1962), 205–217; O. A. Davis and A. Whinston, "Welfare Economics and the Theory of Second Best," *Review of Economic Studies*, **32** (January 1965), 1–14; O. A. Davis and A. Whinston, "Piecemeal Policy in the Theory of Second Best," *Review of Economic Studies*, **34** (July 1967), 323–331; and William J. Baumol, "Informed Judgment, Rigorous Theory and Public Policy," *Southern Economic Journal*, **32** (October 1965), 137–145.

[22]See Mishan, ibid.; Baumol, ibid.; and Davis and Whinston, "Piecemeal Policy in the Theory of Second Best," ibid.

likely to be inhibited by the fact that there may be monopoly in the production of pinwheels.[23]

It also must be emphasized that the case against monopoly in the United States has never rested exclusively on resource misallocation. Americans historically have objected to monopoly on other grounds—for example, high prices and income transfers that are viewed as unfair. These objections would support piecemeal efforts to curb monopoly even if one were to accept the second best argument in its strongest form.

What, then, does the theory of second best tell us? The broad lesson is significant: we cannot be sure that "more" competition is allocatively better than "less," even though we accept universal competition as the ideal. Second best, however, does not provide an unqualified or specific challenge to competition-promoting policies. Rather, it demands our recognition of the fact that policies aimed toward one sector of the economy can have ramifications in other sectors; and the **possibility** that the introduction of competition in one area might reduce allocative welfare overall.

"WORKABLE" COMPETITION AND THE STRUCTURE–CONDUCT–PERFORMANCE HYPOTHESIS

If we accept that perfect competition is an unrealistic, and in some circumstances an undesirable, policy objective, the question becomes: What kind and degree of competition ought to be pursued? Presumably we should seek the best arrangement that is practically attainable. Rather than chasing perfection, we may aim for a market system that is **workably** competitive. Definitions of workable or effective competition represent efforts to provide a more meaningful and useful policy goal than can be drawn from the competitive ideal.

Once we depart from the ideal, the question is how an acceptable alternative is to be defined. The father of the term workable competition, John Maurice Clark, contended that both the competitive **process** and its **results** are important.[24] In judging a competitive situation, then, we might look at rather distinctive sorts of indexes.

What is sometimes termed the structure–conduct–performance hypothesis in industrial organization now becomes relevant. Briefly, this hypothesis states that within any industry, existing structural characteristics determine the conduct patterns of constituent firms; that conduct, in turn, determines industry performance. **Structure** refers to the relatively stable organizational aspects of a market—most notably concentration, the extent of product differentiation, and the ease of entry. **Conduct** denotes the behavioral patterns of firms within the market; it embraces their objectives, policies, and the ways in which they interact with one another. Decisions about where to set price, what products to produce, and whether to collude with rivals are all part of the conduct realm.

Finally, market **performance** may be defined as the observable end results in such areas as price, quantity, and product quality. It is the composite of the conse-

[23] Davis and Whinston, ibid.

[24] "Toward a Concept of Workable Competition," *American Economic Review*, **30** (June 1940), 241–256.

quences produced by the conduct decisions of firms. Of particular interest are such magnitudes as profitability, production efficiency, and the rate of innovation in new products and techniques.

When we ask whether a market is workably competitive, then, we might look to any or all of these dimensions. Many writers since the 1940s have attempted to formulate standards of workable competition. An exhaustive review of the literature by Stephen H. Sosnick has cited, among others, the following common suggestions:[25]

1. Conditions of structure.
    a. Moderate and price-sensitive quality differentials.
    b. No artificial handicaps on mobility.
    c. Adequate access to information.
    d. Some uncertainty about whether price reductions will be met.
2. Conditions of conduct.
    a. Firms should not shield permanently inefficient rivals, suppliers, or customers.
    b. There should be no unfair, exclusionary, predatory, or coercive tactics.
    c. Sales promotion should not be misleading.
3. Conditions of performance.
    a. Efficiency in operations.
    b. Promotional expenses should not be excessive.
    c. Profits should reach levels that reward investment and efficiency and induce innovation.
    d. Output should be consistent with a good allocation of resources.
    e. Quality should conform to consumers' interests.
    f. Opportunities for better products and techniques should not be ignored.
    g. Conservation should not be disregarded.

These proposed criteria of workable competition are among those mentioned most frequently by writers on the subject. There is, as Sosnick points out, some "clustering" of proposals, that is, some agreement that certain attributes are relevant. At the same time, there is considerable diversity in the views expressed. Some observers stress workable market structures, whereas others place a higher priority on performance or conduct. Few have actually suggested, however, that workable competition can be defined adequately within any single category. Many would agree with Sosnick that performance is of "ultimate importance" in the economy, and that the primary question we ought to ask about competition is: What do we want it to **do** for us? Like Sosnick and Clark, however, few would accept a **pure** performance criterion of workability. As Ben W. Lewis has put it:

*Results alone throw no light on the really significant question: have these results been **compelled** by the system—by **competition**—or do they represent simply the dispensations of managements which, with a wide latitude of policy choices at their*

---

[25] "A Critique of Concepts of Workable Competition," *Quarterly Journal of Economics,* **72** (August 1958), 380–423.

disposal, happened at the moment to be benevolent or "smart?" This points up the real issue.[26]

In a sense, then, we demand not only good performance, but good performance for the right reasons. The well-behaved monopolist may, like the benevolent despot, perform splendidly; but if he does so at his own discretion, society cannot be certain that a similarly good record will continue in the future. Structure or conduct norms, however, are also not fully acceptable, in part because they may not imply satisfactory performance.

The categories of structure, conduct, and performance are logically related. Certain market structures are associated with particular patterns of conduct and performance, specific types of conduct bear on performance, and performance may influence both structure and conduct. But these relationships are not necessarily precise and are not well defined. A comprehensive definition of workable competition, even in the broadest terms, is thus difficult to formulate. Certain aspects of structure, conduct, and performance may seem desirable, but the ordering of these aspects by degree of importance and the resolution of conflicts among them present us with difficult dilemmas.

If we attempt to define in more specific terms the market conditions that imply a satisfactory level of competition, further problems arise. Suppose, for example, there is general agreement that innovation is an important aspect of workability; that is, for a market to be judged effectively competitive, it must demonstrate an acceptable rate of development and introduction of new processes and products. The first problem is how to measure these magnitudes. But assuming that meaningful observations of inventiveness are possible, a fundamental difficulty remains. This is simply the **assessment** of what is observed. What constitutes a "good" innovative record? Against what standard can it be measured? It is not only conceivable but highly probable that different individuals will evaluate a given set of observations in different ways. The problem of evaluation is one that runs through all criteria of workability. What is meant by a "considerable" number of firms? by an "efficient" productive record? by "independence" in firm policymaking? Without answers to such questions, there is no way to form judgments of industries. The most common notions of workable competition, although they specify the relevant dimensions of workability, do not generally tell us how acceptable levels of these dimensions are to be defined.

A somewhat distinctive approach to workable competition was suggested by Jesse W. Markham:

An industry may be judged to be workably competitive when, after the structural characteristics of its market and the dynamic forms that shaped them have been thoroughly examined, there is no clearly indicated change that can be effected

---

[26] "The Effectiveness of the Federal Antitrust Laws: A Symposium," Dexter M. Keezer, Ed., *American Economic Review*, **39** (June 1949), 706–707; emphasis in original.

through public policy measures that would result in greater social gains than social losses.[27]

Markham's view is essentially pragmatic and contains two important virtues. First, it makes clear that there can be no uniform standard of workability applicable to all industries. What is workable in one set of circumstances may be wholly unacceptable in another. This might mean, for example, that a particular rate of innovation would be satisfactory in an industry in which the state of the art is not conductive to new developments but unsatisfactory where existing technology and the nature of products and processes seemed to invite innovation.

The second, and perhaps most useful, aspect of Markham's definition is that it requires no subjective assessment of what is "good" or "bad" in the structure, conduct, and performance of industries. The relevant question is never: Are the various characteristics of a market "good"? Rather, the question becomes: Are these characteristics **improvable** by public policy? An industry that everyone agrees is well behaved will not be judged workably competitive under Markham's approach if public action could force it to behave still better. Similarly, an industry that appears to do poorly by accepted standards might be found workably competitive if no public policy offered hope of improvement.

Despite these virtues, formulations of workable competition, such as Markham's, suffer from much the same difficulty that has plagued earlier definitions. The central problem is that, lacking precise and agreed-upon criteria, definitions of workability tend to be tautological. That is, they are redundant, stated in such a way that the definition adds relatively little to the meaning of the term. To say, for example, that workable competition requires a "considerable" number of firms, is not much different from saying that workable competition requires a "workable" number of firms. As Ben W. Lewis has stated more generally: "Workable competition is competition that works."

The tautological nature of many definitions of workable competition does not mean that the concept is a useless one. In the first place, the definitions are not usually **pure** tautology. Specifying the dimensions of workability—number of firms, innovation and profit rates, and the like—is itself an addition to knowledge. It is also possible that in some cases agreement on the ranges of workable values in the various dimensions will be possible. Ultimately, however, the question of what is and is not workably competitive depends upon subjective judgments. The notion of workable competition may therefore be useful not so much as a guide—for it cannot easily surmount this dependence—but, rather, for the questions it **raises**. The idea of workable competition, however vague it may be, makes it quite clear that those concerned with public policy must decide what is important. Given an imperfect world, there is a need for priorities. We cannot have everything; therefore, we must define what it is that we can attain and what we are willing to settle

---

[27] "An Alternative Approach to the Concept of Workable Competition," *American Economic Review,* **40** (June 1950), 361.

for. Mere invocation of the words "workable competition" will not provide us with a specific idea of appropriate policies, but the term does help to focus attention on the problems that must be resolved.

PRODUCT COMPETITION

Traditional market theories, as we have seen, are primarily theories of **price** competition. Firms within any market sell a defined product; what they must decide is the "best" price or, equivalently, the best output level for that product. Descriptively, this view is plainly unrealistic in many cases. Corporations are typically concerned with the nature of the products they sell, and may devote more resources to defining and developing the "right" product than to calculating the best price for that product. We must therefore consider the possibility that markets that are not highly competitive in traditional (price) terms may, nevertheless, foster active competition in product characteristics.

This possibility clearly harks back to Schumpeter's view of the economic system, which is, as we have noted, quite different from that of the orthodox body of theory.[28] His concern was with innovation in products and techniques rather than with the traditional problem of resource allocation, and he saw as the basic virtue of the capitalist system its ability to introduce the "perennial gales" of "creative destruction" that imply change and improvement. Schumpeter attributed this strength to large companies with some monopoly power. Such firms, according to Schumpeter, are likely to engage in inventive activity for several reasons.[29] First, they have the financial wherewithal to do so. The invention and introduction of new products and techniques often requires extensive financial capital, and possibly the ability to absorb losses over some time period. Even if the inventive process is simple and does not require much research, it may be costly to place new items on the market under conditions that offer a reasonable chance of success. The kind of small, zero-profit firm that exists in pure competition would not, in the Schumpeterian view, have sufficient funds to bring about major changes. Furthermore, Schumpeter argued, a large potential payoff is required to induce inventive activity.[30] Unless a firm can see some prospect of a large, essentially **monopolistic,** reward, it may find little reason to experiment with new developments, which are, by virtue of their untested nature, risky. Finally, Schumpeter noted that although the large firm may operate in what are termed noncompetitive markets, it is not free from competitive pressures. Such a firm may be very insecure in markets in which it confronts powerful opponents. Accordingly, invention and innovation may be stimulated by the desire to survive against firms that are similarly motivated. The

---

[28] Joseph A. Schumpeter, *Capitalism, Socialism, and Democracy,* 3rd ed. (New York: Harper, 1950).

[29] A distinction is usually made between **invention,** the development of a new product or technique, and **innovation,** the actual introduction of the novelty to the market.

[30] It is interesting to note that the American patent system presupposes precisely the requirement of a large payoff. The assumption of the current system is that invention will be stimulated by granting the inventor a monopoly on his development for a specified number of years. During this period, the inventor may exploit his invention or profit by licensing it to others.

threat of failure in a market populated by a few innovators is seen as potentially greater than that posed by a market of many small competitors, none of whom are active innovators; and the purpose of innovation in the concentrated market thus may be not monopolization but simply maintenance of an established position.

The Schumpeterian thesis, as stated in *Capitalism, Socialism and Democracy,* is rather general. His position is that the strength of the capitalistic system lies not in traditional price competition but in the competition of invention and innovation. Such activity flourishes in imperfectly competitive markets; thus the good performance of the modern capitalistic economy is a result not of adherence to the strict competitive ideal but of **divergence** from it. There are, of course, objections to this position. It can be argued that large firms generally are **not** under severe pressure to innovate and that smaller firms in more competitive market settings are more likely to be subject to the kinds of pressure that encourage innovation. It also is possible that the large firm, although induced by competitive pressures to "do something," may not concentrate on meaningful or genuine change. Rather than introducing a new product or improving an old one, the firm may decide that it is profitable instead to alter the packaging or styling of the product. Rather than attempting to develop cost-saving productive techniques, it may choose to alter its demand curve by increased advertising.

One of the necessities in evaluating the Schumpeterian hypothesis is a definition and specification of terms. We need to know what is and what is not a true innovation; and we must define more precisely the implied relationship between firm size, degree of market power, and innovation. We need to know more than that a large firm will engage in more inventive activity than a smaller firm. The real question is: **How much more**? It is necessary to determine how inventiveness relates to firm size, and in what patterns. Possibly, for example, firms must attain a certain size before they become active inventors and innovators, but they will not respond to **further** size increases with more innovation. These questions are empirical, and the accuracy and significance of Schumpeter's contention must be established by facts rather than speculation.

Some observers view product competition as something even broader than the Schumpeterian contention suggests. What firms desire is **product differentiation**— the belief among consumers that one's offerings are different from and, ideally, better than rivals'. One way to differentiate is through "actual" change in the quality or performance of the product. This is Schumpeterian innovation: the wonder drug; the car with comfort **and** better gas mileage; the tasty, low-calorie beer.

Alternative routes to differentiation may exist, however: changes in styling or packaging, which some people regard as "artificial" product distinctions (e.g., we may put our ordinary beer in a fancy bottle, or give our uncomfortable, mediocre-performance car a new "look"); or advertising and other promotional efforts, which may involve no "real" change in the product itself (e.g., we try to convince people to drink our unchanged beer because some famous athletes profess to do so with enormous pleasure).

One may be inclined to regard "genuine" innovations as socially "good," and "artificial" distinctions as wasteful, but the issue is seldom clear-cut. Consider an example. I may buy a Volkswagen Rabbit because of a television commercial that shows Wilt Chamberlain driving one. The ad convinces me that I am more comfortable in the Rabbit; it has created a "real" product difference for me, even though you may believe that I am a gullible fool. Who is to distinguish between product differences that are "real or fancied," in Edward H. Chamberlin's phrase? If one believes in consumer sovereignty, every individual must decide for himself. Whether I believe that your decisions are based in "reality," or vice versa, is of no importance.

Virtually all product competition is like any form of economic activity. It has both costs and benefits. The issue is therefore **not** whether the activity is socially "good" or "bad," but whether the market provides an appropriate amount of it. This is an important question, but it will not be settled deductively. One may construct a perfectly logical theory that predicts **either** "too much" **or** "too little" product differentiating effort.[31] The problem is in part that, to be useful, the theory must apply to oligopoly markets where (as we well know) the prospects for firm analytical conclusions are not bright. Thus it is that further statements about product competition must be based on some appeal to observed facts.

SUMMARY

Interpretations of the market system vary widely in the roles they envision for competition and monopoly, and even more basically in the meanings they assign to these terms. There is agreement that competition in the strict sense of our pure model cannot be achieved, but the status of structural competition as a norm for public policy is still vigorously debated. In the view of some, such a standard is not merely unattainable but a positive danger—an ideal the pursuit of which is likely to damage our economic welfare.

Competition as a theoretical construct has a clear meaning, but it is evident that the kind of "competition" toward which we may reasonably aspire in practice, is not an unambiguous concept. Under the circumstances, it should not be surprising to find that our attitudes as reflected in public competition policies are marked by some inconsistency.

---

[31] For example, the popular view that there is too much advertising receives support from Nicholas Kaldor's classic article, "The Economic Aspects of Advertising," *Review of Economic Studies,* **18** (1949–1950), 1–27. Yet there are also common arguments that markets **under**-allocate resources to the "production" and distribution of information (usually because information is seen to have aspects of a public good). The theories thus conflict (although one may argue cogently that not all advertising conveys much information).

CHAPTER 6

Competition Theory and Policy: Some Implications

Barring Utopia, the basic economic problem of all societies is much the same: Human beings need or want more than they can have, and a way must be found to use limited resources to obtain the best level of satisfaction. One framework within which decisions about resource utilization can be made is the private enterprise system. As we have seen, the rationale for such a system is closely related to the optimality of resource allocation that competitive markets tend to yield. Few individuals, however, would insist on the laissez-faire view that such a system is capable of running itself. Evidence of imperfection is abundant, and the vulnerability of the system to distortion and abuse is widely recognized. This is the general rationale for government intervention in economic matters. Where the system is abused or does not run smoothly, government as the representative of the people enters to protect society's welfare.

In the United States, governmental intervention in the economy takes many forms and is justified by a wide variety of special circumstances. Certain activities (e.g., national defense) are handled by the government because they present problems that are not amenable to market-type solutions. Other activities may be subsidized positively or negatively by government because there is reason to expect that the market will chronically misestimate their benefits or costs. (For example, it is thought that the market would underestimate the value of education and thus produce too little; similarly, it would underestimate the cost of air pollution and thus produce too much.) Antitrust—or, more precisely, public competition—policy[1] is one of the more inherently conservative forms of governmental intervention. It does not ordinarily attempt to substitute social preference for those of the private market, nor does it alter private valuations by subsidization or taxation of activities. Quite the contrary, antitrust policy is intended to preserve the conditions under which the private market functions best. It is designed to protect an environment in which individual judgment reigns supreme.

---

[1]The term **antitrust** is something of a misnomer today. A trust is a legal arrangement that was widely utilized in the nineteenth century by business rivals who wished to avoid competition and to pursue common policies. Statutes designed to reestablish competition and prevent the spread of such arrangements were thus called "antitrust" laws, and the term persists, although the applicability of the laws is much broader.

107

Accordingly, the attention of antitrust focuses primarily on those areas of the economy in which the market system is thought to be workable. It is obvious, however, that even here market conditions do not conform to a strict competitive ideal and that public policy has not attempted to implement the ideal. This suggests that, for some reason or reasons, a clear theoretical conclusion about the desirability of competition has not been capable of straightforward translation into public policy. This difficulty is not surprising in light of challenges to the competitive norm such as those discussed in Chapter 5. In considering the reasons that theory has not provided a clear and detailed blueprint for policies toward competition, it may be helpful to note the following general positions:

1. The theoretical superiority of competition is logically established but is largely irrelevant for public policy because of the extremely restrictive assumptions under which the conclusion of superiority is reached. Policymakers cannot ignore the costs of competition that exist in the real world simply because such ignorance makes abstract analysis easier.
2. The conclusion of competitive superiority is useful for some policy decisions but is limited by the fact that the theoretical apparatus does not tell us enough. We know, for example, that pure competition is the ideal; but there is little in the theory to indicate which among numberless **imperfect** alternatives we ought to prefer.
3. Competition maximizes economic efficiency, but it may also yield results (for example, in the distribution of income) that we regard as "unfair." The problem of translating theory to policy lies not so much in the inadequacies of the theory as it does in our inability to attach clear priorities to efficiency and equity.

Each of these positions may have some claim to truth. For various reasons, the theoretical superiority of competition does not imply a ready-made prescription for public policies. This failure indicates immediately that the role of theoretical conclusions in policy formulation is inherently limited. For the present at least, we cannot simply take economic models, plug in real-world values, and expect to derive optimal policies.

What, then, is the role of economic theory in antitrust? Most broadly, the theory contributes a series of data or clues as to what may occur when certain dimensions of firms and markets are altered. That is, the theory associates a number of characteristics with expectations—albeit imprecise expectations—about firm and market behavior. Public policy can in some ways influence these characteristics, and the primary role of economic analysis is to provide predictions about the consequences of alternative policy actions. We know, for example, that behavior depends to some degree upon the concentration of power among firms in a market. Accordingly, it should be possible to say something about the behavioral consequences of policies that affect the concentration of power.

There are a number of characteristics in addition to power concentration that may be termed policy variables, that is, they are amenable to policy manipulation. Given some notion of the kinds of goals we would like to attain, it may be possible to define (at least roughly) the policy manipulations that are most likely to be successful. Is the kind of market behavior that we desire associated, for example, with a high degree of market concentration? If so, there are policy moves that will tend to produce the concentration levels that are thought to be appropriate. Does market performance deteriorate when firms conspire? If so, then it may be possible through public action to prevent conspiracy from occurring.

In practice, the issues that come before policymakers are likely to be more narrow. Will the merger of two large steel producers, say, have a significant impact on the structure of the steel industry? And if so, is the implication for industry performance such that the merger ought to be prohibited?

The role that is envisioned here for economic analysis is both important and limited. It is important in that governments—state as well as federal—continually make decisions that will affect the future organization of markets. Even something as seemingly far removed as the awarding of defense contracts, for example, may determine the size structure of a defense-oriented industry. In choosing among alternatives, the theoretical apparatus may yield very helpful information about the economic effects that will result.

Limitations on the role of theory arise for two general reasons. The first is that theory alone may not be capable of answering many questions. The merger of the steel companies above, could have several effects. It might increase the efficiency of the merged firm; but it might also increase concentration and affect the condition of entry into the industry for new firms. The likelihood of these possibilities and the importance of each are not questions that can be answered adequately on the basis of abstract reasoning. It is necessary to estimate the relevant magnitudes, that is, to lend empirical content to the possibilities suggested by the analysis. The role of theory in antitrust policy is, then, largely informational; and the information provided tends to be incomplete. The clues and suggestions to be drawn from theoretical constructs are invaluable; but those who might expect to derive categorical policy statements are likely to be disappointed.

A second restriction on the role of theory in policymaking is that the definition of desired goals cannot be aided by objective analysis. To this point we have referred to appropriate or desirable policies as if the meanings of the words presented no difficulty. In fact, this is hardly the case. If policy goals are well defined, it is still necessary to determine what policies will satisfy the goals, and such a determination may prove to be difficult. The difficulty is compounded, however, when—as in antitrust policy—the definition of objectives is itself unclear. There is nothing in economic analysis that can help much with this problem. Our theoretical structures can illuminate the implications of alternative policy moves, or, perhaps more frequently, suggest ways in which we can test for implications. But there is nothing in objective analysis that can tell us what our goals **ought** to be.

The definition of policy goals seems to be especially difficult in antitrust policy. Broadly speaking, of course, the goals are little different from the general economic and political objectives of society. Antitrust policy seeks to promote economic progress and efficiency and to protect individual liberty and freedom of choice. Many governmental policies are designed to encourage precisely the same things.

What is unique to antitrust policy is the lower-order, more immediate objective which serves as the **means** to the final ends. The proximate objective is to maintain a competitive market system, in the belief that such a system ultimately yields progress, efficiency, and freedom. But although it is easy to **list** these noble aims, with which no one is likely to disagree, such a listing does not represent a meaningful "definition of objectives." A meaningful definition must go beyond more general enumeration of goals to (1) state specifically what is meant by each, and (2) specify the **relative importance** of each.

A hypothetical example may be helpful. Suppose it were agreed that technical efficiency and limitations on economic power are the only goals of antitrust policy. By itself this statement does not tell us very much about what antitrust policy ought to do. Perhaps there is one set of policy measures that will increase efficiency and another that will tighten the limits on power. The two goals cannot be simultaneously maximized. If we take steps to advance efficiency we shall necessarily ignore other steps that would have limited power. What is the proper "mixture" of policy steps? There is no way to be sure, as long as we have specified only that we are concerned with both objectives.

Suppose we now go a bit further and specify that efficiency is to be the primary objective. That is more helpful since it tells us that efficiency-increasing moves are to be more heavily emphasized than moves that limit power, but there is still an area of ignorance. We do not yet know **how much more** efficiency is to be stressed relative to power limits. Should we devote 51 percent of our resources to efficiency-promoting policies and 49 percent to policies that limit power? Or is the proper ratio 75 to 25 or 90 to 10? The two objectives are competitive in that both require resources. They may also compete in the more direct sense that policies which create efficiency simultaneously increase power (i.e., decrease its limits). In any event, to get more efficiency we must give up some limit on power and vice versa.

To pursue the best possible policy, some further guidance is necessary. Specifically we need to know:

1. The actual trade-offs between efficiency and retardation of power, that is, the amount of one that must be sacrificed in order to obtain some specified incremental amount of the other. We must determine, in other words, the "price" or "marginal cost" of each characteristic in terms of the other.
2. A more precise statement of our relative preferences. That is, how much is efficiency **worth** to us in terms of lesser restraints on power and vice versa?

When stated in this way, our knowledge requirements are clearly demanding. Indeed, it can hardly be surprising that economic analysis fails to provide a blueprint for public policy. At best, our theoretical framework can do little more than to show us what kinds of variables to examine, and to give us an idea of what kinds of relationships to expect. We know, for example, that where economies of scale are important there is likely to be a direct conflict between our interest in efficiency and our interest in restraining power. To get greater efficiency we may have to accept a high concentration of power; but to restrain power we may have to give up efficiency.

This much may be drawn from the theory, but it is now evident that the knowledge we require for policy purposes is much broader. What economics must do to assist the antitrust policymaker is, most basically, to price his alternatives; that is, to specify the price, or cost, of any policy in terms of alternatives foregone. Do we wish more efficiency? Certainly! But this does not necessarily mean that we will pay any price, in terms of increased power or something else, in order to get it.[2] A prime objective of the economist is to define for the policymaker the prices of efficiency, or any other objectives. This presupposes an ability to predict the effects of policy moves both on the objectives in question and its alternatives.[3]

There is no question that economic theory itself cannot provide the necessary information. It should, in fact, be obvious that the kind of information we lack can be obtained only by measuring relevant magnitudes. Theory may suggest, for example, that high market concentration could imply both an efficiency gain and a welfare loss. If we wish to formulate policies toward a particular market, however, the theoretical suggestion does not tell us what to do. Is existing concentration such that an increase (or decrease) would imply relatively large losses or relatively large gains? There is no substitute for empirical estimates of these magnitudes. For this reason, it is necessary to consider in some detail the approaches to and problems of empirical measurement.

---

[2] The analogy to the consumer should be obvious. Perhaps each of us would like to own a new Rolls Royce, but will each of us buy one? The question simply cannot be answered without specifying the price of the car (and of its alternatives). At current prices, few people buy a Rolls Royce, but imagine the demand if price were to fall, say, to $5000. Of course there may be some Rolls owners who would get rid of their cars if "anyone" could afford to buy one!

[3] This ability would contribute to knowledge under item 1 above; it would not, however, clarify the preference information requirement of item 2.

PART TWO

EMPIRICAL
PROBLEMS
AND
EVIDENCE

The ultimate test of an economic theory is its ability to predict or explain actual events. A theory may be subtle, sophisticated, and even intrinsically interesting, but if it can do nothing to help us understand "the way things are," its usefulness is limited. The usefulness of the body of economic theory that has been discussed in Part One for purposes of public competition policy depends to an extent on its ability to meet such a test. This is so if only because the direct inferences of theory for policy are both incomplete and somewhat ambiguous. It would be extremely difficult to formulate a public policy on the basis of our current theoretical understanding of the workings of markets, and there is a clear need for further clues.

A wide variety of empirical methods is employed in testing economic theories. The suggestions of theory are used to explain or predict observed behavior, and attempts then are made to determine whether and in what way the theoretical explanation "works." If the explanation does work, the theory is supported or verified. If it does not—and if we are satisfied that our specification of relationships, observations of reality, and methods of testing are correct—it may be considered an invalid explanation, one that is rejected on the basis of the evidence.

There are several steps in the empirical testing process. First, it is necessary to select meaningful suggestions from the theory and to formulate them carefully. These suggestions, usually termed hypotheses, are the explanations or predictions of events that we draw from the theory and wish to verify or reject. The hypotheses must be developed into testable propositions, statements that can be measured against observed events. For example, we might make the statement: "Large firms innovate more than small firms." This is a rather general assertion that needs to be further specified, but it is potentially testable. What is needed is some measure of firm size and of innovation.

Suppose that the statement had instead been: "Oligopolists charge higher prices than firms in competitive markets." This statement is again testable in principle;

however, it may turn out to be a far less useful hypothesis in terms of our ability to apply meaningful tests. We could formulate an index of competition and oligopoly, apply it to various firms, and examine the prices they charge. But the prices charged depend so heavily on other factors such as cost and demand conditions that we may not be able to isolate that part of the price variation that is attributable to the difference in the nature of the markets. The statement is, in fact, so imprecisely framed that it is not useful. It would be better put: "Oligopolists charge higher prices than they would under competitive market conditions, other factors remaining constant."

Still other statements may not even be susceptible in principle to empirical verification. If we state, for example, "Large firms try harder to maximize profits than small firms," there is probably no meaningful way to proceed, for "trying hard" is not something that can be readily measured in an objective way.

Once a hypothesis is framed in a testable fashion, numerous data problems may arise. Measures of relevant magnitudes may be unavailable. The variables that are measurable may be conceptually less than ideal, and a host of measurement difficulties may cause an investigator to question the accuracy of the information that is utilized. A thorny problem in empirical investigation often is involved in the decision as to whether available data are "good enough" to permit meaningful tests of hypotheses. Here an element of subjective judgment is probably unavoidable.

A final difficulty in the process of hypothesis testing is the selection of an appropriate methodology. This refers in part to the problems already noted: specification of the hypothesis and assembly of data. It also pertains to the type of statistical tests that will be applied to the data. Many methods exist for determining relationships among two or more variables, and it is necessary to select those that are conceptually appropriate to the problem at hand.

Quite obviously, the subjection of theoretical propositions to empirical tests can be a difficult and tricky job, one that often requires a thorough understanding of statistical techniques. Not the least of the task, however, lies in the initial choice of problems to be studied. It is necessary to develop hypotheses that are not only susceptible to empirical techniques but that are also meaningful and of some general interest. In short, a sound conceptual basis is required. Aimless hunting for correlations among variables is likely to add nothing to our knowledge.

The question of what constitutes an "interesting" problem or hypothesis cannot be answered with complete objectivity. In the area of industrial organization, interests tend to be policy oriented. The selection of problems for study, therefore, depends in part on the presence of implications for public competition policy. But what is important for policy, in turn, depends upon what the actual or ideal goals of policy are seen to be. Since individuals hold different views, we should expect some disagreement about what constitute the most pressing empirical questions. It appears, however, that the attention of economists in industrial organization focuses on a rather well-defined subset of problems having to do with the behavior of firms and industries.

This section reviews the nature of measurement difficulties and some of the empirical evidence on firm and industry behavior. It should be recognized—as was stressed earlier—that the role of the evidence is purely informational. It can tell us about the economic consequences of alternative policies but cannot define for us what an appropriate or ideal policy is.

CHAPTER 7

The Conceptual Problem: Deciding What to Measure

There is no scarcity of interesting hypotheses in industrial organization. Economic theory engenders expectations about the behavior of firms and markets that form the basis for many potentially testable statements; tests of such statements often provide information that is pertinent to public competition policy. The formulation of a testable hypothesis requires initially that variables relevant to the hypothesis be defined. That is, it is necessary to identify the kinds of magnitudes that need to be measured in order to examine the validity of the idea in question. Initially, the task is largely conceptual, involving specification of what ought to be measured. More practical problems concerning the nature of available data must also be considered; however, it is sometimes useful first to define the ideal measures, and to isolate partially the problem of what measures are actually possible.

What kinds of hypotheses ought we to test? There are, of course, no rigid rules. In industrial organization, policy interests lead most frequently to hypotheses that seek to explain the performance of firms and industries. An important policy objective is to secure the kinds of economic results that we consider desirable; accordingly, it is necessary to determine what factors seem to determine desirable behavior patterns.

Our theoretical structures are very helpful in this regard. It is clear, for example, that an industry that is "competitive" in the strict sense is expected to act differently from one that is "monopolistic." Should an industry contain elements of both competition and monopoly—and this is almost always so—expectations about its behavior may be less precise. But even here, it may be possible to formulate some expectations concerning the degree to which the industry deviates from truly competitive or monopolistic conditions. The important point is that the way in which firms and industries function has something to do with the **state of competition** present. Moreover, this is precisely the element with which our antitrust laws are designed to deal.

The first problem, then, concerns the ways in which the competitive status of an industry can be described and measured. We may expect that "competitive" and "monopolistic" industries will perform in different ways, but in order to test specific hypotheses we must be able to decide which industries fit various categories. At the extremes the question may prove to be relatively easy, but for mixed cases, in which elements of competition and monopoly coexist, it becomes more troublesome. What is needed is a measure or measures of the degree of competition or monopoly present. Clearly, such measures, even if they are perfect, cannot imply the end of our conceptual problems. But if the degree of competition in markets can be described meaningfully, some useful predictions about behavior become possible.

Unfortunately, the measurement of competition and monopoly is not a straightforward problem. As we noted in Chapter 5, the traditional structure–conduct–performance hypothesis suggests three broad approaches. These are represented in Table 7.1.

Market structure refers to the relatively stable organizational characteristics of the market and is the starting point of most theories. Recall that the competitive model, for instance, begins with a set of structural specifications: many small firms, free entry, and a homogeneous product. Structure is of critical importance because it implies something about the likely conduct and performance of the market. Accordingly, we might seek to assess the competitiveness of any given market by examining its structural elements.

Alternatively, one might view the competitiveness of a market in terms of its **conduct**: the behavioral patterns of its constituent firms, including the stratagems that the companies adopt in dealing with one another. Some observers regard a market as competitive as long as it is characterized by independent conduct; that is, firms "fight it out" rather than collude. In this sense a market may be competitive even though its structure looks nothing like perfect competition. A small number of rivals will suffice, provided that they "go at each other" aggressively.

Notice, however, that in Table 7.1 market conduct is placed in brackets. The reason is twofold: First, the theoretical role of conduct is not always clear-cut. We may agree, for example, that "independent" action by firms will lead to a different market outcome than "collusion," but what can we say about the tight-knit oligopoly in which firms do not explicitly collude but cannot really act independently either? A second, somewhat related, reason for placing conduct in brackets is that it frequently proves difficult to measure. This problem will be discussed further below.

Finally, we might define the competitiveness of a market by referring to its **performance**—the end results as manifested in prices, output levels and qualities, costs, and innovations. This approach suggests that a market is competitive when it produces those **outcomes** that we associate with competition.

Table 7.1 The Traditional Industrial Organization Paradigm

Market Structure ⟶	(Market Conduct) ⟶	Market Performance
1. Number and relative size of firms	(1. Firms' strategies: collude or fight?)	1. Prices and output quantities
2. Condition of entry	(2. Firms' goals: profits sales, growth . . .?)	2. Profits
3. Product differentiation		3. Innovations and costs

As is often true in economics, the desirability of a particular empirical approach depends heavily upon the type of problem that is under investigation. Each of the possibilities noted above has a number of shortcomings, however, that may influence their potential usefulness:

1. Measures of market structure are both obtainable for many industries and theoretically relevant; but the imprecision of structure-based predictions is troublesome. It is not always possible to draw accurate inferences about conduct or performance from structural variables.
2. Market conduct is notoriously difficult to observe, much less to measure in precise fashion. Recall, for example, the discussion of collusive oligopoly in Chapter 3. Even to define what collusion means is not entirely simple; to determine whether and to what extent it exists in a market may not be possible in many instances.
3. Market performance is observable, but it may be difficult to interpret what has been observed. (For example, we see a particular rate of innovation in an industry. Is this a ''competitive'' or ''monopolistic'' rate? There may be no firm theoretical benchmark.) Moreover, performance tends to be invulnerable to policy control since public officials would probably be reluctant to direct companies to perform in specific ways. This smacks more of the controlled economy than the private enterprise systems.

There is now an obvious quandary: What do we look at? Where do we begin? To answer such questions, it is helpful to consider again **why** we are interested in measuring ''monopoly'' and ''competition.'' From an economic point of view, the significant test of an economy, or of the markets within an economy, is whether it secures for us the sort of results that are desired. This central concern indicates that our ultimate interest must have something to do with economic **performance.**

This orientation of our interests implies a strong motive to discover what **determines** performance patterns, and especially to identify determinants that are amenable to public policy influence. Since performance is usually not subject to direct policy control, discussions of competition and monopoly often proceed in terms of market structure and, upon occasion, conduct. Indeed, if the structure–conduct –performance hypothesis is valid, we should be able to secure competitive performance by means of policies that affect structure.

THEORETICAL INDEXES OF "COMPETITION" AND "MONOPOLY": THE POWER OF FIRMS

The most direct way of measuring the degree of monopoly or competition focuses on the power of firms within relevant industry groupings. In some areas firms have little control over the price they charge. Any deviation from the market-determined level is likely to prove insupportable. In such circumstances the firms may be termed ''powerless,'' a condition in accord with our idea of pure competition. In most markets, however, some leeway exists. Firms can ''get away with'' lesser or greater pricing deviations, and are thus said to hold power or control over price—a condition associated with economic notions of monopoly.[1]

The first difficulty in attempting to measure this kind of control is the fact that it is not one dimensional. That is, there is no **single** magnitude that comprehensively reflects market power. The problem has been compared by Chamberlin to that of measuring a person's health:

Some aspects of health can be measured and others cannot. Among the former we have body temperature, blood pressure, metabolism, weight, etc. But these do not lend themselves to the construction of a single quantitative index of health.[2]

It turns out that a number of practical measures, while providing useful clues to the state of monopoly, cannot be taken as definitive statements. Furthermore, there exist measures that are potentially useful but are impractical because of difficulties in quantifying the relevant magnitudes. Economists have expanded considerable effort in trying to define meaningful indexes of competition and monopoly, and the results, although not fully satisfactory, include several valuable suggestions.

Simple Measures of Elasticity

The degree of pricing power held by a firm obviously depends in some way upon the shape of its demand curve. The most convenient way of characterizing the curve is by its price **elasticity,** that is, the extent to which quantity demanded responds to price changes made by the firm. The price elasticity of demand for a product, X, is defined as:

$$\frac{\text{percentage change in quantity demanded of } X}{\text{percentage change in price of } X}$$

The fraction ordinarily has a negative sign, since price **increases** lead to quantity **decreases** and vice versa.[3]

---

[1] Readers may observe a conceptual difficulty even here, however. For given demand and cost functions, there exists (in all likelihood) only one profit-maximizing price. If the firm is a maximizer, it has pricing "leeway" only in the sense that its position is not enforced by the market. That is, the firm's decision to maximize is itself a matter of choice. Once this decision is made, however, the firm's appropriate behavior is closely prescribed by market forces.

[2] Edward H. Chamberlin, "Measuring the Degree of Competition and Monopoly," in Edward H. Chamberlin, Ed., *Monopoly and Competition and Their Regulation* (London: Macmillan, 1954), p. 267.

[3] To compute the elasticity of a demand curve, the following formula is derived:

$$E = -\frac{\Delta\%Q}{\Delta\%P} = -\frac{\Delta Q/Q_0}{\Delta P/P_0} = -\frac{\Delta Q}{\Delta P} \cdot \frac{P_0}{Q_0}$$

where E is elasticity; ΔQ and ΔP are changes in quantity and price; and Q_0 and P_0 are original quantity and price, respectively. This formula is used to compute **arc elasticity**—the average elasticity of some segment of the curve. Such a measure may be adequate when the arc in question is relatively small. It is often desirable to compute elasticity for a

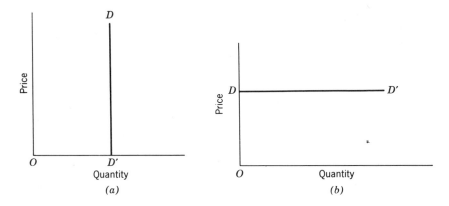

Figure 7.1(*a*) Perfectly inelastic demand. (*b*) Perfectly elastic demand.

This simple measure of quantity responsiveness to price provides one clue to the pricing power of the firm. The more inelastic (less elastic) the firm's demand curve, the more power or control over price the firm may be said to possess. This is true in the sense that the firm is freer to manipulate its price without regard to implications for the quantities demanded. In the case of a **perfectly inelastic** demand curve, as shown in Figure 7.1*a*, the firm has complete pricing control. Given demand curve *DD'*, it can charge any price it wishes without affecting the quantity it is able to sell. The opposite extreme of a **perfectly** or **infinitely elastic** demand curve—as shown in Figure 7.1*b*—occurs, it may be recalled, in the case of the firm in pure competition. The firm confronting such a demand curve faces the ultimate in price sensitivity in that the slightest price increase will result in the loss of all sales.

Although demand elasticity tells us something about pricing control, it is neither a sufficient nor an especially convenient index of monopoly power when considered alone. In the first place, the elasticity values may not be readily translatable into degrees of monopoly. It is true that in pure competition elasticity is infinite; however, there is no corresponding value for the case of pure monopoly. The monopolist's demand elasticity is simply that of the industry. The firm and industry demand curves are identical. For any firm, price elasticity of demand measures a combination of two factors:

---

point on a demand curve by examining the response of quantity demanded to an infinitesimally small price change. The formula for point elasticity is

$$E = -\frac{dQ}{dP} \cdot \frac{P_0}{Q_0}$$

where *dP* is an infinitesimal change in price, and *dQ* is the response of quantity demanded. The fraction *dQ/dP* is the first derivative of quantity demanded with respect to price and represents the inverse of the slope of the demand curve.

1. Industry demand elasticity, a function of consumer preferences for the products of the industry, and the closeness of substitute products outside the industry.
2. The firm's power within the industry.

Measures of price elasticity of demand may also ignore factors relevant to an assessment of a firm's power. Demand curves are constructed under a *ceteris paribus* assumption that holds constant the prices of other commodities (among other factors). Conceivably, a firm that has some pricing power within its defined market when "other things are equal" will nevertheless be sensitive to changes in the prices of other goods. This type of sensitivity is measured by the **cross elasticity** of demand. If we wish to examine the impact of the prices of goods X and Y upon each other's demands, we would try to estimate:

$$\text{Demand cross elasticities} = \frac{\Delta Q_x}{\Delta P_y} \cdot \frac{P_y}{Q_x} \quad \text{and} \quad \frac{\Delta Q_y}{\Delta P_x} \cdot \frac{P_x}{Q_y}$$

These measure the percentage change in the demand for good X (or Y) that results from some percentage change in the price of good Y (or X).

Despite some conceptual difficulties, both demand-elasticity and cross-elasticity information is extremely useful to an appraisal of firm power. The major problems are practical. Elasticity measures are highly sensitive to the way in which a firm's market is defined. As we shall see, market definition problems are themselves formidable and at times may force us to make rather arbitrary choices; thus the demand-elasticity values would also contain an arbitrary element.

Finally, and perhaps most important, there is a paucity of reliable data. Actual elasticity values are just extremely difficult to isolate and observe in most circumstances.

The Lerner Index of Monopoly

Abba P. Lerner in 1934 proposed a measure of monopoly that is related to price elasticity of demand.[4] Noting that "the mark of the absence of monopoly is the equality of price or **average** receipts to marginal cost,"[5] Professor Lerner suggested that monopoly be measured by the extent of divergence of price from marginal cost. Specifically, the Lerner index is defined as:

---

[4] Abba P. Lerner, "The Concept of Monopoly and the Measurement of Monopoly Power," *Review of Economic Studies*, **1** (June 1934), 157–175.

[5] *Ibid.*, p. 161.

$$\frac{\text{Price} - \text{Marginal cost}}{\text{Price}}$$

In pure competition price equals marginal cost, and the value of the index is zero. The greater the ability of the firm to price above marginal cost, the higher the value of the Lerner index, and the greater the degree of monopoly inferred.

The relation of the Lerner index to demand elasticity is evident when we consider ordinary demand and cost functions. For a given marginal-cost curve, the extent to which the price charged by a firm can exceed marginal cost, that is, the vertical distance between price and marginal cost, will have something to do with the shape of the demand curve. Yet price elasticity also has something to do with the shape of the demand curve. It turns out that for profit-maximizing firms **in equilibrium,** the index is precisely the reciprocal of the price elasticity of demand,[6] a situation that Lerner treats as a special case.

The Lerner index is conceptually appropriate for a wide range of welfare problems. By examining the extent of deviation from optimal (marginal cost) pricing, it serves as a gauge of exercised, as opposed to potential, market power, and reflects the misallocation cost of monopoly. Attempts to apply the Lerner index have yielded only limited results,[7] however, largely because of the difficulty of estimating actual cost and demand functions.

The Rothschild Index

A distinctive approach to the measurement of monopoly was offered by K.W. Rothschild some time ago.[8] Rothschild starts with the situation shown in Figure 7.2. The CC' curve is "the familiar cost curve of a single firm" that produces a commodity differentiated from those produced by rivals. Curve dd' is the demand curve for the firm's product assuming that prices charged by rival producers are held constant, while DD' is the firm's demand curve assuming that rivals' prices respond in some consistent way to the price of the firm in question. These curves are similar to the d and D curves of the Chamberlin model. In fact, the only difference is that whereas Chamberlin's D curve assumes that the prices of all firms move together, Rothschild's DD assumes that "other firms change their price . . . in the same **or**

---

[6] At equilibrium, marginal revenue equals marginal cost. Thus the Lerner index can be written $(P-MR/P)$. But it can be shown that price elasticity of demand is equal to $P/P-MR$. See, for example, George J. Stigler, *The Theory of Price,* 3rd ed. (New York: Macmillan, 1966), pp. 333ff.

[7] For an effort to apply the index to the economy as a whole, see M. Kalecki, "The Determinants of the Distribution of the National Income," *Econometrica,* **6** (1938), 97–112. This effort is criticized in R. H. Whitman, "A Note on the Concept of 'Degree of Monopoly'," *Economic Journal,* **LI** (June–September 1941), 216–269. An attempt to apply the index to individual industries is provided by John T. Dunlop, "Price Flexibility and the 'Degree of Monopoly'," *Quarterly Journal of Economics,* **LIII** (August 1939), 522–533. See also Rufus S. Tucker, "The Degree of Monopoly," *Quarterly Journal of Economics,* **LIV** (November 1940), 167–169.

[8] K. W. Rothschild, "The Degree of Monopoly," *Economica,* **9** (February 1942), 24–39.

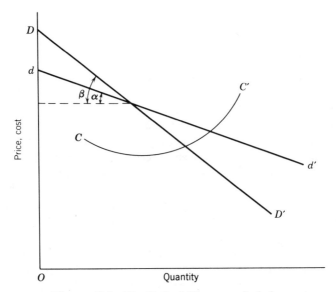

Figure 7.2 The Rothschild monopoly index.

some other predetermined way. . . ."[9] Rothschild's DD' thus may coincide with Chamberlin's, but it is left open to a wider variety of possible assumptions.

In terms of Figure 7.2 Rothschild proposes the following index of monopoly: $m = (\tan \alpha)/\tan \alpha$[10] that is, the **slope** of dd' divided by the slope of DD'. In pure competition, dd' has zero slope, and $m = 0$.[11] In pure monopoly dd' and DD' coincide, and $m = 1$. Between these extremes,[12] the value of m will reflect "the infinite possibilities of a mixture" of monopoly and competition. The distinctive quality of the Rothschild index is its exclusive focus on the strength of the firm within the market. The index does not tell us whether the market is itself "strong" in the sense that its demand is relatively inelastic. Rather, it tells us how much control of the

---

[9] Ibid., p. 24. Italics added.

[10] For readers unfamiliar with trigonometry, the tangent of an angle β is defined as ac/cd. Thus in the Rothschild example, the tangent of each angle is the slope of the associated demand curve.

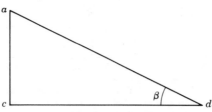

[11] The tangent of α (or its slope) is zero. Thus, $m = (\tan \alpha)/(\tan \beta) = 0$, regardless of the value of $\tan \beta$.

[12] As Rothschild points out, there are exceptional circumstances under which dd' might have a steeper slope than DD'. Here m would have a value greater than 1, but we need not be concerned with such a possibility.

market the firm has, regardless of the character of marketwide demand. The Rothschild index also is somewhat different in that it measures not the actual effects of monopoly but purely the potential of the firm for exercising monopoly power.

Summary

The foregoing indexes attempt to measure monopoly by defining in somewhat different ways the degree of market power or discretion possessed by firms. In this respect, the indexes may be as appropriate theoretically as any measure designed for this purpose. Yet they suffer from two common problems. The first difficulty, which is conceptual, is shared by virtually all measures of competition and monopoly: they are one dimensional, that is, they take account of a single aspect of monopoly or competition. The degree of monopoly or competition present in a market, however, is not a simple thing to define, and it is therefore unlikely that any such measure can provide an adequate description.

The second problem with the indexes is more practical. Each requires that values be assigned to one or more variables that are extremely difficult to measure. In view of these difficulties, it is unlikely that any of the monopoly indexes would be utilized as a full description of the competitive state of industries.

STRUCTURAL INDICATORS OF COMPETITION AND MONOPOLY

The structure of a market refers broadly to the way in which it is organized. The number of firms in the market, their relative sizes, and the condition of market entry are the primary structural elements. The degree of product differentiation is also an important characteristic of structure, although one could argue that to the extent that firms can control differentiation it might be considered a reflection of performance.

Rather than quibbling over such semantic distinctions, however, the meaning of market structure can be defined in a more pragmatic way. It is limited to those elements of organization that are theoretically significant in that they create expectations about market behavior. Indeed, this is precisely the reason for discussing structure. Our various market models are presented in essentially structural terms. (Perfect competition, for example, "means" many small firms, ease of entry, and product homogeneity.) Such models posit chains of causation that originate in these structural conditions. Our attention is, accordingly, focused upon those elements that support predictions about the ways in which firms may behave and the market results that may be forthcoming.

Concentration

If we wished to predict market behavior and could observe only one structural fact, that fact would probably be the number of firms in the market. The presence of only one firm would suggest monopoly, a few could denote oligopoly, and many might point to the possibility of something akin to pure or perfect competition. Although knowing the number of firms in a market is better than having no knowledge whatever, this is obviously a most unsatisfactory clue to the state of competition. Counting firms tells us nothing about their relative positions in the market. An industry that contains several hundred companies may be dominated by a small handful. If so, it could be considered "more monopolistic" structurally than an industry containing fewer firms in which no single company or small group dominates. What is needed in addition to information on the number of firms is some measure of their size distribution, where it is assumed that size is a reasonably good indicator of a firm's position or power within the market. Measures that take account of such information are usually referred to as concentration indexes.

Bases of Concentration Measures The base of a concentration index is the element that is used to measure the size of firms and markets. If, for example, we take the dollar value of assets, the large firm is one whose asset value is high, and the concentration index will tell us something about the distribution of assets among firms within a defined industry. A variety of bases might be appropriate, and although the values an index yields using different bases may be highly correlated, different bases may give somewhat different concentration rankings of industries. For this reason the choice of a base is a decision that deserves some attention.

1. **Sales.** Sales revenue is a commonly mentioned base for concentration measurement. The major objection to using sales is that this measure may neglect intrafirm transactions. If reported figures reflect only sales to "outsiders," the base may fail to take account of part of the relevant market activity generated by some firms. Specifically, the size of vertically integrated firms may be understated relative to their "true" significance in the market, and this understatement may affect the concentration index. It is not clear that counting all intrafirm transactions would be the proper method of weighting vertical integration; but complete neglect of such activity may produce somewhat inaccurate estimates of firms' positions in markets where there are large differences in degree of integration among companies.

2. **Employment.** A frequently utilized base is employment. Here the size of firms is defined in terms of the number of employees. The employment base may be even less acceptable than sales revenue, for it introduces a systematic bias into virtually any measure of concentration. It is known that the degree of capital intensity (and labor intensity) tends to vary with firm size. Larger firms often rely more on capital and less on labor than smaller firms, a fact that may be casually confirmed by thinking of the relative extent of "automation" in large and small enterprises. In light of this fact, an employment base will consistently understate the size of large firms relative to small firms, for the larger organization is likely to employ fewer workers per unit of output. Since concentration measures are heavily influenced by the size of the largest firms, the employment base will understate the degree of concentration. It is also true that the way in which capital and labor intensities vary with firm size differs from industry to industry and from firm to firm. Thus, although the direction of the bias intro-

duced by the employment base is known, there would be no simple way of adjusting concentration findings for all industries to reflect a truer result.

3. **Assets.** Another commonly used base, the value of assets, presents somewhat the opposite problem to that encountered with employment. The size of larger, more capital-intensive firms may be overstated by taking asset value as the measure, and the result may be a general overstatement of concentration. Once again, although the direction of the bias is known, the bias is not so completely consistent that it would permit us to apply a simple adjustment. If the asset base is applied to a group of industries, we would know only that the concentration level of some industries is probably overstated by unknown and varying degrees. There are additional problems with the valuation of firms' assets. Several valuation methods are possible, and to the extent that firms' accounting practices differ, random distortions would be introduced into an asset-based concentration index.

4. **Value Added.** Some writers have suggested that value added would be a useful base for measuring concentration. Value added is the difference between sales revenue and the cost of goods and services purchased from other firms. It measures in effect the difference between the value of the product when it enters the firm and the value when it leaves. Such a measure would be affected by the profit rate of the firm and by interindustry differences in the raw materials component of final value.

The Broad Spectrum of Concentration Indexes.   Concentration measures are based on the premise that the centralization of power in a market can be described in terms of the number and relative sizes of firms. One begins ideally with a list of each company in the market and its share of the market base, i.e., its market share. This is all the information that is needed.

What all concentration measures do in one way or another is to summarize such information in shorthand form. The objective is, ideally, to define a single statistic that tells us something about the distribution of power in the market and that also permits comparisons among markets. The task is thus straightforward, but the best solution is not obvious.

The Concentration Curve.   The concentration curve is simply a diagrammatic representation of the data contained in a distribution listing. In Figure 7.3 three concentration curves are illustrated. The vertical axis measures the cumulative percentage of the base, here the value of shipments. The horizontal axis measures the number of firms in the industry, where the firms are arrayed from largest, at the left, to smallest. The concentration curve does not itself yield a single statistic that characterizes the distribution; it does, however, permit a number of statements to be made conveniently. From such a curve, we can (1) specify any percentage of the base and see how many firms account for it or (2) specify any number of firms and see what percentage of the base they possess.

The concentration curve begins at the origin (no firms have 0 percent of the value of shipments) and reaches the 100 percent level at the total number of firms in the

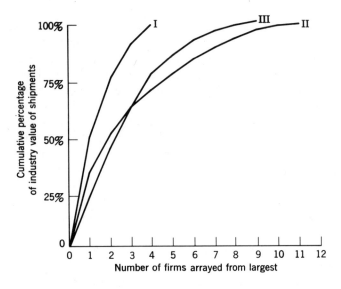

Figure 7.3 Concentration curves.

	Industry				
	I		II		III
Firm	Percent of Industry Value of Shipments	Firm	Percent of Industry Value of Shipments	Firm	Percent of Industry Value of Shipments
1	50	1	35	1	25
2	25	2	20	2	20
3	15	3	9	3	18
4	10	4	8	4	16
		5	7	5	10
		6	6	6	5
		7	5	7	3
		8	4	8	2
		9	3	9	1
		10	2		
		11	1		

industry (all firms have all of the shipments). In between, the curve increases at a decreasing rate, except for the special case in which all firms are the same size. In that instance the curve is a straight line, increasing at a constant rate. Generally, short and steep curves reflect high concentration, whereas long, flat curves reflect low concentration. The degree of concentration, however, is not precisely or unambiguously stated by the curves. In Figure 7.3, curves II and III intersect. Which of the industries represented by these curves may be ''more concentrated'' is not clear, although both are less concentrated than the industry represented by curve

I. The two largest firms in industry II have 55 percent of the value of industry ship-ments as compared with 45 percent for the top two in industry III. At this point, industry II is more concentrated. However, the four largest firms have 79 percent of industry III and 72 percent of industry II, indicating that at this point III is more concentrated.

Concentration curves present a great deal of useful information in a convenient form and may thus provide an excellent means for initial examination of industry structure. They do not, however, provide the kind of shorthand description that would enable meaningful comparisons to be made among all industries.

The Top-Four Concentration Ratio.   The most common concentration index sim-ply gives the percentage of the market base held by the four largest firms (or some-times the top 8 or 20). If, for example, it is stated that "the concentration ratio of the widget industry is 55 percent," this means that the specified number of firms ac-counts jointly for 55 percent of the market base. The information conveyed by the top-four ratio is simply that given by the fourth-firm level of a concentration curve.

The ratio is useful because it makes a simple statement about the condition of "fewness" (or "manyness") in an industry, while yielding considerably more knowledge than a simple counting of firms. It is possible to get an idea from the top-four ratio whether a market is clearly dominated by a small group. The index is also most convenient in that its value is unaffected by relatively insignificant changes in market structure. Entry or exit of firms, for example, does not influence the top-four percentage unless it perceptibly alters the distribution of market shares among existing firms.

A shortcoming of this ratio is that it fails to take account of differences in struc-ture **within** the top group. Table 7.2 shows three industries each of which has a top-four concentration ratio of 80 percent. Quite obviously, the structural situation differs considerably among the three. Industry A's 80 percent ratio is accounted for by four equal-sized firms. Industry C has the same ratio, but is dominated by a single firm, while industry B lies somewhere between. We would likely expect somewhat different behavior from these three industries, but nothing in the simple 80 percent ratio permits distinctions of this kind. The top-four ratio thus neglects an

Table 7.2   Industries with Identical Top-four Concentration But
Different Size Structures

	Industry A		Industry B		Industry C	
	Firm	Market Share	Firm	Market Share	Firm	Market Share
	1	20%	1	40%	1	75%
	2	20	2	15	2	3
	3	20	3	15	3	1
	4	20	4	10	4	1
Top four		80%		80%		80%

important bit of information: the degree of equality or inequality in firm size within the leading group.

The upper limit of the top-four ratio is 100 percent, attained whenever there are four firms or fewer in the market. The lower limit varies with the number of firms in the market and is achieved whenever all firms are of precisely equal size. If the market consists of 100 firms, the minimum concentration is 4 percent; if it consists of 10 firms, the minimum concentration is 40 percent. The ratio reflects both the number of firms within a market and the degree of inequality in their sizes. It is a useful, simple, understandable statistic that implies a modest data requirement (one need know only the size of the market and of the **largest** firms). If data exist for all firms, however, the ratio does not make full use of the information. It ignores all firms **other** than the largest.

The Gini Coefficient.[13]   The Gini coefficient is a type of concentration index based on a classic device for measuring distributions, the **Lorenz curve.** The Lorenz curve is illustrated in Figure 7.4, in which the vertical axis measures the cumulative percentage of industry value of shipments, or any other market base. The horizontal axis measures the cumulative percentage of firms, where the firms are arrayed from smallest, at left, to largest. With the Lorenz curve constructed in this fashion for an industry, it is possible to select any percentage of firms and read off the percentage of value of shipments they account for; or, alternatively, to select any percentage of value of shipments and read off the percentage of firms that supplies it. The Lorenz curve bears some similarity to the concentration curve; it differs in relating the **percentage** of firms, rather than the number of firms, to the percentage held of the industry base.

The Gini coefficient is a statistic that summarizes the information of the Lorenz curve. It is defined as the area between the Lorenz curve and the diagonal OC in Figure 7.4, divided by the area of triangle OBC,[14] or Area X/Area OBC. If all firms in the industry are the same size, the Lorenz curve will coincide with the diagonal. Ten percent of the firms will have 10 percent of the shipments, 20 percent will have 20, and so forth. In this case, there is no area between the curve and the diagonal, and the value of the Gini coefficient is zero. The greater the **inequality** in firm size, the greater the area between the curve and the diagonal, thus the higher the value of the coefficient. In the extreme case in which there is a large number of firms, one of which has virtually the entire value of shipments, the value of the Gini coefficient approaches 1.0. The coefficient is, then, a measure of **inequality** in distribution.

The weakness of this index is that it does not really measure the condition of fewness in the market. For example, if the Gini value is zero, this tells us simply that all firms are of equal size. But it does not indicate whether there are two firms or two thousand. Further, the introduction of a very small firm into an industry character-

---

[13] C. Gini, "Sulla misure della concentrazions della variabilitia dei caratters," *Atti del Reals Istitute Veneto di Scienze, Lettere ed Arti,* Tome LXXIII, Paete Seconda (1913–1914).

[14] The Lorenz curve is frequently discrete, that is, composed of straight-line segments as in Figure 7.4. Where the number of firms is large, however, these straight-line segments become numerous and may be smoothed into a continuous curve.

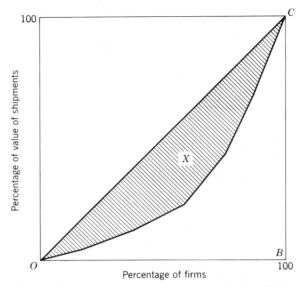

Figure 7.4 The Lorenz curve and the Gini coefficient.

ized by some inequality may substantially alter the value of the coefficient even though the structure of the market is not altered in an economically significant way. The Gini measure is thus too responsive to structural changes that may be theoretically trivial for an industry.[15]

This is not to imply that the Gini coefficient is conceptually inferior to an index such as the concentration ratio. But because it focuses purely on inequality, ignoring numbers of firms, it is an inappropriate measure for certain kinds of market comparisons.

The Herfindahl Index.[16]   The Herfindahl index is a concentration measure that takes account both of the number of firms in an industry and of the size inequality among the firms. It is defined as:

$$H = \sum_{i=1}^{n} \frac{x_i^2}{X}$$

where x_i is the size of firm i (in terms of value of shipments, assets or any other market base), and X is the total "size" of the industry, that is, the market base held

---

[15] It should be pointed out that the major application of the Gini coefficient is in the measurement of **income** distributions. Since the number of units is likely to be very large, with no single unit holding a signficant portion of total income, the problem of overresponsiveness to "small" units is absent. This problem appears when we attempt to apply the index to industries consisting of varying, but relatively small, populations.

[16] Although this measure is commonly referred to as the Herfindahl index, after Orris C. Herfindahl, it was developed independently by Albert O. Hirschman. See Hirschman's "The Paternity of an Index," *American Economic Review,* **54** (September 1964), p. 761.

by all firms. In other words, H is the sum of the squares of the size of each firm in an industry, where firm size is expressed as a percentage of the industry—**the sum of the squares of the market share of each firm.**

The upper limit of the index is 1.0, attained when one firm has 100 percent of the market. Regardless of the number of firms in the industry, the value of the index approaches 1.0 whenever the largest firm's share of the market approaches 100 percent. The lower limit of the index is reached when all firms are the same size; however, the limit varies with the number of firms. In a two-firm industry, the minimum value of H is $(0.50^2 + 0.50^2) = 0.5$. With three firms, the minimum is 0.33, and with ten it is 0.10. The lower limit of H generally is $1/n$, where n is the number of firms in the industry. This limit approaches zero as n becomes very large.

The Herfindahl index has two major advantages as a concentration measure. First, it is a summary measure, making use of all data points (in this respect it is like the Gini coefficient but unlike the concentration ratio). Second, the index reflects both numbers of firms and size inequalities (like the concentration ratio but unlike the Gini coefficient) in a theoretically reasonable way.

There also are some drawbacks to H. As a summary (i.e., comprehensive) index, it imposes a heavy data requirement; in principle, one must know the size of every firm in the market, although as a practical matter very small firms can be omitted without perceptible effect. In addition, the Herfindahl measure has no obvious intuitive interpretation. It is simply the sum of the squares of firms' market shares. What, one might ask, is **that** supposed to tell us? An industrial organization economist can provide an answer; but most public policymakers are not trained economists, and the lack of intuitive clarity is thus troublesome.

The Numbers Equivalent. Morris A. Adelman has suggested translating H into a "numbers-equivalent" measure: $N = 1/H$.[17] It is obvious that N, the reciprocal of H, adds no new information and will have properties similar to H itself. One possible advantage, however, is a somewhat more intuitive interpretation: N is the number of equal-sized firms that generates the observed value of H. It is a "translation" measure in the following sense: the value of H has been translated into an equivalent hypothetical market of equal-sized firms. If $H = 0.10$ then $N = 10$. The value of H (0.10) is thus the competitive equivalent of a market of 10 equal firms.

The Entropy Index.[18] The entropy measure of concentration is defined as:

$$E = \sum_{i=1}^{n} p_i \log \left(\frac{1}{p_i}\right)$$

---

[17]Morris A. Adelman, "Comment on the 'H' Concentration Measure as a Numbers Equivalent," *Review of Economics and Statistics,* **51** (February 1969), 99–101.

[18]See, for discussion of the development and properties of the index, Michael O. Finkelstein and Richard M. Friedberg, "The Application of an Entropy Theory of Concentration to the Clayton Act," *Yale Law Journal,* **76** (March 1967), 677–717. An application of the entropy measure is provided by Ann and Ira Horowitz, "Entropy, Markov Processes, and Competition in the Brewing Industry," *Journal of Industrial Economics,* **16** (July 1968), 196–211.

where p_i is the market share of the ith firm and n is the number of firms in the market.

Some similarities to the Herfindahl measure are apparent. Both are summary indexes—that is, they reflect every firm's market position—and both are constructed as sums of firms' market shares. They differ in the weights attached to the shares: H weights each firm's share by squaring it, while E weights according to the logarithm of the share. Each index assigns heavier weight to larger firms, but in differing degree; comparisons among industries will accordingly differ somewhat as well.

Both E and H possess defensible theoretical rationales. But whereas some economists may have a decided preference for one or the other, the choice is not clearcut.

Summary.   None of the concentration measures discussed above provides an ideal index of market structure. The number of indexes that could be constructed is indefinitely large, and we have looked at only a few examples.[19]

A basic problem in formulating concentration measures is that the object of measurement is obscure. In order to predict market behavior, we wish to describe the condition of fewness or manyness that prevails. But these are subtle notions that depend on both firm numbers and on the degree of size inequality among them. A useful concentration measure must combine and weight both kinds of information. The proper way of doing so, however, is not obvious.

To put the point a bit differently, the ideal concentration index would be derived directly from a rigorous theory of oligopoly that relates structural information to conduct and performance expectations. But, as we saw in Chapter 3, no such theory exists. For this reason, most concentration measures are essentially empirical, with little analytical grounding.[20]

It is commonly observed that the various concentration indexes are highly correlated with one another. If, for example, we were to apply each index to data for 100 industries, the concentration rankings would be very similar for each. Perhaps, then, we should not worry too much about which measure is best—after all, each one tells us roughly the same thing.

Unfortunately, this sanguine view is not very sound. John E. Kwoka, Jr., shows, for example, that if concentration is used for purposes of statistical prediction (which is precisely how economists use these measures) it may make a difference which of several highly correlated indexes is chosen.[21]

---

[19] Many concentration indexes are in effect **weighted sums** of firms' market shares. (H weights by squaring the shares; E weights by logarithms; the concentration ratio assigns a weight of 1 to the top firms' shares, and 0 to all others.) There is clearly no practical limit to the number of weights that could be devised.

[20] Only the Herfindahl index among those discussed above has some foundation in microeconomic theory. See George J. Stigler, "A Theory of Oligopoly," *Journal of Political Economy,* **72** (February 1964), 44–61. For a useful but rather technical discussion of the implicit weights in some common indexes, see Stephen Davies, "Choosing Between Concentration Indices: the Iso-Concentration Curve," *Economica,* **46** (February 1979), 67–75.

[21] "Does the Choice of Concentration Measure Really Matter?" *Journal of Industrial Economics,* **29** (June 1981), 445–453.

Apart from statistical issues, however, a basic problem remains. It is not clear that **any** concentration index, taken alone, is a reliable guide to the state of competition. Conceivably firms will compete fiercely in a highly concentrated market; or compete ineffectively in a market where concentration is low. The difficulty, once again, is that we are looking for a simple and convenient measure of something that is in reality complex. Concentration and competition are not synonymous, and a key question is just how much the one implies about the other. In light of this problem, arguments about which particular measure of concentration does the best job may be reduced to their proper perspective; such arguments are not trivial, but neither are they central to our concerns.

Barriers to Entry

A second structural element with important implications for market behavior is, as we have seen, the condition of entry. If it is easy for new firms to come into the market, then the degree of pricing discretion for established firms may be limited even though they appear to occupy a strong position in the market. Prices designed to limit entry may be adopted, with the result that profits are forced toward competitive levels. Such a scenario suggests that it may be misleading to examine market concentration without also considering entry barriers.

The literature on entry barriers raises a definitional issue. Writers such as Bain and Shepherd are inclined toward a broad view: A barrier to entry is "anything that decreases the likelihood or speed" of actual entry.[22] Stigler's definition is somewhat narrower: entry barriers are costs "borne by a firm which seeks to enter an industry, but . . . not . . . by firms already in the industry."[23] One's preference for either approach may be dictated by the problem under consideration, as will be seen shortly.

Various kinds of entry barriers are commonly observed, and we may look at each briefly.

Absolute Cost Advantages   Absolute cost advantages for established firms will obviously have some inhibiting effect on prospective entrants. Such advantages may be conferred by patents, trade secrets, or other sorts of know-how; by money market imperfections that work against new entrants; or by contracts under which existing firms "tie up" superior factor inputs or distribution outlets. The implication is much the same in any case: New firms will produce at higher unit costs than "old" firms. Their chances of successful entry are thus diminished; indeed, if the established companies react to entry by cutting price to a level close to their own costs, the life expectancy of the entrant may be quite short.

Economies of Scale   These may deter entry if they are sufficiently important. For they imply that the new entrant must come into the market at a relatively large size

[22] William G. Shepherd, *The Economics of Industrial Organization* (Englewood Cliffs, N. J.: Prentice-Hall, 1979), p. 182.

[23] George J. Stigler, *The Organization of Industry* (R. D. Irwin, 1968), p. 67.

in order to operate efficiently (the market will support only a "small" number of "big" firms). Such large-scale entry, however, will have two predictable effects in the market, both of which work against the new firm: It will tend to push up the prices of factor inputs by raising their demand and to push down the price of market outputs by increasing their supplies. Notice, however, that scale economies are not an entry barrier in Stigler's sense, because they are likely to apply to old and new firms alike.

Product Differentiation   This is an important structural attribute that may at times serve as an effective entry barrier. If consumers are "loyal" to established brands and companies and, concurrently, skeptical about new, untried items and suppliers, entry is plainly more difficult than it otherwise would be.

This situation is illustrated in Figure 7.5, in which both established firms and prospective entrants are assumed to have cost curve $AC = MC$ (notice this means that no scale economy or absolute cost barriers exist). Suppose further that an established firm faces demand curve D. (Some assumptions about the price policies of other firms are needed to derive this curve, but we may ignore these for the moment.) If the established firm sets price P_1, the demand curve of the strongest potential entrant is d_1. Because of the entrant's product differentiation disadvantage—consumers simply will not pay as high a price for the goods of the new firm—this company cannot profitably enter the market. No quantity of output can be sold at a price above average cost. If, however, the established firm were to raise price to P_2, the entrant's demand curve would shift upward to d_2, and profitable entry positions would exist.

The sources of such advantages are once again varied. Product differentiation may be based on "real or fancied" distinctions, to use Chamberlin's phrase, and some bases may appear more useful socially than others.[24] The implications, however, may be quite similar in most instances. Strong consumer loyalties to established suppliers are necessarily discouraging to would-be rivals.

One should not assume, though, that a product-differentiated market is always inhospitable to new firms. Differentiation may be a means of entry as well as a deterrent. The chance to offer a commodity that is distinctive from those already on the market may provide the "foot in the door" for a new firm. Product differentiation is in a way a double-edged sword, defying ready generalization.

The topic, however, is one of continuing controversy and deserves a bit more attention. The purely competitive model assumes a homogeneous product, that is, one that is not only physically identical throughout the market, but that buyers regard as identical in all relevant ways. Although we might find a few examples that approach such homogeneity—agricultural markets are frequently cited as a case in point—consumers commonly do distinguish between the closely substitutable offerings of different sellers.

---

[24] The firm that has loyal customers because it produces an "objectively" superior product, is preferred to the one whose customer loyalties attach to heavy (and "subjective") advertising. Bear in mind, however, that the objective/subjective distinction may be very difficult to draw.

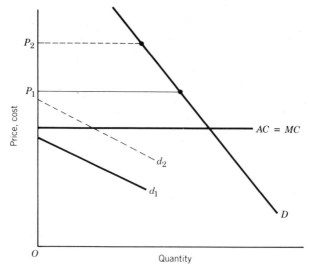

Figure 7.5 Product differentiation as an entry barrier.

The distinction may originate in a number of ways. Products may be physically different. A Ford is not physically identical to a Chevrolet, nor is the 16 cubic-ft. refrigerator produced by Westinghouse precisely the same as the General Electric model. In each case the competing products serve the same function in much the same way. They are close substitutes that clearly deserve to be grouped in the same markets. Yet the differences between them, while they may not appear objectively crucial, are important to the type of competition that is present.

This importance is not reduced even when the origin of product differentiation seems somehow less than genuine. Such products as beers, whiskeys, cigarettes, and detergents are not physically identical in the strict sense. It would seem, however, that the degree of product differentiation in such markets is due more to the promotional efforts of sellers than to "real" product differences. True, the connoisseur may be able to tell the difference between a "good" bourbon and a "cheap" one, but many who could not tell the two apart may nevertheless insist on the "better" brand.[25] At times even physically identical products can be differentiated through advertising and other means of promotion, as the famous case of aspirin has shown.

To the extent that product differentiation exceeds the level that is justified by "real" product differences, it could be viewed as a function of ignorance and as an imperfection in the market. It has been suggested that consumer goods are subject to greater differentiation than producer goods precisely because greater ignorance is present in consumer markets. Regardless of the truth of this suggestion, product dif-

---

[25] A cartoon several years ago made this point forcefully. A woman ordering a meal in a restaurant said to the waiter: "Now be **sure** you bring me the imported wine because I can't tell the difference."

ferentiation in any market has substantial implications for firm behavior. As we have seen (in Chamberlin's theory of monopolistic competition), the primary effect of differentiation is to yield a degree of pricing control to sellers. No longer must the firm fear that any price increase will cause its sales to disappear; nor is the incentive for price decreases blocked by the fact that the firm can sell all it produces at the prevailing price. In a weak sense, the seller of a differentiated product is a monopolist. It is the sole supplier of its product, although its effective control over price may be circumscribed by relatively close substitutes.

How does product differentiation alter the state of competition? As we have seen, differentiation of products in the presence of all other competitive conditions causes an industry to become less efficient. If entry is free, firms will not earn long-run monopoly profits, but their production will be restricted. Consumer preferences will be exploited, and as a result less will be produced at greater per unit cost, and higher prices will be charged.

Perhaps the most important implication of product differentiation has been noted earlier (see Chapter 5). This is the possibility that differentiation may itself become the primary battleground of competition. Rather than concentrating on the optimal pricing strategy for a defined product, the firm's efforts may be directed toward redefinition of the product itself, no longer a "given" in the company's calculations.

Since consumers have preferences among products, the manager's task becomes in part the selection of the optimal set of product characteristics, that set which appeals "best" to consumers relative to its own costs of development. Once again, such efforts may yield varying policies that range from development of a new product (the better mousetrap) to heavier advertising (promote the existing mousetrap).

It is apparent that the nature of competition will be altered if firms see as their objective the selection of optimal product characteristics (real or imagined) rather than the selection of optimal prices. At a more basic level, it may be argued that product differentiation implies a "less competitive" situation than product homogeneity, other factors being constant. Each seller in the differentiated market has more pricing power than it would otherwise. Moreover, if the degree of differentiation is high, that is, if consumers have strong preferences among the products sold within the market, then potential competition, as we have noted, may be discouraged. The would-be competitor may be deterred by the fact that its product is likely to be regarded initially as inferior to established brands.

Although product differentiation has been cited as an element of market imperfection, this should not be interpreted to mean that heterogeneity is necessarily "bad." Differences among products imply, *ceteris paribus,* greater diversity and more choices for consumers. The desire to differentiate has undoubtedly led sellers both to develop valuable product improvements and to waste resources in an effort to create artificial product differences.

It is not terribly useful, however, to argue about whether existing differences in particular products are "real" or "fancied," "important," or "trivial." For these judgments are themselves quite subjective. If the market responds to product differences, then those differences are meaningful to someone—even though you or I might disagree.[26]

Other Barriers to Entry. These encompass everything from legal obstacles that arise occasionally (a fixed number of liquor or taxicab licenses in a community) to the existence of heavy capital requirements. Whether the latter ought to be called a "barrier" is, again, subject to debate. If the existing technology of an industry is capital intensive, entry is likely to require a substantial money investment. But this requirement does not apply only to new firms; existing companies presumably have been faced with similar obstacles, and have managed to overcome them. Even if the new entrant faces relatively high costs of obtaining financing, these may only reflect rational market judgment. Entry carries risks, which are accentuated if the entrant is small or untested.

Measurement. It should be no surprise in light of the discussion above that measurement of entry barriers is a delicate art. It may be possible to identify the presence of a particular barrier—assuming that we can first sort out the disagreements about the meaning of the term—and even to say whether it seems important in a given market. But to reduce the various obstacles to entry to more precisely quantified indexes is no simple task.

In 1956 Bain developed comprehensive estimates of barriers to entry for 20 manufacturing industries.[27] These estimates were based on painstaking study and relied heavily on what are termed "engineering estimates," that is, answers to questionnaires by industry experts. The result was not a quantitatively precise index but a broad ranking. These findings, combined with the work of Mann[28] and extended by Shepherd, are reproduced in Table 7.3.

Despite the crudeness of measurement, entry-barrier estimates have been found to be positively and significantly correlated with profitability in a number of instances.[29] This is a plausible finding since high barriers, all things being equal, imply that firms can pursue profitable policies with at least relative freedom from the threat of entry. The topic remains controversial, however, with some economists contending that the term **entry barrier** is misused and even confused at times with competitive activity.[30]

[26]I may believe, for example, that there is no "real" difference between *Perrier* sparkling water and the local supermarket club soda, although *Perrier* commands a much higher price. It goes without saying that I am entitled to my opinion, but my opinion does not change the facts: many consumers do see a real difference and are prepared to pay the higher *Perrier* price for it. Even I am not arrogant enough to argue that their opinions should not count!

[27]Joe S. Bain, *Barriers to New Competition* (Cambridge: Harvard University Press, 1956).

[28]H. Michael Mann, "Seller Concentration, Barriers to Entry and Rates of Return in Thirty Industries, 1950–1960," *Review of Economics and Statistics, 48* (August 1966), 296–307.

[29]See Mann, ibid., and William G. Shepherd, *The Treatment of Market Power* (New York: Columbia University Press, 1975), p. 96.

[30]See, for example, Yale Brozen, "Entry Barriers: Advertising and Product Differentiation," in Harvey J. Goldschmid, H. Michael Mann, and J. Fred Weston, Eds., *Industrial Concentration: The New Learning* (Boston: Little Brown, 1974), 115–137. See also Robert H. Bork, *The Antitrust Paradox* (New York: Basic Books, 1978), Chapter 16.

Table 7.3   Estimated Barriers to Entry in 58 Selected
Manufacturing Industries

High Barriers to Entry

Distilled liquors	Steel
Wood pulp	Copper
Newspapers	Tractors
General periodicals	Computers
Drugs	Copying equipment
Soaps	Heavy electrical equipment
Explosives	Electrical lamps
Glass and glass products	Telephone equipment
Automobiles	Buses
Aircraft and parts	Locomotives
Photographic supplies	Shipbuilding

Moderately High Barriers to Entry

Cereals	Books
Flour mixes	Gases
Bread	Organic chemicals
Sugar	Inorganic chemicals
Soft drinks	Synthetic rubber
Cigarettes	Toilet preparations
Lumber	Fertilizers
Paper	Petroleum refining
Periodicals	Tires and tubes
Gypsum products	Aluminum
Metal cans	Heavy industrial machinery
Typewriters	Large household appliances

Low Barriers to Entry

Meat-packing	Wooden furniture
Flour	Corrugated containers
Canned fruits and vegetables	Printing
Woolen and cotton textiles	Footwear
Clothing	Cement
Brick and tile	Foundries
Small metal products	

Source: William G. Shepherd, *The Economics of Industrial Organization*, (Prentice-Hall, 1979), p. 204.

OTHER INDICATORS OF COMPETITION AND MONOPOLY

Market Conduct

Conduct refers to the actual stratagems and policies employed by firms. Price leadership is an example of conduct, as is conspiratorial price fixing or independent pricing. It is obvious that the conduct of companies is the most proximate cause of their performance. Nevertheless, as we have noted, there is disagreement as to whether conduct itself is a meaningful explanation of performance, or even a real clue to the state of a market's competitiveness. It may "cause" performance in much the same sense that stepping on the accelerator causes an automobile to move and turning the steering wheel causes it to turn. if we wish to know why someone has followed a particular route at a particular speed, it will be insufficient to examine the behavior of the car's accelerator and steering wheel.

Market conduct is often an unobservable phenomenon. Consider, for example, the common question of whether firms in a market behave independently or conspiratorially. In many instances this question is simply unanswerable. There is no reliable way to tell how independent or interdependent firms' decisions may be. And the determination of whether something called conspiracy has occurred is ordinarily difficult. Even if we could agree on the significance of market conduct, then, there may be no objective means of measuring it.

In light of these problems, it is somewhat surprising that conduct occupies an eminent role in antitrust enforcement. Fully accurate breakdowns are not readily available; it appears, however, that the bulk of antitrust resources in recent decades has been employed so as to restrict "anticompetitive" practices. A partial explanation may lie in the very broad social consensus that some forms of conduct are undesirable. An important early motivation of the antitrust laws was to protect individuals against the ruthless and predatory acts of powerful firms and groups. Such protection may have an economic justification, but it is not a purely economic matter.

The government's emphasis on restriction of undesirable conduct may, indeed, have relatively little to do with economic considerations. This seems plausible when it is realized that antitrust policy is often viewed as a tool of justice or fairness. The point is not that the conduct restrictions are economically useless but, rather, that noneconomic motivations may explain why so much emphasis has been placed on the enforcement of restrictions whose economic effects may be small. It may well be that the absence of anticompetitive conduct is a good thing economically as well as on other grounds. But it should be clear that good conduct—whatever that may mean—does not alone satisfy the requirements of competition.

Market Performance

The theoretical significance of performance in discussions of competition and monopoly is self-evident. If a market model can be described in structural terms—number and size of firms, condition of entry, degree of product differentiation—so, too, can it be meaningfully described in terms of results such as prices, outputs, and profits.

Market performance is also of great interest on general economic grounds. Our ultimate concern is with policies that, by encouraging competition, will yield beneficial results. We desire, for example, efficiency in production and responsiveness of the market to consumer desires. These are among the benefits that we expect competition to provide, and it may be argued that the presence of such results is the most sensible definiiton of competition. In this view, competition **is** what competition **does;** and the test of a market's competitiveness is whether it yields results that are themselves "competitive."

The most widely used performance measure of competition and monopoly is the profit rate, frequently the rate of return to owners' equity. It is theoretically clear, as Bain argued some time ago, that **persistent excess profits** may well reflect monopolistic elements in the market.[31] Profitability is thus a plausible "symptom" of monopoly power.

Profit-based indexes of monopoly are initially appealing because, in addition to theoretical relevance, data are more readily available than for many alternative measures. There is, however, an important difficulty. Economic theory yields hypotheses about **economic** profits, that is, those **in excess** of the normal rate of return to an activity. This is not quite the same as the accounting profits reported by companies.

In Bain's words, "accounting profit is 'not all profit' in the economic sense."[32] the former refers simply to total revenues minus allocable current costs and past costs (depreciation and amortization). A valid measure of economic profit must remove the "normal" rate of return from these calculations. Conceptually, this return is the alternative, or opportunity, cost of investment; that is, the receipts foregone because business owners' investment cannot earn a return elsewhere. Bain defines accounting profit as $R - C - D$, where R is total receipts, C is current costs, and D is depreciation. Economic or excess profit is then

$$R - C - D - (iV)$$

where V is the value of owners' investment and i is the rate of return that this investment could earn if it were not "tied up" in its present use.

The profit rate is in effect a measure of the deviation of price from average cost, and may thus appear similar to the Lerner index. There is, however, a fundamental difference between the two. The Bain profit index of monopoly is a less certain measure than either the Lerner index or measures of price elasticity. The reason for this relative uncertainty is clear when it is recalled that although a pure or partial monopolist **may** earn persistent excess profits, such profits are not inevitable. The partial monopolist in the Chamberlin model, for example, earns zero excess profits in the long run. More generally, no monopolistic firm can earn better than normal profits if sufficient demand for the product does not exist. There is absolutely no reason that profits would accrue to a monopolist of some product that consumers do not desire.[33] Profit indexes are therefore uncertain in the following sense: a high rate of excess profits persisting over a reasonably "long" period may well reflect the presence of monopoly power, but the absence of excess profits does not necesarily mean that no monopoly power is present. Such indexes, then, fail to distinguish between some competitive and some monopoly cases. They may indicate the **likelihood** of some monopoly power, but do not measure it directly.

---

[31] Joe S. Bain, "The Profit Rate as a Measure of Monopoly Power," *Quarterly Journal of Economics,* **55** (February 1941), 293–324.

[32] Joe S. Bain, *Industrial Organization* (New York: Wiley, 1959), p. 365.

[33] A monopolist may also squander funds on wasteful expenditures. If so, reported profits may appear quite low. See Richard A. Posner, "The Social Costs of Monopoly and Regulation," *Journal of Political Economy,* **83** (August 1975), 807–827.

One final word of caution is in order. When we discuss the profit rate as an index of "monopoly," it is well to bear in mind precisely what this term means. "Monopoly power" is simply control over price or the other terms at which goods are supplied to the market. Although monopoly may have negative connotations in common forms of discussion, it is an analytically neutral condition. Control over price **may** result from socially detestable conditions such as collusion by a group of firms; but it may also result from beneficial activity, for instance, development of a valuable innovation. Profitability that is persistently high signals "monopoly" only in this catch-all sense. The **desirability** of such monopoly is quite a separate issue.

Other aspects of performance, such as efficiency and rates of innovation, are also relevant to an assessment of competition; but such indicators have not been extensively employed. The problem is not only that the actual patterns may be difficult to measure precisely, but that once measured there may be no way of defining the ideal pattern with which the actual could be compared.

It is possible, for example, to examine the actual price–cost combinations for various commodities and industry groups; but it is far more difficult to specify what these patterns **would have been** in the "ideal" competitive situation. Even if it can be determined that performance in an industry deviates from purely competitive performance, the knowledge gained may be of limited usefulness. Purely competitive performance need not be the appropriate yardstick, especially for industries in which cost structures preclude large numbers of small firms.

One of the foremost objectives of economists concerned with industrial organization is to establish better measures of performance, and to learn more about the ways in which performance varies with other characteristics of the market. It may be, however, that performance standards will never be heavily relied upon by public policymakers. The obstacle to heavy reliance is, again, the fact that performance itself is not amenable to direct policy control. In the case of market conduct, the courts can order undesirable manifestations stopped and can penalize violators. In the case of structure, sanctions such as dissolution of firms can influence future trends strongly. No similar measures could be easily invoked in dealing with undesirable performance, however.

A court could not, for example, expect to achieve much by ordering inefficient firms to be more efficient, or poor innovators to increase their innovative activities. Conceivably, a court could "require" that excessive profits be reduced, but such action might violate accepted principles of antitrust policy. The idea of an antitrust program, as conceived in the United States, implies faith in and dependence upon the free market. Where markets do not function well, the usual approach is to attempt to create an environment in which better operations are likely, whether this implies structural change or simply the curtailment of practices that cause malfunction. To attempt to "order" the results of "free" markets is a contradiction in terms. Indeed, such a procedure might imply a kind of public regulation that has thus far been reserved for sectors of the economy in which the free-market principle has been found unworkable.

SUMMARY

The degree of competition present in any industry is a peculiarly difficult quantity to define and measure. If the strict economic definition of competition were accepted, it would be simple enough to classify virtually all modern markets as "noncompetitive" or "monopolistic," but this would convey little information. It is necessary to know more about the origins and extent of monopolistic elements before meaningful statements can be made.

Measurement of these elements can be approached in various ways, none of which is entirely satisfactory. The economist's approach to this problem has been largely structural. Competition and monopoly in economics are concepts that refer to market power, and the degree to which power is centralized can be inferred— although only in a rough and imperfect way—from structural data. Moreover, the interests of economists lie in the testing of theoretical predictions. The predictions of market theories move conceptually from structure to performance, possibly with an intermediate role for conduct; and while the direction of causation might be questioned, tentative definitions of the competitiveness of markets in terms of their structure is usually consistent with the suggestions of the underlying analysis.

Can we, by specifying structural (and possibly conduct) conditions, make reasonable predictions about the performance of industries? Much of the remainder of this section will discuss the evidence that has been marshaled to date. The importance of the question in a policy context is enormous. The antitrust laws have been used for many years to influence the conduct of business and the structure of markets, but neither structure nor conduct is the ultimate and complete goal of policy. The effects of changes in structure and conduct upon performance must be defined, although "good" performance also is not the sole objective of policy. Whatever the goals of antitrust may be—and there is considerable disagreement here—knowledge of structure–conduct–performance relationships is necessary. No policy that affects one or more of these areas can be sensibly pursued without knowledge of the consequences.

CHAPTER 8

Measurement: Some Practical Pitfalls

Our discussion has thus far ignored some problems that arise when actual measurement of market structure and behavior is attempted. Such problems will be of special interest to those who wish to conduct empirical studies. They are of more general interest as well, however, since some understanding of the difficulties is necessary to an assessment of the findings presented by others. The practical problems of measurement seem to fall into the following general groups:

1. Studies of market structure and behavior are sensitive to the way in which the market is defined. Yet the "correct" definition of the market may not be obvious; even when it is, available data may not correspond closely to that definition.
2. Certain variables that are conceptually appropriate to a study may not be directly measurable; the task is then to find (if possible) proxies that do a reasonable job of indirect measurement.
3. Almost all measurement occurs subject to error, and measures are at times biased. Although these problems may be inescapable, it is important to understand their nature and severity.

PROBLEMS OF MARKET DEFINITION

Any measurement of market structure, conduct, or performance obviously presupposes that the "market" is known. The definition of an appropriate market, however, may not be a simple matter. A market is sometimes defined as a group of **firms** producing identical or closely related products.[1] Such a definition has drawbacks, however, especially in an economy in which many firms are diversified. In the United States today we find companies that produce both chemicals and spaghetti, farm machinery and rayon, and aircraft and bathroom fixtures. Although diversification, or conglomeration, is not always so dramatic, it is sufficiently widespread that it is often inappropriate to define a market simply as a group of firms. To do so would be to lump together all the unrelated products of companies that happen to produce something in common.

[1] Firm groupings are sometimes referred to as industries rather than markets.

144

A preferable approach is to define the market as a group of closely substitutable **products**. But how is "closeness" to be defined and measured? Goods and services may be closely related in that they are regarded as substitutes by consumers. This implies positive and significant **cross elasticities of demand** among the products. For example, an increase in the price of Coca Cola, other things equal, may well induce a relatively large increase in sales of Pepsi Cola. On the other hand, products may be closely related in that the factors and techniques of production used in each are similar; that is, there is substitutability on the producers' side of the market, and positive and significant **cross elasticities of supply** exist. If products are closely substitutable both for consumers and producers, we are likely to have no trouble deciding that they should be classified in the same market. In many instances, however, the degree of substitutability on the two sides is very different.

A consumer contemplating leisure time, for example, might see a restaurant meal, a concert, or a baseball game as the relevant choices; but is this the proper set of substitutes upon which to base a market definition? Notice that the supply cross elasticities will be low, although it is conceivable that a single company would produce all three services. To cite another example, men's shoes are a poor substitute for women's shoes from the standpoint of most consumers. Yet all shoes are produced in much the same way, utilizing similar labor, materials, machinery, and distribution systems, and are produced by the same firms. Should these products be grouped in the same market even though demand cross elasticities are negligible?

Consumer substitutability would seem to be of prime importance in defining the market, and very misleading conclusions could be drawn on the basis of product groupings that exclude close substitutes or include nonsubstitutes. Yet producer substitutability cannot be ignored. The behavior of the maket in which some product *A* is produced, will be affected if producers of products *B, C,* and *D,* which are **not** consumer substitutes, could easily produce *A* as well.

One approach to market definition is to take account of producer substitutability in terms of potential entry, and to define the market primarily according to relationships on the consumer side. That is, markets could be said to consist of consumer substitutes, with producer substitutability considered in its implication for the condition of entry rather than as a dimension of the market boundary. Another possibility is to define the market so as to include products that qualify **either** as producer **or** consumer substitutes. The trouble with this kind of definition is that we may wind up with "markets" composed largely of commodities that are not close consumer substitutes. Such a problem is illustrated by the Census industry grouping "pharmaceutical preparations." It is true that within narrowly defined submarkets, there are drugs that are competitive: various pain-killers or tranquilizers, for example. But aspirins are not a substitute for antibiotics, and a vitamin A tablet is not a substitute for a vitamin B tablet.

This example raises a more general, and very important, question for market definition. How broad or narrow should the scope of the market be? Perhaps the difficulty with the pharmaceuticals classification is not that it is based on producer rather than consumer considerations but, rather, that the definition of the market is so wide that it encompasses many nonsubstitutes. That is, it may make sense to speak of a market for headache remedies or for stomachache remedies, yet be quite misleading to combine such markets, among others, into the general pharmaceutical preparations category.

A market definition that is theoretically appropriate should meet two criteria.

1. It must be sufficiently narrow so as to exclude all nonsubstitutes.
2. It must be sufficiently broad so as to include all substitutes.

It turns out that these reasonable criteria are difficult to satisfy simultaneously, although either criterion alone can be met. Any market grouping may encounter the problem that there exist outside products that are substitutes for some but not all of the products within the group. If such outside products are included in the market definition, then the first criterion is violated; but if they are excluded, the second criterion is breached.

An example is shown is Figure 8.1. Companies A, B, and C sell similar but differentiated products, that is, imperfect substitutes. The differences may arise from physical dissimilarities or from varied seller locations, thus the distances in Figure 8-1 could be thought of in terms of geography or product characteristics. Suppose that sellers A and B are close competitors, as indicated by the oval around them. Many customers are willing to switch from one to the other in response to small relative price changes, and the demand cross elasticities between them are accordingly "very high." Sellers B and C are also close competitors in the same sense (they also have an oval around them). But A and C are **not**—there is so much distance between them that relatively few customers of one can be captured by the other.

How should this market be defined? If we take (A + B) or (B + C), we have in each case excluded a relevant competitor for one of the firms within; but if we define the market broadly (A + B + C), we have included two noncompetitors. The problem lacks a solution.

In practice, it turns out that we may not be certain whether the criteria for an appropriate market definition have been met. The question of whether various products are closely substitutable for one another is essentially empirical. In some cases we may be able to make reasonable guesses—for example, a radio is not a close substitute for a head of lettuce—but a priori notions inevitably leave many relationships in doubt. Is tea a good substitute for coffee or wine for beer? Some basic economics textbooks say yes, but confident conclusions would require us to find out to what extent consumers actually make the substitutions—not a simple task, although empirical investigation of relevant behavior at times provides some useful clues.

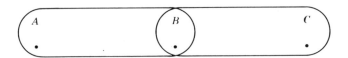

Figure 8.1

Problems of market definition are particularly troublesome when we deal with structural measures such as concentration, for the procedures adopted in defining markets may systematically bias the calculations. In general, the narrower is the market definition, the higher measured concentration tends to be. The reason is that companies, even though each may pursue diverse activities, are usually specialized to some degree. If, for example, we consider producers of beverages, we would expect to find that some firms specialize in beer, others in soft drinks, and still others in distilled liquors, coffee, and milk. Measurement of a broadly defined "beverage market" probably would disclose a rather low concentration figure—likely much lower than would be found for the "beer," "soft drink," "distilled liquor," "coffee," and "milk" markets individually. Similarly, **within** a market such as "distilled liquor," we might find that some firms specialize in Scotch, others in gin. Accordingly, concentration in the still narrower Scotch and gin markets would be higher than in "distilled liquors."

The general relationship between the measured concentration of a broadly defined market and that of its narrower components is illustrated in Table 8.1. In this example, 10 firms (A through J) operate in each of 10 narrow submarkets (no. 1 through no. 10). The various submarkets could represent distinct but related products (e.g., various beverages or drugs), or different geographic locations in which a single product is sold.

Submarket 1 is dominated by firm A, which sells 100 units, while the nine other firms sell only a single unit each. Similarly, submarket 2 is dominated by firm B. Each of the submarkets is dominated by a different seller. The top-four concentration ratio (CR_4) in every submarket is roughly 94.5 percent (the four largest firms account for 103 of the total 109 units sold). Yet CR_4 for the combined market

Table 8.1 Market Definition and Measured Concentration

Firm	Units Sold in Submarket										Units Sold in Combined Market (No. 1 through No. 10)
	No. 1	No. 2	No. 3	No. 4	No. 5	No. 6	No. 7	No. 8	No. 9	No. 10	
A	100	1	1	1	1	1	1	1	1	1	109
B	1	100	1	1	1	1	1	1	1	1	109
C	1	1	100	1	1	1	1	1	1	1	109
D	1	1	1	100	1	1	1	1	1	1	109
E	1	1	1	1	100	1	1	1	1	1	109
F	1	1	1	1	1	100	1	1	1	1	109
G	1	1	1	1	1	1	100	1	1	1	109
H	1	1	1	1	1	1	1	100	1	1	109
I	1	1	1	1	1	1	1	1	100	1	109
J	1	1	1	1	1	1	1	1	1	100	109
Total sales	109	109	109	109	109	109	109	109	109	109	1090
CR_4 (Top-four concentration ratio)	94.5%	94.5%	94.5%	94.5%	94.5%	94.5%	94.5%	94.5%	94.5%	94.5%	40%

consisting of submarkets 1 through 10 is only 40 percent (the four largest firms— any four, in this example—sell 436 of 1090 total units).

This is plainly an artificial example, but the underlying relationship is generally valid: the concentration ratio for a broad market will "understate" the concentration of component submarkets in this fahsion whenever the dominant firms in each submarket **are not the same firms**.[2]

One way of avoiding the problem of understatement of concentration in the broad market is to take a weighted average of the ratios of the various submarkets. Instead of "adding up" the submarkets individually it is possible to attribute to the broad market the typical concentration level of its component parts. Thus, for example, should each submarket display a concentration ratio of 94.5 percent, the typical concentration level of the broader market is also 94.5 percent, without reference to the identity of the leading firms in each segment.

Unfortunately, neither the adding-up nor the weighted-average procedure of deriving concentration measures for broad groupings provides an entirely satisfactory method of concentration measurement.[3] If the former approach may understate true concentration levels, so too may the latter approach **overstate** the degree of concentration in a broadly defined market. What is needed, however, is not so much good arithmetic procedures as good theoretical definitions of markets. In the absence of meaningful definitions, no mechanical operation will transfer deficient concentration information into something more useful.

How widespread is the problem of market definition in concentration measurement? It is possible to paint either a fairly optimistic or a fairly pessimistic picture. If one examines the concentration data of the Bureau of the Census—the most readily available source of ratios for a large number of groupings—it appears that the underlying definitions are in most cases less than ideal.[4] At the same time, however, it is possible to find for many purposes a rather large number of groupings that seem to represent at least reasonably well-defined markets. Some of the worst problems of concentration measurement can be avoided in empirical studies by deliberately restricting one's sample of markets to those that are well defined.

Census concentration measures nevertheless involve several problems of which it is well to be aware. The Bureau publishes every few years top-4, top-8, top-20, and top-50 concentration ratios based on value of shipments and on employment for a wide variety of manufacturing groupings. Groups range from the broadest two-digit

---

[2]The problem of understatement is summarized admirably by Fritz Machlup as follows: "If the broad industrial classifications are taken for measurement of concentration, concentration in industries more narrowly defined is hidden, for the chances are greater that firms which control only a negligible proportion of the whole production of the broadly defined industry produce a large proportion of the output of one particular article, which may not directly compete with any other product of the industry. The broader the definition of the industry, the greater the likelihood that the group includes some specialized firms. The concentration index for the broad industry would never reveal this monopoly power." *The Political Economy of Monopoly* (Baltimore: The Johns Hopkins Press, 1952), p. 483.

[3]For a detailed discussion of the issues, see Stanley E. Boyle, "The Average Concentration Ratio: An Inappropriate Measure of Structure," *Journal of Political Economy,* **81** (March/April 1973), 414–426.

[4]William G. Shepherd examined 1966 Census concentration ratios in light of this problem, among others, and found that significant adjustments were necessary in more than half the industries covered. *Market Power & Economic Welfare* (New York: Random House, 1970), Appendix Table 8.

Table 8.2

Standard Industrial Classification Code	Designation	Name
20	Major industry group	Food and kindred products
201	Industry group	Meat products
2011	Industry	Meak packing (slaughtering) plants
20111	Product class	Fresh beef
20111-12	Product	Whole carcass beef

Source: Concentration Ratios in Manufacturing Industry, 1963, Report Prepared by the Bureau of the Census for the Subcommittee on Antitrust and Monopoly, Part I, 89th Congress, 2d. sess., (Washington: G.P.O., 1966).

industry classification to seven-digit product classes, as shown in Table 8.2 (concentration ratios are not published at the seven-digit level, however).

Under the Bureau's **industry approach,** each plant (or "establishment") for which data are gathered is assigned to one of 430 four-digit industry groups. A plant is assigned to an industry according to its **primary** product or activity, and its **entire** output is included in that classification. Thus, all shipments of a plant classified in an industry are assigned to that industry, even though some (minor) portion of those shipments may be of a different kind.

These classification procedures permit two kinds of discrepancies that are best discussed by example. Suppose that a number of plants engaged in the production of "petroleum refining products" also produce, as a secondary output, "lubricants and greases." The entire output of these plants is assigned to petroleum; thus the calculation of the concentration ratio for the petroleum products industry is based in part on **irrelevant output**—the lubricants and greases. Similarly, when the concentration ratio for the "lubricants and greases" industry is calculated, it **excludes** some **relevant output**—those lubes and greases that are the secondary products of petroleum-refining plants.

The situation in, say, the meat-packing industry is precisely analogous. The four-digit group (1) includes the non-meat products of plants whose primary output is meat and (2) excludes the meat production of any plants whose primary output is in another industry. The industry data on which concentration measures are based **generally** exclude some relevant output and include some irrelevant output.

The Census Bureau provides two measures that permit us to see whether these discrepancies are in any case large enough to be troublesome:

1. The **coverage ratio** describes the extent to which the primary product of an industry originates in plants classified in that industry. It is simply the ratio:

$$C = \frac{\text{Shipments of industry A that come from plants classified in A}}{\text{Total shipments of industry A}}$$

A ratio of 0.86 in meat packing, for example, indicates that 86 percent of meat packing output originates with plants classified in the meat packing industry, and 14 percent comes from "outside."

2. The primary product specialization ratio describes the extent to which plants classified in an industry specialize in making the products primary to that industry. It is simply the ratio:

$$PPS = \frac{\text{Shipments of industry A that come from plants classified in A}}{\text{Total shipments of plants classified in A}}$$

A primary product specialization ratio of 0.98 in meat packing indicates that 98 percent of the output of plants classified in the industry actually consists of meat products—or that 2 percent of the output of meat packing plants consists of something else.

A low specialization ratio indicates that plants classified within an industry are diversified; that is, a good deal of what they produce is outside the product lines that define the industry. An example is "paints and allied products," an industry with a specialization ratio of 0.60; this means that 40 percent of the output of plants in the industry does not consist of anything that could be called "paints and allied products." Similarly, a low coverage ratio implies that much of an industry's output is produced in plants whose primary activity lies elsewhere. The 0.47 ratio for "surface active agents," for example, means that most (53 percent) of the output of this industry originates in plants whose primary business is making something other than surface active agents.[5] Used together, the primary product specialization and coverage ratios yield a reasonably good idea of the degree of correspondence between the industry and product groupings.

Problems of market definition have been noted in detail because so much empirical work is attempted at this level. If definitions are deficient, then hypotheses about market behavior may be confirmed or (more likely) rejected because the wrong facts have been examined. Many of the definitional problems can be avoided by judicious sample selection; but neither empirical investigation nor the interpretation of investigation by others can proceed meaningfully without an understanding of the actual and potential pitfalls.

THE IMMEASURABILITY OF MARKET CONDUCT

As we have noted, the conduct or actual stratagems of firms in a market have some bearing on ultimate performance. Although many economists would not place primary emphasis on conduct as an explainer or predictor of performance, this element of behavior has been emphasized in antitrust enforcement. It is certainly true that conduct directly "causes" some kinds of performance. For example, a conspiracy among producers to set the price of their product at an agreed-upon level causes the price to go to that level. It may be, however, that this conspiratorial conduct is not the most important underlying factor that determines the price. The conspiracy

---

[5]The low coverage ratio does not necessarily mean that the category is a poorly defined market; but the concentration ratio for that market may have ignored some major producers, and cannot be assumed to be reliable.

might never have been possible except for structural conditions that made it easy, or even inevitable, for producers to get together. And the prices that have been determined might have come about in any case through purely tacit reactions, without an "agreement."

If we wish to make generally reliable statements about firms' conduct, information in two areas in necessary.

1. The goals of firms and the way in which they perceive and measure relevant quantities.
2. The existence and extent of mutual interdependence, as seen by firms, and their reaction to it.

Unless we can say something about what firms are trying to accomplish and how they take account of each other's presence, it will be extremely difficult to interpret their actions. Is a firm that raises its prices trying to earn greater profits or greater revenue? Is it raising price under specific expectations about the reaction of its rivals? Or is it simply ignoring them?

Meaningful definition of conduct patterns may not always be possible. Indeed, conduct itself is rarely observable directly. What we usually see is performance, to which we attempt to attach a conduct interpretation. The correct interpretation, however, may depend upon what goes on in the minds of business managers— something we are not likely to be able to judge with confidence.[6] Does a particular pattern of price response in an industry reflect independence or interdependence? Possibly several firms will charge the same price because they have carefully conspired to do so; and possibly they will charge the same price because they have independently decided to do so. Our observations of the pricing pattern may not enable us to discern which of these alternatives is the "true" one.

Some efforts have been made to determine whether a particular mode of conduct—collusion—is systematically related to structure or performance.[7] These studies attempt to finesse the problem by stating, in effect: "collusion exists when—and only when—the courts say it exists." This approach yields some interesting results, but does not advance our understanding of how collusion ought to be identified and measured.

The difficulty of measuring conduct is such that empirical studies of firms and industries frequently ignore it, focusing exclusively on structure and performance. Just how great a loss of knowledge may be implied by this short-circuiting is not obvious. Certainly there are hypotheses concerning market conduct that would be well worth testing, and it is to be hoped that measurement will improve to permit

---

[6] As we shall see, however, the courts have held that "intent" must be judged in order to decide the legality of certain types of business conduct.

[7] For an early examination, see James M. Clabault and John F. Burton, *Sherman Act Indictments, 1955–1965* (New York: Federal Legal Publications, 1966). More recent studies include Peter Asch and J. J. Seneca, "Is Collusion Profitable?" *Review of Economics and Statistics,* **53** (February 1976), 1–12; Asch and Seneca, "Characteristics of Collusive Firms," *Journal of Industrial Economics,* **23** (March 1975), 223–237; George A. Hay and Daniel Kelley, "An Empirical Survey of Price Fixing Conspiracies," *Journal of Law & Economics,* **17** (April 1974), 13–38.

further tests. At the same time, however, it is not clear on a priori grounds that business conduct is necessarily an important independent determinant of either market structure or market performance. Indeed, if the chain of causation runs from structure to conduct to performance—that is, if structural conditions lead to certain modes of conduct that, in turn, lead to particular performance patterns—then the loss of knowledge that results from our inability to measure conduct directly may be limited.[8]

INADEQUACIES IN EXISTING DATA

Efforts to test hypotheses are beset by a variety of measurement problems. In some instances these are of a very basic nature. It may be that relevant data are unavailable, or that data are available only in deficient forms.

In many cases, problems with existing data are specific and mundane, but are nevertheless important. The available data may measure something similar to, but not precisely the same as, the variable we would like to measure. Data may be compiled in forms that are so inconvenient as to be unusable, or compilations across industries or time may not be fully comparable. These kinds of problems can prove extremely troublesome, but they possess the virtue in most instances of ready visibility.

Potentially more obscure difficulties often lie within the measurement procedures that have been used to compile basic data, and it is in this area that special care must be exercised. Even if data appear to describe the appropriate variables, significant errors can arise. The compilation of data may be in some way haphazard so that essentially random errors of measurement are introduced. Worse yet, the compilation may introduce a systematic bias into the measure. It is important to be alert to these problems, for if they are ignored, misleading interpretations of observed facts may follow.

Some Obvious Data Problems

Some of the glaring deficiencies in economic data are readily illustrated by referring to measures of market structure and performance. Suppose, for example, that we wish to define the structural characteristics of a number of markets. If the previously noted problems of market definition and concentration measurement can be handled, it probably would be useful to proceed to some description of factors such as degree of product differentiation and ease of entry. Here some new measurement problems arise.

Product differentiation is not easily reduced to a precise index. Not only is there no obvious way of quantifying actual physical differences, but the extent of differentiation is a largely subjective question; that is, it is a matter of how different consumers **think** products are. It is most unlikely that we would be able to produce a

---

[8]For some arguments and evidence that conduct itself is important, see William L. Baldwin, "The Feedback Effect of Business Conduct on Industry Structure," *Journal of Law & Economics,* **12** (April 1969), 123–153.

specific index that assigns meaningful cardinal values to the differentiation of product classes. Yet we do have certain relevant information. It is evident that some products are physically more similar than others; the former may well be less differentiated, other things equal. Similarly, some product groups are more heavily advertised, and it is likely (although not inevitable) that these will be relatively more differentiated. If a cardinal index is not possible, it may nevertheless be feasible to attempt a less ambitious index that **ranks** products by degree of differentiation. Even a complete ranking may be impossible if there are many instances in which the proper ordering is unknown. For example, we may be confident that steel bars as a product class are less differentiated than cigarettes, yet not be at all sure whether steel bars are more differentiated than aluminum conductor, or whether cigarettes are more differentiated than tooth pastes. It may be necessary to rank products broadly by placing them in a small number of categories (steel and aluminum conductor might be categorized as products of ''low'' differentiation, cigarettes and tooth pastes as products of ''high'' differentiation).

The situation with respect to measurement of other entry barriers is somewhat similar. Suppose that one wishes to define the importance of economies of scale in various industries. Two elements are involved: (1) the minimum efficient or optimal size of an operation, sometimes termed MES or MOS; and (2) the degree of cost disadvantage experienced by nonoptimal-sized operations. We are asking in effect, where—at what quantity level—does the cost curve bottom out; and how steeply does it rise from the bottom?

Given sufficient time and resources, one might obtain reasonable estimates from industry experts, or from detailed analyses of cost data for different-sized plants. Such procedures are cumbersome, and many investigators have looked at shorthand proxies instead. Reasoning that efficient size is likely to be the size that actually characterizes the market, some have looked at such readily available measures as midpoint plant size or the average size of the largest plants accounting for 50 percent of industry output. Such proxies are imperfect, for actual plant sizes may respond to factors other than true scale economies; but even less-than-ideal measures are quite useful.

The steepness or gradient of industry cost curves presents an equally thorny problem. One would like to know the **difference** in unit costs between large and small plants. Extensive cost studies might provide some answers on a case-by-case basis. Alternatively, an available proxy such as output or value added per worker in large versus small plants might be employed.[9]

The measurement of inventive and innovative activity has presented difficulties, primarily because there is no observable magnitude that seems to describe precisely the variable in question. Some writers have taken firm and industry **expenditures** on research and development as the best measure. But the expenditure figures describe in effect the **effort** that is being made to be inventive, whereas our interest

---

[9]For use of the value-added measure, see R. E. Caves, J. Khalilzadeh-Shirazi, and M. E. Porter, ''Scale Economies in Statistical Analyses of Market Power,'' *Review of Economics and Statistics,* **57** (November 1975), 133–140.

may lie more with the end **results** of such effort. Does not a highly successful R&D program imply more ''inventiveness'' than one that fails?

An alternative approach is to measure inventive output by looking at the number of patents taken out by firms and groups of firms. It is obvious, however, that patents are often noncomparable. Some are important, and others are trivial; and two comparable developments may result in different numbers of patents assigned. In a sense, both R&D expenditures and number of patents are relevant to the magnitude investigators would like to describe, but they do not constitute a fully accurate description. Such data may be utilized as the best available, but their shortcomings must be noted carefully, and conclusions qualified accordingly.

A host of data problems involve the simple incomparability of many statistics and the unavailability of information. One source of difficulty is the fact that government statistics are often gathered in different ways, by different agencies or by the same agency over a long period. If one wishes to study, say, price, production, profit, and concentration data for certain industries, it is quite possible that the industry definition will be slightly different for each of the variables. The Bureau of the Census, for example, uses one set of classifications (the S.I.C.), and the Internal Revenue Service another. In many instances the differences are small, and industries are easily matched, but such is not always the case. Time series data gathered by a single agency may also change so that recent information is not entirely comparable with that provided for past years.

In many cases, these obvious kinds of data problems are not terribly serious, and it may be sufficient to note that certain possible discrepancies qualify the conclusions that can be drawn. In other instances, however, it becomes necessary to decide whether existing data—even if they are the best available—are sufficiently accurate and reliable to be useful. No objective rules of thumb exist, and the decisions become matters of judgment.

Some Less Obvious Data Problems

A variety of nonobvious problems arise in connection with economic data.[10] Rather than attempting to survey all possible pitfalls, it may be relatively efficient to illustrate such problems by referring to one kind of widely used information: price statistics. Economists concerned with industry structure and behavior have an obvious interest in examining price patterns. Accordingly, much attention is paid to the major price measures published by the Bureau of Labor Statistics: the Consumer Price Index (CPI) and, especially, the Producer Price Index (PPI), previously known as the Wholesale Price Index (WPI).[11] These indexes provide a detailed pic-

---

[10]For a general discussion of problems in economic data, see Oskar Morgenstern, *On the Accuracy of Economic Observation*, 2nd ed. (Princeton, N.J.: Princeton University Press, 1963).

[11]The PPI (or WPI) is a more relevant measure for manufacturing industry questions. One reason is that the CPI reflects the combined effect of behavior at various levels of production and marketing, and is therefore a less ''pure'' measure of what occurs at the manufacturing level.

ture of price movements in a large number of product categories (many of which can be matched with SIC product and industry groups).

The availability of such information is, of course, most fortunate for any economist who wishes to compare the pricing patterns of different industries, or to analyze the patterns within an industry over time. But there are also significant drawbacks to the data. Certain of these drawbacks affect the goodness of the indexes in toto, and may not be relevant for questions with specific industry patterns.[12] Other shortcomings, however, affect the measures in quite specific ways.

The most familiar problem associated with price measures concerns changes in the quality of products. When we look at the price of something over a period of time, the changes that we observe are meaningful only if that "something" is constant. If the product itself undergoes changes, then the prices we observe are in effect associated with **different** products. This is clear if it is recognized that the demand for any product can be viewed as a demand for the attributes or characteristics of that product. Quality changes yield a different set of attributes and, in some meaningful sense, a different product. Presumably, then, some adjustment in the price measure is required. If product quality improves and its nominal price also increases, the "true" price increase, if any, will be less than the nominal amount; for although we must pay more money to buy the product, we are buying a better product. Examples of quality increases are legion. Ballpoint pens, when first introduced, were cumbersome, short-lived, and highly unreliable compared with what they are today. The television and stereo sets, fishing reels, and typewriters of today simply perform better than "the same" products did decades ago. Of course, it is also true that some products perform less well today. The statement, "They just don't make them the way they used to!" unquestionably has some applicability.

Whatever the direction of quality change, such change must enter into a true measure of price. Conceptually, one measure of true price may be defined as: Observed index of price/index of quality change.[13] Thus a product whose observed price index moves from 100 to 150, but whose quality has "doubled" over the same period, has a true current price index of 75. If price and quality both double, true price does not change; and if price falls while quality rises, true price falls by more than the observed change.[14] The Bureau of Labor Statistics is, of course, aware of quality change problems, and attempts to make appropriate adjustments where possible. But quality change is immensely difficult to quantify, and for many changes there is no objective method of doing so. Consequently, quality trends may be ignored or inadequately treated, with definite implications for indexes such as the CPI and PPI. To the extent that quality improvement goes unrecorded, the indexes generally overstate price increases and understate decreases. If we observe that prices

[12]For example, it has been argued that the CPI is a poor measure of general prices because its weights are somehow unrepresentative of the economy. This problem would in no way affect the ability of the index to measure price movements in specific industries.

[13]See, for instance, Zvi Griliches, "Hedonic Price Indexes for Automobiles: An Econometric Analysis of Quality Change," Staff Paper 3 in *The Price Statistics of the Federal Government*, A report to the Office of Statistical Standards, Bureau of the Budget, Prepared by the Price Statistics Review Committee of the National Bureau of Economic Research (National Bureau of Economic Research, 1961).

go up in some industries but not in others, we cannot be sure that relative prices have changed in this fashion; perhaps quality has risen more in one sector than the other.

Very similar problems are raised by the introduction of new products and changes in the specifications of existing products. How, for example, should the introduction of subcompact cars or self-cleaning ovens or color television have been taken account of? As the Price Statistics Review Committee has pointed out:

The treatment of new products presents a serious problem for any price index. An attempt to introduce all innovations into an index as soon as they appear would clutter the index with the failures that never attain appreciable importance. On the other hand, if new products are introduced only when the old items are completely displaced, the index will become seriously obsolete. . . .[15]

Changes in product specifications are very much like other quality changes. Many cameras today have built-in light meters, and some radios have alarm mechanisms and clocks. It would clearly be inaccurate to interpret the increased prices that result from the addition of such components as true price increases. Once again, however, there may not be an adequate procedure by which to measure such changes.

These problems, troublesome as they are, do not exhaust the fundamental shortcomings of price measures. Studies by Harry E. McAllister[16] and John M. Flueck[17] cast serious doubt on whether the old WPI represented actual transactions prices. McAllister has shown that the frequency of price change for some commodities in the WPI was closely related to the number of firms reporting prices; Flueck found substantial differences between the behavior of some WPI commodity prices and the prices of the same commodities on government purchase contracts (these differences hold for amplitude as well as frequency of change). Such findings led the Price Statistics Review Committee to suggest "that the price quotations obtained from manufacturers do not faithfully measure the movements of prices, quite aside from the usualy problems of measurement."[18] At this point, one cannot be sure whether the WPI was quoting transactions prices, list prices, some combination of the two, or something quite different!

This list of pitfalls in price data does not imply that indexes such as the PPI and CPI are of no value. The measures do contain some potentially important inaccuracies and biases that would reduce their usefulness for certain tasks. But for other kinds of jobs, the data, although imperfect, will still be serviceable. Some examples are discussed below in reference to studies of industrial pricing patterns.

---

[14]There is, however, a question about the adequacy of such indexes under some circumstances. See F. M. Fisher and K. Shell, "Taste and Quality-Change in the Price Theory of the True Cost-of-Living Index," in J. N. Wolfe, Ed., *Value Capital and Growth: Papers in Honor of Sir John Hicks* (Edinburgh: At the University Press, 1968).

[15]See *Price Statistics*, footnote 13, p. 37.

[16]"Statistical Factors Affecting the Stability of the Wholesale and Consumers' Price Indexes," Staff Paper 8 in *The Price Statistics of the Federal Government*, pp. 373–418.

[17]"A Study in Validity: BLS Wholesale Price Quotations," Staff Paper 9 in *The Price Statistics of the Federal Government*, pp. 419–58.

[18]Ibid., p. 69.

Problems With Profit Data

The profit rate is the most basic measure of firm and market performance, and, as we shall see in Chapter 9, it has been the object of very extensive empirical investigation. For this reason, it is important to be aware of the limitations of available profit data.

We have previously noted the distinction between economic and accounting definitions of profit. (Accounting profits include whatever rate of return is normal for the activity in question; the normal return, treated as a cost, is excluded from economic profits.) Our hypotheses, drawn from the theory, relate to the economic notion of profit, but it is reported or accounting profits that we can observe directly. Attention commonly focuses on two accounting profit rates:

$$\text{The return to stockholder's equity} = \frac{Y - T}{E}$$

where Y = net income, T = taxes, and E = stockholders' equity or net worth.

$$\text{The return to capital} = \frac{Y - T + I}{TA}$$

where Y = net income, T = taxes, I = interest payments, and TA = total assets.

These rates of return are closely correlated with one another and do focus on the type of profits with which investors are concerned. The use of such accounting profits, however, introduces several difficulties.[19]

1. Accepted accounting procedures permit a good deal of flexibility (some would say "creativity") in what is reported. Asset valuation is a major area subject to varied treatments; such items as depreciation, inventory values, and taxation are also manipulable. It would therefore be unsurprising to find that several companies in very similar circumstances report substantially different profit rates.[20]

2. A more specific problem concerns certain "investmentlike" expenditures such as advertising and research and development. These activities yield returns over relatively long periods, and are thus referred to as "intangible assets." Yet accountants typically write off advertising and R&D as current expenses, thus misstating company asset values.[21]

3. Company funds may flow into enlarged managerial salaries and perquisites and thus never show up in reported net income.

---

[19] For good discussions of the issues raised, see Harold Demsetz, "Accounting for Advertising as a Barrier to Entry," *Journal of Business,* 52 (July 1979), 345–360; Stanley I. Ornstein, "Concentration and Profits," *Journal of Business,* 45 (October 1972), 519–541; and Leonard W. Weiss, "The Concentration–Profits Relationship and Antitrust," in Harvey J. Goldschmid, H. Michael Mann, and J. Fred Weston, Eds., *Industial Concentration: The New Learning* (Boston: Little, Brown, 1974), 184–223.

[20] As Weiss argues, high-profit firms may have an incentive to understate their returns, whereas low-profit companies overstate theirs. If so, the true *differences* in profitability will not be fully observable. Ibid., p. 197.

[21] Moreover, the misstatement will not be consistent across firms, if only because the importance and spending path on such intangible assets varies greatly from company to company.

4. Profits are generally reported at the firm level, but most sizable firms are diverse. As a result, the single profit rate that we observe is likely to reflect the average outcome of numerous activities in various markets. If our interest is with a particular activity or market, the overall profit rate of firms may tell us little.[22]

In part because of these difficulties, some investigators prefer to work with the price–cost margin (PCM), or (Price − Cost)/Price. Census industry statistics permit the calculation of an average margin, defined as:

$$PCM = \frac{\text{Value added} - \text{payroll}}{\text{Value of shipments}}$$

(Recall that value added is value of shipments minus the cost of goods and services purchased from other firms.) The PCM is a useful measure that has the advantage of being drawn from precisely the same groupings as other Census data. It is not, however, a precise measure of the profit rate,[23] and it cannot be calculated for a specific firm (Census data permit calculation only for an industry or for groups of firms within it).

How severe are problems of measuring profits? Some economists take a dim view and believe that what firms report is hardly worth examining. Others—probably the majority if one can judge from the volume of research that employs profit data—are more optimistic. Whereas reported profits are clearly subject to serious distortion, the importance of some disturbances can be reduced by examining profits over relatively long time periods, several years at least.

Furthermore, some important difficulties with profit data are of an essentially random nature much of the time. Random distortions are a serious problem but, as we shall see, they may not be fatal to the testing of certain hypotheses.

CONCLUSIONS

Although imperfections in economic data are almost inevitable, the lesson to be drawn is one of caution rather than despair. A large number of data deficiencies are random or unsystematic in character. As we have just seen, the profit rates that are examined, for example, may contain some inaccuracies because of variation in accounting practices among firms; but the inaccuracies go both ways—some understatement here, some overstatement there. Provided that the errors are not so large or frequent as to render the data worthless, this sort of problem is usually not crippling. It tends to work against the finding of significant relationships among variables, but if one is aware of the problem, conclusions will be qualified accordingly.

---

[22] Since 1970 many large companies have been required to report the profits of their various divisions separately. This requirement, however, has not yielded a generally available data set of superior reliability.

[23] One reason is that the Census Bureau compiles data at the establishment or plant level. Certain costs that are not specifically "attached" to any particular plant are therefore ignored.

More serious is the existence of a systematic (or nonrandom) **bias** in one's data.[24] Suppose, for instance, that all firms over a certain size use an accounting procedure that tends to depress the reported profit rate on assets or equity; while no firms under this size use similar procedures. A study of the relationship between firm size and profit rates based on this information would be subject to obvious distortion, and one would be better off using an alternative profitability measure.[25]

The kinds of difficulties discussed above are not, as a rule, avoidable. Perfect measures of the magnitudes we would like to examine are seldom (if ever) available. What is important is not to search for ideal data, which would be utterly futile; but to understand as fully as possible the potential shortcomings of the information that can be gathered. At times, the available measures may be too distorted to be useful. More often, however, we can proceed even with serious data deficiencies provided that we know precisely what those deficiencies are.

[24]Perhaps the most infamous example of bias via incorrect sampling occurred in the *Literary Digest* poll prior to the 1936 presidential election. The *Digest* poll concluded that Alf M. Landon would defeat Franklin D. Roosevelt, a conclusion that was in retrospect not merely wrong but incredible. The error was caused by the *Digest's* sampling procedure: it took names from telephone directories, thus excluding from its poll all persons unable to afford telephones. These persons comprised in 1936 a very large and very pro-Roosevelt group.

[25]Even if we were forced to use the biased profits measure, all might not be lost. If we found, say, that large firms were **more** profitable than smaller ones, the bias would actually strengthen our conclusion. That is, a relationship would be observed even though distortions in the data "work against" that observation.

CHAPTER 9

The Empirical Clues

The first edition of this book in 1970 described the volume of empirical work in industrial organization as "immense." Since that time, the volume has not merely increased, it has exploded—partly as a function of widespread access to computers within the economics profession. There is no way to "cover" here all that has been done, nor would that be a worthwhile undertaking. For interested readers, the best course is to sample selectively the primary literature itself.

It is useful nevertheless to report the empirical findings on a limited number of important issues. These results are frequently of interest on two separate grounds: first, as tests of hypotheses suggested by economic theory, second, as clues to the probable effects of public competition policies.

EXPLANATIONS OF PROFITABILITY

Profitability, or simply the profit "rate," is the life's blood of the firm and the central measure of its success. Unless a normal return or better can be earned, companies are unlikely to survive for long. Furthermore, as we have seen, there is a strong rationale for the demise of unprofitable concerns, as sad as the event may be. If the market functions properly, the absence of profits suggests that firm or market activities are not sufficiently valuable; consumers are not willing to pay for the full cost of resources used in providing the goods or services.

Our interest, in both a private and public sense, in explaining what determines varying profit rates among firms and markets, is thus strong. And the empirical effort devoted to the definition of the determinants has been prodigious.

Structural Determinants: Concentration, Shares, and Entry

As we have seen, economic theory suggests that firms in monopolistic markets may reap persistent excess (i.e., above normal) profits. Many investigators have therefore tested the hypothesis that measures of monopoly will explain statistically some of the variation among firm and market profit levels; specifically, that the monopolistic areas will enjoy higher returns, other things being equal.

The pioneering work on this issue is Joe S. Bain's examination of relationships between industry profit rates and the eight-firm concentration ratio during 1936 through 1940. Bain used a sample of 42 Census industries and hypothesized specifically that:

. . . the average profit rate of firms in oligopolistic industries of a high concentration will tend to be significantly larger than that of firms in less concentrated oligopolies or in industries of atomistic structure.[1]

Bain reasoned that highly concentrated oligopolies are relatively likely to collude effectively, thus driving the profit rate toward the pure monopoly level, whereas less concentrated markets are characterized by less effective coordination and lower profits on average.

Bain found no "conclusive indication" of a strong linear relationship between the variables, but noted instead "a rather distinct break in average profit-rate showing at the 70 percent concentration line." The distinction is shown in Figure 9.1. The simple linear relationship of panel *a* shows a constant response of profit rate to concentration at all levels of concentration. What Bain saw was something more like the step function of panel *b;* profits were distinctly higher above the 70 percent level of eight-firm concentration (CR_8) than below it, but when the full spectrum of industries was examined no smooth linear relationship was apparent.

Although Bain's study was somewhat ad hoc—the 70 percent cutoff level of CR_8 was apparently suggested by the data rather than any prior theory of market structure and profitability—it has been enormously important in stimulating further research.[2] Later studies have added methodological refinements. The principal ones include:

1. Examination of numerous other profit rate determinants, useful in permitting us to isolate the concentration–profits relationship under some approximation of *ceteris paribus* assumptions.
2. Experimentation with different definitions of both profit rates and concentration.
3. Determination of relationships at the firm level.
4. Tests of more precisely specified statistical relationships—usually linear but occasionally more complex.

It has been found that introduction of a second structural variable, barriers to entry, improves the predictions of profit rates.[3]

William G. Shepherd has found that the market share of the firm is a more powerful statistical determinant of its profit rate than the top-four concentration ratio for the firm's primary industry.[4] And John E. Kwoka, Jr., in a study of industry

[1] Joe S. Bain, "Relation of Profit Rate to Industry Concentration, American Manufacturing, 1936–1940," *Quarterly Journal of Economics,* **65** (August 1951), 293–324, quotation at p. 294.

[2] A 1974 survey by Leonard W. Weiss cites at least 46 studies, and a conservative guess would be that the number doubled by the end of the decade. "The Concentration–Profits Relationship and Antitrust," in Harvey J. Goldschmid, H. Michael Mann, and J. Fred Weston, Eds., *Industrial Concentration: The New Learning* (Boston: Little, Brown, 1974).

[3] See H. Michael Mann, "Seller Concentration, Barriers to Entry and Rates of Return in Thirty Industries, 1950–1960," *Review of Economics and Statistics,* **48** (August 1966), 296–307. Mann, following Bain's methodology, utilized broad rankings of industries according to height of barriers. More specific measures sometimes encounter the statistical problem of collinearity with concentration indexes.

[4] "The Elements of Market Structure," *Review of Economics and Statistics,* **54** (February 1972), 25–37.

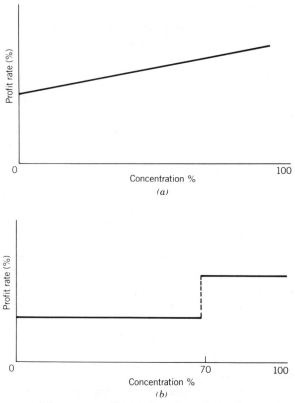

Figure 9.1 Two possible concentration–profitability relationships. (*a*) Linear. (*b*) Step function.

price–cost margins—an alternative profit-"type" measure—has reported that the joint share of the top **two** firms is "generally decisive."[5]

There is now a very extensive body of evidence on the hypothesis that profitability is linked to structural variables such as concentration, shares, and entry. Although findings are not uniform, the most frequent conclusions are that:

1. Concentration and certain entry barrier measures exert a statistically significant and positive effect on firm and industry profit rates.
2. The firm's market share (when it can be measured adequately) exerts an important influence on its profits.[6]

[5]"The Effect of Market Share Distribution on Industry Performance," *Review of Economics and Statistics,* **61** (February 1979), 101–109.

[6]Measurement of market share is difficult because of corporate diversification. It is easy to find the overall sales of many firms, but not the proportion of sales that take place within any given market. In order to use a shares measure, one must either have access to independent data prepared by research firms (as did Kwoka) or else be prepared to do much painstaking estimation, probably including some judicious guesswork (see Shepherd, footnote 4).

The broad results thus tend to confirm theoretical expectations. This is an impressive conclusion for two reasons. First, the patterns seem to hold over a variety of industry, firm, and time-period samples, strongly suggesting that there exists both a real and relatively stable relationship. Second, the results appear despite the existence of some important data problems. The shortcomings of concentration, entry barrier, and profit-rate measures have been noted above. These factors tend to work against the observation of statistically significant relationships; they appear as "noise" that will to some degree obstruct our view of what truly exists. In view of such disturbances, Leonard Weiss observes that "any relationships between profit and concentration [or] barriers . . . that we observe are real and are probably badly underestimated."[7]

Despite this rather clear picture, a number of important qualifications must be mentioned. The results reported above are typical but not universal, and some studies fail to find a significant role for concentration or structure generally.[8] Moreover, readers should note carefully that a **statistically** significant result need not be economically **important**. Quite a few studies report a concentration–profitability association that could be described as "significant but weak." This means in effect that the relationship between the variables is quite consistent but quantitatively small. Change the concentration level by X percent, *ceteris paribus,* and one can make a reliable prediction about what happens to profits; but the prediction is that only "a little" will happen.

This is not a surprising result, and it may be, as Weiss says, that the true effect is understated. It is well to keep things in perspective, however. Economic theory clearly suggests that the degree of monopoly will affect the profit rate, but does not imply that it is the sole, or even the primary, determinant.

One final qualification to the empirical results requires brief mention now and will be discussed in more detail below. This is the fact that even a well-defined link between concentration and the profit rate is subject to varied interpretation. Persistent excess profits point to monopoly.[9] But "monopoly"—that is, power over price—may itself originate in different ways. At one extreme, the firm that reaps "high" profits may do so because the market offers no effective competition; price is raised above cost so as to exploit consumers. At the other extreme, the firm may earn profits because it is efficient; price exceeds cost because, in a broad sense, the

---

[7]"Quantitative Studies of Industrial Organization," in M. D. Intriligator, Ed., *Frontiers of Quantitative Economics* (Amsterdam: North-Holland, 1971), pp. 370–373.

[8]See, for example, George J. Stigler, *Capital and Rates of Return in Manufacturing Industries* (Princeton: Princeton University Press, 1963). Norman R. Collins and Lee E. Preston find some support for the relationship amidst mixed results. *Concentration and Price–Cost Margins in Manufacturing Industries* (Berkeley: University of California Press, 1968). See also Stanley I. Ornstein, "Concentration and Profitability," *Journal of Business,* **45** (October 1972), 519–541.

[9]Yale Brozen has argued with reference to Bain's original study that "high" profits in concentrated industries did **not** persist over time. "Bain's Concentration and Rates of Return Revisited," *Journal of Law & Economics,* **14** (October 1971), 351–369.

firm has managed to push costs down. It has simply performed in superior fashion.[10]

Both cases, as well as intermediate mixtures of the two, are consistent with an observed relationship between concentration and profit rates. Clearly, however, our social judgment of and public policies toward the two would be markedly different.

Advertising as a Determinant of Profits

Advertising is a controversial activity regarded as useful by some and wasteful (or worse) by others. It is related to product differentiation, an element of market structure, but is also, as we have noted, a behavioral variable over which firms exert some control. Our question at this point, however, is quite specific: Does the level of advertising systematically affect the profit rate?

Some rather strong statistical evidence has been gathered, but it turns out that the proper interpretation of what is observed is not a simple matter. A number of major studies find that advertising variables—frequently defined as advertising dollars divided by sales dollars—are a strong statistical determinant of firm and industry profit rates.[12] Comanor and Wilson, for example, report that industries characterized by heavy advertising outlays have profit rates nearly 4 percentage points higher than other industries. The significant and positive impact of advertising persists when other determinants of profitability, such as concentration, growth of demand, and entry barrier measures, are included in the analysis.

The meaning of this statistical association has been hotly debated. Bloch, for example, has argued that the observed relationship results from improper accounting treatment of advertising; firms treat it as a current expense, yet most advertising is in effect an investment in a (longer-term) capital asset.[13] Weiss, responding to this point, concludes that a correction for accounting problems does not make an "earthshaking" difference to the results, but debate persists about the nature of an appropriate correction.[14]

Even if one accepts that the advertising–profits relationship is real, no mere fluke of the data, questions of interpretation remain. What is the chain of causation? Tra-

[10]Some economists contend that a firm that becomes dominant by means of superior performance ought not to be called a "monopolist." For the present, however, we use the term without pejorative connotation to describe any company that can regularly hold price above (average and marginal) cost.

[12]See, especially, William S. Comanor and Thomas A. Wilson, "Advertising Market Structure and Performance," *Review of Economics and Statistics,* **49** (November 1967), 423–440; Leonard W. Weiss, "Advertising, Profits, and Corporate Taxes," *Review of Economics and Statistics,* **51** (November 1969), 421–430; and Shepherd, footnote 4.

[13]Harry Bloch, "Advertising and Profitability: A Reappraisal," *Journal of Political Economy,* **82** (March/April 1974), 267–286. As noted, the argument is that the effects of advertising occur over a relatively long period; the "purchase" of an advertising campaign is therefore akin to the purchase of any other long-lived asset.

[14]Leonard W. Weiss, footnote 12. See also L. W. Weiss and John J. Siegfried, "Advertising, Profits, and Corporate Taxes Revisited," *Review of Economics and Statistics,* **56** (May 1974), 195–200; Harold Demsetz, "Accounting for Advertising as a Barrier to Entry," *Journal of Business,* **52** (July 1979), 345–360; and Robert Ayanian, "Advertising and Rate of Return," *Journal of Law & Economics.* **18** (October 1975). 479–506.

ditional arguments associated with Bain and Kaldor[15] run roughly as follows: Advertising is a product-differentiating activity that, if successful, creates monopoly power. This power, in turn, leads to higher profit rates.[16] The purpose of advertising, after all, is to convince consumers that one's products are better than those of rivals, that is, to create one's own partial monopoly. Bain also stresses the role of advertising as a barrier to entry. Heavy expenditures raise the "ante" that new firms must meet to enter the market, and may imply that entry carries a high risk of failure.

These arguments suggest that heavy advertising may diminish competition, yet counterarguments may be made on both conceptual and empirical grounds. Advertising may be **pro**competitive, in Brozen's words, "much more a means of entry than a barrier to entry."[17] A priori, both possibilities make sense. One can envision cases in which advertising enhances monopoly power by increasing the inelasticity of demand and heightening entry barriers, but also cases in which advertising is used to attack established monopoly. The issue thus cannot be settled "theoretically." We must instead appeal to the evidence.

The evidence, however, is far from clear. If advertising creates monopoly power that, in turn, yields high profits—the traditional hypothesis—then some relationship should be seen between advertising and measures of market power. In fact, a connection between advertising and concentration, the common proxy for such power, is not easy to establish.

In 1964 Lester G. Telser found a positive but statistically insignificant correlation: advertising and concentration in manufacturing industries were "virtually independent."[18] This result was one of several that led Telser to conclude that there is "little empirical support for an inverse association between advertising and competition." Three years later, Mann, Henning, and Meehan reported a positive and significant association between firm advertising and market concentration.[19] This finding, which has been subject to some methodological criticism, has stimulated considerable debate.[20]

Telser, building on the Mann et al. sample, found insignificant correlations[21];

---

[15] See Joe S. Bain, *Barriers to New Competition* (Cambridge: Harvard University Press, 1956); and Nicholas Kaldor, "The Economic Aspects of Advertising," *Review of Economic Studies*, **18** (1949–1950), 1–27.

[16] Comanor and Wilson note the possibility of reverse causation (footnote 12 at p. 439): "A plausible case can be made that a significant feedback exists from profits to advertising expenditures, since advertising reflects the discretionary behavior of firms. . . ."

[17] Yale Brozen, "Entry Barriers: Advertising and Product Differentiation," in Goldschmid, Mann, and Weston, footnote 2, p. 115.

[18] "Advertising and Competition," *Journal of Political Economy*, **72** (December 1964), 537–562.

[19] H. M. Mann, J. A. Henning, and J. W. Meehan, Jr., "Advertising and Concentration: an Empirical Investigation," *Journal of Industrial Economics*, **16** (November 1967), 34–45.

[20] See Stanley I. Ornstein, *Industrial Concentration and Advertising Intensity* (Washington, D.C.: American Enterprise Institute, 1977), p. 16ff; "Symposium on Advertising and Concentration," *Journal of Industrial Economics* **18** (November 1969), 76–94.

[21] "Another Look at Advertising and Concentration," in "Symposium," ibid., 537–562.

and John M. Vernon in a careful study of promotional spending in therapeutic drug markets could uncover "no evidence" of a link to concentration.[22]

The empirical picture remains truly mixed. Some investigators conclude that advertising exerts an influence on concentration, whereas others, viewing somewhat different samples and time periods, find the opposite to be true.[23] Moreover, the uncertain nature of these results appears again when the **change** in concentration over time is examined.[24]

We are thus left with an ambiguous picture. Advertising intensity appears to influence profit rates; but its relationship to concentration—the element through which its influence is usually expected to run—is questionable. The difficulty may lie partly with data problems; both concentration and advertising measures are imperfect. It also may be, however, that the effects of advertising are in fact inconsistent, promoting competition in some places while discouraging it in others.

Other Determinants of Profit Rates

Quite a few other variables have been tested as possible determinants of profitability in statistical studies. Among the more prominent are **growth rates,** usually of sales or physical output. Growth is a likely proxy for shifts in demand and, as expected, shows a positive and frequently significant impact on profits.

The effect of **firm size** on profitability is less clear. Large size could signal scale economies and difficult entry, both of which suggest higher profits; but it might alternatively suggest diseconomies of scale, possibly reflecting efforts by corporate managers to become large, even at some sacrifice of profits. Empirical findings most frequently show size to be an insignificant factor in profitability.[25]

Richard A. Miller has examined the effects of **marginal concentration** ratios, defined as $CR_8 - CR_4$, that is, the joint market share of firms 5 through 8.[26] He finds that for a **given** value of CR_4, marginal concentration exerts a negative and significant effect on profits, presumably because a larger "fringe" of firms offers more effective competition to the top four.

---

[22] "Concentration, Promotion, and Market Share Stability in the Pharmaceutical Industry," *Journal of Industrial Economics,* **19** (July 1971), 246–266.

[23] For some useful discussions, see Douglas F. Greer, "Advertising and Market Concentration," *Southern Economic Journal,* **38** (July 1971), 19–32; C. J. Sutton, "Advertising, Concentration and Competition," *Economic Journal,* **84** (March 1974), 56–69; and Allyn D. Strickland and Leonard W. Weiss, "Advertising, Concentration, and Price–Cost Margins," *Journal of Political Economy,* **84** (October 1976), 1109–1121.

[24] High advertising intensity is associated with increasing concentration in two studies: Matityahu Marcus, "Advertising and Changes in Concentration," *Southern Economic Journal,* **36** (October 1969), 117–121; and Willard F. Mueller and Larry G. Hamm, "Trends in Industrial Market Concentration, 1947–1970," *Review of Economics and Statistics,* **56** (October 1974), 511–520. No relationship is found by Peter Asch, "The Role of Advertising in Changing Concentration, 1963–1971," *Southern Economic Journal,* **46** (July 1979), 288–297.

[25] One exception is Marshall Hall and Leonard W. Weiss, "Firm Size and Profitability," *Review of Economics and Statistics,* **49** (August 1967), 319–331.

[26] "Marginal Concentration and Industrial Profit Rates," *Southern Economic Journal,* **24** (October 1967), 259–267. The marginal concentration ratio has some peculiar statistical properties; notice that its value is constrained by the value of CR_4.

Risk is another element with important theoretical implications for profitability. It is plausible to suppose that most investors do not wish to take risks with their funds, and must therefore be compensated by higher expected returns when they do so. If this is the case, then part of the variation in profit rates that we see among firms (and perhaps among industries) may well be due to varying risk.

Attempts to test this expectation encounter some substantial difficulties. Both firm risk and profitability are likely to be influenced by market structure, a circumstance that suggests troublesome collinearities if we examine the hypothesis:

$$\text{Profit rate} = f(\text{Market structure; risk})$$

Furthermore, accurate and observable proxies for risk are hard to devise. Risk, after all, is an *ex ante* magnitude—something that investors anticipate for the future, perhaps in a partially subjective way. Yet we can only infer it after the fact by looking at *ex post* data.

Plausible empirical measures of risk have centered on the variability, most frequently the standard deviation, of company profit rates over time.[27] The rationale is that a highly volatile profit record is likely to be associated with greater perceived risk. The findings to date present a mixed picture. Shepherd, for example, finds no relationship between risk, so defined, and profitability; whereas Fisher and Hall and Sullivan report the expected (positive and significant) association. The common point of agreement is that risk measures based in profit variability are unlikely to reveal the full story.

Are Profits Stochastic?

Could it be that profit-rate variations among firms are at least partly stochastic, that is, the result of random forces or "mere" chance? Richard B. Mancke suggested such a possibility in 1974, aruguing that all the observed relationships we have described are consistent with a world in which corporate success is a matter of sheer luck.[28] Firms that are lucky, for example, earn high profits, grow rapidly, and attain large market shares; investigators may (improperly) attribute causal significance to growth and shares as determinants of profits.

Caves, Gale, and Porter have shown that certain implications of Mancke's argument are contradicted by analysis of actual data[29]; Albin and Alcaly conclude on

---

[27] For discussion of the issues and presentation of evidence, see I. N. Fisher and G. R. Hall, "Risk and Corporate Rates of Return," *Quarterly Journal of Economics,* **83** (February 1969), 79–92; Paul H. Cootner and Daniel M. Holland, "Rate of Return and Business Risk," *Bell Journal of Economics and Management Science,* **1** (Autumn 1970), 211–226; William G. Shepherd, *The Treatment of Market Power* (New York: Columbia University Press, 1975), especially pp. 106–113; and Timothy G. Sullivan, "A Note on Market Power and Returns to Stockholders," *Review of Economics and Statistics,* **59** (February 1977), 108–113.

[28] "Causes of Interfirm Profitability Differences: A New Interpretation of the Evidence," *Quarterly Journal of Economics,* **88** (May 1974).

[29] R. E. Caves, B. T. Gale, and M. E. Porter, "Interfirm Profitability Differences: A Comment," *Quarterly Journal of Economics,* **92** (November 1977). See also Mancke's reply in the same issue.

the basis of a simulation study that randomness is an unlikely explanation of some observed relationships.[30]

The point suggested by Mancke is nevertheless an important one. We may not believe that all observed links between profit rates and other variables result purely from luck (indeed, it may not be completely obvious what "luck" means). But randomness may enter. The more general lesson should be remembered well: interpretations of statistical relationships can be subjective. The way in which one "reads" regression equations to explain profitability depends importantly on one's underlying beliefs about the functioning of markets.

EXPLANATIONS OF PRICING: THE "ADMINISTERED-PRICE" CONTROVERSY

Rudimentary analysis suggests that monopoly prices will be higher than competitive prices at any given time.[31] Considerable attention has also been paid to the effect of monopoly power on pricing patterns through time. Some prominent hypotheses that have been suggested are associated with what has been known as the administered-price controversy, and represent an unusual episode in the study of industrial organization.

Market prices are expected to respond to changes in both supply (i.e., cost) and demand conditions. In practice, however, it appears that many prices in the American economy are inflexible or "sticky," changing—if at all—only at infrequent intervals. This occurs depsite the fact that it is unreasonable to think that cost and demand conditions remain stable over long periods.

Price inflexibility may be detrimental. It means that the market mechanism is failing to take account of changes in the cost of resources and in consumer preferences, or that it is doing so only after significant time lags. Inflexible prices received special attention during and after the Great Depression of the 1930s, for had prices generally fallen faster and farther, it is at least possbile that much of the severe and self-feeding unemployment of the period could have been avoided. Any tendency for prices to be sticky implied a lower quantity of goods demanded (than would have been demanded at lower prices), and as a direct result, lower output and fewer jobs.[32]

A study by Gardiner C. Means in 1939 examined the behavior of industrial prices during the depression period 1929 through 1932.[33] Means, however, did not treat

---

[30]Peter S. Albin and Roger E. Alcaly, "Stochastic Determinants of Interfirm Profitability Differences," *Review of Economics and Statistics,* **61** (November 1979), 615–618.

[31]Studies of profitability examine the divergence of price from average cost under conditions of varying market power and, therefore, touch on this suggestion indirectly.

[32]Flexible (downward) prices, however, might have been associated with flexible wage levels. Had lower prices been accompanied by lower wages, the result could have been to depress aggregate demand. For this reason, the macroeconomic desirability of flexible prices is arguable.

[33]*The Structure of the American Economy,* Part I (Washington, D.C.: National Resources Committee, 1939).

price inflexibility during this period as either a general or a random problem. Rather, he suggested that the phenomenon of inflexibility was associated with particular industry characteristics and was confined largely to what have come to be known as "administered-price" industries. The term **administered price** has been used in somewhat different ways throughout the controversy. Means originally defined it as:

. . . a price which is set by administrative action and held constant for a period of time. We have an administered price when a company maintains a posted price at which it will make sales or simply has its own price at which customers may purchase or not as they wish.[34]

Such a definition would appear to encompass all prices except those negotiated for every individual transaction (e.g., the retail sale of most automobiles) or set in auction-type markets such as the stock exchanges. In contrast to this extremely broad definition, however, administered-price industries are frequently defined as those in which control over price by firms is substantial.

Means found a positive relationship between industry concentration and percentage increase in price for the period 1929 through 1932, and a negative relationship between concentration and frequency of price change—both based on an examination of 37 selected manufacturing industries. The findings suggested that the more highly concentrated industries resisted pressures for price decreases during the Depression, or, conversely, that the lower an industry's concentration level the larger its price decreases (i.e., the lower its rate of increase). If accepted, this conclusion would tie the price-inflexibility problem primarily to highly concentrated industries.

The Means finding stimulated an extensive debate over Depression price behavior. Willard E. Thorp and Walter F. Crowder concluded in an independent study that no measurable relationship between concentration and amplitude of price change existed during 1929 to 1933.[35] Alfred C. Neal found that industry price changes were closely correlated with changes in cost, stating:

. . . amplitude of price decline in depression is for the most part explained (in the statistical sense) by amplitude of direct cost decline, a matter over which particular industries have little if any discretion. This evidence completely controverts Means' contention so far as manufacturing industry is concerned.[36]

Thus the evidence on Depression price patterns was in conflict. Means found a "rough" relationship between concentration and the failure of prices to decline; Thorp and Crowder saw no relationship; and Neal concluded that price declines could be explained adequately without reference to concentration. A number of crit-

---

[34] "Industrial Prices and Their Relative Inflexibility," Senate Document 13, Washington, D.C., January 17, 1935.

[35] *The Structure of Industry* (Washington, D.C.: Temporary National Economics Committee, 1941).

[36] *Industrial Concentration and Price Inflexibility* (American Council on Public Affairs, 1942), p. 124.

icisms of the three studies, based largely on methodology and reliability of data, have been made,[37] but the issue has never been fully resolved.

In the late 1950s occurred what Stigler has termed "the second life" of the administered-price theory,[38] this time in a somewhat different form. The newer version of the hypothesis sought to explain not the failure of prices to decline during a depression but, rather, the tendency of prices to rise during a period (the middle 1950s) of apparent stability in aggregate demand. Gardiner Means presented evidence before the Senate Antitrust and Monopoly Subcommittee[39] showing that "administered-price" industries, which he had found to be price "insensitive" during depression, were now, in a sense, too price **sensitive**. If Means's evidence was correct—and whether correct or not it was scanty—then administered-price industries were again to "blame" for a formidable but different economic problem: inflation.

More detailed studies of "administrative" or "oligopolistic" inflation, as it was sometimes called, were forthcoming in the 1960s. Horace DePodwin and Richard Selden examined a large number of Census industry and product classes for the period 1953 through 1959, and reached the following conclusions.

1. *The relationship between price change and concentration for 322 five-digit SCI product classes is extremely low. . . . The best one can do is to explain 9 percent of the price variation by referring to economic concentration.*

2. *On a four-digit industry class basis the best that one can do is to explain 10 percent of price variation in terms of economic concentration.*[40]

The DePodwin–Selden study employed linear and curvilinear regressions of a specially constructed price index for product classes, both weighted and unweighted, on various measures of concentration. The results of the statistical analysis uniformly supported the hypothesis that there was no significant relationship between concentration and price change during 1953 through 1959, and the authors concluded by saying that "we suggest that it is time to put the administrative inflation hypothesis to rest."

In 1966, however, Leonard W. Weiss presented new evidence that lent some credence to the administered-price inflation arguments.[41] Using the DePodwin–Selden price and concentration data, Weiss constructed measures of cost and demand

---

[37] See, for example, John M. Blair, "Means, Thorp and Neal on Price Inflexibility," *Review of Economics and Statistics*, **38** (November 1956), 427–435; Jules Backman, "Economic Concentration and Price Inflexibility," *Review of Economics and Statistics* **40** (November 1958), 399–404; and Blair, "Rejoinder," *Review of Economics and Statistics*, **40** (November 1958), 405–406.

[38] George J. Stigler, "Administered Prices and Oligopolistic Inflation," *Journal of Business*, **35** (January 1962), 1–13.

[39] *Hearings* Before the Subcommittee on Antitrust and Monopoly of the Committee of the Judiciary, United States Senate, 1958, Parts I, IX, and X.

[40] Horace J. DePodwin and Richard T. Selden, "Business Pricing Policies and Inflation," *Journal of Political Economy*, **71** (April 1963), 116–127; quotation at p. 125.

[41] "Business Pricing Policies and Inflation Reconsidered," *Journal of Political Economy*, **74** (April 1966), 177–187.

change for 81 four-digit industries. He found that once these other significant explanatory variables were introduced, the coefficients for concentration also became significant in explaining price changes. Weiss' explanation of this finding is highly instructive for any approach to empirical hypothesis testing. It was clear, he noted, that simple correlations between concentration and price change were unimpressive. This had been convincingly demonstrated by DePodwin and Selden. But such results, Weiss argued, were to be expected, because concentration is at most a secondary determinant of price movements. Once the primary determinants, cost and demand change, were taken account of in his regression equations, the existing relationship between concentration and price change became visible. This relationship, which appears to be significant, had been previously "swamped" and thus hidden by the effects of cost and demand change in the simple analysis.

The administered-price controversy has proceeded on both the empirical and theoretical levels. Economists such as Stigler have argued strongly that the empirical demonstrations of distinctive behavior in administered-price industries have been based on faulty data and methodology. The Wholesale Price Index, as we have noted, is subject to a variety of errors, some of which may introduce bias into examinations of price behavior. This would be especially damaging if the bias tends to work in favor of the hypotheses proposed by Means. If, for example, the WPI (now the PPI) systematically understates price declines and overstates increases in administered-price industries, many findings would have to be fully discounted. Means and Blair, on the other hand, have argued that some of the shortcomings of the WPI are irrelevant for questions of price **change,** although they may render the index useless for comparing the **height** of prices at a point in time.

A further methodological objection raised by Stigler concerns Means's classification of administered-price industries. It is not fully clear, even now, what an "administered-price" industry is. Means's categorization seems to have something to do with market power, but he has also utilized infrequency of price change as a measure of "administrativeness."[42] Here it appears that the WPI may do a poor job of measuring frequencies,[43] and this method of assigning industries to the administrative category is therefore questionable.

More recent evidence on administered-price hypotheses has failed to provide a definite conclusion. P. David Qualls, for example, has found support for the hypothesis that prices in highly concentrated industries are "less flexible."[44] Weston and Lustgarten have examined the proportion of price increases and decreases within industry groups categorized by concentration level, and report results "over-

---

[42] See also Gardiner C. Means, "The Administered Price Thesis Reconfirmed," *American Economic Review,* **62** (June 1972), 292–307. It is not clear that Means's definition of an administered-price industry has remained constant over time.

[43] See, for an extensive analysis of WPI prices, George J. Stigler and James K. Kindahl, *The Behavior of Industrial Prices* (New York: Columbia University Press, 1970).

[44] "Price Stability in Concentrated Industries," *Southern Economic Journal,* **42** (October 1975), 294–298.

whelmingly in disagreement'' with Means's version of the administered-price hypothesis.[45]

The variation in empirical findings is in some degree attributable to the testing of distinct (although similar) hypotheses. *The* administered-price argument is not in fact a single, well-defined statement. And even at this late date, it is pertinent to ask whether anything that could be called an administered-price phenomenon has been convincingly demonstrated.

A different but also important question is whether the notion of administered pricing or administered-price behavior has theoretical content. As we have seen, it is expected that monopolistic industries will charge higher prices than competitive industries in comparable circumstances. But there is no expectation in the orthodox body of economic analysis that patterns of price change will consistently differ among industries.

The way in which the prices of monopolistic and competitive firms change over time will depend upon the ways in which their cost and demand functions may change. Should costs and demand increase in an industry, price increases will presumably be forthcoming. There is no obvious reason to expect, however, that prices charged in concentrated or monopolistic industries will generally rise more (or fall less) than other prices. Moreover, the kind of argument presented by Means is not fully convincing. He has stated, for example, that in the mid-1950s inflation occurred simply because large firms raised their prices; and that the prices were raised ''because'' the firms had the power to do so. This begs the obvious question: Why, during such a period, were firms in administered-price industries motivated to raise prices more than other firms? The fact that they had the power to do so is hardly an explanation.

Several explanations of administered-price or oligopolistic inflation have been advanced by those who accept the existence of the phenomenon. One possibility, which has had some currency among economists, is that the kinds of industries that fit most administered-price descriptions are peculiarly vulnerable to increases in labor cost. Such vulnerability may be traced to a specific form of the countervailing power hypothesis: Powerful firms breed powerful opposing trade unions that then formulate and press relatively heavy wage demands. The labor component of these firms' cost structures rises by more than the average and, *ceteris paribus,* larger overall cost increases and price increases will be evidenced by such companies and by their industry groups.

The vulnerability of administered-price firms and industries to labor union demands may be argued without reference to the empirically questionable countervailing-power hypotheses. If these industries earn higher-than-average profits—and we have seen some evidence that they may—then union wage demands and bargaining positions are likely to be enhanced. Moreover, the companies as possessors of substantial pricing power may regard a wage hike as a cost that is

---

[45] J. Fred Weston and Steven H. Lustgarten, ''Concentration and Wage–Price Changes,'' In Goldschmid, Mann, and Weston, footnote 2.

readily transferable to consumers by means of price increases.[46] The granting of union demands may therefore not be viewed as an especially costly action. On the contrary, it might even be taken by some nonmaximizing companies as an excuse for **profitable** upward revisions in price.

A second possible explanation of oligopolistic inflation has been offered by Galbraith, who argues that oligopolists typically make imperfect price adjustments in periods of rising demand.[47] Specifically, Galbraith contends that as demand rises, oligopoly prices rise by less than an appropriate amount. After a period of demand increase oligopolists find themselves charging suboptimal prices and confront what Galbraith calls the unliquidated monopoly gain. Price increases during periods of stable demand can then be interpreted in Galbraith's terms as an effort to liquidate this gain, that is, to move from suboptimal to optimal (profit-maximizing) prices several years after a period of rising demand. This argument is an ingenious one; its policy implications, however, may be rather disappointing to many who accept the administrative inflation hypotheses. If upward price movements are in fact an attempt by oligopoly firms to compensate for earlier imperfect adjustments, then these firms can hardly be held "responsible" for inflation. Under this line of reasoning, such price increases are economically justified by demand conditions, and the companies that impose them are not saddling the economy with a somehow illegitimate inflation. One could argue to the contrary that such firms actually behaved with considerable pricing *restraint* during the earlier period of demand expansion.

A third interesting explanation of administered-price inflation, formulated by Adams and Lanzillotti, suggests that firms with considerable market power set prices in a way that differs basically from conventional profit-maximizing behavior.[48] According to Adams and Lanzillotti powerful firms are likely to act as **target-return** pricers (or "statisficers") seeking a defined long-run return on investment; whereas less powerful concerns behave more in conformity with the usual maximization calculus. Such a dichotomy carries several implications for price patterns. For example, target-return pricers will respond positively in the short run to increases in overhead costs, whereas profit-maximizing pricers will not. It has been shown by Charles L. Schultze that the period 1955 through 1957 was characterized by rapid increases in fixed overhead.[49] Thus the Adams–Lanzillotti hypothesis, although it has not been proved, is consistent with any observed tendency for the prices of powerful firms and concentrated industries to rise at higher than average rates.

[46] Such a consideration makes good sense, for at the very least a powerful firm will be able to pass on cost increases in the form of higher prices more quickly than a firm that can only react to a market-determined price.

[47] John Kenneth Galbraith, "Market Structure and Stabilization Policy," *Review of Economics and Statistics,* **39** (May 1957), 124–133.

[48] Walter Adams and Robert F. Lanzillotti, "The Reality of Administered Prices," *Administered Prices: A Compendium on Public Policy,* Subcommittee on Antitrust and Monopoly (Washington, D.C.: G.P.O., 1963).

[49] "Recent Inflation in the United States" Study Paper No. 1 in *Employment, Growth and Price Levels,* Joint Economic Committee, 86th Congress, 1st Session (Washington, D.C.: G.P.O., 1959).

These arguments all contain plausible elements, but each is in the nature of an ad hoc, after-the-fact hypothesis. The administered-price patterns that have been observed, in other words, were not predicted by the orthodox body of theory. New theories have therefore been devised to explain what has already been observed. Useful analysis may, of course, emerge from this sort of chronology; but the particular hypotheses described above have proved difficult to subject to categorical tests.

Perhaps the most remarkable fact about the administered-price controversy is that it persists. More than four decades of sporadic data gathering and debate have failed to establish the presence of a well-defined phenomenon, or to rationalize the possibility of its presence in satisfactory theoretical terms. At the very least, it must be concluded that administered pricing is not a readily demonstrable event. The evidence that administered-price industries—meaning those that are "oligopolistic" or "monopolistic" or "highly" concentrated—pursue pricing patterns inimical to the interests of the American economy, is scanty. A harsher judgment might be that the debate itself has been wasteful, centering around a possibly nonexistent occurrence. In the words of Morris A. Adelman, it may be that:

'Administered prices' is a catchy phrase which promises everything, explains nothing, and thereby gets in the way of our learning something.[50]

EXPLANATIONS OF "PROGRESSIVENESS"

As noted earlier, a number of arguments have been made that inventive and innovative activity flourish in large firms and highly concentrated industries. Among these arguments, most often associated with Schumpeter, are the following:

1. Significant inventions in a world of complex technology require a substantial outlay of resources, which only large companies can provide.
2. The riskiness of inventive effort is such that only large firms, with the ability to sustain losses or to pursue so many inventive efforts that risk is effectively pooled, can undertake major programs.
3. The primary motivation for inventive activity is the profits that may ultimately accrue to new innovations; for this motivation to be sufficient, firms must occupy a strong enough market position to ensure that the fruits of inventive activity will be exploited.

Attempts to examine patterns of inventive activity are hampered by two important problems. Primary is the difficulty of measurement. The "amount" of "inventiveness" that occurs in a firm or market simply is not quantifiable in any fully satisfactory way; and the available proxies, such as patents and research and development expenditure, have significant drawbacks. Second, but also important, is the theoret-

---

[50] "A Commentary on 'Administered Prices,'" *Administered Prices: A Compendium on Public Policy*, Subcommittee on Antitrust and Monopoly (Washington, D.C.: G.P.O., 1963), p. 22.

ical vagueness of the Schumpeterian "hypothesis."[51] That **some** relationship between inventiveness, on the one hand, and firm and market structure, on the other, exists may be inferred from Schumpeter's writings. But the relationship, apart from its general direction, is formless. How it should be tested is therefore unclear.

Despite these difficulties, the importance of defining the influences on inventive activity has produced extensive empirical research. One of the early contributions, by Henry H. Villard, was based simply on the following observation.

The percentage of companies undertaking research increases steadily with the size of the firm: 8 percent of those with fewer than 100 employees, 22 percent of those with fewer than 500, 42 percent of those with fewer than 1,000, 60 percent of those with fewer than 5,000, and 94 percent of those with more than 5,000 employees were reported by a National Science Foundation Survey for 1953–1954 as conducting research and development.[52]

This information, in addition to Villard's intuitive sympathy with the Schumpeterian position, led him to conclude that large, oligopolistic firms engage in relatively more research effort than their smaller counterparts in competitively structured industry.

Such fragmentary evidence, while unpersuasive, does raise pertinent questions about the meaning and appropriate measurement of inventive activity. Jacob Schmookler in an article critical of Villard, showed that, within the group of firms conducting research, **expenditures** on such programs were proportionately about the same for "small" as for "large" companies.[53] A study by James S. Worley indicated that although larger companies hire **more** research and development personnel than do smaller firms, their staffs do **not** in general consist of **proportionately more** R&D employees than the staffs of smaller companies.[54] And Hamberg, utilizing a similar measure of R&D "intensity," concluded that ". . . there is no solid evidence in support of the 'Schumpeterian' hypothesis."[55]

The measures of inventive activity utilized by these authors all reflect in some way the inventive **effort** or **input** of firms. Such indexes are suggestive but have serious drawbacks. What companies define as "R&D" spending may have little to do with attempts to invent or innovate; in some industries, for example, much R&D is devoted to compliance with government regulations affecting such things as product safety and environmental effects, or it may reflect public subsidies. This sort of

---

[51] Readers of Schumpeter's main work may be surprised to see how little he had to say on the issue. The hypothesis has been defined and refined largely by his followers. See Joseph A. Schumpeter, *Capitalism, Socialism and Democracy*, 3rd ed. (New York: Harper, 1950).

[52] "Competition, Oligopoly and Research," *Journal of Political Economy*, **66** (December 1958), 483–497; quotation at p. 486.

[53] "Bigness, Fewness and Research," *Journal of Political Economy*, **67** (December 1959), 628–635.

[54] "Industrial Research and the New Competition," *Journal of Political Economy*, **69** (April 1961), 183–186.

[55] D. Hamberg, "Size of Firm, Oligopoly and Research: The Evidence," *Canadian Journal of Economics and Political Science*, **30** (February 1964), 62–75.

spending may prove socially useful, but it is unlikely to coincide with technological progress.

The second difficulty with R&D measures is that, even if they are a tolerable index of inventive input, they may tell us little about results or output. A given proportion of research spending or employment is likely to yield widely varying outcomes across firms and industries. Yet is may be suggested quite cogently that it is precisely the outcomes in which society is interested.

A study by Edwin Mansfield attempted to utilize a more direct measure of inventiveness by examining the relationships between innovations and firm size and market structure in three industries (iron and steel, petroleum refining, and bituminous coal).[56] Mansfield's findings do not support any simplified hypothesis about inventive activity. In petroleum and coal, for example, the largest firms accounted for "a disproportionately large share of the innovations," but this was not the case in steel, where their contribution was disproportionately small.

In a study of the ethical drug industry, William S. Comanor used the proportion of company sales accounted for by new products as a proxy for inventive output.[57] His conclusion was that substantial **diseconomies** of scale in R&D were encountered "even by moderately sized firms." The Schumpeterian hypothesis, in other words, did not do a good job of describing new product patterns in this industry.

More general evidence on inventiveness has been presented by F. M. Scherer,[58] who took **patents** as a measure of inventive activity. This measure contains shortcomings—different firms or industries may, for example, have different propensities to patent a given "quantity" of invention. Scherer's findings failed almost uniformly to support the hypothesis that large, semimonopolistic firms are "more" inventive than other companies. He concluded that the major determinant of inventive output is technical opportunity. Inventive output was found to increase with firm sales, "but generally at a less than proportional rate." And no systematic relationship to market power or a number of other factors was discovered. In a later study,[59] Scherer found somewhat more ambiguous results in testing for relationships between market concentration and employment of research scientists and engineers.

There is some theoretical reason to believe that the effect of competition on inventive activity is dichotomous. At one extreme, the Schumpeterian contention holds. That is, firms in highly competitive markets have neither the funds nor the incentive to undertake the ambitous R&D programs that are likely to yield important

[56] "Size of Firm, Market Structure, and Innovation," *Journal of Political Economy,* **71** (December 1963), 556–576.

[57] "Research and Technological Change in the Pharmaceutical Industry," *Review of Economics and Statistics,* **47** (May 1965), 182–190.

[58] "Firm Size, Market Structure, Opportunity, and the Output of Patent Inventions," *American Economic Review,* **55** (December 1965), 1097–1125.

[59] "Market Structure and the Employment of Scientists and Engineers," *American Economic Review,* **57** (June 1967), 524–530.

progress. At the other extreme, however, the well-insulated monopolist also lacks a strong incentive to invent and innovate; the spur of competition, actual or potential, is missing.

The expectation is, then, that inventiveness will flourish in the "in between" cases where neither "too much" nor "too little" competition is present. This is an oversimplified argument, but it has found some empirical support. Specifically, it appears that the threat of entry, rather than the current level of market concentration, may be the critical determinant of inventive efforts.[60]

It is difficult to draw clear-cut conclusions about firm size, market structure, and inventive activity on the basis of the evidence to date.[61] Several suspicions emerge, however. The relationship between technological progress and structural variables may be highly idiosyncratic in the sense that it is quite different in one type of industry than another.[62] This implies that firm and market structures do not exert a consistent influence on inventiveness across industries and that attempts to test for general patterns will therefore show the kind of inconsistent results we have seen.

A second suspicion is that the shape of the progress–structure relationship is not only variable but in some instances quite complex. Relatively simple statistical tests, for example, for linearity or threshhold effects, might therefore prove inappropriate in certain places and times.

When all is said and done, however, it must be noted that evidence in support of the Schumpeterian hypothesis is very meager. It simply does not appear that increasing the size of firms or the concentration of markets yields generally disproportionate gains in inventive inputs or outputs. As usual, however, some caveats are very much in order. Empirical investigators have, of necessity, used highly imperfect data to test a contention that is not very well specified.[63] As weak as the evidence may be to date, we cannot be certain that clearer and more useful results will not emerge in the future. Surely, few observers would contend that firm size and market structure have **no** impact on progressiveness anywhere in the economy. The question—still open—is whether such impact follows any regular or systematic pattern.

---

[60] See William S. Comanor, "Market Structure, Product Differentiation and Industrial Research," *Quarterly Journal of Economics*, **81** (November 1967), 639–657.

[61] Lucid surveys of the evidence will be found in John M. Vernon, *Market Structure and Industrial Performance: A Review of Statistical Findings.* (Boston: Allyn and Bacon, 1972); and Morton I. Kamien and Nancy L. Schwartz, *Market Structure and Innovation* (Cambridge: Cambridge University Press, 1982), Chapter 3. Even the best surveys in this area, however, may become quickly dated.

[62] Such an interpretation fits Scherer's findings (footnote 58), and is supported in a recent study by Ronald E. Shrieves, "Market Structure and Innovation: A New Perspective," *Journal of Industrial Economics*, **26** (June 1978), 329–347. Shrieves discerns an "ambiguous" role for concentration that varies with the characteristics of industry groups.

[63] Franklin M. Fisher and Peter Temin have argued that empirical tests of the Schumpeterian hypothesis have been inappropriate and that the implications commonly drawn from the hypothesis are inconsistent with Schumpeter's own statements. "Returns to Scale in Research and Development: What Does the Schumpeterian Hypothesis Imply?" *Journal of Political Economy*, **81** (January/February 1973), 56–70.

EXPLAINING STRUCTURE ITSELF

The traditional

$$\text{Structure} \rightarrow \text{Conduct} \rightarrow \text{Performance}$$

paradigm of industrial organization tended to ignore what is now recognized as a crucial question: what determines structure itself? We shall take a brief look first at the factual picture and then proceed to the empirical causal clues.

The Factual Picture

Aggregate Concentration   Aggregate concentration refers to the share of **national** economic activity accounted for by the largest firms (frequently the top 100 or 200). It is thus computationally similar to the top-4 or top-8 ratio for an industry, but conveys a much different type of information.

A frequently posed question is whether aggregate concentration in the United States is increasing over time. Perhaps surprisingly, the answer is unclear, varying somewhat with (1) the sector(s) of the economy examined, (2) the years that are compared, (3) the measure of activity size that is used, and (4) the number of top firms included. Table 9.1, for example, shows little increase in the value-added share of the top 50, 100, or 200 manufacturing corporations between 1963 and 1972; but a sharp increase between 1947 and later comparison dates; and a perceptible, if smaller, rise between 1958 and subsequent years. In contrast, William S. Comanor's data show that the asset shares of the largest nonfinancial corporations were "relatively stable, and perhaps even declined slightly" during the period 1958 through 1975.[64] This discrepancy is apparently attributable more to the scope of Comanor's sample—nonfinancial corporations include sectors other than manufacturing—than to the different size measures (assets versus value added). A considerable number of series confined to manufacturing have shown mild to moderate increases in aggregate concentration for subperiods within 1909 through 1968[65]; but the manufacturing sector itself has declined in importance relative to the economy as a whole.

The most recent findings, by Lawrence J. White, indicate that whatever may have occurred since the early part of the century, aggregate concentration has been stable during the past two decades.[66] White concludes a review of various sectors of the economy by observing that aggregate concentration "has not increased in the 1960s and 1970s," and "if anything . . . has probably decreased."

[64]"Conglomerate Mergers: Considerations for Public Policy," in Roger Blair and Robert F. Lanzillotti, Eds., *The Conglomerate Corporation: A Public Problem?* (Cambridge: Oelgeschlager, Gunn, and Hain, 1981).

[65]Several are reproduced in John M. Blair, *"Economic Concentration"* (New York: Harcourt Brace Jovanovich, 1972), Chapter 4.

[66]"What Has Been Happening to Aggregate Concentration in the United States?" *Journal of Industrial Economics,* **29** (March 1981), 223–230.

Table 9.1   Percentage of Value Added Accounted for
by Largest Manufacturing Corporations

	Year					
	1972	1970	1967	1963	1958	1947
50 largest	25	24	25	25	23	17
100 largest	33	33	33	33	30	23
200 largest	43	43	42	41	38	30

Source: 1972 Census of Manufacturers (Washington, D.C.: GPO, 1972)

It is clear from the data that, whether or not aggregate concentration has been rising at certain times, it is in some absolute sense extremely high. There were, as of the middle 1970s, about 1.7 million active corporations in the United States. The top 100 of these—roughly six thousandths of 1 percent of the population—account for one quarter of value added and more than 30 percent of the assets. The degree of size inequality is large indeed!

The obvious question concerns the implications of this apparent concentration of economic resources. Should it cause us concern? Some observers contend that in a strict economic sense the answer is no. Aggregate concentration tells us essentially nothing about the state of competition **within markets**. Substantially higher levels of aggregate concentration than we now see would be quite consistent with a highly competitive market system (and, incidentally, with low market-concentration ratios). Moreover, increasing concentration nationally need not imply similar market increases.[67] Since our notions of competition are tied to markets, one might argue that data on the aggregate are irrelevant to competitive considerations.

The objection to this sort of argument is made on what is sometimes termed ''noneconomic'' grounds,[68] more a matter of social or political ideology than of concern about competitive effects. Comanor, for example, refers to ''an instinctive fear of large aggregations of private power'' in America, even where the aggregation cannot be shown to inflict immediate economic damage. Many regard the basis of such fear as quite real, although theories linking corporate size to social and political control or ''clout'' are not especially well developed.[69]

---

[67]The absence of any necessary link between aggregate and market concentration may be seen as follows. Suppose that the economy is dominated by 200 huge corporations scattered among 2 million minuscule companies. If the huge ones are highly diversified, each competing against most or all of the others across a broad range of markets, each and every market may be extremely competitive, containing scores of equally matched rivals. Yet the relative size of the top 200 will appear as a very high level of aggregate concentration. For some pertinent observations, see Sanford Rose, ''Bigness is a Numbers Game,'' *Fortune,* **80** (November 1969), 113ff.

[68]The quotation marks are intended to suggest that the distinction between ''noneconomic'' and ''economic'' arguments are less clear than many believe. Some economists—though perhaps a small minority—contend that virtually all human decisions can be usefully treated as economic decisions.

[69]For some evidence on this issue, see Lester M. Salamon and John J. Siegfried, ''Economic Power and Political Influence: The Impact of Industry Structure on Public Policy,'' *American Political Science Review,* **71** (September 1977), 1026–1043.

One's reaction to high aggregate concentration is thus, at least partly, a matter of judgment and values. A pertinent question, regardless of values, is whether existing concentrations of power are **efficient**. If so, we may well tolerate the concentrations; if not, the issue is muddier. As we shall see, however, to determine whether particular levels of size or power are justified by efficiency, is no simple task.

Market Concentration Market concentration ratios for some important manufacturing industries are shown in Table 9.2. Although the information in this table is fragmentary, two observations turn out to be generally quite accurate. First, concentration is in some absolute sense high; the ratios we see clearly do not reflect "atomistic" structures akin to the competitive model. Second, the changes over time point to no obvious trend; some concentration ratios increase, others fall, but most do "nothing much."

Table 9.2 Concentration Ratios: Percentage of Value of Shipments Held by the Largest Firms in Selected Manufacturing Industries

S.I.C.	Industry	Year	Top Four Firms	Top Eight Firms
2043	Cereal breakfast foods	1972	90	98
		1963	86	96
		1954	88	95
2111	Cigarettes	1972	84	N.A.
		1963	80	100
		1954	82	99+
3334	Primary aluminum	1972	79	92
		1963	N.A.	100
		1954	100	100
3635	Household vacuum cleaners	1972	75	91
		1963	81	96
3011	Tires and inner tubes	1972	73	90
		1963	70	89
3331	Primary copper	1972	72	N.A.
		1963	78	98
2892	Explosives	1972	67	86
		1963	72	86
		1954	79	92
3411	Metal cans	1972	66	79
		1963	74	85
		1947	78	96
2841	Soap and other detergents	1972	62	74
		1963	72	80
2082	Malt beverages	1972	52	70
		1963	34	52
		1954	27	41
2085	Distilled liquor, except brandy	1972	47	68
		1963	58	74
		1954	64	79

Table 9.2   (*continued*)

S.I.C.	Industry	Year	Top Four Firms	Top Eight Firms
3312	Blast furnaces and steel mills	1972	45	65
		1963	48	67
		1954	55	71
2522	Metal office furniture	1972	42	54
		1963	33	50
		1954	46	63
2041	Flour and other grain mill products	1972	33	53
		1963	35	50
		1954	40	52
3161	Luggage	1972	39	50
		1963	31	40
2911	Petroleum refining	1972	31	56
		1963	34	56
		1954	33	56
2051	Bread, cake, and related products	1972	29	39
		1963	23	35
		1954	20	40
2011	Meatpacking plants	1972	22	37
		1963	31	42
		1954	39	51
2851	Paints and allied products	1972	22	34
		1963	23	34
2026	Fluid milk	1972	18	25
		1963	23	30
		1954	22	28
2721	Newspapers	1972	17	28
		1963	15	22
		1954	18	24
2086	Bottled and canned soft drinks	1972	14	21
		1963	12	17
		1954	10	14
2335	Women's and misses' dresses	1972	9	13
		1963	6	9
2752	Commercial printing, lithographic	1972	4	8
		1963	6	10

Source: U.S. Census of Manufacturers (1972)

Scherer calculates a weighted four-firm concentration ratio for all manufacturing industries of 39.2 percent in 1972,[70] and the median appears to be slightly lower. The bulk of four-digit industries fall into the CR_4 range 20% to 59%, and there is a good deal of variation within broader (two-digit) industry groups. Electrical ma-

[70] F. M. Scherer, *Industrial Market Structure and Economic Performance*, 2d ed., (New York: Rand McNally, 1980), p. 69.

chinery and transportation equipment, for example, are characterized by highly concentrated four-digit industries for the most part; while apparel, lumber, and leather products are much lower.

Intensive statistical analyses reveal few consistent trends over time. Slight increases in the average value of CR_4 have been noted by Scherer and others; yet Scherer also observes that the proportion of value added in manufacturing that originates in industries with CR_4 above 50 percent has declined slightly since 1954.[71] Most writers would no doubt agree with Mueller and Hamm that large samples of manufacturing industries "display a remarkable degree of stability" in concentration.[72]

Do existing levels and trends of market concentration pose a public policy problem? The answer to this important question depends crucially upon the determinants of existing concentration. If concentration is "dictated" or "justified" by efficiency considerations, then even the Jeffersonians among us may be willing to put up with it. If not, however, the question is then whether public efforts to deconcentrate industry should be seriously considered.

Determinants of Concentration and Concentration Change

Consider the following specific questions:

1. Why are there more than 1400 domestic manufacturers of farm machinery but only 5 of automobiles?
2. Why do 4 companies dominate industries such as cereals, cigarettes, and aluminum, but not dresses, butter, or cardboard boxes?
3. Why has concentration been increasing somewhat in consumer goods industries, but not in producer goods?

The Causal Question.   These questions suggest the more general task: to explain variations in the level of concentration among industries and in changes over time. Before examining the evidence, it will be useful to note again the underlying arguments. We would expect to find concentration ranging from "very high" in some industries to "very low" in others, for several reasons.

Scale or Size Economies.   This is perhaps the most obvious possibility. In some industries it is more efficient to operate on a relatively large scale. The reasons vary: for example, increased specialization or better use of "lumpy" capital. If such efficiencies are important in the sense that an economic scale for the firm is large relative to the market, then large firms and a concentrated structure will tend to result. In terms of Figure 9.2 (a rather extreme case), we might expect to find one large firm operating in the area of quantity q, or perhaps two in the area of q'. But it would be unlikely, and undesirable, to have several smaller companies producing at

[71] Ibid., p. 68.
[72] See footnote 24.

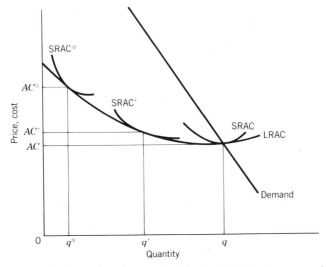

Figure 9.2 A market characterized by important scale economies.

q^*. One possibility, then, is that different levels of market concentration reflect differences in efficient size structures across markets.

Pecuniary Economies. As we have noted, pecuniary economies send the same message to firms: size is efficient. This "efficiency," however, may be largely private rather than social; thus the desirability of the concentration that occurs where pecuniary gains are important will be dubious.

Collusion. Collusion (or other forms of abusive conduct) may play a role in market concentration, but cause and effect is difficult to sort out. Recall that firms might collude, for example, to set prices so as to discourage entry; this could tend to preserve and enhance the concentration of affected markets. Traditional analysis, however, postulates that high concentration leads *to* collusion (this is the link upon which many studies of concentration and profitability rely).

"Competitive Superiority." Certain firms may do a better job than others of serving consumer tastes or lowering costs. If so, they are likley to grow at the expense of less efficient rivals, increase their shares of the market, and contribute to higher concentration.[73] We shall therefore observe variations in concentration not because size as such is more efficient in some markets, but because in some markets efficient firms attain large size. Why does this happen only in certain markets? One possibility is that executive talent exists in limited supply. There may simply be few managers capable of driving their firms to excellent performance (and the opportu-

---

[73] See Harold Demsetz, "Industry Structure, Market Rivalry, and Public Policy," *Journal of Law & Economics,* **16** (April 1973), 1–9; and Sam Peltzman, "The Gains and Losses from Industrial Concentration," *Journal of Law & Economics,* **20** (October 1977), 229–263.

nities for doing so may not exist equally in all markets). Where they do, a degree of dominance and high concentration emerges.

"Market Failure." High concentration may result from the failure of certain markets to check accumulations of power, where such power is **not** the result of efficient performance.[74] One possibility is what Williamson refers to as "default failure." Certain firms may rise to the top not because they are efficient in absolute terms, but because their rivals are inept. Alternatively, firms may enjoy current dominance because of "historic accident"—some "old" event propels a company to the forefront, from which it is never dislodged.[75] Where such market failures occur, we are likely to see high concentration.

Stochastic Processes (or "Luck"). This might work to yield large firms and high concentration in some markets but not others.[76] The argument here is precisely the same as that discussed earlier in relation to profit rates. Indeed, a single stochastic process (string of luck) could produce a few dominant firms, high market concentration, *and* high profits.

Mergers. It is readily observed that concentration levels and trends in certain industries are directly affected by merger waves. Steel and petroleum refining, for example, became highly concentrated in this fashion many decades ago. This sort of causality is of limited interest, however, for it says little more than that increases in concentration follow events that increase concentration. The more pertinent question is why concentration-raising mergers occur at some times and places but not at others.

The Evidence. It is apparent that varying levels and trends of industry concentration may be due in principle to numerous causes. We turn now to the empirical evidence, which is extensive but far from definitive.

Attempts to measure the importance of scale economies (discussed in Chapter 8) have been actively pursued since Bain's early (1956) work.[77] The significance of these efforts within the context of this discussion, is plain: If existing firm and industry structures are closely tied to the need for efficient scale, then there is a strong presumption that these structures are economically necessary. If, on the other hand, a clear efficiency justification of observed structures does not exist, the question of their desirability—and of appropriate public policies—remains open.

Bain's initial study presented "engineering estimates" based on expert opinion. The major finding was that the minimum efficient size (MES) of an optimal plant was typically small relative to the industry as a whole; and that economies of

---

[74] For detailed discussion, see Oliver E. Williamson, "Dominant Firms and the Monopoly Problem: Market Failure Considerations," *Harvard Law Review*, **85** (June 1972), 1512–1531.

[75] One might (and should) ask why the firm is not dislodged if its current dominance is "undeserved." This is presumably where the market fails. A properly functioning market will not permit dominance to persist through sheer inertia.

[76] For an interesting experiment suggesting that this alternative has some plausibility, see F. M. Scherer, footnote 68, pp. 145ff.

[77] Joe S. Bain, *Barriers to New Competiton* (Cambridge: Harvard University Press, 1956).

Table 9.3 Plant Scale Economies: Selected Estimates of Minimum Efficient Size (MES) by Industry[a]

Industry	MES as Percentage of U.S. Market Demand	Average Size of Top Four U.S. Firms (As Percentage of Market)
Chewing gum	6.7	21.8
Distilled liquor	4.2	11.8
Cigarettes	6.6	21.0
Tires and tubes	5.0	18.3
Tufted rugs	0.7	5.0
Meatpacking	0.7	5.5
Petroleum refining	1.8	7.5
Steel	1.8	11.3
Shoes	0.3	7.0
Glass containers	1.5	13.8

[a]Notice that in each of the industries shown, the average size of the four top firms is far larger than the MES suggests is needed for efficient operation. This does not necessarily mean that such firms are inefficiently large, but only that their size cannot be explained by plant-based scale economies as reflected in these MES estimates.

Sources: Joe S. Bain, *Barriers to New Competition* (Cambridge, Mass.: Harvard University Press, 1956): William S. Comanor and Thomas A. Wilson, ''Advertising, Market Structure, and Performance,'' *Review of Economics and Statistics,* **49** (November 1967), 423–440; H. Michael Mann, ''Seller Concentration, Barriers to Entry, and Rates of Return in Thirty Industries,'' *Review of Economics and Statistics,* **48,** (August 1966), 296–307; Leonard W. Weiss, ''Optimal Plant Size and the Extent of Suboptimal Capacity,'' in Robert T. Masson and P. David Qualls, Eds., *Essays on Industrial Organization in Honor of Joe S. Bain* (Cambridge, Mass.: Ballinger, 1975); and Roger Sherman and Robert Tollison, ''Advertising and Profitability,'' *Review of Ecnomics and Statistics,* **49** (November 1971), 397–407.

multiplant operation were in most instances slight, nonexistent, or not readily estimated. Other investigators have reached conclusions that are not markedly different.[78] Most recently, Scherer et al. have estimated minimum optimal plant scales for 12 industries in several countries.[79] The results for the United States point to a minor role for scale economies in most cases, and to multiplant efficiencies that are ''at most slight.'' Some examples of MES estimates are shown in Table 9.3.

Efficient size estimates have also been attempted using other methodologies. The ''survivor technique,'' for example, examines the output shares of plants in different size categories, and terms ''efficient'' those categories that are increasing their shares (i.e., ''surviving'') over time.[80] Some typical findings of ''survivorship''

[78] See, for example, C. F. Pratten, *Economies of Scale in Manufacturing Industry* (Cambridge: Cambridge University Press, 1971); Leonard W. Weiss ''Optimal Plant Size and the Extent of Suboptimal Capacity,'' in Robert T. Masson and P. David Qualls, Eds., *Essays on Industrial Organization in Honor of Joe S. Bain* (Cambridge, Mass.: Ballinger, 1976); and F. M. Scherer, Alan Beckenstein, Erich Kaufer, and R. D. Murphy, *The Economics of Multi-Plant Operation: An Internation Comparisons Study,* (Cambridge, Mass.: Harvard University Press, 1975).

[79] *Ibid.*

[80] This technique was suggested by George J. Stigler, ''The Economies of Scale,'' *Journal of Law & Economics,* **1** (October 1958), 54–71.

studies are that (1) the MES is small where it can be estimated, but that (2) estimates frequently are impossible.[81] Still other types of studies based in the similar assumption that **existing** plant sizes are **efficient** tend also to show relatively small MES estimates.[82]

The evidence relating levels of industry concentration to scale economies is thus unimpressive. Estimates of minimum efficient plant size seldom suggest that existing firms are inefficiently small. It is, of course, possible that multiplant rather than within-plant economies account for observed firm size, but here again the evidence is weak. Problems with the data are legion, and confident efficient-size estimates are lacking for many industries. But with these qualifications in mind, the fact remains that a forceful scale-economies argument for existing levels of market concentration can seldom be made. Truly atomistic market structures in most manufacturing industries would be inefficient; but it does not appear that size-related efficiencies require the **degree** of concentration that we see in most cases. At the very least, the empirical justification has not yet been made.

As we have noted, the absence of a strong scale-economies argument does not preclude the possibility that existing firm sizes and market structures are in some sense efficient (it simply means that the efficiency, if it exists, is not "size specific"). Unfortunately, however, alternative hypotheses are not often amenable to straightforward empirical tests.

Statistically, it is possible to obtain reasonably "good" explanations of variations in concentration among industries. Similarly, changes in concentration over time appear quite closely correlated with factors such as net entry, initial concentration level, advertising intensity, industry growth, and change in the midpoint plant size of the industry.[83] Some of these relationships are interesting (e.g., the tendency for concentration to fall in rapidly growing industries), but in many cases they tell us little about cause and effect. Indeed, some of what we see is mere tautology: Changes in concentration are related statistically to entry and changes in midpoint plant size simply because these are elements **of** the concentration index. A recent study by Caves and Porter deliberately avoids such "identities" but is largely unsuccessful in finding an alternative empirical explanation of changes in concentration.[84]

One curious fact is the tendency of concentration to increase more in consumer goods industries than in producer goods during recent years. Although some writers

---

[81] William G. Shepherd, "What Does the Survivor Technique Show About Economies of Scale?" *Southern Economic Journal,* **34** (July 1967), 113–122. See also Thomas R. Saving, "Estimation of Optimum Size of Plant by the Survivor Technique," *Quarterly Journal of Economics* **75** (November 1961), 569–607.

[82] Comanor and Wilson, footnote 12. See also Roger Sherman and Robert Tollison, "Advertising and Profitability," *Review of Economics and Statistics,* **49** (November 1971), 397–407.

[83] Mueller and Hamm, footnote 24. Asch, footnote 24. William G. Shepherd, "Trends of Concentration in American Manufacturing Industries, 1947–1958," *Review of Economics and Statistics,* **46** (March 1964), 200–212; Leonard W. Weiss, "Factors in Changing Concentration," *Review of Economics and Statistics,* **45** (February 1963), 70–77.

[84] Richard E. Caves and Michael E. Porter, "The Dynamics of Changing Seller Concentration," *Journal of Industrial Economics,* **29** (September 1980), 1–15.

have attributed this to heavier advertising in the consumer sector, neither the evidence nor the theory underlying this interpretation is fully convincing. The fact is that our ability to explain variations in market structure is to date quite limited—a most unfortunate failing in light of the policy significance of the issue.

An important question now becomes whether the determinants of structure are in fact empirically distinguishable. That is, have our efforts fallen short because we have not (yet) done the job properly? Or is the job one that cannot, in principle, be done? We shall return to this question in Chapter 10.

EQUITY

In recent years a pertinent criticism of much economic research has begun to surface with some frequency. Economics has focused largely on **efficiency** of production and of resource allocation. Yet the interest of citizens extends to issues of **equity** or "fairness," something about which most economists have had little to say. The economics discipline may thus be in danger of examining certain questions in minute detail, while largely ignoring other issues that are of great—perhaps primary— importance to many people.

What is "fair" or "unfair" is, of course, a subjective matter. This is undoubtedly one reason that economists, often loathe to impose "value judgments" that may appear "unscientific," have stayed away from the subject. In two areas, however, there has been some investigation of empirical relationships that bear on issues of equity: the distribution of wealth and discrimination in employment.

Comanor and Smiley published in 1975 the first major attempt to measure the effect of monopoly power on the distribution of wealth.[85] Although forced to make some important assumptions about unobservable magnitudes, the authors were able to conclude that monopoly profits have contributed substantially to the severe inequality of the wealth distribution; that is, the disproportionate share of all wealth controlled by the very wealthiest families is in significant degree a monopoly phenomenon. Although the Comanor–Smiley assumptions are admittedly "heroic," their procedures were conservative. Assumptions were chosen that would, if anything, tend to understate the monopoly–wealth effect. One's view of these findings will depend upon one's definition of the "fair" or "correct" distribution of wealth (the dreaded value jdugment!); but the findings are surely relevant to people with an interest in the topic, regardless of viewpoint.[86]

Discrimination in employment as it relates to industry organization has been studied more extensively. Is there more discrimination, say, against women or blacks, where power is concentrated? Economic theory suggests that this might be the case.

---

[85] William S. Comanor and Robert H. Smiley, "Monopoly and the Distribution of Wealth," *Quarterly Journal of Economics*, **89** (May 1975), 177–194.

[86] If, however, monopoly profits were largely dissipated in the effort to obtain and maintain monopoly positions, the conclusions of Comanor and Smiley are subject to challenge. See Richard A. Posner, "The Social Costs of Monopoly and Regulation," *Journal of Political Economy*, **83** (August 1975), 807–827.

Companies with the discretion to exploit via high prices or to waste some resources also have the ability to pursue biased hiring, salary, and promotion policies. Competitive firms, on the other hand, can do only what the market dictates. They do not have the leeway to choose to discriminate.

The empirical question is whether firms with monopoly power do, in fact, take advantage of their ability to discriminate. The answer to date is mixed. Some studies suggest an association between market power and discrimination, while others find no clear-cut pattern.[87] The true picture is uncertain, in part because discrimination is a rather elusive empirical magnitude.[88] But this is one area in which more detailed and sophisticated empirical analysis may well yield a more definitive conclusion in the near future.

MARKET CONDUCT

As we have seen, there are reasons to expect market structure to influence conduct (the particular stratagems adopted by firms) and conduct, in turn, to act as a proximate cause of performance. Difficulties in observing conduct directly, however, make these expectations almost impossible to test in a fully reliable manner.

To define market conduct in such a way that it can be measured—expressed in quantitative terms—is the primary task. One interesting effort, by James M. Clabault and John F. Burton, related the incidence of Sherman Act penalties to industry concentration, as shown in Table 9.4.[89] Penalties under the Sherman Act are largely those assessed upon conviction for price fixing and other kinds of conspiratorial conduct, and thus constitute a rough index of collusive conduct **as defined by Federal antitrust agencies and the courts**.

Column 1 shows the distribution of all industries by concentration groups. If Sherman Act violations are essentially random with respect to concentration, that is, if the propensity of an industry to violate has nothing to do with concentration level,

---

[87] For interesting and somewhat varied findings, see William G. Shepherd and Sharon G. Levin, "Managerial Discrimination in Large Firms," *Review of Economics and Statistics,* **55** (November 1973), 412–422; William S. Comanor, "Racial Discrimination in American Industry," *Economica,* **40** (November 1973), 363–378; Sharon M. Oster, "Industry Differences in the Level of Discrimination Against Women," *Quarterly Journal of Economics,* **89** (May 1975), 215–229; Sharon G. Levin and Stanford L. Levin, "Profit Maximization and Discrimination," *Industrial Organization Review,* **4** (1976), 108–116; and William R. Johnson, "Racial Wage Discrimination and Industrial Structure," *Bell Journal of Economics,* **9** (Spring 1978), 70–81.

[88] Discrimination in employment means, roughly, that treatment of employees is based upon some economically **irrelevant** factor (such as race or sex). But this can be a difficult circumstance to isolate. Suppose, for example, that women and blacks are paid relatively low salaries in a particular firm or industry. Does this indicate discrimination, or does it mean that white males have stronger job qualifications in this area? Measurement of qualifications is a tricky task, yet it must be done in order to reach a conclusion. (For an instructive approach, see Burton G. Malkiel and Judith A. Malkiel, "Male–Female Pay Differentials in Professional Employment," *American Economic Review,* **63** (September 1973), 693–705). Notice that even a finding that salary differences reflect differences in qualifications would raise a further question: Why does a particular group have inferior qualifications on average? And is this perhaps the result of discriminatory treatment elsewhere? The empirical problems raised by these questions may be reduced in importance, but not fully avoided by examining large samples of industries or firms.

[89] *Sherman Act Indictments 1955–1965: A Legal and Economic Analysis* (New York: Federal Legal Publications, 1966).

Table 9.4 Distribution of Manufacturing Industries by Concentration Ratios and Sherman Act Penalties

Concentration Ratio, Top 4 Firms	(1) All Industries		(2) Industries with Criminal Penalties		(3) Industries with Criminal Penalties Weighted by Cases	
	Number	Percentage	Number	Percentage	Number	Percentage
80—100	14	3.6%	2	3.1%	2	1.6%
70— 79	15	3.9	2	3.1	5	3.9
60— 69	30	7.8	1	1.6	1	0.8
50— 59	31	8.0	3	4.7	13	10.2
40— 49	47	12.2	5	7.8	8	6.3
30— 39	59	15.3	14	21.9	26	20.5
20— 29	88	22.8	19	29.7	39	30.7
0— 19	102	26.4	18	18.1	33	26.0
Total	386	100%	64	100%	127	100%

Source: Burton and Clabault, footnote 90, p. 130.

then the distribution of violations, both unweighted, as in column 2, and weighted as in 3, should be about the same as the distribution of industries. It appears, however, that the distributions are different. Column 3 shows that only 6.3 percent of the cases in which penalties were imposed were in industries with concentration of 60 percent or above; yet 18.3 percent of all industries fall within this concentration range. In other words, there seems to be a disproportionately low incidence of violations among industries of very high concentration. This fact may be interpreted in various ways. One possibility is that these industries are so close-knit that the kind of formal, overt conspiracy most often punished by the Sherman Act is unnecessary. Where the concentration level is extremely high, collusive modes of conduct may be sufficiently subtle and informal to escape prosecution. A second possibility is that highly concentrated industries may tend to be under relatively close antitrust scrutiny, which in itself deters firms from entering into clearly illegal actions.

Studies by this author and Joseph J. Seneca have tried further to define the links between collusive conduct and structure and performance patterns.[90] Among the main findings are:

1. Collusive firms are less profitable and slower growing than noncolluders.
2. The colluders are also larger than noncolluders, and tend to be located in industries of low advertising intensity.

[90]Peter Asch and Joseph J. Seneca,"Characteristics of Collusive Firms," *Journal of Industrial Economics,* **23** (March 1975); 223–237; "Is Collusion Profitable?" *Review of Economics and Statistics,* **58** (February 1976), 1–12. See, for some further empirical explorations; W. Bruce Erickson, "Economics of Price Fixing," *Antitrust Law and Economics Review,* **2** (Spring 1969), 83–122; George A. Hay and Daniel Kelley, "An Empirical Survey of Price-Fixing Conspiracies," *Journal of Law & Economics,* **17** (April 1974), 13–34.

3. Consumer goods firms are **more** likely to collude if their primary markets are highly concentrated; but producer goods firms collude **less** where concentration is high.

Although the results are of interest, however, the fundamental measurement problem remains. We cannot examine "collusion" in any pure economic sense but must, rather, observe episodes in which a **legal** finding of collusion has occurred. This limitation greatly complicates the interpretation of findings, in part because one cannot know whether observed relationships are a function of collusive conduct or of legal policies undertaken in response to that conduct.[91]

CONCLUSION

As this relatively brief survey suggests, many empirical questions concerning the structure and behavior of firms and markets remain unanswered today. In some instances, better answers will emerge as evidence mounts; in others, the picture is likely to remain unclear, either because measurement problems are insoluble given existing data limitations, or because the relationships being investigated are themselves obscure.

A final, important, category of questions will remain open simply because no amount of evidence (no matter how high in quality) can provide answers. This has to do with the **interpretation** of observed relationships and specifically with matters of cause and effect. The debates frequently revolve around empirical findings, but are not empirically resolvable. Some of the more important issues for public policy fall into this category, and are the main subject of the next chapter.

---

[91] For example: do the low profit rates of colluding firms mean that collusion is an unprofitable activity, or that the Justice Department tends to prosecute unsuccessful (thus unprofitable) kinds of collusion? One possible way of sorting out such complications is pursued by Robert M. Feinberg, "Antitrust Enforcement and Subsequent Price Behavior," *Review of Economics and Statistics,* **62** (November 1980), 609–612.

CHAPTER 10

Empirical Evidence and Public Policy

The empirical evidence bearing on industrial oranization and behavior serves two distinct purposes. First, it tells us something about the validity of the theoretical framework from which our hypotheses are drawn. Second—and more important in the context of this discussion—it provides some indication of the consequences of policies that affect the organization and behavior of markets.

As we have seen, empirical measurement is beset by a range of conceptual and practical problems. Theoretical suggestions may be difficult to translate into testable hypotheses. Data deficiencies are common. And even hypotheses that are in principle testable may prove difficult to examine. For these reasons alone the interpretation of empirical findings is often not straightforward. Given such problems, mild optimism seems justified when one considers the relationship of existing evidence to the theoretical apparatus. In the words of Clabault and Burton:

If one were to be generous about the justifiable conclusions which can be drawn from the empirical studies made of the American economy . . . it could be argued that there is a relationship between structure and performance, and this relationship seems to be roughly what the neoclassical economist expected: i.e., the more firms in an industry the better.[1]

Although other observers might disagree vigorously with this conclusion, it is apparent that some support for, and little outright contradiction of, a variety of theoretical suggestions has been found.

Of more direct concern to us, however, are the policy implications of evidence, and here the picture is far from clear. Empirical relationships are imprecise. Moreover, public policies are influenced by a number of distinct goals. Thus, even the most clear-cut evidence on the direct market effects of alternative policies might not prove decisive. The most we can say is that the evidence will carry weight as long as policy formulation is **in some degree** responsive to its purely "economic" implications.[2]

---

[1] James M. Clabault and John F. Burton, *Sherman Act Indictment, 1945–1967* (New York: Federal Legal Publications, 1966), p. 127.

[2] It should be noted once again that the distinction between "economic" and "noneconomic" implications is not always clear-cut.

An even more troublesome problem than imprecision concerns the cause-and-effect relationships that underlie our observations. To know that two or more variables are correlated with each other (i.e., that their values move together in some regular fashion) is often to know little or nothing about causation.[3] Where causation is unclear, however, policy implications are seriously limited. Public policies, after all, are designed to bring about, or **cause**, certain effects. Gaps in our understanding of causation may therefore be critical, preventing us from predicting what the results of particular policies are likely to be.

POSITIVE IMPLICATIONS OF THE EVIDENCE

Public competition policy is concerned with both market power and behavior. Should policy be used to limit the concentration of power? Is it sufficient instead to impose constraints on the conduct of firms, thereby leaving market power intact but circumscribing the ways in which it is exercised? These are, in general terms, the key questions.

It is quite clear from the discussions above that the existing evidence on firm and market structure and behavior will not yield very specific policy guidelines. If we ask, for example, what the socially optimal structure of markets or size of firms is, there can be no answer. What is "best" will not only vary from market to market (a statement that could have been made confidently without any evidence), but is also difficult to define in specific cases.

The large body of data that has been assembled and analyzed does contribute to policy formulation, but somewhat less directly. Empirical investigations have identified variables that are of policy concern. We cannot, for example, define precisely the "correct" concentration level of the domestic steel industry; however, we can be quite sure that policymakers ought to be concerned about prospective changes in industry concentration. Empirically, concentration and market share do have implications for market performance; and policies that will affect concentration must be considered in this light.

The point may be pursued a bit further. Suppose, for example, that administrators of antitrust policy begin with a social and political predisposition against high market concentration. On the basis of evidence gathered thus far, it can at least be stated that observations of economic consequences do not lead us generally in the opposite direction; in other words, there is no clear indication that highly concentrated areas display consistently superior economic performance.

This is a limited conclusion, but it is by no means trivial. In a society that has long viewed concentrated power with suspicion, the absence of a solid empirical case in favor of high market concentration has real policy significance. Some will be quick (and correct) to point out that the case **against** high concentration is also far

---

[3] A correlation (even a very close one) between variables X and Y is consistent with X as a cause of Y, Y as a cause of X, or no causal connection whatever. An example of the last possibility is a correlation between people's height and ability to spell. Neither characteristic "causes" the other. Rather, both are related to other factors such as age and education, which presumably do have causal significance.

from clear empirically. One could not, for example, base a general program to reduce industry concentration on the empirical evidence gathered to date.

Other bits of information also tend to be suggestive rather than conclusive. The evidence of the effect of advertising on profit rates, for example, is strong statistically. This may well reflect an entry barriers phenomenon; that is, heavy advertising creates high barriers to entry that, in turn, facilitate high profits. Possibly, however, the relationship reflects a more competitive phenomenon, or, possibly, it is merely spurious.[4] We may each have our suspicions, but we cannot be certain about what is really going on.

It seems fair to observe that the contributions of empirical evidence to our thinking about public competition policy are just that. The evidence stimulates thought, but it does not provide anything close to precise prescriptions. In virtually no area is the weight of our observations so overwhelming as to change the mind of someone with strong a priori beliefs about the desirable state of market structure or behavior. This situation may testify both to the weakness of the evidence and to the strength of people's beliefs about competition!

WHAT DOES THE PROFITS-CONCENTRATION RELATIONSHIP MEAN?

The observed link between profit rates and market concentration (or firms' market shares) has been debated extensively by economists. At issue is not the existence of a relationship—almost all observers concede that there is one—but its proper interpretation.[5] Why is it that higher profits and higher concentration tend to go together? Consider two possible explanations.

1. The relationship between profitability and concentration reflects monopolistic behavior. In highly concentrated markets, firms effectively collude and force prices well above marginal and average costs. What we see, then, is plain and simple misallocation of resources—exploitation of consumers.
2. The relationship simply reflects the fact that in some markets certain firms do a superior job. They, therefore, take over the bulk of market activity; and we observe high market shares, high concentration, and high profits. This is not really "monopoly" but, rather, the fruits of successful **competition**.

These possibilities are extreme, not because they lack plausibility but, rather, because each alone is unlikely to serve as a **full** explanation. The marketplace is not a

---

[4] Notice that the direction of causation (if any) is not fully obvious. Advertising may cause profits in one way or another, but the level of profits also may influence advertising expenditure. For relevant discussion, see Robert Dorfman and Peter O. Steiner, "Optimal Advertising and Optimal Quality," *American Economic Review*, **44** (December 1954), 826–836.

[5] Yale Brozen has argued for a number of years that observed relationships reflect disequilibrium rather than the effects of concentration on profitability. If so, then properly designed studies should show a weakening or disappearance of the link. See, for example, Brozen's "The Antitrust Task Force Deconcentration Recommendation," *Journal of Law and Economics*, **8** (October 1970), 279–292.

simple organism, and its behavior is unlikely to conform to very simple descriptions of cause and effect.

The immediate question, however, is whether such alternatives are empirically distinguishable. Can we determine whether monopolistic behavior (1) or competitive superiority (2), in fact, contributes to the profits-concentration relationship? And, if so, can we determine whether one or the other weighs more heavily? This is no simple task; however, one inventive effort, by Harold Demsetz, has come down squarely on the side of competitive superiority as the causal link.[6] Demsetz shows, generally, that the association between profit rates and concentration is a large-firm phenomenon; that is, the higher profitability of concentrated industries is confined mainly to the largest firms. The profit rates of small firms (those with assets under $500,000) do not rise with concentration; and the gap between small-firm and large-firm profits is positively and significantly related to concentration.

These results, according to Demsetz, are inconsistent with the view that high profits are the consequence of ''collusion'' or other monopolistic abuse. If that were the case, he argues, **all** firms should show higher profits under the collusive umbrella of the highly concentrated industries. That only the large ones do better in these industries indicates to Demsetz their competitive superiority.

Demsetz's findings are provocative but not completely persuasive. One must ask first whether other factors could account for the difference in the profit-concentration relationship between large and small firms. Ronald S. Bond and Warren Greenberg, commenting on Demsetz's study, have redefined size categories and added an advertising intensity variable (advertising/sales) to explain the difference in profitability between the largest and next-to-largest firms within industries.[7] They have found that advertising intensity, but **not** concentration, is a significant determinant of this profit-rate gap, thus casting some doubt on Demsetz's conclusions.

An important study by Sam Peltzman poses in a different way the question of whether concentration reflects competitive superiority.[8] Peltzman has attempted to decompose the concentration-profits relationship into a price effect—the traditional argument that where power is concentrated prices are pushed up—and a cost effect—the possibility that it is the introduction of cost-saving techniques that enhances both concentration and profits. The central finding is a significant association between concentration increases and cost decreases, taking into account other explanatory factors. Although Peltzman has found some tendency for prices to rise with concentration, the negative cost effect is dominant—a further point in favor of the competitive superiority hypothesis.

---

[6]Harold Demsetz, ''Industry Structure, Market Rivalry, and Public Policy,'' *Journal of Law and Economics*, **16** (April 1973), 1–9.

[7]Ronald S. Bond and Warren Greenberg, ''Industry Structure, Market Rivalry, and Public Policy: A Comment,'' *Journal of Law and Economics*, **19** (April 1976), 201–204. See also Demsetz's ''More on Collusion and Advertising: A Reply,'' in the same issue.

[8]Sam Peltzman, ''The Gains and Losses from Industrial Concentration,'' *Journal of Law and Economics*, **20** (October 1977), 229–263.

Peltzman's conclusions have been criticized by F. M. Scherer, who contends that "the chain of causation linking concentration and unit cost changes" has been misspecified.[9] Scherer points out that industries undergoing increases in concentration may be qualitatively different from others in Peltzman's sample (e.g., they are predominantly consumer-goods industries). If so, then influences on concentration other than cost change are not fully accounted for. Peltzman's evidence does not prove cause and effect, but the results are striking. They suggest strongly (at the very least) that the behavior of concentration and profits is not, for the most part, random.

The issue addressed by each of these writers in a sense involves the proper interpretation of "profits." In the traditional, market-oriented view, profits are the reward for valuable activity: efficient production, risk taking, innovation, and so forth. The profitable firm is one that is doing socially useful things; thus, it would make little sense for public policy officials to worry about, much less to act against, the phenomenon. Alternatively, high profits can be seen as a symptom of monopoly power, reflecting the absence of consumer choice—the position of some populists and consumer advocates. If this is so, policymakers ought to regard high returns on investment skeptically and perhaps act to curtail them.

There are unfortunately several reasons why a definitive interpretation is likely to remain elusive. First, the two views that we have cited are not **exhaustive;** variations in profitability may be caused by factors other than valuable activity or monopolistic exploitation. Moreover, these alternatives are not **exclusive;** the profitable organization may be pursuing useful activities and misallocating resources simultaneously. Trying to determine the degree to which each factor influences profits is likely to be an especially difficult task.

Finally, and perhaps most troublesome, straightforward empirical analysis is relatively impotent in defining the type of cause-and-effect issue that confronts us here. We know that concentration and market shares (among other variables) "determine" profit rates (imperfectly, to be sure) in a statistical sense. But this knowledge alone tells us nothing about **why** the connection exists. Accordingly, the social desirability and policy significance of both profit patterns and market structure remain debatable. Quite simply, the facts are consistent with diametrically opposed interpretations of what is "really" happening. To define causation in a more satisfactory way may not be impossible, but it will require considerable ingenuity.

THE CAUSES OF CONCENTRATION

Why does concentration vary from market to market? This question is in a sense the same as "Why do high concentration and high profits go together?"; for if we could answer either question, the answer to the other would also be obvious. Indeed, we

---

[9]F. M. Scherer, "The Causes and Consequences of Rising Industrial Concentration: A Comment," *Journal of Law and Economics,* **22** (April 1979), 191–208. See also in the same issue Steven Lustgarten, "Gains and Losses from Industrial Concentration: A Comment," 183–90; and Sam Peltzman, "The Causes and Consequences of Rising Industrial Concentration: A Reply," 209–211.

might pose the query a bit more generally: **Why do firms "succeed" or "fail"?** A reasonable measure of success is likely to reflect both profits and market shares. Successful firms, those that are profitable and relatively large—thus suggesting relatively high market concentration—may emerge for the various reasons we have noted earlier.

1. Scale economies in the market dictate large size for efficiency reasons.
2. Successful firms simply do a better job than their rivals: competitive superiority.
3. Although not absolutely superior, these firms maintain relative superiority over inept rivals.
4. Some "old" event leads to market dominance, that then persists over time: historic accident.
5. The firms engage in collusion or other forms of monopolistic conduct.
6. They have luck.

The great difficulty of sorting out these possibilities may be illustrated with a hypothetical example.[10] Suppose that a small group of firms emerge as leaders of the highly concentrated market in ceramic brick. Their success has nothing to do with size-based economies, collusion, or historic accident. Rather, the companies have emphasized precisely those elements of color and texture in ceramic bricks that have become most popular in the market; they have succeeded because their products appeal better than those of their rivals to consumer tastes. Although rival firms have now attempted to produce very similar brick, the market shares of the leaders have remained high. These shares are unlikely to fall substantially in the near future, both because consumers have developed brand loyalties to the leaders and because little price competition exists in this market.

One might interpret the success of these firms in (at least) three ways.

1. The leading firms' position reflects superior competitive performance; these companies have done the better job of anticipating and meeting consumer desires.
2. Consumer preferences in this market could have been identified easily by any competent market researcher. The leading firms have, therefore, succeeded not because of any particular skill but simply because their rivals were too negligent and inept to figure out what the market would demand.
3. The leaders' position resulted from luck. No one could have predicted what colors and textures of brick consumers would prefer; and the successful firms were merely the ones whose uninformed guesses turned out to be the most accurate.

This example is both simplified and extreme in that the success of the leading firms is purely and unambiguously attributable to their ability to appeal to market tastes. Yet even knowing the immediate reason for their success—information that we seldom have in practice—is insufficient.

---

[10]This discussion follows closely that in Peter Asch, "Industrial Concentration, Efficiency, and Antitrust Reform," *Antitrust Bulletin*, **22** (Spring 1977), 137 ff.

Alternative interpretations of underlying cause remain plausible; which one is correct may not be obvious. Does the company that succeeds because it is in the "right" place at the "right" time exhibit skill or luck? Without an answer to this and similar questions, we may not be able to define very precisely the social costs and benefits of leaving dominant firms intact or of using public policy to restrict their power or behavior.

PUBLIC POLICY: WHERE NOW?

In assessing the contribution of empirical evidence to public policy, one can take either a pessimistic or an optimistic view. The pessimist could paint a rather dismal picture along the following lines.

We have failed to answer the questions of primary policy significance. (1) How precisely do various structural attributes of firms and markets affect their performance? and (2) Are existing market structures economically "justified" in the sense that they yield efficiencies of some sort? The failure to answer these questions means that we cannot tell whether policies that influence existing structures will have "good" or "bad" effects.

While the pessimist has a point, the situation may be realistically viewed in a more positive fashion. It is true that we cannot predict precisely the effects on performance of policies toward market structure (or conduct, for that matter). But whereas we cannot say much about the **magnitude** of policy effects, our empirical data do provide some **directional** presumptions.[11] To be sure, these give us less information than we ideally would like to have; but the directional clues are of considerable importance in shaping public programs.

Attitudes toward public competition policy tend to be grounded in ideological considerations. Believers in the unvarying correctness of market decisions may regard all policy restrictions with skepticism if not hostility. Others, believing that imperfect markets tend to exploit and to act "unfairly," are more prone to view public policy as a source of protection. Empirical evidence is unlikely to convert those who hold strongly to either position. But it is nevertheless useful to those searching for improved policies, even if policy formulation remains in part an act of faith.

---

[11] Consider, for example, a policy that will permit an increase in the concentration of a market (perhaps via merger of two large firms). Evidence suggests that such a change will probably (though not certainly) enhance the profit rate earned in this market, though it is hard to say by how much. Whether one regards this prospect as desirable depends on other considerations; but the expectation itself is a pertinent one.

PART THREE

ANTITRUST POLICY

This section deals with the nature and economic interpretation of antitrust policy. As we have seen, neither economic theory nor the existing body of empirical evidence provides very precise prescriptions for public policy. General theoretical arguments in favor of competition are often difficult to apply to specific situations. The implications of existing theory and evidence for imperfectly competitive markets, especially oligopoly, are often weak; and the problem is compounded when one attempts to judge the probable effects of "small" policy changes. Any economic evaluation of antitrust, then, does not have a well-defined ideal with which to compare actual policy.

To point out that economics has not provided antitrust policy with comprehensive guideposts is **not** to imply that it has provided nothing at all. Indeed, the clues to policy contained in the theory and evidence that is discussed above are both abundant and important. If we do not have a theoretical road map for policy, we at least have a large number of road signs and signals. Economic theory and evidence are most useful in predicting—albeit imprecisely and with limited confidence—the consequences of alternative policies. For example, if the government were to consider a major effort to lower market concentration in the manufacturing sector, it would be possible to suggest some possible results of such a policy move. Even if the contemplated policy were much more limited—say, an effort to lower concentration in steel production—there exists an analytical framework within which the possible effects can be evaluated. Objective analysis stops short, however, of defining the "rightness" or "wrongness" of any policy. This kind of judgment depends on the **goals** of policy, an element beyond the scope of economic theory or empirical measurement.

The goals of antitrust policy are not much different from the broader economic and political objectives of society. Antitrust policy seeks to promote economic progress and efficiency and to protect individual liberty and freedom of choice. Such objectives are hardly unique. What is special to antitrust policy is the more proximate objective of maintaining competitive markets. This is the lower-order goal that constitutes the means toward the ultimate ends. Although it is easy to list objectives on which some general consensus exists, the problem of defining antitrust goals is not so simple. This is because a meaningful definition must be more than a listing. It

199

must include, at least, some **ordering** or ranking of objectives; and ideally it should provide an even more specific notion of the relative importance accorded to each.

It may be helpful to resurrect an earlier example in somewhat greater detail. Let us suppose, quite plausibly, that society desires both efficient production and the absence of concentrated economic power; and suppose further, a bit less plausibly, that the concentration ratio measures power concentrations reliably. To make the example specific, consider the hypothetical widget manufacturing industry in which technical efficiency and atomistic market structure are known to conflict. In other words, large firms, whose existence implies high concentration, will enjoy lower unit costs, but they will also impose a welfare loss on the community.[1] The conflict is clear-cut: To raise efficiency, society must accept some concentrated power; whereas to erode concentration will cost society some efficiency.

The problem is illustrated in Figure 1. Curve *TT* is somewhat akin to a transformation function. It tells us the unit cost of output at different levels of concentration. *II* is a community "indifference" or "welfare" curve showing the efficiency–concentration combinations among which society is indifferent.

The slopes of these curves have familiar interpretations. The slope of *TT* is the "marginal rate of transformation," at which atomism can be sacrificed for efficiency (or vice versa). Note the implication of the concave shape of *TT*: At high levels of concentration, additional concentration gains us little in terms of efficiency; and the reverse is true at low concentration levels. The slope of *II* is the "marginal rate of substitution" between the two "goods," that is, the rate at which the community is **willing** to trade atomism for efficiency (or vice versa). Apart from the fact that the slope will be negative at all points, little can be said about the likely shape of the community welfare function.[2]

Point *E,* a tangency between *TT* and *II,* represents the community's equilibrium or welfare-maximizing position.

Presentation of the problem in these terms does not resolve the policy issue. Indeed, the problem here may be atypical, since in other industries it may be that efficiency and atomism are more compatible (*TT* might in such cases be positively sloped through some range). Given our assumptions about the widget industry, however, these terms do allow us to define the problem more clearly. The slope of *TT* is, in a sense, the ratio of the marginal costs of efficiency and competitiveness, with each cost expressed in terms of the other characteristic or "commodity." The slope tells us how much competitiveness must be sacrificed in order to gain some additional cost savings. This information is essentially economic. Given ideal measurement, this slope—the real trade-offs between efficiency and atomism—could be defined; and it is precisely this kind of information that economics strives to provide. The slope of the indifference curves reflects the preferences of the community.

---

[1] One can think of this loss as strictly "economic"—as the restrictive behavior of the partial monopolists who dominate the market—or as an array of costs resulting from the social and political power of such firms.

[2] The curve will have a negative slope for much the same reasons that ordinary consumer indifference curves are negatively sloped.

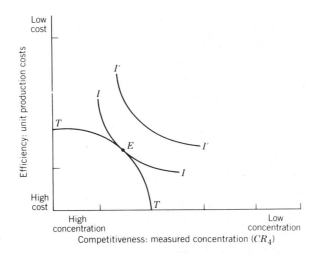

Figure 1 Production efficiency and competitiveness: a hypothetical example.

It tells us, at any given efficiency–competition point, how much of one commodity the community is willing to sacrifice in order to obtain one more unit of the other. This kind of information would be included in an ideal statement of policy goals and priorities, but it is not the kind of information that economic theory and measurement provide.

It goes almost without saying that the state of our definition of antitrust goals, as well as of our economic facts, is far from ideal. Indeed, it is not clear that more than the most general and vague kinds of criteria have been established. The example of efficiency and competition is a prime case in point. A system in which power is highly concentrated limits competition in one traditional sense, and such a limitation may impose social and political, as well as economic, costs. At the same time, it is possible, although not inevitable, that the productive efficiency that we desire is tied in part to large producing units that, in turn, imply some concentration of power. There is, thus, a possible direct conflict of goals, as in the widget example. Efficiency and competitiveness compete not only in the sense that they bid for the common resources of public policy programs, but also in the sense that a high level of one may be incompatible with a high level of the other.

This is not the only possible conflict in policy objectives, and it may not even be the most common one. Perhaps our desire for progressiveness (invention and innovation) will lead to patterns of income distribution that are thought to be less than ideal. It is possible that by placing a high value on individual freedom, we shall incur the waste of some resources or that in seeking "fairness" and "justice," we may seem to limit individual freedom. Thus, the pursuit of any particular objective may imply costs in addition to the obvious direct costs of supporting a public policy program to obtain that objective.

The need for clear and well-established priorities is manifest; yet there is little reason to think that consistent priorities exist in antitrust enforcement. At the same time, the real trade-offs (or technical marginal rates of substitution) between objectives are not fully known. We often cannot say just how much of one goal we would have to give up to attain a specified level of another. We may not, in other words, know precisely how much our objectives cost. Thus, even a well-defined system of priorities might not lead to ideal policies.

Many descriptions of antitrust objectives retreat into discussions of more immediate goals, such as the preservation of ''competition'' and the prevention of ''anticompetitive'' practices. These more proximate goals are, of course, both real and important, but to discuss objectives in these terms is not to mitigate the problem of confused priorities. ''Competition,'' as we have seen, is an ambiguous term, and it may well be that a person who sees efficiency as the ultimate objective of policy will interpret competition quite differently than one who stresses economic freedom.

The objectives of antitrust policy may at times appear confused and even in disarray. This is not because policymakers are bent on pursuing the wrong goals, but rather because the assignment of priorities and reconciliation of conflicts are difficult tasks. One should not be too pessimistic, however. Although a clear social consensus does not exist on every issue, agreement about our broad objectives is wide enough to be helpful. When it comes to specifics, moreover, our national history yields some clues about the priorities we may wish to assign.

CHAPTER 11

The Language
of the Antitrust Laws

The stated policy of the U. S. government is to maintain a competitive economy. Many deviations from this policy can be observed, but there is a large sector of the economy within which the principle is genrally pursued. This is the segment that is thought to be amenable to competition, that is, areas in which market-type solutions are feasible.

Legal challenges to monopolistic or anticompetitive practices began, even in the United States, long before the adoption of federal antitrust laws. Certain kinds of contracts and agreements have long been unenforceable because of their anticompetitive and socially undesirable nature. The immediate precedent for the legal framework of United States is found in the body of English common law. During the nineteenth century extensive private litigation in the United States drew on and expanded earlier notions of "restraint of trade." Various sorts of market-rigging agreements, such as price fixing, output limitation, and territorial division, were viewed by the courts with disfavor.

As antimonopoly sentiment increased in the period following the Civil War, there was some legal recourse open to injured parties. The support of competition in American courts, however, faced obvious limitations, most notably the absence of **public** action. Litigation was confined largely to instances in which persons acting in their private capacity could demonstrate direct harm from agreements of a re-straining nature. The first public reaction to this situation was the adoption of state antitrust laws in the 1870s and 1880s. These laws, however, were notable primarily for the fact that were rarely enforced. This impotency, exemplified by the formation and behavior of large trusts, alarmed the American public and paved the way for federal intervention. When it came, intervention did relatively little to expand the existing law of monopoly. Rather, its significance lay in the face that restraints of trade were now to be opposed by federal action.

THE SHERMAN ACT[1]

The Sherman Act, passed in 1890, carried the following important provisions.

[1]26 Stat. 209 (1890).

Section 1. "Every contract, combination in the form of trust or otherwise, or conspiracy, in restraint of trade or commerce among the several states, or with foreign nations, is hereby declared to be illegal."

Section 2. "Every person who shall monopolize, or attempt to monopolize, or combine or conspire with any other person or persons to monopolize any part of the trade or commerce . . . shall be guilty of a misdemeanor."

The act reflected the language of the common law; yet it is interesting to note precisely how vague its provisions are. There is no definifion of either "restraint of trade or commerce" or of "monopolization" (although the terms did carry meaning within the common law). Section 2 is the broader provision, applying to individuals as well as to combining or conspiring groups of individuals.

THE CLAYTON ACT[2]

It did not take long for some disillusionment with the Sherman Act to appear. Various kinds of "monopolistic abuses" were known to go unchallenged under the law, and the result was the adoption of the Clayton Act in 1914. The Clayton Act prohibits or limits a number of specific practices.

Section 2. Makes it illegal "to discriminate in price between different purchasers" but does allow for price differences where the differential reflects "only due allowance for differences in the cost of selling or transportation."

Section 3. Forbids sellers to lease or sell "on the condition, agreement or understanding that the lessee or purchaser thereof shall not use or deal in the goods . . . of a competitor or competitors of the lessor or seller."

Section 7. Prohibits corporations from holding the stock of another company or of two competing companies "where the effect . . . may be substantially to lessen competition."

Section 8. Prohibits interlocking directorates for corporations larger than $1 million.

The first three Clayton Act prohibitions are limited to cases in which the result of the practice in question may be "to substantially lessen competition or tend to create a monopoly in any line of commerce." The act further provides, in Section 4, that any individual "who shall be injured in his business or property by reason of anything forbidden in the antitrust laws," may sue to recover "threefold the damages by him sustained . . ."

THE FEDERAL TRADE COMMISSION ACT[3]

Section 5 of the Federal Trade Commission Act states: ". . . unfair methods of competition in commerce are hereby declared unlawful." The remainder of the act is largely devoted to establishing the Federal Trade Commission.

[2] 38 Stat. 730 (1914).
[3] 38 Stat. 717 (1914).

Passed at about the same time, the Federal Trade Commission and Clayton acts targeted a variety of abusive practices. Once again, little new substantive matter was added by these laws. The Clayton Act did, however, clarify somewhat the legal status of specific practices, and it provided the government with a potentially important preventive measure.

THE ROBINSON–PATMAN ACT[4]

The Robinson–Patman Act amended Section 2 of the original Clayton Act. The original provision was designed primarily to prevent large manufacturers from driving out smaller competitors by means of selective, discriminatory price cuts. Prior to Robinson–Patman, however, many complaints were heard from small wholesale and retail sellers whose existence was threatened by large chain organizations. The mass distributors were underselling the smaller independents by obtaining preferential prices from suppliers. Various devices were employed. The chains, for example, often received "broker's commissions" in the form of a price discount on sales in which no broker was employed. Similarly, they received "allowances" for services rendered (e.g., promotion of the supplier's commodities) or received services without charge. The Robinson–Patman Act is aimed directly at such discriminatory practices.

Section 2(a). Restates and broadens somewhat the language of original Section 2.

Section 2(b). Provides that a seller charged with price discrimination may defend his actions on the grounds that they were made in good faith to meet an equally low price of a competitor or the services or facilities furnished by a competitor.

Section 2(c). Prohibits discriminatory brokerage commissions.

Section 2(d). Prohibits allowances for services rendered "unless such payments or consideration is available on proportionally equal terms to all other customers."

Section 2(e). Forbids sellers from performing services for customers, unless such services are available to all on "proportionally equal terms."

Section 2(f). Forbids any person from knowingly inducing or receiving a discriminatory price.

The Robinson–Patman amendments thus provide extensive and specific coverage of discriminatory pricing practices.

THE WHEELER–LEA ACT[5]

The Wheeler–Lea Act of 1938 amended Section 5 of the Federal Trade Commission Act to read as follows.

Unfair methods of competition in commerce, and unfair or deceptive acts or practices in commerce, are hereby declared unlawful.

[4] 49 Stat. 1526 (1936).

[5] 52 Stat. 111 (1938); 15 U.S.C. Sec. 41.

The addition of the phrase ''and unfair or deceptive acts or practices in commerce'' was stimulated by an earlier court decision that indicated that the Commission could not curb ''unfair methods'' unless harm to *competitors* was demonstrated.[6]

"FAIR TRADE" LAWS

From 1937 through 1975 there existed federal laws exempting certain resale price maintenance agreements from antitrust prosecution.

The *Miller–Tydings Act* of 1937, amending Section 1 of the Sherman Act, stated in part:[7]

Provided: That nothing herein contained shall render illegal, contracts or agreements prescribing minimum prices for the resale of a commodity which bears, or the label or container of which bears, the trademark, brand, or name of the producer or distributor of such commodity and which is in free and open competition with which commodities of the same general class produced or distributed by others.

The act, thus, provided that such ''fair trade'' arrangements could not be prosecuted as restraints of trade under Section 1.

The *McGuire Act* of 1952 amended Section 5 of the Federal Trade Commission Act to allow enforcement of nonsigners' clauses in resale-price maintenance agreements.[8] A nonsigners' clause binds all sellers within a state to follow a manufacturer's resale price specification once one seller in that state signs a contract and the others are notified.

The impact of resale-price maintenance was widespread through the 1960s; only eight states had failed to enact or had repealed enabling statutes. State courts, however, had been invalidating nonsigners' provisions with some consistency. By the end of 1975, when Congress repealed the Miller–Tydings and McGuire acts, the influence of fair trade had already waned considerably. In 1981, however, the Justice Department indicated that it will not ordinarily prosecute ''vertical price fixing'' of the fair trade variety. It may thus be that even in the absence of federal enabling legislation, the practice will continue to affect some American markets.

THE CELLER–KEFAUVER ACT[9]

Section 7 of the Clayton Act prohibited corporate stock acquisitions where the effect might be a substantial lessening of competition. In 1950, the Celler–Kefauver Act amended Section 7 to include asset acquisitions. The act provides that:

. . . no corporation engaged in commerce shall acquire, directly or indirectly, the whole or any part of the stock or other share capital . . . [or] the whole or any part

---

[6]*FTC* v. *Raladam Co.,* 283 U.S. 643 (1931).

[7]50 Stat. 693 (1937); 15 U.S.C. Sec. 1.

[8]66 Stat. 632 (1952); 15 U.S.C. Sec. 45.

[9]64 Stat. 1125 (1950); 15 U.S.C. Sect. 18.

of the assets of another corporation engaged also in commerce, where in any line of commerce in any section of the country, the effect of acquisition may be substantially to lessen competition, or to tend to create a monopoly.

Rather few corporate acquisitions had been challenged under original Section 7, and the amendment, by closing a loophole of gargantuan proportions, marked the beginning of a new era in public policy towards corporation mergers.

SUMMARY

The statutes described above comprise the principal antitrust laws of the United States. As we have noted, the term "antitrust" is today a misnomer. It would be more accurate to speak of "public competition" or even "antimonopoly" laws and policies. In general, the Clayton and Federal Trade Commission acts cover anticompetitive practices that, if left untouched, might lead to monopoly. The Sherman Act also deals with practices involved in attempts to monopolize, but this law stands as the principal means of treating the fait accompli of established monopoly positions. The fair trade statutes—Miller–Tydings and McGuire—provided for a time one of the most significant and controversial exemptions from the competition-encouraging provisions of antitrust.

Although the antitrust laws are relatively brief and, for the most part, are worded in straightforward fashion, associated litigation has been both voluminous and complex. The simple wording of the laws is a bit misleading, for numerous terms—for example, "restraint of trade," "monopolization," and "unfair methods"—are capable of innumerable interpretations. The task of interpretation falls largely to the courts, and for this reason our attention will be focused on court decisions. What the courts say about the meaning of various terms, however, is not the entire sum and substance of antitrust. Public policy is also deeply influenced by the behavior of federal agencies charged with enforcement of the laws, most notably the Federal Trade Commission and the Department of Justice. Of course, the kinds of legal action taken by the agencies depend partly on what the courts have previously said; however, the process works in both directions. That is, the thrust of public policy is determined by court interpretation of the laws, but it is also affected by the kinds of situations that the agencies bring before the courts. A timid approach by executive agencies can effectively limit the impact of even the boldest judicial outlook.

Even within the decisions of the courts, interpretation of the law is not the only important aspect of antitrust. A separate question concerns the relief or remedy imposed upon the finding of a violation of law. There are many instances in which sweeping interpretations by the courts are significantly modified by a relatively weak remedial policy. To look only at the language of interpretation in such instances could, thus, grossly overstate the real result of antitrust policy.

CHAPTER 12

Restraint of Trade
and Conspiracy to Monopolize

It is somewhat misleading to classify antitrust policies according to subject. Specific cases and episodes often fail to fit any single category precisely but, rather, overlap several. The process of categorization, thus, conveys the impression of a much neater and more orderly antitrust record than, in fact, exists. In the case of restraint of trade, however, the classification is reasonably distinct; for as we shall see, the courts have been careful to draw a line between the abuse of power and its "mere" existence.

The Sherman Act has been utilized extensively to deal with certain kinds of anticompetitive practices such as conspiracy to fix prices, to restrict output, or to divide markets among competitors. Such practices have been interpreted both as conspiracies to restrain trade, a violation of Section 1, and as conspiracies to monpolize, a violation of Section 2. Unlike the Section 2 infringements that we discuss below, market-rigging conspiracies raise no question of whether companies succeed or fail to achieve positions of monopoly power. Traditionally, the focus is on the action itself as distinct from the market power of participating firms.

Conspiratorial behavior, which often takes the form of price-fixing agreements, falls within the collusive oligopoly pattern discussed in Chapter 3. Mutually dependent firms may attempt rationally to avoid the consequences of unlimited price competition, and an obvious method is to agree on pricing policies. Any such tendency raises two basic policy questions. First, should conspiratorial behavior be condemned in general, or should it be treated on a case-by-case basis? And second, how is conspiratorial behavior to be defined—in other words, at what point does a taking account of mutual interdependence by firms become a violation of law?

The courts have provided a relatively clear answer to the first question. The second, however—which goes to the fundamental meaning of conspiracy—continues to plague antitrust policy; and the disposition of cases in the courts has raised questions about economic rationality in this area of policy enforcement.

A REVIEW OF RELEVANT CASES

Outright Price-Fixing and Market-Rigging: Development of the Per Se Doctrine

The legal status of obvious conspiratorial conduct is well established by several Supreme Court decisions on relatively open agreements among competitors to fix prices or divide markets. There is typically little disagreement about the facts surrounding these cases, and the existence of conspiratorial behavior is usually not in doubt. Rather, the issue has been whether extenuating circumstances of any kind can justify such agreements.

The Addyston Pipe and Steel Case (1899).   One of the earliest conspiracy cases pursued after enactment of the Sherman Act involved a bid-rigging cartel formed by six leading producers of iron pipe. The companies had divided the market into regional monopolies ("pay territories"), and had fixed prices within each. The winner of a particular bidding was determined in advance by the cartel, with other cartel members submitting essentially fraudulent bids to give the appearance of competition.

The companies offered two contentions in their defense.

1. The purpose of their agreement was to avoid ruinous price competition, a condition attested to by a high mortality rate among firms.
2. The prices at which cast iron pipe was being sold were reasonable and, thus, should be held legal under common-law standards.

Judge Taft in the Circuit Court of Appeals found the defense unconvincing.[1] Restraints of trade, he observed, may be permissible—but only where they are "merely ancillary" to another, legitimate purpose. (The formation of a business partnership, for example, entails an allowable restraint: the agreement of the partners not to compete with one another.) Where, however, there is no other purpose than "mutual restraint of the parties," the restraint cannot stand; and courts that attempt to weigh the reasonableness of such practices, the judge observed, "have set sail on a sea of doubt."

Although Judge Taft did not regard the prices fixed by this cartel as "reasonable," he clearly believed that the issue of reasonableness was not an important one and, under common-law precedent, was not a question left open to the courts. His decision was upheld by the Supreme Court in 1899, with the statement that "the facts . . . show conclusively that the effect of the combination was to enhance prices beyond a sum which was reasonable."[2]

---

[1] *U.S.* v. *Addyston Pipe and Steel Co.*, 85 F. 271 (6th Cir. 1898).

[2] *Addyston Pipe and Steel Co.* v. *U.S.*, 175 U.S. 211 (1899).

The *Addyston* case was the precursor of an unqualified, or per se, prohibition on conspiracy to rig markets. The Supreme Court did not state such a doctrine explicitly, but its approval of Judge Taft's decision and language pointed to it.[3]

The Trenton Potteries Case (1927).   The first unequivocal statement of a *per se* doctrine with respect to price fixing was enunciated in a case that reached the Supreme Court in 1927.[4] Twenty individuals and 23 corporate manufacturers of vitreous china belonged to an association that had fixed prices for the sale of sanitary pottery, and had limited sales to so-called legitimate jobbers. The defendants, who held 82 percent of the market, had been convicted in a district court trial but had won a reversal in a circuit court of appeals. The reversal was based on the grounds that the trial judge had incorrectly instructed the jury that it could return a verdict of guilty without considering the reasonableness of prices fixed by the conspiracy.

The issue presented to the Supreme Court did not concern the facts of the case or any question as to whether a finding of guilt was supportable. Rather, the issue was the propriety of the judge's instructions. Justice Stone, speaking for the Court, stated simply that:

The aim and result of every price-fixing agreement, if effective, is the elimination of any one form of competition. . . . The reasonable price fixed today may through economic and business changes become the unreasonable price of tomorrow. Once established, it may be maintained unchanged because of the absence of competition secured by the agreement for a price reasonable when fixed. Agreements which create such potential power may well be held to be in themselves unreasonable or unlawful restraints, without the necessity of minute inquiry whether a particular price is reasonable or unreasonable.[5]

Thus, said the Court, price fixing violates the Sherman Act, "despite the reasonableness of the particular prices agreed upon." Under this doctrine the establishment of the existence of a price-fixing agreement ends the responsibility of the prosecution. There is no need to show that the prices fixed are in any way unreasonable or damaging, and, by similar token, there can be no showing that the fixed prices are justifiable.

The Supreme Court thus held that the trial judge had correctly charged the jury. There was no need for the reasonableness of fixed prices to be considered, and, apparently, any such consideration would have been out of order. This is the basic statement of the *per se* approach: The action is **by itself** illegal; the circumstances surrounding the action, and the consequences flowing from it, are irrelevant.

---

[3] The Court had previously held illegal a rate-making agreement among competing railroads on the grounds that under such agreement "competition is allowed no play." This language also suggested that it is the agreement itself—not the particular price agreed to—that runs afoul of the law. *U.S.* v. *Trans-Missouri Freight Association*, 166 U.S. 290 (1897).

[4] *U.S.* v. *Trenton Potteries Co.*, 273 U.S. 392 (1927).

[5] Ibid., p. 397.

The Appalachian Coals Case (1933).   The condition of the bituminous coal industry in the United States was one of persistent depression during the early part of
this century. Excess capacity was chronic, the use of substitute fuels was growing,
bankruptcy was common, and aggregate net income for the industry was at times
actually negative. Faced with such conditions—which were clearly not to be
remedied by "natural" economic forces—coal producers had sought government
assistance in reorganizing the market. When such aid was not forthcoming, 137
companies joined together to form Appalachian Coals, Inc. This company, owned
jointly by participants in accordance with their shares of total production, was to act
as exclusive selling agent for the 137 participants, and it was to seek more effective
marketing systems and obtain the "best prices" possible. The 137 producers accounted for about 12 percent of national coal production in 1929, but they held almost 75 percent of the output in the Appalachian region. One purpose of the combination was, manifestly, the elimination of price competition among the 137
producers.

The combination was challenged by the government, which won its case in a district court in 1932.[6] Judge Parker, writing for the three-man court, adhered closely
to the principles set forth in *Trenton Potteries*. The combination, he stated, was designed to eliminate competition, and it could not be interpreted as a "bona fide corporate organization resulting from normal growth and development." The decision
was appealed to the Supreme Court, and final disposition made in 1933.[7]

The Court was obviously responsive to the "deplorable" economic conditions of
the coal industry and to the obvious need for reform and reorganization. Citing the
Sherman Act's "essential standard of reasonableness," Chief Justice Hughes
stated:

. . . *a close and objective scrutiny of particular conditions and purposes is necessary in each case. Realities must dominate the judgment. The mere fact that the
parties to an agreement eliminate competition among themselves is not enough to
condemn it.*[8]

If the conditions surrounding the case were evident, the Court found the defendants'
purposes to be equally clear. The agreement was intended, according to the producers, to foster "a better and more orderly" marketing system, and not to restrict output. The Court majority saw no reason to question this statement of motivation, but
it held that the issue of legality ultimately rested on the likely effects of the agreement rather than on the intentions of its participants.

Here the Court placed emphasis on the competitive conditions of the industry.
The cooperating firms were relatively small in the national market even when their
production was pooled. Although the producers held most of the Appalachian area

---

[6] *U.S.* v. *Appalachian Coals, Inc.,* 1F. Supp. 339 (W. D. Va., 1932).

[7] *Appalachian Coals, Inc.* v. *U.S.,* 288 U.S. 344 (1933).

[8] Ibid., p. 360.

coal production, much of this coal was sold in other parts of the country. Chief Justice Hughes found it impossible to conclude that the plan would enable the coal producers effectively to fix prices. Moreover, he noted, a merger of the producing companies, involving actual integration of facilities, would have been regarded as natural and acceptable under the law. The device of a common selling agency, although not quite the same as a merger, could not thus be judged abnormal.

The *Appalachian Coals* decision was obviously a departure from the *per se* doctrine of *Trenton Potteries*. Chief Justice Hughes's conclusion that the coal producers' agreement was reasonable, in light of industry conditions and the intent of the companies, remains cogent. But under the *per se* approach, reasonableness simply could not have been considered.

The Socony-Vacuum Case (1940).[9] The Supreme Court decision in *Appalachian Coals* left the legal status of price fixing in considerable doubt. This doubt was resolved in a case that reached the Court in 1940, involving price rigging in the oil refining industry.

Oil refining was a depressed industry during the 1930s, and independent producers were experiencing particularly difficult times. Refiners sold gasoline to jobbers, who, in turn, resold to retail service stations. During this period of depressed prices, several major oil refiners including Socony-Vacuum embarked on coordinated programs of gasoline purchasing from the independents. Purchases made were of "distress gasoline," for which the independents had no regular outlets. Buying in coordination, under an informal gentleman's agreement, the major refiners managed to maintain and even to drive up the spot market price of gasoline. The spot price directly determined the price at which gasoline was sold to jobbers in tank car lots. This price, in turn, influenced gasoline prices charged to retail service stations and, ultimately, the retail price paid by consumers. Each of the major refiners was fully integrated, from wells to retail stations. By manipulating the relatively thin spot market, the conspirators managed to support prices throughout the various distribution stages of the industry. In effect, they kept prices above that level which competitive conditions in the industry would otherwise have dictated.

The major refiners argued that their buying programs were designed to maintain order in a weak and deteriorating market. The problem of depressed demand had been aggravated by new oil discoveries, and the companies argued that their actions were a necessary stabilization measure. This defense was in some ways similar to that accepted in *Appalachian Coals*. Moreover, the refiners' buying arrangement was authorized under the National Industrial Recovery Act, and it almost certainly would have passed the *Appalachian* test.

Nevertheless, the Supreme Court rejected the refiners' arguments. Justice Douglas held that the buying programs of the companies constituted a combination designed to raise prices, stating:

---

[9] *U.S.* v. *Socony-Vacuum Oil Co.*, 310 U.S. 150 (1940).

The elimination of so-called competitive evils is no legal justification. . . . If the so-called competitive abuses were to be appraised here, the reasonableness of prices would necessarily become an issue in every price-fixing case. In that event the Sherman Act would soon be emasculated; its philosophy would be supplemented by one which is wholly alien to a system of free competition.[10]

Furthermore, Justice Douglas said:

The Sherman Act places all such schemes beyond the pale and protects . . . our economy against any degree of interference. Congress . . . has not permitted the age-old cry of ruinous competition and competitive evils to be a defense to price-fixing conspiracies. . . .

    Under the Sherman Act a combination formed for the purpose and with the effect of raising, depressing, fixing, pegging, or stabilizing the price of a commodity . . . is illegal per se.[11]

    Socony-Vacuum thus returned price fixing to the status of a *per se* offense. The last quotation notwithstanding, the Court had clearly stated that any effort to fix prices directly is illegal regardless of surrounding circumstances or effects. Justice Douglas made some effort to distinguish the situation in *Socony-Vacuum* from that of *Appalachian Coals.* It is evident, however, that the *Appalachian* decision was a temporary aberration in the development of price-fixing law, consistent neither with *Trenton Potteries* nor with more recent cases affirming the *per se* doctrine.[12]

The Topco Case (1972).[13] In *Topco,* the Supreme Court extended the *per se* rule to a market-dividing scheme that did not include an agreement to fix prices directly. Topco was a cooperative association of about 25 small and medium-sized supermarket chains, which served as a purchasing agent for its members. The association supplied members with more than 1000 products, which the members sold under various brand names owned by Topco.

    At the heart of the government's complaint was a "continuing agreement" under which

. . . each . . . member firm will sell Topco-controlled brands only within the marketing territory allocated to it, and will refrain from selling Topco-controlled brands outside such marketing territory.

The association licensed each member to sell within specified areas. Most of the licenses were effectively exclusive; a Topco member was thus able to sell the affected products without competition from other members. In its defense, Topco ar-

---

[10]Ibid., pp. 220–221.

[11]Ibid., pp. 221, 223.

[12]Among the decisions affirming the *per se* doctrine are *U.S.* v. *Frankfort Distilleries,* 324 U.S. 293 (1945); *Schine Chain Theaters, Inc.* v. *U.S.,* 334 U.S. 110 (1948); and *Kiefer-Stewart Co.* v. *Joseph E. Seagram and Sons,* 340 U.S. 211 (1951).

[13]*U.S.* v. *Topco Associates, Inc.,* 405 U.S. 596 (1972).

gued that such territorial restrictions were necessary for its relatively small companies to compete effectively with major supermarket chains.

Justice Marshall observed for the Court that horizontal limitations had been characterized previously as "naked restraints of trade with no purpose except stifling of competition."[14] The Topco restraints, he said, were clearly horizontal—involving competitors at the same level of market activity—"and therefore a per se violation of Section 1."

Trade Association Cases.

Despite the fact that price-fixing and similar agreements are clearly established to be *per se* violations of the Sherman Act, difficulty is often encountered in defining the circumstances under which such agreements can be said to exist. One of the borderline areas concerns trade association activities. Typically, these associations are formed to pursue legitimate activities such as the dissemination of information among producers and sellers. The question that has arisen under the Sherman Act concerns the point at which such activities may invite, or actually amount to, market rigging. The courts have thus been faced with the difficult task of assessing practices that serve a legal and beneficial purpose but that may simultaneously facilitate illegal patterns of conduct.

The American Column and Lumber Case (1921).[15]   The first major trade association case to reach the Supreme Court involved an association of 400 hardwood manufacturers. Of the 400 members of the American Hardwood Manufacturers' Association, 365 participated in what was known as the "Open Competition Plan." Under the plan, each participant supplied extensive information about his business activities, including daily reports on prices and shipments, documented by actual invoices; monthly production and stock reports; and price lists. According to the plan, any member failing to report such information could not **receive** the reports of the association, which summarized and condensed the data supplied by all members.

Justice Clarke for the Supreme Court held that:

This elaborate plan for the interchange of reports does not simply supply to each member . . . the data for judging the market on the basis of supply and demand and current prices. It goes much farther. It not only furnishes such information . . . but also significant suggestions as to both future prices and production. . . . It is plain that the only element lacking in this scheme to make it a familiar type of the competition suppressing organization is a definite agreement as to production and prices. But this is supplied: By the disposition of men "to follow their most intelligent competitors," especially when powerful.[16]

[14]*White Motor Co.* v. *U.S.*, 372 U.S. 253 (1963).

[15]*American Column and Lumber Co. et al.* v. *U.S.*, 257 U.S. 377 (1921).

[16]Ibid., pp. 398–399.

The plan was thus interpreted as something that went beyond a simple interchange of market information. Referring to pricing suggestions of the association and the actual course of price changes in the industry, the Court found that the plan amounted to a subtle kind of conspiracy, designed to "procure 'harmonious' individual action."

The decision was an important one in two respects. First, it made clear that an illegal scheme could not be legalized by tying it to the legitimate function of disseminating information. Second, the demonstration of illegality did not necessitate proof of a formal or tangible overt agreement. The Court was willing to infer such agreement from the provisions of the plan, in conjunction with evidence showing the forcefulness with which the price and production "suggestions" of the association were presented.

The Maple Flooring Manufacturers' Association Case (1925)[17]. A different decision was reached by the Supreme Court in a case involving the 22-member Maple Flooring Manufacturers' Association. Members had supplied information on prices, costs, and stocks, which was circulated by the association. However, there was evidence that after the earlier court decision, prices were not discussed at association meetings. Moreover, pricing patterns among member firms did not give the appearance of conspiracy. Prices were as a rule nonuniform, and in many instances the prices charged by members were lower than those of nonmember firms in the industry.

The Supreme Court held that a distribution of commercial information does not in itself impose a restraint on competition. The judgments obtained in the earlier trade association cases, the Court said, turned not on the distribution of information but, rather, on the Court's ability to infer "that concerted action had resulted or would necessarily result." The distinction also depended on the role of the trade association apart from gathering and circulating information. The Maple Flooring group had put together market data similar to that gathered by the association in *American Column and Lumber*. But unlike the first, this association had made no suggestions or recommendations concerning future price and production policies of members. Moreover, the association had freely publicized the information it gathered, in contrast to the earlier group, which had withheld information from interested buyers.

There is some question as to whether the *Maple Flooring* decision reflected "real" distinctions between circumstances surrounding this case and those of earlier cases. If it did not, then the Supreme Court had shifted toward a more lenient view of trade association activities.

The Sugar Institute Case (1936).[18] The Sugar Institute was a trade association of 15 firms, which controlled 70 to 80 percent of the production of domestic refined sugar. The industry had been characterized by chronic excess capacity since the end

---

[17] *Maple Flooring Manufacturers' Association* v. *U.S.*, 268 U.S. 563 (1925).

[18] *Sugar Institute* v. *U.S.*, 297 U.S. 553 (1936).

of World War I, a condition that led some producers to give secret price concessions in an effort to expand sales. The purpose of the institute was to end these concessions, which were regarded by members as "vicious and discriminatory."

Under the workings of the institute, members entered into an agreement whereby they announced in advance prices to be charged and adhered to those prices. There was no provision for agreement on price announcements—that is, each member could presumably determine his announced price independently. But once announced, the price was to be honored until altered by a subsequent announcement. The agreement was, apparently, effective in ending the secret price concessions and in raising profit margins for the industry.

The Supreme Court, referring to "the essential standard of reasonableness" embodied in the Sherman Act, stated that concerted action to curb competitive abuses does not always violate the law. Rather, Chief Justice Hughes said, the issue is whether coordinated policies go so far as to amount to an unreasonable restraint of trade. In the present case, the Court held that the gathering and distribution of information by the Sugar Institute was not inherently offensive, but that the requirement of **adherence** to price announcements was an unreasonable restraint on competition. This requirement curtailed "deviations in price which fair and open competition might require or justify." This finding by the Court was not independent of conditions in the sugar refining market. The defendant companies comprised a dominant group, and, since the products were physically standardized, price was seen as the critical variable of market competition. The relief granted by the Court prohibited the institute from pursuing its plan insofar as adherence requirements were concerned; however, the Court modified a lower court decree that would have forbidden the sugar refiners from pursuing **any** program involving "the sale, marketing, shipment, transportation, storage, distribution or deliver of refined sugar."

In its effect, the Supreme Court decision seemed consistent with earlier cases. The association was barred only from going beyond the information-gathering and dissemination processes. But the rule-of-reason orientation of the decision served, along with *Appalachian Coals,* to create uncertainty about the legal status of price fixing agreements.

The Tag Manufacturers Institute Case (1949).[19]   The Tag Manufacturers Institute, whose members accounted for 95 percent of tag products sales, gathered from participating firms list prices for each component of various products—strings, wires, eyelets, and so forth. Since the actual products were largely "custom-made," prices were generally quoted on a component basis.

The Federal Trade Commission filed suit against the institute under Section 5 of the FTC Act, charging unfair methods of competition. The Commission cited the institute's system of fines to be levied against firms that did not comply with its procedures. The circuit court, however, absolved the insitute of any violation of law, citing two decisive factors. First, the system of fines was for failure to **report**

---

[19]*Tag Manufacturers Institute et al.* v. *Federal Trade Commission,* 174 F. 2d 452 (1st Cir., 1949).

list prices—there was no requirement to **adhere** to announced lists. Second, the institute had freely publicized the data it gathered, making no effort to withhold information from customers or its members. Further, the court pointed out, real transaction prices could easily deviate from list prices by means of discounts. The treatment of the case was, thus, broadly consistent with that of *Sugar Institute*. Concerted action pursued through the device of a trade association was to be judged on its reasonableness; and that action would likely be found reasonable as long as information was made available to all who might want it, and as long as no agreement to adhere to announced prices could be inferred.

The Container Corp. Case (1969).[20] In *Container Corp.*, the Supreme Court extended legal prohibitions to an exchange of price information among competitors that involved no agreement to adhere to specified prices. Eighteen manufacturers of corrugated boxes, accounting for 90 percent of shipments from the southeastern United States, had agreed to supply each other with data on prices charged to specific customers. Information of a highly detailed nature was provided on request, and customers were identified by name.

Although the Court acknowledged that there was no agreement to follow a price schedule, Justice Douglas observed, "The exchange of price information has had an anticompetitive effect . . . . Price is too critical, too sensitive a control to allow it to be used even in an informal manner to restrain competition."

The *Container Corp.* decision may have signaled some change in attitude from that of the early trade association decisions, for the Court here struck down a plan "merely" to exchange information. It was evident, however, that the data that the box manufacturers provided to each other was unusually detailed—far more than one would expect rivals to exchange ordinarily. Further, the structural conditions of the market were quite competitive; the exchange of data may, therefore, have been necessary to facilitate pricing coordination under circumstances that were not otherwise favorable to effective collusion.

It is worth noting that despite occasional references to *per se* prohibitions, the Court applied a rule-of-reason test. The purpose, market power, and conduct of the group were all examined, as was the effect of the agreement on market performance.

Implied Conspiracy and Conscious Parallelism: the First Phase

Although the status of conspiratorial conduct under the Sherman Act is well established, the question of what constitutes a conspiracy remains troublesome. As is clear in a number of cases cited above, the courts have not required direct proof of overt conspiracy to find that defendants have conspired in violation of the law. The courts have, rather, been willing at times to infer agreement from the surrounding circumstances. The pertinent question now becomes: What are the circumstances? In other words, how far will the courts go, or how far ought they to go, to find that a conspiracy is implied by facts in the absence of direct evidence?

[20] *U.S.* v. *Container Corp. of American et al.*, 393 U.S. 333 (1969).

The Eastern States Retail Lumber Dealers' Association Case (1914).[21]   The origins of the "implied conspiracy" doctrine are usually traced to this early trade association case. The facts were simple. The association circulated lists of wholesale lumber dealers who were known to be selling at retail as well. After the association lists were circulated, members generally stopped buying from the companies that had been named. This action was a type of group boycott, a concerted effort on the part of lumber retailers to punish those wholesalers who were bypassing them in the market.

As clear as the behavior of association members seemed, however, there was no known "agreement" to boycott the firms named on the lists. The lists were merely circulated, and it could be argued that each retailer made an "independent" decision after seeing the lists to cease dealing with the companies whose names appeared there. The Supreme Court, however, saw the facts as sufficient to find an unlawful agreement, noting that "conspiracies are seldom capable of proof by direct testimony, and may be inferred. . ." The existence of conspiracy, in other words, could be inferred from the behavior of participants.

The Interstate Circuit Case (1939).[22]   The implied conspiracy doctrine, which received at least tacit support in the trade association cases, was clearly reaffirmed by the Supreme Court in a case involving the distribution of movies. The manager of Interstate Circuit, Inc., a major chain of movie theaters in Texas, sent identical letters to each of eight movie distributors. The letters demanded that the distributors not release their first-run films to any theater charging admission of less than 25 cents or showing the films on double bills. If these demands were not met, the letters stated, Interstate Circuit would no longer place the distributors' films in its first-run movie theaters. Each distributor complied with these demands, and, as a result, admission prices in many movie houses underwent "drastic" increases.

The situation that existed represents a classic case of what has come to be known as **conscious parallelism**. Each movie distributor acted in identical fashion, placing the same restrictions on first-run films. Moreover, every letter sent to distributors by the manager of Interstate Circuit named all distributors as addressees; each distributor knew, therefore, that all the others were receiving identical letters and might well accede to the demands. Yet, although each distributor pursued the same course of action knowing that the others were likely to do the same, there was no direct evidence of an "agreement" among them.

The Supreme Court held that the absence of direct evidence did not preclude the finding of an unlawful agreement, as actual testimony that an agreement exists is the exception rather than the rule in such cases. The question, said the Court, is whether circumstances point to the likely existence of conspiracy. In this regard, Justice Stone stated:

[21] *Eastern States Retail Lumber Dealers' Association* v. *U.S.*, 234 U.S. 600 (1914).

[22] *Interstate Circuit, Inc.* v. *U.S.*, 306 U.S. 208 (1939).

It taxes credulity to believe that the several distributors would . . . have accepted and put into operation with substantial unanimity such far reaching changes in their business methods without some understanding that all were to join, and we reject as beyond the range of probability that it was the result of mere chance. . .

Acceptance by competitors, without previous agreement, of an invitation to participate in a plan, the necessary consequence of which . . . is restraint of interstate commerce, is sufficient to establish an unlawful conspiracy under the Sherman Act.[23]

Two significant points, then, emerge. First, the test of an agreement need not involve direct evidence of its existence; the issue can turn on the actions of competitors. In the present case, the Court could not reconcile the actions of the eight distributors with an assumption of independence. Second, it appears that even if there is **no** agreement in the sense of an overt joint decision, competitors can act so as to imply unlawful conspiracy. Under the *Interstate Circuit* approach, it appears that proof of conspiracy may be divorced from questions of overt or formal agreement. In this case, the issue had become one of judging the market behavior of competing firms. If such behavior seemed consistent only with a mutual "understanding" of some kind, the Sherman Act was breached without any need to demonstrate the mechanics involved.

The American Tobacco Case (1946).[24]   The *American Tobacco* case of 1946 again raised the question of when conspiracy can be inferred, in the absence of a demonstration of actual agreement. Three major tobacco products manufacturers— American, Liggett & Meyers, and R. J. Reynolds—and several company officials had been charged with multiple violations of the Sherman Act.

1. Conspiracy in restraint of trade.
2. Monopolization.
3. Attempt to monopolize.
4. Conspiracy to monopolize.

The defendants were convicted on all counts in a district court jury trial.

The trial court's findings against the companies were based on extensive evidence of market behavior, which the Supreme Court reviewed. The defendants, known as the Big Three of the tobacco industry, had accounted for 91 percent of cigarette sales in 1930, but their joint share had fallen to 68 percent by 1939. The main factor in this drop was the introduction of economy brand cigarettes, which sold for about 10 cents per pack as compared with the 14 to 16 cent price of the "regular" brands. Although the Big Three continued to dominate regular brand sales, they had no share of the growing economy brand portion of the market. The actions of the major

---

[23] Ibid., pp. 223, 227.
[24] *American Tobacco Co.* v. *U.S.*, 328 U.S. 781 (1946).

companies, which comprised the alleged violations of law, were undertaken in response to this threat from economy brand producers. Among these actions, the following were considered by the courts.

1. The Big Three had entered the market for low-grade tobacco and bid up prices (this tobacco was the type used in economy, but not in regular, brands of cigarettes). It was never known what the major companies did with the cheap tobacco they purchased, but the effect of the purchases was to raise the cost of materials to the economy producers.
2. Although the Big Three all bought and used the same kinds of tobacco in their regular brands, they seemed to avoid direct competition in purchasing; that is, they rarely, if ever, bid against each for the same tobacco.
3. Price differentials among the regular brands had been the rule in the industry up to approximately the time when the threat of economy brands was recognized; but there had been no price differentials since that time.
4. In 1931, during the Great Depression, Reynolds had raised the price of Camels, and the other major companies followed suit. This price increase was, in retrospect, the error that opened the way for the economy brands. By 1933, the economy brands held over 20 percent of the market, and at that point the majors, led by American, introduced a series of price cuts. During 1933, both Lucky Strike and Camels were sold at a loss; but when the threat of the economy brands appeared to subside, the Big Three again raised prices. The pattern of pricing, thus, appeared closely coordinated to drive out the smaller competitors.

Did such behavior amount to an illegal conspiracy? Detailed evidence on the above points persuaded the Court that it did. Said Justice Burton:

It is not the form of the combination or the particular means used but the result to be achieved that the statute condemns. . . . No formal agreement is necessary to constitute an unlawful conspiracy. Often crimes are a matter of inference deduced from the acts of the person accused and done in pursuance of a criminal purpose. Where the conspiracy is proved, as here, from the evidence of the action taken in concert by the parties to it, it is all the more convincing proof of an intent to exercise the power of exclusion acquired through that conspiracy. The essential combination or, conspiracy in violation of the Sherman Act may be found in a course of dealing or other circumstances as well as in an exchange of words. . . . Where the circumstances are such as to warrant a jury in finding that the conspirators had a unity of purpose or a common design and understanding, or a meeting of minds in an unlawful arrangement, the conclusion that a conspiracy is established is justified.[25]

Once again, then, conspiracy was found without direct evidence of overt agreement. If the actions of competitors reflect collusion, it is not necessary to show that an "exchange of words" also took place.

---

[25] Ibid., pp. 809–810.

The *American Tobacco* decision was widely hailed as a new departure in antitrust law. An illegal conspiracy had been found on the basis of evidence showing only that the companies had acted in parallel ways. Their prices had moved together. They had entered markets and made purchases that, in combination, could only have helped their cause and hurt their competitors. And they had avoided any "hard" competition with each other in the purchase of tobacco. To some, the Big Three had done no more and no less than rational oligopolists normally attempt to do. Yet if this were the case, then the courts had, in effect, condemned ordinary oligopoly. As William H. Nicholls put it, ". . . . the courts have at last brought oligopolistic industries within reach of successful prosecution under the antitrust laws."[26]

Although this conclusion appears in retrospect to have been premature, the Court did go beyond its decision in *Interstate Circuit*. Rather than proving that rivals had accepted an invitation to participate in a restraint of trade, the government here had only to show actions implying a "unity of purpose" among the tobacco manufacturers.

The Paramount Case (1948).[27]   The conscious parallelism doctrine was applied again in a case involving five major integrated movie companies. The companies demonstrated a long history of parallel behavior in various aspects of their businesses: They specified the same minimum admission prices in licenses granted to exhibitors of their copyrighted films; the clearances—that is, time periods separating the first run of a film from subsequent runs—were substantially the same; and in dealing with exhibitors, identical terms were frequently imposed by the five.

The Supreme Court decision in *Paramount* ratified the earlier doctrine of *Interstate Circuit* and *American Tobacco*. Justice Douglas stated:

It is not necessary to find an express agreement in order to find a conspiracy. It is enough that a concert of action is contemplated and that the defendants conformed to the arrangement.[28]

The conclusion that conspiracy may be inferred from parallel practices was the same as that in *American Tobacco*, but the remedial action was more significant. In addition to prohibiting specific trade practices, the Court ordered a review of the theater holdings of the major producer-distributors. By 1952, all major companies had agreed to consent decrees requiring divestiture of their theater interests. It is widely agreed that the divorce of exhibition from distribution and production created a more vigorous competitive environment, and some observers consider the *Paramount* remedy one of the most successful in recent antitrust experience.[29]

---

[26]"The Tobacco Case of 1946," *American Economic Review*, **39** (May 1949), 284–296.

[27]*U.S.* v. *Paramount Pictures, Inc.*, 334 U.S. 131 (1948)

[28]Ibid., p. 142.

[29]For a useful discussion, see Donald Dewey, *Monopoly in Economics and Law*, (New York: Rand McNally, 1959), pp. 260–263.

The Cement Institute Case (1948).[30]   The *Cement Institute* case involved the operation of a multiple basing-point system and raised a number of issues distinct from that of conspiracy under the Sherman Act. Under the system, the delivered price quoted to buyers was determined by the base price—that is, price at point of origin—plus freight charges from the relevant basing point, rather than from the seller's location. The Federal Trade Commission had also brought suit under the FTC Act—for unfair methods of competition—and under the Clayton Act—for price discrimination. The issue raised by the Sherman Act was whether adherence to the basing-point system by sellers amounted to conspiracy, in the absence of any demonstrable overt agreement to do so. The Court's finding on this point was in keeping with earlier decisions. It ruled that the Commission was justified in finding an implied agreement, in light of evidence that members of the institute had acted so as to maintain the multiple point pricing system.

The importance of conscious parallelism was emphasized additionally in the *Rigid Steel Conduit* case, also decided in 1948.[31] Here, an appellate court held that general use of a basing-point pricing system constitutes circumstantial evidence of conspiracy. Said the Court:

. . . each conduit seller knows that each of the other sellers is using the basing point formula; each knows that by using it he will be able to quote identical delivered prices and thus present a condition of matched prices under which purchasers are isolated and deprived of choice.[32]

Implied Conspiracy: Recent Developments

By the end of 1948, any highly detailed parallelism of action among competing firms was suspect. The courts had not gone so far as to say that uniform pricing by companies that are aware of the uniformity is itself illegal; but uniformity had been the key to a demonstration of illegal conspiracy in numerous cases. In retrospect, however, it appears that, whatever the courts may have meant, 1948 was the high watermark of the conscious parallelism doctrine. Beginning in 1949, the trend of judicial opinion seemed to turn in a different direction.

The Pevely Dairy Case (1949).   The *Pevely Dairy* case raised in a graphic way the question of whether consciously parallel action by competitors violates the law. Two St. Louis dairies, which accounted for almost two thirds of relevant market sales, behaved identically in many aspects of their businesses. The companies charged identical prices, and when one changed its price, the other followed within 48 hours. Moreover, the companies' frequency of delivery was the same, and the cooling equipment that they provided to retailers was identical. In short, there was no deviation in pricing, products, or services. The parallelism between the two was virtually complete.

---

[30] *Federal Trade Commission* v. *Cement Institute*, 333 U.S. 683 (1948).

[31] *Triangle Conduit and Cable Co.* v. *Federal Trade Commission*, 168 F. 2d 175 (7th Cir. 1948).

[32] Ibid.

A trial court found, on the basis of parallel behavior, a conspiracy in violation of the Sherman Act. This decision, however, was reversed in circuit court.[33] This court held that the behavior of the companies, although it might have implied conspiracy, was also compatible with innocent, nonconspiratorial action. Since criminal charges were involved, the doubt was resolved in favor of the defendants. The court's position was that the observed behavior of the companies could have resulted from a conspiracy, but it also could have resulted from "independent" decisions. The two dairies offered a standardized—physically identical, if not "homogeneous"—product. Both firms paid the same (government controlled) prices for fluid milk, and they paid identical wages (having bargained with the same labor union). In the view of the court:

. . . *milk* . . . *was a standardized product. Its cost items being substantially identical for both appellants, uniformity in price would result from economic forces. . . . We are clear that mere uniformity of prices in the sale of a standardized commodity is not in itself evidence of a violation of the Sherman Act.*[34]

This decision represented a step back from the strict conscious parallelism doctrine. It raised clearly the argument that in certain market circumstances, competitors can "independently" arrive at identical policies. Such a possibility was not explicitly denied by the courts in earlier decisions; nevertheless, *Pevely* did appear to represent something of a break with earlier doctrine.

The Milgram–Loew's Case (1951).[35] The *Milgram–Loew's* case was initiated by Milgram, an independent drive-in theater operator. Eight major film distributors refused to supply the drive-in with first-run films, even though the operator offered to pay more than the prevailing market price for such films. Milgram charged that distributors had conspired to boycott him. In response, the distributors argued that their actions, although identical, had not been conspiratorial. Rather, they maintained, their classifications of theaters were based on independent business judgment; and their refusals to place first-run films in the drive-in were based on such factors as the seasonal nature of the drive-in business, the threat of bad weather, and the relatively limited audience to which such theaters appeal.

The trial court held that the denial of films by the eight distributors demonstrated a conspiracy in violation of the Sherman Act. This decision was upheld by a circuit court, which noted the rarity of direct evidence in conspiracy cases. Said the court:

. . . *There is no dispute over the proposition that circumstantial evidence will sustain a finding of conspiracy. . . . Uniform participation by competitors in a particular system of doing business, where each is aware of the others' activities, the effect of which is restraint of interstate commerce, is sufficient to establish an unlawful conspiracy.*[36]

---

[33] *Pevely Dairy Co.* v. *U.S.*, 178 F. 2d 363 (8th Cir. 1949). The decision of the circuit court became final when the Supreme Court refused certiorari, 339 U.S. 942.

[34] Ibid., pp. 368–369.

[35] *Milgram* v. *Loew's, Inc.*, 192 F. 2d (3rd Cir., 1951), certiorari denied 343 U.S. 929.

[36] Ibid., pp. 583–584.

Conscious parallelism, then, played a role in establishing conspiracy; but this finding, the circuit court continued, was limited.

This does not mean, however, that in every case mere consciously parallel business practices are sufficient evidence in themselves, from which a court may infer concerted action.[37]

Milgram–Loew's seems to have reasserted the doctrine of conscious parallelism; however, the qualification of the appeals court was a significant one. Parallel behavior may help to establish conspiracy in some cases; yet it may be insufficient in others. This kind of judicial outlook suggests that clear rules for establishing the existence of conspiracy may be impossible. It is at least conceivable that in marginal cases, the courts will simply have to "get the feel" of the situation, rather than rely on well-established guides to illegality.

The C-O Two Case (1952).[38]   In the *C-O Two* case, four manufacturers of fire extinguishers were accused of conspiracy. The companies charged uniform prices for extinguishers of identical size and design. They had uniform licensing agreements with distributors and a history of identical bids submitted to public agencies. In their defense, the companies claimed that, as in *Pevely,* parallelism is natural when products are standardized. This defense was rejected by the circuit court, which cited an "artificial standardization" of the product, the detailed parallelism in all aspects of the businesses, and the companies' history of coordination. The court refused to believe that this record could be explained other than by conspiracy. The companies' actions, it stated, were "inconsistent with any other reasonable hypothesis."

The Theatre Enterprises Case (1954).[39]   In *Theatre Enterprises*, a suburban Baltimore theater located in a shopping center, was unable to obtain first-run films from distributors and sued for treble damages. The distributors limited these films to eight downtown theaters, three of which they themselves owned. The arguments of the suburban theater operator and the distributors were similar in substance to those in *Milgram–Loew's*. Here, however, the Supreme Court found in favor of the distributors, holding that their behavior was consistent with independent business judgment.

The distributors had indeed acted uniformly, restricting first-run status to the downtown houses. The Court, however, found that such uniformity did not amount to a conspiracy, as charged by the theater operator. Justice Clark, speaking for the Court, stated:

To be sure, business behavior is admissible circumstantial evidence from which the fact finder may infer agreement. . . . But this Court has never held that proof of

---

[37] Ibid., p. 583.

[38] *C-O Two Fire Equipment Co.* v. *U.S.,* 197 F. 2d 489 (9th Cir. 1952), certiorari denied, 344 U.S. 892.

[39] *Theatre Enterprises, Inc.* v. *Paramount Film Distributing Corp. et al.,* 346 U.S. 537 (1954).

parallel business behavior conclusively established agreement or, phrased differently, that such behavior itself constitutes a Sherman Act offense. Circumstantial evidence of consciously parallel behavior may have made heavy inroads into the traditional judicial attitude toward conspiracy, but "conscious parallelism" has not yet read conspiracy out of the Sherman Act entirely.[40]

Although the language of the Court seems clear, the precise status of parallelism after *Theatre Enterprises* remains somewhat ambiguous. "Mere" parallel behavior is not sufficient to show conspiracy; yet it may constitute part of such a demonstration. The pertinent question in conspiracy cases is apparently whether parallel business behavior could have been the product of independent decisions. If an independence hypothesis does not tax the credulity of the court, a conclusion of innocence may be reached.

The Eli Lilly Case (1959).[41]   During the 1950s, six drug manufacturers had contracted with the National Foundation for Infantile Paralysis to produce Salk polio vaccine. After expiration of the agreement, the companies submitted competing bids to government agencies for new orders of vaccine. The prices quoted on these bids were uniform, and similar price changes were undertaken by various companies within weeks of each other. A district court dismissed conspiracy charges against the companies on the grounds that their behavior could have been the result of independent action; that is, their behavior was consistent with a hypothesis of innocence.

This decision serves to emphasize the difficulties that federal, state, and local governments frequently encounter in their roles as purchasers. The purpose of competitive sealed bidding is to force potential suppliers to quote their best price. If bidding is truly competitive, a supplier can only quote a high price at the risk of losing business. In many instances, however, government agencies receive identical bids. The existence of such uniformity often must raise the suspicion of conspiracy. One economist, Vernon A. Mund, has argued that conspiracy is the **only** plausible explanation of identical bidding under some circumstances.[42] Yet as the *Lilly* decision indicates, it is difficult to show that such bids imply a violation of law. As long as the product is standardized, bidding companies face similar costs, or there is some "traditional" pricing system in the industry, then the hypothesis of innocent parallelism may well be accepted.

The Pfizer (Tetracycline) Case (1973).   A prolonged test of legal conspiracy doctrine began in 1961, when the government charged three large drug companies— Charles Pfizer, American Cyanamid, and Bristol-Myers—with violating Sections 1 and 2 of the Sherman Act. What was specifically alleged was a conspiracy by the three to confine tetracycline production and sales to themselves under "substantially identical and non-competitive prices."

---

[40]Ibid., pp. 540–541.

[41]U.S. v. *Eli Lilly & Co.*, Crim. No. 173-58, D.N.J. (1959).

[42]Vernon A. Mund, "Identical Bid Prices," *Journal of Political Economy*,**68** (April 1960), 150–159.

The factual picture was unusually complicated, even for an antitrust case. Representatives of Pfizer and Cyanamid had met in 1953 to settle conflicting claims to the patent rights for tetracycline production; and later meetings occurred between Pfizer and Bristol executives to settle a patent infringement action brought by Pfizer. Although the government did not attack the specific agreements reached by the companies, it claimed that these meetings and agreements were "initial evidence" of a broader conspiracy to exclude competitors from the tetracycline market and to fix prices therein.

The companies were convicted by a district court in 1968;[43] but they won reversal of the conviction on appeal.[44] The appellate decision held, in part, that the district court judge had erred in emphasizing to the jury such "inflammatory issues" as profits and "high prices." Although the district court judge (Judge Frankel) had been careful to note that the reasonableness of prices (or profits) was not itself the legal issue, he had pointed out to the jury that price or profit behavior might be relevant in indicating the existence of an illegal agreement.

The case was appealed to the Supreme Court, which remanded the case following a tie (3 to 3) vote.[45] In the most recent district court decision, Judge Cannella held simply that the government "failed to meet its burden of proof."[46] Despite the evidence of meetings, high prices, and uniform prices, the court was not convinced "beyond the 'hesitation' point" that "anything other than the exercise of independent business judgment" had occurred.

Refusals to Deal

We have already seen one case, *Eastern States Retail Lumber Dealers,* in which the proximate objective of an agreement was not to fix price but rather to boycott certain sellers. Although individual firms have a right to refuse to deal with others, concerted boycotts by groups of firms have long been regarded as *per se* violations of Section 1 of the Sherman Act.

The beginnings of a *per se* doctrine may be traced to *Montague & Co. v. Lowry.*[47] The defendants in this case were an association of wholesale dealers in tiles, mantels, and grates in the San Francisco area, and of manufacturers of these products located in other states, who sold to dealer-members. The bylaws of the association provided that no dealer-member should purchase from any manufacturer who was not also a member and that sales at less than list price not be made to any nonmember. The penalty for violation of these laws was expulsion from the association. The Supreme Court held that the association "constituted or amounted to an

[43] *U.S.* v. *Chas. Pfizer & Co., Inc. et al.,* 281 F. Supp. 837 (SDNY, 1968).

[44] *Chas. Pfizer & Co., Inc.* v. *U.S.,* 426 F. 2d 41 (1970).

[45] 404 U.S. 548 (1972).

[46] *U.S.* v. *Chas. Pfizer & Co., Inc.,* 367 F. Supp. 91 (SDNY, 1973).

[47] 193 U.S. 38 (1904).

agreement or combination in restraint of trade''; and it termed the defendants' contention that the amount of commerce involved was negligible "not very material.''

Later rulings have followed a similar approach. In *Paramount Famous Lasky Corp.* v. *United States,* a group of motion picture distributors and producers had adopted standard contracts with exhibitors.[48] The contracts provided that any disputes were to go to arbitration; but they also stated that the failure of an exhibitor to agree to arbitration, or to abide by an arbitrated award, would result in common punitive action by the group. The Supreme Court held that, despite the usefulness of arbitration in the industry, the agreement suppressed competition and was illegal. The Sherman Act, said the Court, cannot "be evaded by good motives.''

In *Fashion Originators' Guild of America, Inc.* v. *Federal Trade Commission,* the guild, an association of textile manufacturers and designers, had entered into an agreement with a group of garment manufacturers.[49] Under the agreement, members of the guild were to supply textiles to the garment makers only on condition that the makers did not use the textiles of "pirate" suppliers—those whose textile designs were copied from the designs of guild members. Further, the garment manufacturers were to supply only those retailers who similarly refused to buy garments from pirates. This was, then, a group boycott by guild members of both manufacturers and retailers who dealt with pirate suppliers.

The guild argued that its original designs could not be protected under existing patent or copyright laws and that the agreement was "reasonable and necessary to protect against the devastating evils growing from the pirating of original designs.'' The Supreme Court held, however, that the guild's plan was in conflict with the principles of all major antitrust laws—the Sherman, Clayton, and Federal Trade Commission acts. Justice Black observed that the guild had gone well beyond the agreement; it had, for example, attempted to control the advertising, sales, and discount policies of members and local guilds. Yet the plan itself was sufficiently anticompetitive to justify FTC findings of illegality. Said the Court:

. . . *the reasonableness of the methods pursued by the combination to accomplish its unlawful object is no more material than would be the reasonableness of the prices fixed by unlawful combination.*[50]

The *per se* illegality of group refusals to deal has been repeatedly reaffirmed. In *Klor's, Inc.* v. *Broadway-Hale Stores, Inc.,* Broadway-Hale, a department store chain, had used its buying power to induce major appliance companies not to deal with Klor's, a retail price-cutter, or to sell to Klor's at "highly unfavorable" terms.[51] In striking down this practice, the Supreme Court observed:

[48] 282 U.S. 30 (1930).
[49] 312 U.S. 457 (1941).
[50] Ibid., p. 468.
[51] 359 U.S. 207 (1959).

Group boycotts, or concerted refusals by traders to deal with other traders have long been held to be in the forbidden category. They have not been saved by allegations that they were reasonable.[52]

The legal status of refusals to deal thus seems clear. An individual seller may refuse to deal with anyone, but it **may not join with others** to boycott any supplier or customer. Moreover, there has been relatively little difficulty in establishing the existence of concerted boycotts, which are, by their nature, difficult to effect on a tacit and informal basis.

THE CURRENT LEGAL STATUS OF CONSPIRACY

As we have seen, certain kinds of restraints and conspiracies are considered illegal *per se* under the Sherman Act. The apparent simplicity of the *per se* doctrine, however, is somewhat misleading. It condemns market-rigging agreements without defining them. As a result, the courts are faced with a rather strange dilemma. Certain areas of behavior are clearly proscribed by legal precedent; at the same time, however, the existence of the offensive behavior can be extremely difficult to establish. Consequently, the courts are required to consider not so much the legal fate of conspiracy as the meaning of the term.

The reaction of the courts to this task has been unsurprising. Cases of obvious conspiracy are dealt with uniformly: Where there is direct evidence of agreement, conviction is virtually certain. At the other extreme, mere similarity of behavior on the part of competitors is unlikely to result in legal action, much less conviction for violation of the Sherman Act, unless it is accompanied by other incriminating evidence. Price leadership, for example, is a mode of parallelism that has not commonly been brought within the act's coverage.

In general, the more elaborate a conspiracy is, the greater is the likelihood of legal sanctions. This is simply because complex and detailed agreements will usually require conspirators to communicate. When evidence of communication can be produced in court, the outcome of a trial is no longer in doubt; but such direct information is seldom obtained.

A crucial question is how far the courts are willing to go to infer conspiracy from circumstantial evidence. In other words, what do the courts do in the absence of direct proof that accused firms overtly agreed to terms? This question can be answered only tentatively, for recent decisions are ambiguous. *Theatre Enterprises* indicated that parallel business behavior does not *itself* violate the Sherman Act—something more is necessary; but the courts have not defined precisely what "something more" means.

In some cases involving conscious parallelism, the courts have stated that a judgment must be made about the possible independence of firms' actions. If the parallel behavior is such that it could have resulted from independent decisions, then it is legally acceptable; if, on the other hand, it could only have resulted from conspir-

[52]Ibid., p. 212.

acy, it violates the law. The difficulty with this on-the-surface plausible standard is its vagueness. Although it may be simple enough to categorize extreme cases, there is, at times, no obvious way to distinguish innocent from guilty parallelism.

If it is difficult to say precisely what the courts' standards of conspiracy **are,** it is somewhat easier to note what they are **not.** Certainly the past 20 years of litigation do not bear out the late-1940s notion that rational oligopoly is somehow illegal. The courts have not moved to condemn "normal" oligopolistic behavior, and they have given no indication that similar action by firms will be generally presumed to violate the law. At the same time, it would be incorrect to conclude that conscious parallelism no longer plays a role in conspiracy cases. Identical behavior by firms is legally significant **in conjunction** with other factors. Almarin Phillips has suggested, for example, that parallelism in a context that is somehow "unreasonable" will be condemned more quickly than similar parallelism without undesirable implications.[53] And it may be that when uniformity of action is complete and highly detailed, it will likely be found inconsistent with a hypothesis of independent action.

The language of conspiracy cases is, at times, extremely vague. It is evident, however, that the judicial definition of conspiracy is now a rather narrow one, and it is certainly narrow compared with the definitions implicit in decisions through 1948. Although the courts have continued to note that direct evidence of overt agreement is rare, they are less hospitable to indirect inferences than they once were. Much tacit conspiracy—that is, the type of collusive behavior that proceeds without overt agreement—seems today to be beyond the reach of the Sherman Act.

THE ECONOMIC MEANING OF THE CONSPIRACY DOCTRINE

Having reviewed the legal status of conspiracy, it is now pertinent to ask whether this area of public competition policy has been developed in an economically sensible way.

Definitions of Conspiracy

As we have seen, the courts have tried to distinguish between independent and interdependent (conspiratorial) behavior. Phillips points out, however, that such a distinction may be more semantic than real.[54] In certain markets the actions of any firm affect the conditions facing other firms. A decision with respect to price or output by a company a_1 will change the feasible price–quantity combinations for firms a_2, a_3, . . . a_i. Similarly, what any "other" firm does must "react back" on its rivals. This is the meaning of interdependence. Firms may attempt to deal with such interdependence in various ways. But what the courts have failed to realize is that "independent" action is an impossibility in these circumstances. Even if firms

[53] Almarin Phillips, *Market Structure, Organization and Performance* (Cambridge, Mass.: Harvard University Press, 1962), pp. 62 ff.

[54] Ibid., pp 72–73.

should choose to "ignore" interdependence, perhaps in the manner of Cournot duopolists, it simply will not go away!

Consider as an example the automobile manufacturing industry. The prices at which the Ford Motor Company can sell various quantities of new cars depends in part on the price and output policies of General Motors (and also, to a lesser degree, on the policies of Chrysler, American Motors, and a number of foreign manufacturers). Ford has a variety of policy options. But "independence" of its rivals is not one of them—that is, Ford is not free to behave as though General Motors does not exist. No matter how independent the company would like to be, no matter how independent its managers may feel, Ford simply cannot do the things it might be able to if General Motors, Chrysler, and Volkswagen were to disappear. In this sense, the company can act *only* in an "interdependent" way.

Clearly, then, it makes little sense for the courts to search for truly independent behavior in markets whose structure implies interdependence. But what are the implications of the courts' apparent determination to undertake such a search? The immediate result is semantic confusion. Beyond this, however, it is evident that judges are making distinctions of some kind, even if the distinctions are not actually between independence and interdependence in firms' behavior.

What is being distinguished seems, rather, to be the degree of **explicitness** or **formality** in coordinated behavior. The courts have not required direct proof of overt agreement, and convictions have been obtained without transcripts of conversations or reports of meetings among competitors. But it does appear that an important element in conspiracy cases is the presence or absence of a presumption that such overt communication has occurred. The trade association cases, for example, did not yield conclusive evidence of what could be called formal or explicit agreement to fix prices and output levels; but an important factor in these cases was the kind of communication that the associations facilitated. Similarly, the *American Tobacco* case evidenced no open agreement among the industry's Big Three; but their actions were so finely dovetailed that the presumption of overt communication was strong. In contrast, the *Pevely Dairy* case showed a history of complete and precise parallelism. Here, however, it was possible to believe that the two companies had attained their existing state of coordination without explicit communication and agreement.

This distinction cannot be offered as a full interpretation of recent judicial actions. Other factors—for instance, the effectiveness of concerted behavior and the damage suffered by competitors or customers—may enter in. It does appear, however, that the courts proceed from a rather narrow definition of "agreement." An agreement will be found when there is strong reason to believe that companies must have overtly agreed to formulate concerted policies. When concerted policies can be interpreted as the result of purely tacit "understandings"—that is, when communication is not necessary—illegal agreement is much less likely to be found by the courts. In applying this kind of standard, the courts are not distinguishing meaningfully between "independent" and "collusive" behavior, whatever they may claim.

To the extent that the courts search for evidence of classic overt conspiracy, some question about the economic value of the policy must arise. It is quite true, as seen in Chapter 3, that a collusive oligopoly may yield substantially different market results than an oligopoly in which rivals compete actively. But we do not know the extent to which **formal** or **overt** agreement is, in general, necessary to successful collusion. Explicit communication—in effect, overtness—will of course be necessary in some circumstances. As Carl Kaysen has pointed out, the larger the number of firms and the greater the degree of uncertainty and ignorance in the market, the less likely it is that collusive results can be achieved without overt dealings among the rivals.[55] Once the situation becomes sufficiently complicated that firms cannot "naturally" follow a coordinated course, communication is required.[56]

In many of the cases that are discussed above, however, the number of conspirators is small, and it is not clear that explicit agreement is needed. As Kaysen states:

The significance of . . . recognition of mutual dependence . . . is that, given a common goal of action . . . no machinery of reporting or enforcement is needed to secure adherence to the goal by the rivals. Each seller, knowing the common goal, realizes that he can gain nothing by actions not in conformity with it.[57]

Consider an example in which a small group of firms sells closely substitutable products. Each firm may be aware that a price cut will cause the others also to reduce their prices and will, thus, prove to be unprofitable. Indeed, price cuts could lead to price warfare, a contingency that all firms are likely anxious to avoid. Cognizance of the situation may well prevent any company from cutting its price. As market conditions change, the need for price adjustments will become apparent. Some firm or firms may over time assume the role of leading their rivals in such adjustments; but as adjustments occur, each rival will continue to recognize the desirability of "staying in line." Price competition may disappear in this fashion, even though there is no actual communication among the rivals. In fact, it is quite possible that purely informal price leadership will establish the same market results that overt communication would have produced.

This possibility points out the artificiality of the legal standards currently applied to conspiracy. If overt communication occurs, the Sherman Act has certainly been

[55] Carl Kaysen, "Collusion Under the Sherman Act," *Quarterly Journal of Economics,* **65** (May 1951), 263–270. Economists have been interested in determining precisely the market conditions that encourage or discourage collusion. The seminal theoretical treatment is George J. Stigler's "A Theory of Oligopoly," *Journal of Political Economy,* **72** (February 1964), 44–61. Since collusion is difficult to observe, however, the gathering of empirical evidence is seriously hindered. About all that can be done is to examine firms and markets in which **legally defined** conspiracy occurs. For some findings, see George A. Hay and Daniel Kelley, "An Empirical Survey of Price-Fixing Conspiracies," *Journal of Law and Economics,* **17** (April 1974), 13–38; and Peter Asch and Joseph J. Seneca, "Characteristics of Collusive Firms," *Journal of Industrial Economics,* **23** (March 1975), 223–237.

[56] As Chapter 9 notes, this situation may account for the finding by Burton and Clabault of a higher incidence of Sherman Act indictments in industries of lower concentration.

[57] See footnote 55; Kaysen, p. 267. See also F. M. Scherer, "Focal Point Pricing and Conscious Parallelism," *Antitrust Bulletin,* **12** (Summer 1967), 495–503.

violated; without such communication, the behavior of firms is more likely to be legal. Yet there is no necessary **economic** distinction between the two cases. The judgment of the law turns here on the purely mechanical aspect of what is in both instances collusive action.

The important policy question is: How frequently does effective collusion require the kinds of behavior that the law is likely to discover and punish? If the answer is "seldom," then a policy that prohibits such (overt) behavior will have limited economic effects. If the answer is "usually," the impact of such a policy will be stronger. Writers such as Stigler are optimistic, suspecting that the law has curtailed the most effective forms of collusion.[58] Supporting theory and evidence, however, remain fragmentary.

Treatment of Conspiracy

American courts have long accepted the proposition that conspiracy is a bad thing. Firms acting in concert presumably do so to raise prices and profits—in short, to act more as a monopolist would. About the only positive benefit of conspiracy that can be cited is that it may impose order on a market. In the absence of some type of coordination, competition among firms could, at times, become chaotic, and some markets might become unstable. It is also possible that some types of agreement will stimulate technology or otherwise reduce costs. Overall, however, the case for conspiracy is unpersuasive.[59] In condemning conspiracy as a *per se* offense, the courts in effect presume that possible benefits are relatively negligible.

Few economists have argued strongly against the *per se* doctrine as it applies to collusion and restraint of trade, and the benefits of the associated policy are apparent.[60] True cartels simply do not exist in the United States, an absence that one observer calls "the major achievement" of antitrust.[61]

Despite this judgment, it is not clear that enthusiasm for Section 1 policies among American economists is overwhelming. At issue again is the kind of collusive behavior proscribed by the courts. If we succeed in stopping formal cartels while permitting tacit collusion that yields somewhat similar results, how much have we accomplished? Some policy benefits unquestionably exist, if only because tacit agreements may be less efficient, *ceteris paribus,* in achieving their ends. Although we have not eliminated collusive behavior in any broad sense, we have made it more costly to pursue. The size of this gain is not easily defined, however.

Posner has proposed a legal approach to detection and proof that would cover at least some types of tacit collusion.[62] His procedure would first examine whether

---

[58] George J. Stigler, "The Economic Effects of the Antitrust Laws," *Journal of Law and Economics,* **9** (October 1966), 225–258.

[59] Not everyone would agree. See, for example, Donald Dewey, "Information, Entry, and Welfare: The Case for Collusion," *American Economic Review,* **69** (September 1979), 587–594.

[60] Notable exceptions are Phillips (see footnote 54) and Dewey (ibid.).

[61] Richard A. Posner, *Antitrust Law* (Chicago: University of Chicago Press, 1976), p. 39.

[62] Ibid., pp. 55–77.

market conditions favor effective collusion (high seller concentration, inelastic demand at the competitive price, a standardized product, and lower probability of rapid entry, for example, would suggest a propitious environment) and then seek to determine whether behavior is in fact collusive (patterns of pricing, profits, and change in market share over time would be among the factors examined). The feasibility of this interesting proposal is uncertain. One may worry, for example, that a vigorous attack on tacit collusion will, beyond some point, become a futile effort to outlaw rational oligopoly behavior; and it is not obvious that the kinds of evidence examined would consistently lead to clear-cut conclusions about the existence of collusion.[63]

Evidence on the effects of Section 1 policy is fragmentary. W. Bruce Erickson has shown that price-fixing conspiracies may succeed in pushing prices up substantially.[64] Evidence gathered by Asch and Seneca, however, demonstrates that firms convicted of collusion are less profitable than other firms, *ceteris paribus*.[65] Whereas the "true" interpretation of this finding is unclear, one possibility is that Sherman Act prosecutions focus on unsuccessful (thus unprofitable) conspiracies—not a tendency that would inspire great confidence about policy impact.

Two recent studies indicate that prosecution of price fixers induces more competitive behavior among the defendant firms—that is, prices closer to costs—and that this effect may "spill over" to other firms in affected industries.[66] Such results are grounds for optimism, suggesting that antitrust activity has salutory effects on market behavior. How important or widespread these effects may be, however, we do not yet know.

A further issue in public policies toward conspiracy concerns the nature of remedies imposed once guilt is determined. The usual penalty for a criminal conviction is a fine, limited to a maximum of $1 million per defendant per violation. Until 1975 the maximum was $50,000, but actual fines were assessed, for the most part, at much lower levels.

Although it is reasonable to suppose that fines have become heftier since 1975,[67] the basic question is a broader one. Antitrust violators have always faced some probability—frequently a very low one—of punishment. A fine might constitute that punishment, but other possibilities also exist: Treble-damage suits, brought by

[63] See Donald F. Turner, "The Definition of Agreement Under the Sherman Act: Conscious Parallelism and Refusals to Deal, *Harvard Law Review,* 75 (February 1962), 655–706.

[64] "Price-Fixing Conspiracies: Their Long-term Impact," *Journal of Industrial Economics,* 42 (March 1976), 189–202.

[65] Peter Asch and J. J. Seneca, "Is Collusion Profitable?" *Review of Economics and Statistics,* 58 (February 1976), 1–12.

[66] Robert M. Feinberg, "Antitrust Enforcement and Subsequent Price Behavior," *Review of Economics and Statistics,* 62 (November 1980), 609–612; and Michael Kent Block, Frederick Carl Nold, and Joseph Gregory Sidak, "The Deterrent Effects of Antitrust Enforcement," *Journal of Political Economy,* 89 (June 1981), 429–445.

[67] Richard A. Posner, however, points out that "a change in maximum penalities is an indirect, and in magnitude uncertain, method of changing the actual penalities." "A Statistical Study of Antitrust Enforcement," *Journal of Law and Economics,* 13 (October 1970), 365–419. And Kenneth G. Elzinga and William Breit note with regard to the new fines ceiling: "In an expected value sense, its size is small." *The Antitrust Penalties* (New Haven: Yale University Press, 1976), p. 61.

those seeking to prove that the violation harmed them, could result in potentially large financial penalties; and even prison sentences for individuals, although seldom employed, lurk in the background.

The problem of remedies, however, goes beyond the question of how much punishment can be heaped on companies (or persons) that conspire to rig market transactions. The very notion that there is such a thing as a punitive "remedy" hinges again on the proposition that conspiracy is a specific type of conduct. Since the law defines it as such, punitive measures are consistent: A conspirator is someone who behaves badly; therefore, to induce better behavior, the bad behavior is punished.[68] Broader economic notions of collusion, however, suggest that punishment will not solve anything. Generally collusive behavior cannot meaningfully be described as a pure conduct phenomenon. It is not something as simple and precise as a series of meetings. Rather, it is a taking account of the mutual interdependence that is implied by the **structural** conditions of the market.

Viewed in these terms, it is clear that punishment is unlikely to reform a collusive market. It does not matter how great the punishment may be. There is simply no way that a court can order firms to act independently in a market whose structural conditions imply interdependence.

---

[68] Elzinga and Breit argue that fines can be levied so as to induce the socially appropriate level of deterrence; they specifically reject the contention that "more" punishment will produce consistently "better" results. (Ibid., especially chapter 7.)

CHAPTER 13

Antitrust Treatment
of Monopoly

The economic meaning of "monopoly" may be viewed in either a broad or narrow fashion. Any firm that has some control over the terms at which it supplies the market can be said to possess a degree of market power. Clearly, however, not every firm with a degree of power is likely to pose a public policy problem nor are most of those firms likely to be thought of as "monopolists." Indeed, any situation short of **pure** monopoly may also be said to reflect a degree of **competition.**

At what point—at what "level" or "degree" of market control—should society become concerned? How should we measure or infer monopoly so as to determine when that point is reached? And if "monopoly" is, in fact, present, what shall we do about it? These are some of the immediate issues of antitrust policy. As we shall see, the courts have confined their attention largely to dominant firms—not pure monopolists, but companies whose size relative to the market suggests that they have a strong degree of power. This narrow focus, moreover, has been accompanied by judicial reluctance to take strong action, even where the existence of monopoly has been proved to the satisfaction of a court.

The treatment of dominant firms generally falls within Section 2 of the Sherman Act, although other statutes, most notably Section 1, are often involved as well. The issue in Section 2 cases is twofold: First, has monopoly in a legal sense been achieved? Second, if it has been achieved, has the firm in question "monopolized" within the meaning of the law?

In the years immediately following passage of the Sherman Act, the status of monopoly was confused. Few cases were initiated by the government, and of those that were, at least one resulted in a stunning defeat. A legal attack on the sugar trust was dismissed by the Supreme Court on the grounds that, although monopoly has been shown to exist, interstate commerce had not been affected.[1] It appeared that the Court did not regard manufacturing activity as "commerce," an interpretation that came as a shock to supporters of the Sherman Act. In the later 1890s, however, the act was effectively applied to a number of rate and price-fixing agreements.

---

[1] *U.S. v. E. C. Knight,* 156 U.S. 1 (1895).

A REVIEW OF RELEVANT CASES

The Standard Oil Case (1911)[2]

The strength of the Sherman Act was still in question when, in 1906, the government charged the Standard Oil Company of New Jersey with violations of Sections 1 and 2. Standard Oil was a huge and dominant company, which controlled about 90 percent of the nation's refining capacity. During the latter half of the nineteenth century, the company had expanded by driving competitors out of business and, in many cases, absorbing them. Standard Oil had obtained preferential treatment from railroads, thus placing considerable pressure on smaller rivals. In addition, there was evidence of "predatory" price-cutting and other practices that enabled the company to sweep local areas clean of competitors. A district court found that Standard Oil had violated the Sherman Act, and the company appealed to the Supreme Court.

The case presented the Court with a classic example of aggressive monopoly. Indeed, there was no disagreement either about the company's power or the means by which that power had been attained.[3] What was at issue was the legal status of a clear factual situation. The government argued for a literal interpretation of the Sherman Act. Section 1 states that "*Every* contract, combination . . . or conspiracy, in restraint of trade" (italics added) is illegal, and the government's position was that a strict application of this language was appropriate.

Chief Justice White, speaking for the Court, rejected this interpretation. It is not merely the fact of a contract, combination, or conspiracy in restraint of trade that is at issue, he stated. The job of the courts goes beyond fact-finding and must encompass judgments about the "nature and character" of restraints. Said the Court:

If the criterion for judging the legality of a restraint . . . is the direct or indirect effect of the acts involved, then of course the rule of reason becomes the guide.[4]

The courts were, therefore, to apply a "rule of reason" to restraints of trade. The government's contention that all restraints are illegal without reference to their character was denied. Rather, the Sherman Act would be construed to prohibit only unreasonable restraints. Chief Justice White did not spell out clear guidelines under which reasonableness can be judged, but he stressed intent as an important factor. It would thus be necessary to draw inferences about the intentions of individuals and companies accused of violations.

Having asserted the rule of reason, the Chief Justice could find "no cause to doubt the correctness" of the lower court's findings. Standard Oil's power and control of the market were such as to create "a *prima facie* presumption of intent and purpose to maintain dominancy . . . not as a result of normal methods of industrial

---

[2] *Standard Oil Co. of New Jersey* v. *U.S.*, 221 U.S. 1 (1911).

[3] John S. McGee has argued in a well-known article that Standard Oil did not achieve market dominance by means of "predatory" pricing or price discrimination and, further, that predatory strategies are frequently irrational—more costly, for example, than buying out one's rivals. See "Predatory Price Cutting: The Standard Oil (N.J.) Case," *Journal of Law and Economics*, **1** (October 1958), 137–169.

[4] Ibid., p. 66.

development, but by means of combination.'' Moreover, the Supreme Court said, the behavior of the company made evident "the intent to drive others from the field and to exclude them from their right to trade.'' The remedy ordered was dissolution of the combination. When dealing with a fait accompli, the Court said, it is not sufficient to curtail the practices that have created the situation.

The Standard Oil decision was important in two respects. It firmly established the Sherman Act as a mean of dealing with monopolistic combinations; and it made it equally clear that the application of the act would be limited to **unreasonable** combinations. The rule of reason that the Court enunciated marked an apparent break with precedent. In an earlier case, *United States* v. *Trans-Missouri Freight Assn.*, Justice Peckham had specifically rejected a contention by the defense that railroad rate-fixing agreements could be justified by their reasonableness.[5] Peckham argued that the Sherman Act should be taken literally and that the courts ought not to read into "law an exception that is not placed there by the law-making branch of the government.'' To accept a rule of reason, he predicted, would open the floodgates to future litigation in which defendants would plead the reasonableness of their illegal schemes.

Despite the unquestioned importance of the *Standard Oil* case, the decision was a vague one. The strength of the Sherman Act was amply exploited by the Court, not merely in finding against a major corporation, but in following this finding with a remedy designed to reduce the company's power and to restructure the market. What the decision might mean for future cases, however, was not clear. The Court had held that an unreasonable restraint of trade had occurred, but virtually nothing was said about the line that divides reasonableness from unreasonableness. "Abnormal'' behavior stood condemned; however, as Robert H. Bork notes, we were given "no general guide as to what behavior was abnormal.''[6] The significance of the decision, then, is not that it spelled out a rule of reason against which future acts could be judged—for it really failed to do so—but, rather, that it placed on future courts the burden of formulating such a rule.

The economic reasoning implicit in *Standard Oil* is somewhat obscure. Clearly, the Court was not concerned primarily with an economic notion of monopoly. Standard Oil had violated the Sherman Act not because it possessed monopoly power, but because it had acted with "intent" in acquiring and maintaining that power. Said the Court:

> It is remarkable that nowhere at common law can there be found a prohibition against the creation of monopoly by an individual. This would seem to manifest . . . a profound conception as to the inevitable operation of economic forces . . . . That is to say, as it was deemed that monopoly in the concrete could arise only from an act of sovereign power, and, such power being restrained, prohibi-

[5] 166 U.S. 290 (1896).

[6] Robert H. Bork, *The Antitrust Paradox* (New York: Basic Books, 1978), p. 58. For an excellent discussion of the Court's opinion, see William Letwin, *Law and Economic Policy in America* (New York: Random House, 1965), pp. 253–270.

tions as to individuals were directed not against the creation of monopoly, but were only applied to such acts . . . which might result if unrestrained, in some of the consequences of monopoly.[7]

This statement represents a viewpoint that still has wide acceptance. Monopoly is regarded as a condition that cannot arise in what might be called the "natural" course of events. In the absence of sovereign acts of power, it can be created only by the deliberate actions of individuals. Accordingly, in this view, the antitrust laws need not take aim at the **fact** of monopoly. It is sufficient instead for the laws to prohibit those **actions** that, if unrestrained, might lead to monopoly positions.

This argument raises some fundamental questions. Although anticompetitive practices may be important in creating or enhancing monopoly power, it is not at all clear that monopoly can arise only through a particular set of practices. Certainly economists are aware that partial monopolies do arise "naturally," as the result of such factors as significant economies of scale. The tendency is, in fact, so strong in some industries that public regulation is substituted for the "natural" alternative of monopoly.

The *Standard Oil* decision leaves open many important questions about antitrust treatment of monopoly. It is evident, however, that in this case violation involved the power **plus the intent** of the company, as it was inferred from actual methods of business behavior. This point was reiterated by Chief Justice White in a companion case, *United States* v. *American Tobacco Co.*[8] Wrongful purpose or intent in addition to market power is necessary, he stated, to demonstrate a violation of the Sherman Act. In this case, the actions of American Tobacco—most notably ruthless price competition—were interpreted not as the ordinary behavior of a company exercising its right to trade, but as that of a company intending to drive out competitors and monopolize trade.[9] Once again, it was not the company's actual domination of the tobacco market, but the means by which domination was achieved, that was decisive.

The United States Steel Case (1920)[10]

The United States Steel Company was created in 1901 as a combination of 12 concerns that had originally consisted of about 180 separate entities. United States Steel, the holding company that controlled the 12 producing units, was a dominant market force with close to two thirds of total ingot production at the time of its formation. Although its position had weakened, the company still controlled more than 40 percent of the market when the government brought Sherman Act charges against

---

[7]See footnote 2 above, p. 55. Notice that **sovereign** means simply **governmental**.

[8]221 U.S. 106 (1911).

[9]One might suspect, of course, that *any* good business manager will desire (thus "intend") to drive rivals out of the market. The legal issue is not this desire, but the means employed to advance it.

[10]*U.S.* v. *United States Steel Corp.*, 251 U.S. 471 (1920).

it. In its complaint, the government emphasized U.S. Steel's intent to monopolize via coercion and intimidation of its market rivals.[11]

The four-man district court that first heard the case dismissed the charges, but the judges were divided on their reasons for doing so.[12] Two judges (Buffington and McPherson) argued that the corporation was not formed with an intent to monopolize; rather, the company's size and dominance were a natural response to economies of scale and integration in the steel market. The other two judges (Wooley and Hunt) did see monopolistic intent in U.S. Steel's formation, but they concluded that the company never "possessed or exerted sufficient power when acting alone to control prices." The attempt to monopolize, in other words, had failed.

Both district court opinions agreed that U.S. Steel had not monopolized the steel industry. Indeed, evidence that the corporation had conspired with rivals to fix prices was viewed as a sign that monopoly had not been established. A true monopolist, the judges reasoned, would simply have imposed its price on the market.

The Supreme Court opinion, written by Justice McKenna, concurred with the Wooley-Hunt position. U.S. Steel, said the Court, failed to monopolize the market. Whatever its intentions, the corporation, acting by itself, was unable to dictate steel prices.

In one of the most quoted statements in antitrust law—although not a statement on which this decision turned—Justice McKenna said:

. . . the law does not make mere size an offense, or the existence of unexerted power an offense . . . . It, we repeat, requires overt acts.[13]

Here, then, was an apparent carrying forward of the rule of reason. It is size or power **plus** overt acts that may violate the Sherman Act. In the case of United States Steel, the requisite power had not been demonstrated, nor had the company resorted to the ruthless practices of Standard Oil or American Tobacco. Evidence of systematic action to harm or exclude competitors had not been presented. Indeed, the company's behavior was interpreted by the Court as a sign of its weakness. As Eugene M. Singer has pointed out, price-fixing agreements between U.S. Steel and its rivals may have done damage to competition, but competitors were unharmed.[14]

Justice Day dissented from the majority, arguing that although the law does not make mere size an offense, the size of United States Steel had been illegally obtained. In his view, the formation and early practices of the corporation violated the Sherman Act. The company, he suggested, had **attempted** to monopolize, regardless of the success or failure of its venture.

Although the *United States Steel* decision is clearly worded, there is ambiguity in its treatment of the company's intent. Justice McKenna seemed to concede the like-

---

[11] For an argrument that the government mishandled the case, see Donald Dewey, *Monopoly in Economics and Law* (New York: Rand McNally, 1959), p. 232 ff.

[12] 233 F. 55 (1915).

[13] See footnote 10 above, p. 451.

[14] Eugene M. Singer, *Antitrust Economics* (Englewood Cliffs: N.J.: Prentice-Hall, 1968), pp. 40–41.

lihood that U.S. Steel had been formed for the purpose of monopolizing. But if size alone was insufficient to violate the law, it appeared that "intent" of the sort that could be inferred here was also insufficient. Justice McKenna was apparently influenced by the absence of ruthless behavior on the part of U.S. Steel. One can only speculate what the Court might have said had the company acted ruthlessly, yet failed to achieve monopoly.

It does appear that the government may have committed a major blunder in its presentation of the case. The government's complaint rested on the proposition that U.S. Steel held a monopoly. When the Court rejected this "fact," the prosecution was undermined, for it had not built a persuasive argument with respect to the company's **attempt** to monopolize.

The Alcoa Case (1945)[15]

The *United States Steel* decision marked the beginning of a "closed season" on prosecution of dominant firms. It was not until 1937 that the government again mounted a major attack, this time against the Aluminum Company of America.

Alcoa's dominance in the production of virgin, or primary, aluminum traced back to the beginning of the twentieth century. Until 1909 the company had a legal patent monopoly on feasible methods of aluminum production. During the period 1909 to 1912, it had entered into illegal cartel agreements with foreign manufacturers to limit imports of aluminum; however, it had been ordered to abandon such arrangements and had apparently done so. As of 1937, however, Alcoa was still the sole domestic producer of virgin ingot. The government charged that this position violated Section 2 of the Sherman Act and asked that the company be dissolved.

Charges against Alcoa were dismissed by a district court in 1942, and the government appealed.[16] Judge Learned Hand of the appellate court defined two pertinent legal questions: first, whether Alcoa's monopoly of virgin ingot production, which existed in the early 1900s, had, in fact, persisted in subsequent years; second, whether such a monopoly, if it were found to persist, violated Section 2.[17] The first question, in Judge Hand's view, rested on the proper definition of the market and of Alcoa's relevant production. There were at least three distinct ways of calculating the company's position, as shown in Table 13.1.

1. If the market is primary aluminum only and Alcoa's share is based on its total output, then the company had 90 percent of the market (the remaining 10 percent was accounted for by imports).
2. If the market is defined to include secondary (scrap) as well as primary ingot, and if the company's total output is counted, then Alcoa's market share was 64 percent.

---

[15] *U.S.* v. *Aluminum Co. of America*, 148 F. 2d 416 (1945).

[16] 44 F. Supp. 97 (1942).

[17] Final disposition occurred in the court of appeals because the Supreme Court could not provide a quorum of justices qualified to hear the case.

Table 13.1 Alternative Calculations of Alcoa's Market Share

| | The Market | |
Alcoa's Output	Primary Aluminum Only	Primary and Secondary (Scrap Aluminum)
Total Production of Ingot	90%	64%
Total Production **minus** Ingot That Alcoa Retained for Its Own Use	—	33%

Numbers in cells represent Alcoa's market share calculated under each definition of the relevant market and of Alcoa's output.

3. If the market includes primary and secondary ingot, but Alcoa's output **excludes** that aluminum which the company retained for its own fabricating activities, its market share was 33 percent.

These alternatives posed a problem; for, in the judge's view, 33 percent of a market was not a monopoly, 64 percent might be, and 90 percent definitely was.

Judge Hand concluded that the 90 percent figure was appropriate. Virgin ingot produced and fabricated by the company, he argued, affected the ingot market, even though Alcoa did not sell it to other fabricators. Further, although secondary ingot might compete with primary, the judge noted that the majority of the secondary was salvaged from primary that Alcoa had produced in the first place. Alcoa, therefore, had indirect control over secondary ingot production. Said Judge Hand:

The competition of "secondary" must therefore be disregarded, as soon as we consider the position of "Alcoa" over a period of years; it was as much within "Alcoa's" control as was the production of the "virgin" from which it had been derived.[18]

Having excluded secondary aluminum from the market and included Alcoa's production for its own use in the company's output total, Alcoa's relevant market share of 90 percent followed, as calculated above.

This conclusion may be questioned in light of our earlier discussion of market definitions. Judge Hand was correct in counting Alcoa's production for own use as part of its total output; for this primary aluminum was a part of the market supply, even though it was not sold to other firms. But the exclusion of secondary aluminum from the relevant market is more dubious. Secondary and primary aluminum were admittedly substitutes, and this is the essence of a product market. To define the

---

[18]See footnote 15 above, p. 425.

market as if secondary aluminum did not matter was to construct an artificial product grouping.

Considerable secondary aluminum had accumulated in the market by 1937, and whereas Alcoa had originally produced all the primary aluminum from which this scrap was salvaged, it no longer controlled the scrap market. Had Judge Hand included secondary in his market definition, Alcoa's share would have been calculated at 64 percent. This, in Judge Hand's view, would have understated Alcoa's true strength in the market, and he may well have been correct. The exclusion of secondary aluminum from the market nevertheless makes for a contestable definition. Alcoa's market position appears to have been one that simply could not be well represented by a simple market-share statistic.

Once the 90 percent market share was defined, however, the pertinent question was whether "this is a monopoly within the meaning of Section 2." The district court had found that Alcoa's profits during its lifetime had been less than spectacular—on the order of 10 percent on invested capital. Judge Hand, however, refused to accept this figure as evidence that Alcoa had not exerted monopoly control. Noting that the company's overall profit figure might not reflect accurately its profit on ingot, the judge went on to state:

But the whole issue is irrelevant anyway, for it is no excuse for "monopolizing" a market that the monopoly has not been used to extract from the consumer more than a "fair" profit. The Act has wider purposes. Indeed, even though we disregarded all but economic considerations, it would by no means follow that such concentration of producing power is to be desired, when it has not been used extortionately. Many people believe that possession of unchallenged economic power deadens initiative, discourages thrift and depresses energy; that immunity from competition is a narcotic and rivalry is a stimulant, to industrial progress; that the spur of constant stress is necessary to counteract an inevitable disposition to let well enough alone.

Congress . . . did not condone "good trusts" and condemn "bad" ones; it forbad all. Moreover, in so doing it was not necessarily actuated by economic motives alone. It is possible, because of its indirect social or moral effect, to prefer a system of small producers.[19]

Judge Hand asserted, further, that the distinction between the existence and exercise of monopoly power is "purely formal." A monopolist must sell at some price, and the only price at which it can sell "is a price which it itself fixed."

By arguing in this fashion, Judge Hand was stating, in effect, that there are reasons for opposing monopoly **power** as distinct from the **methods** that the monopolist happens to employ. Nevertheless, he stopped short of concluding that Alcoa's power could by itself, violate the law.

*It does not folow because "Alcoa" had . . . a monopoly, that it "monopolized" the ingot market; it may not have achieved monopoly; **monopoly may have been thrust upon it** . . . .*

---

[19] See footnote 15 above, p. 427.

. . . from the very outset the courts have at least kept in reserve the possibility that the origin of a monopoly may be critical in determining its legality . . . . This notion has usually been expressed by saying that size does not determine guilt; that there must be some "exclusion" of competitors; that the growth must be something else than "natural" or "normal"; that there must be a "wrongful intent," or some other specific intent; or that some "unduly" coercive means must be used.[20]

Was the origin of Alcoa's monopoly such as to place it beyond the reach of the Sherman Act? Again, in Judge Hand's words:

It would completely misconstrue "Alcoa's" position in 1940 to hold that it was the passive beneficiary of a monopoly, following upon an involuntary elimination of competitors by automatically operative economic forces . . . continued and undisturbed control did not fall undesigned into "Alcoa's" lap; obviously it could not have done so. It could only have resulted, as it did result, from a persistent determination to maintain the control with which it found itself vested in 1912 . . . . It insists that it never excluded competitors; but we can think of no more effective exclusion than progressively to embrace each new opportunity as it opened, and to face every newcomer with new capacity already geared into a great organization . . . . Only in case we interpret "exclusion" as limited to maneuvers not honestly industrial, but actuated solely by a desire to prevent competition, can such a course as Alcoa's . . . be deemed not "exclusionary." So to limit it would in our judgment emasculate the Act; would permit just such consolidations as it was designed to prevent.[21]

Judge Hand was, then stating that Alcoa's rapid growth—consisting primarily of the development of new applications for aluminum—excluded competitors and amounted to monopolizing conduct. The company denied monopolistic intent; but Judge Hand said: "We disregard any question of 'intent.' " It was sufficient to observe that the company acted deliberately to retain its control of the market, "however innocently it otherwise proceeded."

One may of course question whether corporate growth ought to be an element of an antitrust violation. But whatever the answer, the extent to which the *Alcoa* case broke new ground in the law of monopoly is evident. Given a company of Alcoa's dominance, in Judge Hand's view, it is not necessary to show "specific intent" to monopolize; ruthless practices, for instance, need not be proved. In *Alcoa*, it was enough to demonstrate that the company's position was **deliberately** achieved— even if by "honestly industrial" practices.

Under the *Alcoa* doctrine, dominant market power is not itself a violation of law. The dominant firm may be able to show that monopoly was "thrust upon" it—for example, that the market can support only a single producer, or that rivals have dropped out of the market simply because they were inefficient. The doctrine is

[20] See footnote 15 above, p. 429; italics added.

[21] See footnote 15 above, p. 430.

clearly a stringent one, however. As long as a company holding a "monopoly" has worked to maintain its position, it is likely that it has violated Section 2.

Despite the strong opinion of Judge Hand, unique circumstances in the aluminum industry prevented the adoption of the government's proposed dissolution scheme. The government had built aluminum producing facilities for war-time use, and it had been directed to dispose of these properties at the end of the war so as to maximize "free independent private enterprise." Since Alcoa's market position after the disposal was not predictable, Judge Hand adopted a wait-and-see approach. The company was prohibited from resuming certain restrictive practices cited in testimony, but the government's dissolution proposal was neither accepted nor specifically rejected. Any action with respect to dissolution, said the Judge, would be a matter for the district court to consider, if the disposal of government facilities failed to reestablish competition after the war.

The disposal program did effect changes in the structure of the aluminum industry, as the Reynolds Metals Company and Kaiser Aluminum Company arose as significant competitors. Indeed, by 1948 Alcoa's share of aluminum reduction capacity was 50 percent, with Reynolds holding 30 percent and Kaiser 20 percent. In 1947, Alcoa asked a district court to find that competitive conditions prevailed in aluminum and that its position as a monopolist had therefore ceased. The government contested this petition and asked that Alcoa be required to divest itself of some plants to enhance competition.

In 1950, the court ruled that although Alcoa retained the power to exclude competitors, a further diminution in the company's market position would be likely to harm competition.[22] Judge Knox contended that competition in aluminum depended on the existence of the three major producers, each of which possessed substantial market power. To weaken one of the companies, in his view, could have destroyed the competitive balance. This is an interesting position in that something akin to equality among market leaders—rather than concentration of market shares—is posited as the critical competitive element.

The United Shoe Machinery Case (1953)[23]

In 1918, the United Shoe Machinery Corporation had been acquitted of monopolization charges arising from its acquisition of about 50 shoe machinery producers.[24] The original power of the company was based in patents, but in subsequent years United Shoe had maintained dominance in the shoe machinery field. In a case decided by Judge Charles Wyzanski, the company was again charged with monopolizing in violation of Section 2 of the Sherman Act.

Judge Wyzanski noted that the position of United Shoe, which supplied 75 to 85 percent of the market, had been built up partly through patented inventions both

---

[22] F. Supp. 333 (1950).

[23] 110 F. Supp. 295 (D. Mass, 1953).

[24] *U.S.* v. *United Shoe Machinery Co. of New Jersey*, 247 U.S. 32 (1918).

before and after 1918. The company held 3915 patents, 95 percent of which were "attributable to the ideas of its own employees." Although the judge termed the shoe manufacturing industry itself "highly competitive," and although shoes could be manufactured without United Shoe machines, the company's dominance was apparent.

This dominance derived in part from United Shoe's own research and development effort, but Judge Wyzanski found that the company's position was enhanced by the terms at which it leased machines to shoe manufacturers. Three leasing provisions were central.

1. United imposed a full-use requirement, under which lessees were compelled to use company machinery to full capacity before employing a competitor's machines.
2. United repaired its leased machines without separate charge, a practice that discouraged independent service organizations from entering the market. This meant, in turn, that competing machinery manufacturers either had to offer their own repair services or attempt to market machines to customers who knew that repairs would be difficult to obtain.
3. United leases ran for 10 years, and customers who renewed their leases were given especially favorable terms.

Taken as a group, these provisions tended to "marry" shoe manufacturers to United, and they created formidable obstacles for machinery producers who might contemplate competing with the company. The leases, Judge Wyzanski stated, served to create barriers to entry into the shoe machinery industry and, thus, to limit competition therein.

Did United Shoe Machinery thus violate Section 2 of the Sherman Act? Judge Wyzanski noted that the question could be approached in three distinct ways. One approach, antedating *Alcoa,* would hold that monopolizing in violation of Section 2 requires an unreasonable restraint of trade in violation of Section 1. A more recent approach, adopted by Justice Douglas in *United States* v. *Griffith,* would argue that a company monopolizes if it has the power to exclude competition and exercises or has the purpose to exercise it.[25] Finally, the *Alcoa* doctrine would suggest that any one enjoying an overwhelming share of the market monopolizes "whenever he does business"; however, the doctrine is tempered by Judge Hand's statement that the defendant may not violate Section 2 if existing monopoly power is due solely to superior skill.

Judge Wyzanski concluded that the facts of the case made it unnecessary to choose between the Douglas and Hand approaches. Rather, he stated, the evidence shows that:

1. United's strength is so overwhelming as to constitute control of the market.

---

[25] 344 U.S. 100 (1948). Said the Court: "[M]onopoly power, whether lawfully or unlawfully acquired, may itself constitute an evil . . . even though it remains unexercised." (p. 107).

2. This strength "excludes some potential, and limits some actual, competition."

3. [T]his strength is not attributable solely to defendant's ability, economies of scale, research, natural advantages, and adaptation to inevitable economic laws.[26]

United Shoe was an innovative company, but its control of the market was **not purely** the result of its own superiority. This was, the Judge said, an

> . . . *intermediate case where the causes of an enterprise's success were neither common law restraints of trade, nor the skill with which the business was conducted, but rather some practice which without being predatory, abusive, or coercive was in economic effect exclusionary.*[27]

Although United was "free from any taint of . . . wrongdoing," its monopoly position depended in part upon company policies that had limited competition. These policies, perfectly legitimate in themselves, were nevertheless one instrument by which United gained a monopoly.

Finally, Judge Wyzanski disposed of the question of intent, stating:

> . . . *Defendant intended to engage in the leasing practices and pricing policies which maintained its market power. That is all the intent which the law requires when both the complaint and the judgment rest on a charge of "monopolizing," not merely "attempting to monopolize." Defendant having willed the means, has willed the end.*[28]

United Shoe was thus found to have violated Section 2, despite an exemplary record of performance. The company had contributed greatly to the technology of shoe production, and it had engaged in no acts which could be termed predatory or immoral. Yet in the course of doing business, Judge Wyzanski found, United Shoe had deliberately pursued policies that restricted competition and contributed to monopoly power.

Having found against the company, Judge Wyzanski rejected the government's proposed dissolution scheme, which would have split United into three separate manufacturing companies. All machine manufacturing was centered in one plant; and, the judge said, "It takes no Solomon to see that this organism cannot be cut into three equal and viable parts." Minor divestitures were ordered, but the remedy centered on the leasing practices. The restrictive provisions were ordered purged— the terms of the leases were shortened, full-capacity clauses were eliminated, discriminatory commutative charges were removed, and the company was required to charge separately for repair services. Finally, the remedy required that any machine that the company offered to lease must also be offered for sale. In this way, it was hoped, a secondhand market would ultimately arise to offer "a type of substitute competition."

---

[26] See footnote 23 above, p. 343.

[27] See footnote 23 above, p. 341.

[28] See footnote 23 above, p. 346.

The implications of *United Shoe* have been actively debated. It appears that certain practices that do not alone violate the law may amount to a violation in conjunction with market dominance. The decision thus suggests a double standard of business conduct under the Sherman Act: Certain restrictive practices are permissible for small firms but not for those with substantial market power.

The *United Shoe* decision seems further to limit role of intent in monopolization cases. A company that is accused of **attempting** to monopolize must be shown to have intended to do so—a demonstration that can be inferred from predatory or otherwise anticompetitive acts. But a company accused of **monopolizing** need not have intended to do so in quite the same sense. Under *United Shoe,* it is sufficient to demonstrate that monopolizing resulted in part from exclusionary practices that were deliberate but that would not alone have constituted an "attempt to monopolize." The general thrust of Judge Wyzanski's opinion places it within the spirit of *Alcoa.* A finding of monopolization necessitates some attention to practices, but the power of the company is the controlling factor. At the very least, dominant power suggests that a company's acts must conform to an exceedingly rigid standard to escape a finding of monopolization.

The duPont Cellophane Case (1956)[29]

The *duPont Cellophane* case is notable for its treatment of the market definition problem. E. I. duPont de Nemours & Company was for many years the major producer of cellophane sold in the United States. The company had obtained exclusive patent rights in the early part of the century and, since 1925, had accounted for about 75 percent of the market.

In 1947, the government charged duPont with monopolizing, attempting to monopolize, and conspiracy to monopolize commerce in cellophane and cellulosic caps, in violation of Section 2 of the Sherman Act. The company won its case in a district court, which held that the relevant market was not cellophane but "flexible wrapping materials," a much broader product group of which duPont's market share was only about 20 percent. The government's appeal to the Supreme Court was confined to an attack on the lower court conclusion that duPont had not monopolized trade in cellophane.

The opposing arguments were clear-cut. While not denying that cellophane was a separate product, duPont contended that this product was under severe competitive pressure from substitute flexible wrapping materials such as waxed paper, glassine, and aluminum foil. Because of this pressure, the company argued, it lacked the power to exclude competitors, power that could have violated Section 2. The government's argument was that the other wrapping materials did not offer sufficient competition to affect duPont's control of the cellophane market—in other words, that cellophane itself was the relevant market, although it was subject to competitive pressures from outside products.

---

[29] *U.S. v. E. I. duPont de Nemours & Co.,* 351 U.S. 377 (1956).

The decision of the Court hinged on this point, for under the first market definition duPont very likely had monopolized, whereas under the second it had not. As Justice Reed stated for the court:

Every manufacturer is the sole producer of the particular commodity it makes but its control . . . of the relevant market depends upon the availability of alternative commodities for buyers . . . .

If cellophane is the "market" that duPont is found to dominate, it may be assumed it does have monopoly power over that "market."[30]

The definition of the relevant market, according to the Court, depends on "how different from one another are the offered commodities in character or use, how far buyers will go to substitute one commodity for another."[31] The pertinent question was, then, specific: How are differences or similarities among products to be measured? The court rejected the government's contention that products must be "substantially fungible" and must sell "at substantially the same price" to be considered part of the same market. Rather, the Court stated:

. . . where there are market alternatives . . . illegal monopoly does not exist merely because the product said to be monopolized differs from others. If it were not so, only physically identical products would be a part of the market.[32]

What is needed, according to the Court, "is an appraisal of the 'cross-elasticity' of demand in the trade." If a price change in one product substantially affects the sales of another, both should be classified in the same market.[33]

Having noted the relevance of cross-elasticities, however, the Court did not pursue actual measures. Rather, it pointed out that cellophane, despite distinctive property combinations that gave it market advantages, "has to meet competition from other materials in every one of its uses." The government did not challenge statistics showing that cellophane provided the wrappings for less than 7 percent of bakery products, 25 percent of candy, 32 percent of snacks, 35 percent of meats and poultry, 47 percent of fresh produce, and 34 percent of frozen foods. These data indicated that cellophane shared its markets with other materials and were interpreted by the Court as evidence of competitiveness among wrappings. Further, the Court said:

. . . a very considerable degree of functional interchangeability exists between these products . . . except as to permeability to gases, cellophane has no qualities that are not possessed by a number of other materials.[34]

---

[30] Ibid., pp. 380, 391. The sources of duPont's power were not at issue, since the government's appeal was limited to the finding on monopoly. Had charges of attempting and conspiring to monopolize been relevant, the Court would have had to consider the means by which duPont's market position had been attained.

[31] Ibid., p. 393.

[32] Ibid., p. 394.

[33] The issue is closeness of substitution, a condition inferable from high and positive cross elasticities. At what point a cross elasticity becomes "high," however, may be debated.

[34] See footnote 29 above, p. 399.

The lower court had found that customers for wrapping materials were sensitive to changes in prices and qualities, and it took this as indicative of significant cross-elasticities. The Supreme Court concurred. The government had argued that large price differences between cellophane and other materials indicated the separateness of their markets. To this the Court responded that packaging materials were a small portion of the total cost of packaged goods; hence, large price differentials were not necessarily a significant consideration for customers. Justice Reed concluded that the relevant market was broad. DuPont had done nothing to exclude competitors, he said, and the company's "liberal" profits (15.9 percent net after taxes) did not demonstrate the existence of monopoly, in the absence of evidence that other prosperous industries had not earned similar returns. Justice Reed stated in summary:

. . . The "market" which one must study to determine when a producer has monopoly power will vary with the part of commerce under consideration. The tests are constant. That market is composed of products that have reasonable interchangeability for the purpose for which they are produced—price, use and qualities considered. While the application of the tests remains uncertain, it seems to us that duPont should not be found to monopolize cellophane when that product has the competition and interchangeability with other wrappings that this record shows.[35]

Chief Justice Warren, joined by Justices Black and Douglas, issued a sharp dissenting opinion. It contends that cellophane itself is the relevant market and that the majority's lumping together of cellophane with highly differentiated wrapping materials serves to "emasculate Section 2 of the Sherman Act." The Chief Justice argued that cross-elasticity of demand between cellophane and other materials was not high, as the majority had claimed.

. . . during the period 1933–1946 the prices for glassine and waxed paper actually increased in the face of a further 21% decline in the price of cellophane. If "shifts of business" due to "price sensitivity" had been substantial, glassine and waxed paper producers who wanted to stay in business would have been compelled by market forces to meet duPont's price challenge just as Sylvania [a domestic cellophane producer] was.[36]

The markets for cellophane and other wrapping materials were, in the minority view, quite distinct. The company's power, said Chief Justice Warren, was evident. Moreover, he stated, the majority's findings of fact did nothing to demonstrate the absence of power—rather, they demonstrated that the power was used in a benevolent and enlightened fashion. DuPont was, indeed, a 'good monopolist' in this view, but a monopolist nonetheless.

Was the majority's market definition a correct one? The issue posed was the how-close-is-close-enough question; that is, were other flexible wrapping materials sufficiently close substitutes to be grouped with cellophane? The Court's answer was based on the subjective notion of reasonable interchangeability. Whether a more ob-

[35] See footnote 29 above, p. 404.

[36] Ibid., p. 417.

jective standard, based on cross-elasticities of demand, would have supported this view is questionable.

The cellophane decision has prompted considerable controversy among economists. To some it appeared that the Supreme Court's attention to market performance—"rapidly declining prices, expanding production, intense competition stimulated by creative research, the development of new products"—heralded a new era. Henceforth, the courts might be expected to look at implications for future market activity in deciding questions of monopolization. To other economists, duPont appeared a deliberate and cunning, if progressive, monopolist of a product that was distinct from substitutes.[37] Whatever the view, there was broad agreement that the Court had been influenced by the company's brilliant record of research and innovation.

The Berkey Photo Case (1979)

In a significant private damages suit, Berkey Photo charged Eastman Kodak with using a monopoly position in film manufacturing to gain monopoly control in markets for amateur cameras and photofinishing services. Kodak was, indeed, an overwhelming market force in film and also held major market shares in cameras and color paper. Its early dominance in photofinishing had eroded since a 1954 consent decree ended Kodak's practice of tying finishing services to color film sales. The company was described by an appellate court as "a titan in its field."

Berkey, in contrast, was a major film processor. The company had produced cameras as well, holding an 8 percent market share in the 1970s, but it left this market in 1978. A major issue was Kodak's practice of marketing new film "formats"—that is, particular types of cartridges—that would fit only its own cameras, without "predisclosing" its innovations. The company had, for example, introduced the heavily advertised Kodacolor II (a "remarkable new film") in conjunction with its new 110 camera. Amateur photographers seeking to use the film could do so only with the Kodak camera; rival manufacturers were excluded until they could develop a camera that would take the new film format.

A district court found in favor of Berkey, awarding remarkable damages of $87 million.[38] However, the judgment was partially overturned, and the award reduced, by an appeals court in 1979.[39] This court noted that a firm "may not employ its market position as a lever to create . . . a monopoly in another market." Had Kodak done so? No, said the court. The company's practices were "**solely** a benefit of integration, and not, without more, a use of Kodak's power in the film market to gain a competitive advantage in cameras."

---

[37] See George W. Stocking and Willard F. Mueller, "The Cellophane Case and the New Competition," *American Economic Review*, **45** (March 1955), 29–63.

[38] *Berkey Photo, Inc.* v. *Eastman Kodak Co.*, 457 F. Supp 404 (SDNY, 1978).

[39] *Berkey Photo, Inc.* v. *Eastman Kodak Co.*, 603 F.2d 263 (2d Cir., 1979).

Recent Cases

There has been little development of legal doctrine in the area of monopoly since the early 1950s. The Supreme Court declined an opportunity to say much more in a 1966 decision, *United States* v. *Grinnell Corp.*[40] While noting that "the offense of monopoly under Section 2" requires both "possession of monopoly power" and "the willful acquisition or maintenance of that power," the Court broke no new ground. Grinnell, with an 87 percent share of the relevant market (central station burglary and fire claim services), had the requisite power; moreover, its power was achieved "in large part by unlawful and exclusionary practices." Since the company was a poorly behaved monopolist, the Court did not reach the question of how society ought to deal with the better behaved variety.

Despite the absence of new legal precedent, the disposition of three recent cases may hold some clues to future monopolization policies.

International Business Machines   In January 1969, during the last days of the Johnson Administration, the Justice Department charged IBM with monopolizing the market in "general purpose digital computers" and with a variety of discriminatory practices.[41] Dissolution of the company was requested. IBM responded generally that relevant markets should be redefined (recall that the broader the market, the lower the shares of leading firms are likely to appear), and that its success was the result of superior performance.

Thirteen years later, in January 1982, the Justice Department dropped all charges, observing that the case was "without merit." This change in policy may be attributable to changes in the computer industry; IBM was by 1982 subject to more severe competitive pressures than it had been at the time the suit was filed. Yet the substantive issues in the case had for several years been submerged in an overwhelming volume of documentation; the trial, begun in May 1975, had entered its seventh year before the case was dropped. To some, the lesson was that under current legal procedures, the government cannot promptly and effectively pursue a "key" case that seeks to restructure a major domestic industry.[42]

American Telephone & Telegraph Co.   In 1974, the Justice Department sued AT&T, the communications giant, seeking to break off Western Electric (the company's equipment manufacturing branch), its Long Lines Department, and local operating subsidiaries.[43] In January 1982, the government and the company agreed

---

[40] 384 U.S. 563 (1966).

[41] *U.S.* v. *International Business Machines Corp.*, 69 CIV 200 (S.D.N.Y.).

[42] The problems of sheer volume and time are endemic to antitrust cases—perhaps more so, the higher the stakes involved are. Richard A. Posner has calculated that the average length of a litigated case is about 5½ years. "A Statistical Study of Antitrust Enforcement," *Journal of Law and Economics,* **13** (October 1970), 365–419. And, as William G. Shepherd and Clair Wilcox point out, both the incentive and opportunity for a company such as IBM to delay proceedings are abundant. *Public Policies Toward Business,* 6th ed. (Homewood, Ill.: R. D. Irwin, 1979).

[43] *U.S.* v. *American Telephone & Telegraph Co.*, Civil Action No. 74-1698.

to a settlement: AT&T would divest its 22 operating subsidiaries, which, as a group, accounted for almost two thirds of the corporation's assets; it would retain its other divisions; and it would be free to enter unregulated markets in communications and data processing.

The long-term impact of this settlement on American communications markets is a topic of wide interest, although discussions are rather speculative. Virtually all observers agree that some important competitive changes in both communications and data processing will occur. The precise nature of these events, however, cannot be predicted with great confidence. It is perhaps unfortunate that such a far-reaching decision was taken "out of court," thereby setting no true precedent for future public policy.

Breakfast Cereals.　The Federal Trade Commission in 1972 charged four major producers of ready-to-eat (RTE) cereals with a "shared monopoly" in violation of Section 5 of the FTC Act (as an "unfair" competitive practice).[44] The companies—Kellogg, General Mills, General Foods, and Quaker Oats (later dropped from the suit)—had held a combined market share of more than 85 percent; they had enjoyed a record of high profits (apparently close to 20 percent on stockholders' equity, compared with an average of 11.5 percent for all manufacturers and 10.8 percent for producers of food and kindred products); and they faced little effective entry despite the fact that cereal can be manufactured efficiently on a relatively small scale. The commission argued, in part, that the companies had built artificial barriers to entry by various means, including heavy advertising.

Early in 1982, the FTC dropped the case, approving an administrative law judge's ruling for dismissal. The breakfast cereals suit was unusual in at least two respects: It sought to attack a "shared" (rather than a single-firm) monopoly; and it requested some unusual remedies, such as trademark licensing.[45] Some economists believe the case had merit; yet a number of government officials had soured on its prospects well before the final dismissal.[46]

What do the dispositions of these recent cases, taken together, tell us about future monopoly policy? It seems clear that efforts to break up leading firms and restructure important industries are out of favor (the AT&T settlement notwithstanding). National concern with such problems as growth, productivity, and the international competition faced by American firms has, at least for the moment, subordinated concern about the power of companies within domestic markets. Whereas legal precedent in the monopolization area will no doubt continue to evolve, the prospects for ground-breaking enforcement efforts during the next few years seem dim.

---

[44] *Kellogg Co., et al.*, Docket 8883 (April 27, 1972).

[45] For a relevant discussion see Richard Schmalensee, "Entry Deterrence in the Ready-to-Eat Breakfast Cereal Industry," *Bell Journal of Economics,* **9** (Autumn 1978), 305–327.

[46] The idea of pursuing "shared monopoly" cases was, for a time, a "hot item" in public antitrust discussions. Yet John Shenefield, Assistant Attorney General for antitrust in the Carter Administration—and a strong advocate of such efforts—was unable to find a prosecutable instance during his tenure in office. Shenefield was later quoted as saying, "I believe the problem exists, but we can't deal with it." (*Wall Street Journal*, January 16, 1981.)

MONOPOLY IN LAW AND ECONOMICS: CURRENT STATUS

To define the current legal status of monopoly, it is necessary to ask just how much the doctrines of *Alcoa* and *United Shoe* have altered the old rule of reason. It would appear that the alteration has been a very substantial one.

Alcoa and *United Shoe* established that a firm that has been shown to possess monopoly power may be guilty of monopolizing, even though its power was not based in illegal practices. The company need not have acted ruthlessly, and it need not have demonstrated specific intent to exclude competitors or to monopolize. The practical implication of this doctrine is that a company possessing monopoly power has a far more difficult time proving that it has not "monopolized" within the meaning of Section 2, than it would have had prior to 1945. In the words of the appeals court in *Berkey Photo:*

The mere possession of monopoly power does not ipso facto condemn a market participant. But, to avoid the proscriptions of Section 2, the firm must refrain at all times from conduct directed at smothering competition.[47]

Some words of caution are in order regarding the interpretation of *Alcoa* and *United Shoe*. Whatever these decisions may have done, they clearly did **not** make possession of monopoly power, however defined, a *per se* violation of law. The old rule of reason has been altered, but not eliminated. "Reasonable" restraints on trade are still possible, although "reasonable" does not mean precisely what it may have meant in 1911 or 1920.

One might be inclined to argue that this is a quibble, since companies found to have monopoly power will—especially under the *Alcoa* approach—have great difficulty escaping a charge of monopolization. Why, in other words, should it matter that escape is technically possible if, as a practical matter, it is as difficult as it appears? One answer, which points to a potential economic weakness in legal treatment of monopoly, lies in the implication for appropriate remedies.

If monopoly power itself were defined as a violation of law, the clearly indicated remedy would be some disintegration of that power. But as long as a violation is tied to the practices of a company, a sufficient remedy may be logically confined to termination of those offending acts. As Lucile Shephard Keyes states with respect to *United Shoe:*

. . . a fully adequate remedy for the violation could be found without any direct attack upon the Corporation's share in the shoe machinery market. Where the crime of monopolizing requires, in addition to market control, exclusionary practices for its completion, it can always be extirpated by the simple termination of these practices; and the real operational significance of the law against monopolizing is to provide a basis for a distinct and stricter code of business conduct to be applied to enterprises that exercise market control.[48]

---

[47] See footnote 39 above, p. 275.

[48] Lucile Shephard Keyes, "The Shoe Machinery Case and the Problem of the Good Trust," *Quarterly Journal of Economics*, **68** (May 1954), 287–304. Quotation at pp. 290–291.

As we have seen, the government's victories in *Alcoa* and *United Shoe* have not paved the way for further significant attacks on monopoly. An important reason is, of course, that few companies have the degree of dominance that seems necessary to prove "monopoly power" under the law. But it is also probable that the difficulty of formulating and winning acceptance for an appropriate remedy has discouraged litigation.

Traditionally the courts have been reluctant to break up a going concern. It often appears that no "logical" form of divestiture or dissolution is possible. Large companies are extremely complex organizations, and the task of breaking one apart has been compared with trying to "unscramble scrambled eggs." The courts have at times taken Judge Wyzanski's view that specific dissolution proposals are "unrealistic." This judgment is likely where the government concentrates on winning its case—that is, proving illegal monopoly—but fails to devise a plausible dissolution scheme. The result in such instances may be legal victories of dubious economic impact.[49]

Resistance to corporate dissolution is unquestionably related also to concern about consequences for market efficiency. Even if a sensible scheme were proposed, its effects on efficiency may not be known with certainty. Even a small probability of affecting markets adversely may make judges extremely reluctant to accept a dissolution proposal, and the breaking up of major companies is a course of action with which we have little experience to draw on.

Finally, a powerful argument against dissolution may be advanced in terms of equity.[50] Any company, no matter how "excessive" we might consider its power to be, carries the vested interests of many individuals—most notably investors who are, for the most part, both innocent and ignorant of corporate transgressions. To break up a monopoly is to tamper with, and perhaps to harm, the economic welfare of such people. Thus, we see a further source of judicial reluctance to accept dissolution proposals.

How serious is the problem of "innocent investors?" Malcolm R. Burns, analyzing the 1911 dissolutions of American Tobacco, Standard Oil, and American Snuff, concluded that "judges have experienced undue and largely self-inflicted agony over the fate of 'innocent' shareowners. . ."[51] Later research by Burns, however, demonstrated that the excess profits of a monopolist are capitalized in the prices of its outstanding securities; thus, some innocent investors may suffer capital losses from a dissolution remedy that increases market competition.[52] Systems of

---

[49] This is not to suggest, however, that remedies other than dissolution are necessarily without significant market impact. See William L. Baldwin, "The Feedback Effect of Business Conduct on Industry Structure," *Journal of Law and Economics,* **12** (April 1969), 123–153.

[50] See, for example, Donald Dewey, "Romance and Realism in Antitrust Policy," *Journal of Political Economy,* **63** (April 1955), 93–102.

[51] Malcolm R. Burns, "The Competitive Effects of Trust-Busting: A Portfolio Analysis," *Journal of Political Economy,* **85** (August 1977), 717–739.

[52] Malcolm R. Burns, "An Empirical Analysis of Stockholder Injury Under Section 2 of the Sherman Act," *Journal of Industrial Economics,* forthcoming.

compensation to such individuals may be desirable, although the formulation of such arrangements encounters some complexities.[53]

The current status of monopoly under section 2 of the Sherman Act is, then, something of a potpourri. A company will not be found to have monopoly power unless it has gained overwhelming dominance of a defined market. Once monopoly is found, it may be difficult for a court to avoid the conclusion that Section 2 has been violated. Such a conclusion follows under the doctrine of *Alcoa* and *United Shote* as long as the company has acted deliberately to achieve its market position. Yet even the finding of a violation may result only in the curtailment of those deliberate acts.

The law of monopoly is subject to two economic weaknesses. First, as we have seen, there is a possible inconsistency in the approach to remedies. If monopoly itself poses a problem, then a remedy that merely curtails certain modes of behavior may be inappropriate. It is likely to be inadequate, for example, unless the behavior in question was instrumental to the attainment and maintenance of the monopoly position. If the behavior has had only peripheral impact, its curtailment may well prove ineffective.

The second weakness lies in the courts' definition of monopoly itself. For Judge Wyzanski, a 75 percent market share demonstrated the requisite power. For Judge Hand, 90 percent was sufficient, and 64 percent would have made for a troublesome decision. But wherever the line is drawn, defining monopoly purely in terms of market share encounters some difficulties. Market definition is frequently unclear (recall both *Alcoa* and *duPont*), but it will determine measured market share. Whether the share is "high enough" to comprise "monopoly" may, therefore, depend on some rather arbitrary judgments about market boundaries.

Beyond this, market shares can be a misleading guide to monopoly power. Low shares do not necessarily indicate competition; high shares may create suspicion, but they do not always point to monopoly.[54] The courts may have little choice but to rely on a shorthand index of this sort; however, the pitfalls in equating market share with degree of monopoly should be borne clearly in mind.

Indeed, the broader differences between legal and economic conceptions of monopoly are worth noting. In a classic article written many years ago, Edward S. Mason pointed out that monopoly in economics is a tool of analysis.[55] Monopoly refers to a market situation, the essence of which is control or power. The law, however, tends to define monopoly as a "standard of evaluation"; the relevant question is not whether power exists, but whether it is abused—that is, employed to restrict

---

[53] Furthermore, as Burns points out, compensation schemes would create an inconsistency in the law: protection for investors whose companies were dissolved under Section 2, but none for (equally innocent) investors whose companies were forced to end price-fixing conspiracies under Section 1. The latter may suffer capital losses as well.

[54] For useful discussions, see Franklin M. Fisher, "Diagnosing Monopoly," *Quarterly Review of Economics and Business,* **19** (Summer 1979), 7–33; and William M. Landes and Richard A. Posner, "Market Power in Antitrust Cases," *Harvard Law Review,* **94** (March 1981), 937–996.

[55] Monopoly in Law and Economics," *Yale Law Journal,* **47** (November 1937), 34–49.

competition. A situation that is competitive in the legal sense is, thus, compatible with substantial monopoly elements, economically defined.

Some economists are strongly critical of antimonopoly policy on the grounds that its rules of thumb oversimplify and raise the danger of an attack on efficiency, rather than on monopoly as such. The first part of this objection is surely accurate; yet the second part is difficult to take very seriously in practical terms. For the simple fact is that Section 2 of the Sherman Act has seldom been used to attack directly the power of our largest corporations during the past 70 years.

CHAPTER 14

Antitrust Treatment of Mergers

The corporate merger has long been a common method by which firms grow. A company that desires growth can expand internally, by building a new plant and taking on additional personnel; but acquisition of a going concern is often seen to have important advantages. If uncontested, a merger is faster. The acquired company has established facilities and distribution outlets. Perhaps even more important, it has established good will. When one company takes over another, it acquires not only its physical assets but its intangible assets as well. It is, in effect, purchasing a market position that it otherwise would have to fight to obtain. It is hardly surprising, then, that many firms seeking growth prefer the merger route to internal expansion.

Although mergers may appeal to corporations, however, they are often a matter of concern from the standpoint of public competition policy. Acquisitions frequently change the structure of markets. If the acquiring and acquired firms are in the same market, the merger eliminates a competitor and may enhance the power of the surviving company; if they are in a supplier–customer relationship, the merger may yield to the (now-integrated) survivor certain competitive advantages over its rivals; even if the merging companies operate in unrelated markets, the acquisition may contribute to aggregate concentration and, thus, to a greater degree of power, in some sense, than existed before. Since centralized power may have undesirable implications, it is clear that the merging of two independent companies is, at least, of potential concern for public policy.

BACKGROUND: THE MERGER PHENOMENON

The record of corporate mergers in the United States is an interesting one because of its uneven character. There apparently have been three great "merger waves" in our history.[1] The first covered the approximate period 1897 to 1903. As Ralph Nel-

---

[1] See Ralph L. Nelson, *Merger Movements in American Industry* (Princeton: Princeton University Press, for the National Bureau of Economic Research, 1959); George W. Stocking, "Comment on Mergers," in *Business Concentration and Price Policy* (Princeton: Princeton University Press, for the National Bureau of Economic Research, 1955), pp. 191–212; and Willard F. Mueller, testimony reprinted in *Economic Concentration, Hearings Before the Senate Subcommittee on Antitrust and Monopoly,* 89th Cong., 1st sess., part 2, pp. 501–537.

Table 14.1 Mergers and Acquisitions in Manufacturing and Mining

Nelson Series, 1895–1920			
Year	Annual Total	Year	Annual Total
1895	43	1908	50
1896	26	1909	49
1897	69	1910	142
1898	303	1911	103
1899	1208	1912	82
1900	340	1913	85
1901	423	1914	39
1902	379	1915	71
1903	142	1916	117
1904	79	1917	195
1905	226	1918	71
1906	128	1919	171
1907	87	1920	206

Source: Ralph L. Nelson, *Merger Movements in American Industry, 1895–1956* (Princeton: Princeton University Press, 1959), p. 37.

Thorp Series, 1919–1939			
Year	Annual Total	Year	Annual Total
1919	438	1930	799
1920	760	1931	464
1921	487	1932	203
1922	309	1933	120
1923	311	1934	101
1924	368	1935	130
1925	554	1936	126
1926	856	1937	124
1927	870	1938	110
1928	1058	1939	87
1929	1245		

Source: Willard L. Thorp and Walter Crowder, *The Structure of American Industry,* Temporary National Economic Committee Monograph 27, 1941, pp. 231–234.

son's figures, reproduced in Table 14.1, indicate, more than 2800 mergers in mining and manufacturing took place during these five years, and merger activity did not sharply abate until after 1906. Numerous horizontal consolidations occurred with monopolization the apparent predominant motive, and the effects have been long lasting.[2] Among the corporations created by this movement were Standard Oil, U.S. Steel, and U.S. Rubber.

---

[2] See George J. Stigler, "Monopoly and Oligopoly by Merger," *American Economic Review,* **40** (May 1950), 23–34.

The quantity of assets that changed hands in toto was, in comparison with the size of the economy at the turn of the century, impressive. The magnitude of this merger movement was, in fact, so great that, although some students of history associate its conclusion with the rise of strong antitrust enforcement, others have noted that it may have come to an end simply because so few saleable companies remained.

The second merger wave occurred during (roughly) 1925 to 1930, as shown in Table 14.1. These mergers centered in industries such as petroleum, primary metals, and food products, and they included many vertical and conglomerate extensions.[3] The third wave, according to Willard F. Mueller, began in the closing years of World War II.[4] This movement was heavily conglomerate in nature. The Federal Trade Commission series on large mergers—those in which the acquired firm had assets of at least $10 million (see Table 14.2)—suggests that the latest merger wave gathered strength in the early 1960s, peaked by 1970, but has again become active in recent years.

Although the data on mergers are incomplete (primarily because relatively small acquisitions may escape notice), the existence of these periods of abnormal activity is well established. Precisely why these waves occurred when they did is less certain. An extensive literature suggests many motives for merging: everything from conventional scale economies to tax and stock-price incentives that may have little or nothing to do with "real" economic forces.[5] Whereas many interesting suggestions have been offered, however, merger patterns over time have never been definitively explained.[6]

The history of public policy toward mergers demonstrates sharp change since the beginning of the century. At the time of the first merger wave, the Sherman Act was the only relevant antitrust statute in existence. Its effectiveness in dealing with the movement, however, was less than overwhelming. Although it was possible to charge companies with monopolizing or attempting to monopolize trade by virtue of their acquisitions, such an approach had some success only in areas of dramatic market dominance in the railroad industry.[7] As Chapter 13 shows, the prosecution of major trusts, such as Standard Oil and American Tobacco, was based largely on their "ruthless" practices. The market power of the companies was a relevant fac-

---

[3] For a detailed discussion, see Carl Eis, "The 1919–1930 Merger Movement," *Journal of Law and Economics*, **12** (October 1969), 267–296.

[4] See footnote 1 above.

[5] For a good, thorough discussion, see Peter O. Steiner, *Mergers: Motive, Effects, Policies* (Ann Arbor: University of Michigan Press, 1975), especially chapters 2 through 5.

[6] Michael Gort, for example, has reported some evidence that merger rates are determined by broad economic "shocks," which generate discrepancies in valuations of companies. "An Economic Disturbance Theory of Mergers," *Quarterly Journal of Economics*, **83** (November 1969), 624–642. Earlier speculation along somewhat similar lines suggested that merger waves follow major innovations—for example, the development of the railroad, telephone, radio, and television.

[7] In *Northern Securities Co. v. U.S.*, 193 U.S. 197 (1904), the government successfully sued two major rail companies in the northwest that had formed a joint holding company. A similar result was obtained in *U.S. v. Union Pacific Railroad Co.*, 226 U.S. 61 (1912), involving a merger that the Supreme Court characterized as a "consolidation of two great competing systems of railroad."

Table 14.2 FTC Large Merger Series* (Manufacturing and Mining)

Year	Number of Acquisitions	Assets Acquired ($ Millions)	Percentage of Assets Acquired[a]
1948	4	63.2	0.10
1949	6	89.0	0.08
1950	5	186.3	0.15
1951	9	201.5	0.14
1952	16	373.8	0.22
1953	23	779.1	0.44
1954	37	1,444.5	0.81
1955	67	2,165.7	1.17
1956	53	1,882.0	1.00
1957	17	1,202.3	0.62
1958	42	1,070.6	0.50
1959	49	1,431.1	0.69
1960	51	1,535.1	0.65
1961	46	2,003.3	0.81
1962	65	2,251.9	0.91
1963	54	2,535.8	1.04
1964	73	2,302.9	0.80
1965	64	3,253.7	1.07
1966	76	3,329.1	1.13
1967	138	8,258.5	2.10
1968	174	12,580.0	2.94
1969	138	11,043.2	2.32
1970	91	5,904.3	1.14
1971	59	2,459.9	0.51
1972	60	1,885.5	0.41
1973	64	3,148.8	0.50
1974	62	4,466.4	0.69
1975	59	4,950.5	0.70
1976	81	6,279.2	0.80
1977	100	9,004.2	1.07
1978[b]	110	10,705.5	1.14
Total	1,923	108,786.9	

*Mergers in which acquired firms had assets of $10 millior or more.
[a] Acquired assets as percentage of total assets of all mining and manufacturing corporations.
[b] Figures for 1978 are preliminary.

Note: The final column, **percentage** of assets acquired, is most appropriate for comparisons over time. Both dollar assets and numbers of large mergers will be distorted by inflation.

tor, and merger was one means by which market power had been attained; but the Act was not widely construed as a weapon to be used against mergers as such.

The antimerger provision in the Clayton Act of 1914 was stimulated by the earlier merger movement. The original Section 7 prohibited a corporation from acquiring the stock of another corporation where the effect might be "to substantially lessen competition"; and the language of the law seemed to limit this prohibition to situations in which competition between the acquiring and acquired concerns would be affected. Since stock acquisition was the usual merger mechanism at the time, and since mergers between competitors were common, the provision was apparently a meaningful one. As early as 1927, however, the Federal Trade Commission began to recommend legislative extensions. As it stood, Section 7 could not prevent corporations from making direct acquisition of assets, and this form of merger circumvented the law with some frequency. The FTC suggested—and for years continued to press for—revision of the law to include asset acquisition.

Although these suggestions were not followed quickly, Congress believed by 1950 that a serious gap existed in public merger policy. An important stimulus to this belief was provided by the *Columbia Steel* case of 1948.[8] The United States Steel Corporation had contracted to buy the assets of the Consolidated Steel Corporation, the largest independent steel fabricator on the West Coast. As an asset acquisition, the merger was immune under Section 7, but the government brought suit under Sections 1 and 2 of the Sherman Act, charging restraint of trade and attempted monopolization. The merger was viewed by the Supreme Court in a vertical context. United States Steel, the nation's largest producer of basic rolled steel, was purchasing a fabricator of finished steel products. The government argued that the merger would exclude producers of rolled steel—United States Steel's competitors—from supplying Consolidated with the materials that it used in fabrication. This type of argument refers to **vertical foreclosure:** The merger of a customer and a supplier forecloses other suppliers (or customers) from that portion of the market that the customer (or supplier) controls.

The Supreme Court held that such a merger could not be construed as an unreasonable restraint of trade. Further, since the merged company would not hold ''unreasonable'' market control, and since there was no evident intent to monopolize, the merger did not violate the Sherman Act's prohibition against monopolization. Justice Reed stated that vertical integration raises questions of policy that are not to be decided by the courts.

It is not for courts to determine the course of the Nation's economic development . . . . If businesses are to be forbidden from entering into different stages of production that order must come from Congress, not the courts.[9]

The issue was thus clearly defined. The *Columbia Steel* decision indicated that current antitrust law could provide no meaningful check on corporate mergers. If the nation's leading steel producer could legally acquire an important fabricator, then few significant mergers could be prohibited. Moreover, as Justice Reed made plain, a change in policy could come only from Congress. Congressional reaction to the decision was prompt. A number of committees examined existing merger policy and found it wanting. And in 1950, the Celler–Kefauver Amendment to Section 7 of the Clayton Act became law. The new Section 7 extended prohibitions to asset as well

---

[8]*U.S.* v. *Columbia Steel Co. et al.,* 334 U.S. 495 (1948).

[9]Ibid., p. 526.

as stock acquisitions, and was directed at any merger whose effect ''in any line of commerce in any section of the country . . . may be substantially to lessen competition or to tend to create a monopoly.''

The meaning of a ''substantial'' lessening of competition had yet to be defined by the courts, but it was immediately obvious that the potential importance of the new law was tremendous. It would no longer be necessary to prove, in the case of asset acquisition, monopolization or an attempt to monopolize under the Sherman Act; and the intention of Congress clearly was to provide a more stringent legal obstacle. The amendment was also noteworthy in that it was the first significant attempt to **prevent** the development of concentrated market structures via merger. In the words of a Senate report:

The intent here . . . is to cope with monopolistic tendencies **in their incipiency and before they have attained** *such effects as would justify a Sherman Act pro-ceeding.*[10]

Typically, antitrust policy moved against monopolistic conditions only after such conditions had become established facts of life. It was now conceivable that, in the merger area, the chronology would be reversed.

The questions to be brought before the courts were both important and difficult. What meaning was to be ascribed to a ''line of commerce'' or ''section of the country''? When would a merger be likely to ''lessen'' competition? And what standards of probability and substantiality were to be applied? The language of the amended Section 7 was sweeping, and its translation into workable and effective policy would require nothing less than a definition of both competition and markets.

VARIETIES OF MERGER

The corporate ''merger'' is not a single, homogeneous phenomenon. It is, there-fore, impossible to generalize about the expected economic effects of mergers; both the type of merger and surrounding market circumstances must be considered. As we shall see, however, there is substantial disagreement about probable impacts even within narrowly drawn categories.

A **horizontal** merger is a marriage of rivals. It involves firms doing ''the same'' things in ''the same'' market, such as two national clothing manufacturers or two commercial banks in Oberlin, Ohio. This traditional type of merger carries the strongest potential implications. If there are unexploited economies of scale in the market, the combined firm will be more efficient than independent rivals, thereby saving society some resources. At the same time, such a merger eliminates one competitor from the market and may, therefore, yield increased pricing power to the surviving company. It is this latter possibility that has led American courts to adopt a very stringent position with respect to horizontal acquisition.

---

[10] Senate Report 1775, 81st Cong. 1st sess., 1950.

A **vertical** merger, involving companies in a supplier–customer relationship, was described in the *Columbia Steel* decision above.[11] The issue is again one of possible efficiency gains versus possible harm to competition. If true vertical economies exist, the merger will save resources; at the same time, it is likely to "tie up" the acquired firm in such a way as to foreclose rivals of the acquiring company from some segment of the market.[12] Most people—though by no means all—are likely to regard the first effect as desirable, and the second as unfortunate. Which one predominates, or ought to be accorded the greater weight in policy decisions, is a controversial issue.[13]

Conglomerate mergers raise somewhat different questions than the other, more traditional, types. Initially, there is a problem of definition: Just what do we mean by "conglomerate"? The simplest pragmatic answer is: anything that cannot be placed in the vertical or horizontal categories. This is the approach taken by the Federal Trade Commission, the government's main compiler of statistical data on mergers, and it will suffice for our purposes.

There are, however, some ambiguities. The FTC breaks its conglomerate classification into three subcategories: **market-extension** mergers, in which the acquiring and acquired firms do the same things in different geographic markets; **product-extension** mergers, in which the products (or activities) of the partners do not compete with each other but have some functional relationship in production or distribution;[14] and **other** conglomerates. The "other" category embraces what is sometimes called the "pure" conglomerate merger, in which the activities of the partners bear no apparent relationship to one another.

The boundaries of the first two subcategories are somewhat blurred. A good many market-extension acquisitions—perhaps all—have strong horizontal overtones. Product-extension examples, frequently more difficult to define, may appear either horizontal or vertical in character. It is only in the pure conglomerates that the distinction is a clean one.[15]

Definitional questions aside, the conglomerate merger carries the fuzziest implications among the three major categories. Arguments for horizontal or vertical effi-

---

[11] See footnote 6 above.

[12] Suppose, for example, that a shoe manufacturer buys a chain of retail shoe stores with the intention of having the stores carry only its own brand of shoes. Competing manufacturers are foreclosed from that portion of the retail market. Such an effect, however, does not preclude the possibility that the merged company will be able to market shoes more economically.

[13] Some persons argue that, in practice, likelihood of vertical efficiencies is extremely low, perhaps close to nonexistent; others make precisely the same argument with respect to the possibility of competitive harm. For two sharply opposed, but clearly stated, positions, see Willard F. Mueller, "Public Policy Toward Vertical Mergers," and Sam Peltzman, "Issues in Vertical Integration Policy." Both papers are in J. Fred Weston and Sam Peltzman, Eds., *Public Policy Toward Mergers* (Pacific Palisades, California: Goodyear, 1969).

[14] For example, Procter & Gamble's acquisition of Clorox, if permitted by the courts, would have combined a producer of soaps and detergents with a producer of liquid bleach. These product lines are not competitive with each other, but they do utilize the same distribution systems.

[15] Steiner, for example, groups market extension mergers with horizontal and vertical, and treats product extensions as a separate category rather than as a subset of conglomerates.

ciencies do not appear. Are there efficiencies of "conglomeration" or "diversification"? Perhaps, but the a priori arguments are not especially strong. It is, of course, possible that a merged conglomerate will prove to be more efficient than its separate parts (the term synergy is sometimes invoked to describe this event) or that it will act as more of a risk taker than the conventional, specialized firm. But these are precisely possibilites, not strong expectations, and rather speculative ones at that.

On the other hand, the competitive implications of conglomerate mergers are also difficult to pin down. Because the partners are in different markets, an impact on competition within any market is difficult to predict. Many possible long-term effects of "conglomerate power" on market competition have been noted, but—as is the case with the efficiency arguments—these tend to be somewhat speculative.[16] The empirical evidence of anticompetitive effects, moreover, is to date unimpressive.[17]

This is not to assert, however, that conglomerate mergers pose no public policy problem. The joining of significant numbers of large corporations may well affect power in a broad context—visible perhaps in rising aggregate concentration measures—even though the impacts on specific markets cannot be readily discerned. This result may give rise to social or political rather than economic concerns, but even economists will concede that such worries are real ones. William S. Comanor, for example, has recently observed that popular support for limiting conglomerate mergers

is derived not from evidence of actual harms, however defined, but rather from a fundamental ideological concern with giant aggregations of privately held assets, and the political power which is presumed to flow from them.[18]

This statement suggests, perhaps accurately, that social concern with conglomerate mergers is more closely related to firm **size** than to "conglomerateness" *per se*.

The already formidable tasks of public merger policy have been further complicated by the disproportionate growth of conglomerates in the past three decades. As Table 14.3 shows, conglomerate mergers (defined to include both product-extension and market-extension types) now account for more than 80 percent of the assets transferred in large acquisitions, while the relative importance of horizontal and vertical acquisitions combined has fallen dramatically since the 1950s.

---

[16] For example, the large conglomerate may have easier (and cheaper) access to money capital, more opportunities for reciprocity (or mutual back scratching) with other large concerns, and greater ability to subsidize specific activities, thereby outlasting more specialized rivals. One of the best enumerations of possible conglomerate advantages remains Corwin D . Edwards, "Conglomerate Bigness as a Source of Power," in *Business Concentration and Price Policy* (Princeton: Princeton University Press, 1955).

[17] See Lawrence G. Goldberg, "The Effect of Conglomerate Mergers on Competition," *Journal of Law and Economics*, **16** (April 1973), 137–158. Recently, however, Ronald W. Cotterill and Willard F. Mueller have reported that conglomerate merger activity has had a generally significant impact on concentration in retail food markets. "The Impact of Firm Conglomeration on Market Structure: Evidence for the U.S. Food Retailing Industry," *Antitrust Bulletin*, **25** (Fall 1980), p. 557–582.

[18] William S. Comanor, "Conglomerate Mergers: Considerations for Public Policy," in Roger D. Blair and Robert F. Lanzillotti , Eds., *The Conglomerate Corporation: A Public Problem?* (Cambridge, Mass.: Oelgeschager, Gunn, and Hain, 1 981), quotation at p. 15. Interestingly, Comanor's data do not indicate that conglomerate merger activity has had an impact on aggregate concentraion in recent years.

Table 14.3 Assets Acquired in Large Mergers by Type of Merger 1948–1978 (Percent)

Merger Type	1948–1951	1952–1955	1956–1959	1960–1963	1964–1967	1967–1977
Horizontal	38.8	36.6	27.3	13.3	11.4	13.8
Vertical	23.8	11.5	20.1	23.8	8.9	5.8
Pure conglomerate	—	3.6	14.2	17.1	21.2	42.2
Market-extension	—	2.7	5.0	8.0	8.7	5.7
Product-extension	37.5	45.7	33.5	37.8	49.9	32.5
Total	100%	100%	100%	100%	100%	100%

Sources: FTC, *Economic Report on Corporate Mergers, Current Trends,* and *Statistical Report on Mergers and Acquisitions.*

The conglomerate merger complicates policy in part because it raises difficult questions of concept and measurement, and in part simply because it is a new phenomenon. Such mergers have, of course, existed for many years but not as a quantitatively important event. As we shall see, the explosiveness of the conglomerate movement is itself one result of recent merger policy. While the courts have developed some rather well-defined limitations on horizontal and vertical acquisitions in the past 30 years, conglomerates have emerged relatively unscathed.

The reasons for this uneven treatment have to do with the conceptual problems posed by conglomerates. As is suggested above, most vertical and horizontal mergers carry immediate, predictable impacts on market structure; and it is possible to move from these predictions to inferences about competitive effects. Such is not the case with conglomerates. Structural changes, as a rule, cannot be foreseen. The place of the diversified firm in economic theory is not fully clear. And the ability of the courts to define and adopt appropriate standards has thus been limited.

A REVIEW OF RELEVANT CASES

Although some merger cases refuse to fit neatly into a single category, it is helpful to consider legal developments in terms of the horizontal-vertical-conglomerate distinction. The conglomerate classification includes all cases that do not clearly fit the horizontal or vertical molds.

Horizontal Mergers

In amending Section 7, Congress intended to prevent "anticompetitive" mergers. Congress was, moreover, concerned with what the Supreme Court would frequently refer to as "a rising tide of economic concentration" in the American economy. The most immediate and important implications of the new law would involve mergers between competitors. Under what circumstances would the courts find that such mergers reduce "competition" substantially? Would judges insist on analysis of competitive impact, or would they be satisfied with such shorthand clues as the effect of merger on "economic concentration?" These important questions received much attention—and some reasonably clear answers—in the decades following enactment of the Celler–Kefauver Amendment.

The Bethlehem–Youngstown Case (1958)[19]   The proposed merger of the Bethlehem Steel Corporation and the Youngstown Sheet and Tube Company presented the first "big case" under amended Section 7. Steel is a "key" industry in the American economy. In part because its products are the inputs for many other manufacturing industries, steel price and output behavior carries serious implications for many sectors. The industry has long been characterized by high concentration and the existence of a dominant firm, United States Steel; and the merger at issue involved the second and sixth leading producers. As if this were not enough to focus attention on the case, it was the first new Section 7 prosecution to reach final determination in the courts. Previously, the Federal Trade Commission had ruled on specific acquisitions,[20] and a number of suits had been settled by mutual consent,[21] but *Bethlehem* would provide the first possibility for important legal precedent in the future treatment of mergers.

The facts of the acquisition were clear. Bethlehem, the number two steel producer, accounted for 15.4 percent of national ingot capacity; and Youngstown, the sixth largest firm, held 4.7 percent. Since United States Steel had almost 30 percent of the market, the merger would not have created a new market leader, but it would have strengthened the second largest company. Indeed, the companies argued that the primary effect of the acquisition would be to establish a firm better able to compete with United States Steel. The merger, they contended, would actually increase competition in the industry. The government's contention was the reverse: The merger would increase market concentration, however it was measured. For example, the four largest firms accounted for 58.3 percent of the market prior to the proposed merger, but they would have held 63 percent afterward. Moreover, the strengthening of the number two producer was, as Eugene Singer has put it, "double-edged."[22] A combined Bethlehem–Youngstown might be better able to compete with United States Steel, but such a firm would also become more powerful vis-à-vis smaller competitors (Bethlehem was already much larger than the third largest producer, Republic Steel, which held 8.3 percent of the market).

Not the least of the district court's problems in reaching a decision was the finding of a relevant geographic market. Section 7 requires a showing that competition may be lessened substantially in a "line of commerce" and a "section of the coun-

---

[19] *U.S.* v. *Bethlehem Steel Corp.*, 168 F. Supp. 576 (S.D.N.Y., 1958).

[20] *Pillsbury Co.* v. *Federal Trade Commission*, 50 F.T.C. 1110 (1954). This case ultimately was appealed and decided in Circuit Court: 354 F. 2d 952 (5th Cir. 1965).

[21] At least five challenged acquisitions were settled by mutual consent of the government and defendants prior to the time of the *Bethlehem* decision. The consent agreements generally provided for full or partial divestiture of acquired facilities and/or some limitation on future acquisitions.

[22] Eugene M. Singer, *Antitrust Economics* (Englewood Cliffs, N.J.: Prentice-Hall, 1968), p. 131.

try.''[23] With respect to section of the country, the defendants argued that their businesses were conducted primarily in separate regions, Bethlehem in the eastern and western portions of the nation, and Youngstown in the center. Judge Weinfeld, finding that both actual and potential steel shipments of the companies did overlap geographically, held that there were multiple relevant markets (i.e., "sections of the country"): the United States; the northeastern quadrant of the United States; Michigan, Ohio, Pennsylvania, and New York; Michigan and Ohio; and Michigan.[24]

In concluding that the merger would violate Section 7, the Judge stressed several points: (1) The merger would increase market concentration and would widen the gap between the two largest firms and remaining competitors. (2) An addition to concentration in an already concentrated market such as steel might be especially damaging, and approval of the immediate merger might open the door to further concentration-increasing mergers, each "justified" by the fact that the merging companies would be better able to compete with larger rivals. (3) To allow a merger merely because the emergent company would not be the largest in the industry would violate the purpose of amended Section 7. (4) The merger would eliminate a significant competitor in an industry whose history indicated that replacement by a new entrant was most unlikely.

The most important aspect of the *Bethlehem* decision was, in retrospect, the emphasis placed on market shares and concentration. The merger was horizontal—that is, the companies were, primarily, competitors at the same production stage—and the immediate question concerned the meaning of lessening of competition in such circumstances. Although Judge Weinfeld did not say so explicitly, his underlying notion of lessened competition seems to have been closely tied to measurable increases in the centralization of market power: an increased market share for the emergent firm, an increase in the concentration level of the industry, and a reduction in the number of competitors. These structural indicia have continued to play a prominent role in the evaluation of competitive consequences of horizontal mergers.

The Brown Shoe Case (1962)[25]   Brown Shoe Company's acquisition of G. R. Kinney was considered by the Supreme Court on largely vertical grounds (Brown was primarily a manufacturer and Kinney a retailer). The decision, however, included the first important statements by the Court of rules that would govern future horizontal acquisitions.

Kinney was a major retail shoe chain, although its share of the national market was extremely small (less than two percent). Brown also operated retail outlets, al-

---

[23] The lines of commerce, or product markets, in the *Bethlehem* case were defined by the Judge as (1) the iron and steel industry, (2) hot rolled sheets, (3) cold rolled sheets, (4) hot rolled bars, and (5) buttweld pipe.

[24] M. A. Adelman has criticized this definition of markets on the grounds that they are mutually inconsistent—that is, whereas any one definition may be defensible, the acceptance of one ought logically to preclude acceptance of the others. See his "The Antimerger Act, 1950–1960," *American Economic Review*, **15** (May 1961), p. 237.

[25] *Brown Shoe Co., Inc.* v. *U.S.*, 370 U.S. 294 (1962).

though its main activity was manufacturing. In considering horizontal effects, the Supreme Court focused on cities with populations of more than 10,000 in which both companies had retail stores (these constituted the relevant "section of the country"). The product markets (or "lines of commerce") were defined as men's, women's, and children's shoes.

The Court noted explicitly that the effect of the merger on national concentration in shoe retailing would be unimpressive, but the impacts in specific cities would be more noticeable. In 118 cities, the merger would produce a retailer with more than 5 percent of at least one of the lines of commerce. In some cases, the shares would be substantially higher, reaching 57 percent in Dodge City, Kansas.[26] Said Chief Justice Warren:

In an industry as fragmented as shoe retailing, the control of substnatial shares of trade in a city may have important effects on competition. If a merger achieving 5% control were now approved, we might be required to approve future merger efforts by Brown's competitors seeking similar market shares. The oligopoly Congress sought to avoid would then be furthered.[27]

The Court was suggesting some important guidelines. The competitive effect of horizontal merger was to be judged with reference to its impact on shares and concentration in specifically defined markets. Furthermore, a merger might be prohibited even though, at the national level, resulting shares were miniscule and the market unconcentrated. The key to the Court's reasoning is sometimes termed the incipiency doctrine: Section 7 policy is to be used to curb any tendencies toward concentration in their incipiency. It should be noted that, if carried to a logical extreme, such a doctrine could imply a *per se* prohibition on horizontal mergers.

The Philadelphia National Bank Case (1963)[28] Philadelphia National Bank's attempted acquisition of Girard Trust Corn Exchange presented the Supreme Court with an array of legal and economic questions. The merging banks were, respectively, the second and third largest of 42 commercial banks in the Philadelphia area. The merger would have produced the largest bank in the area, with control of 36 percent of total bank assets, 36 percent of deposits, and 34 percent of net loans. This would have made the emergent company substantially larger than First Pennsylvania Bank, which had been the largest single concern with about 23 percent of the market; and it would have raised the four-firm concentration level in the area to about 78 percent.

Viewed in these terms, the effect of the merger would have been dramatic in raising the concentration of the market. But before the Court could consider this impact, two separate issues required disposition: (1) the vulnerability of bank mergers to the

---

[26] In a scathing critique of this decision, John L. Peterman has pointed out that Brown's shares were apparently miscalculated and were in some instances much lower than the Court believed. "The Brown Shoe Case," *Journal of Law and Economics,* **18** (April 1975), 81–146.

[27] See footnote 25 above, pp. 343–344.

[28] *U.S.* v. *Philadelphia National Bank,* 374, U.S. 321 (1963).

Clayton Act and (2) the definition of the relevant geographic market. It is safe to say that prior to the *Philadelphia National Bank* decision, few individuals in the Justice Department, the Federal Trade Commission, the judiciary, or the banking industry believed that bank mergers were subject to prosecution under Section 7.[29] In fact, the merger was attacked by the government primarily as a violation of Section 1 of the Sherman Act; the argument with respect to Section 7 appears to have been an afterthought. The reason for this confusion is the status of banking as a regulated industry. The Bank Merger Act of 1960 expressly directed the bank regulatory agencies (the Federal Reserve Board of Governors, the Federal Deposit Insurance Corporation, and the Comptroller of the Currency) to consider competitive factors before approving mergers; and it was the defendants' argument that this law effectively removed bank mergers from the scope of the federal antitrust laws.

This contention was denied by the Supreme Court. Justice Brennan noted for the majority that immunity from the antitrust laws is not implied lightly. And, he went on, there was nothing in either the legislative history of the Section 7 amendments, or in the Bank Merger Act itself, that conferred express immunity on the banking industry. Presumably, Congress had the power to confer such immunity, but except in the most extreme circumstances, the Court would not infer it indirectly.

Having established the absence of antitrust immunity for the banking industry, the PNB–Girard merger was to be decided under Section 7. The relevant line of commerce was held to be "commercial banking." More troublesome was the determination of the relevant geographic market. The position of the companies, which had been accepted by the district court, was that the relevant area was a broad one.[30] The emergent bank, it was argued, would compete for business among large customers with banks in New York and throughout the northeastern United States. But, said the Supreme Court:

The proper question to be asked in this case is not where the parties to the merger do business or even where they compete, but where, within the area of competitive overlap, the effect of the merger on competition will be direct and immediate.[31]

The Court went on to note that large bank customers may do much of their banking business outside their "home community," whereas small customers are confined by convenience to the immediate neighborhood, and intermediate sized customers "deal with banks within an area intermediate to these two extremes." What, then, is **the** relevant geographic area? Said the Court:

. . . that . . . the relevant geographical market is a function of each separate customer's economic scale means simply that a workable compromise must be found: some fair intermediate delineation which avoids the indefensible extremes of draw-

---

[29]See, for example, Jesse W. Markham, "Mergers and the New Section 7," in Almarin Phillips, Ed., *Perspectives on Antitrust Policy* (Princeton: Princeton University Press, 1965), p. 178.

[30]It is very common for defendants to argue for a broad market in merger cases, since, as we have seen, this is likely to reduce the impact of the merger on measured changes in concentration.

[31]See footnote 28 above, p. 357.

*ing the market either so extensively as to make the effect of the merger upon compe-
tition seem insignificant, because only the very largest bank customers are taken
into account in defining the market, or so narrowly as to place appellees in different
markets, because only the smallest customers are considered. We think that the
four-county Philadelphia metropolitan area . . . which would seem roughly to delineate the area in which bank customers that are neither very large nor very small
find it practical to do their banking business, is a more appropriate "section of the
country" in which to appraise the instant merger than any larger or smaller or different area.[32]*

The determination of the metropolitan area as a relevant market was, then, the
"compromise" that permitted the Court to decide on the basis of the market share
and concentration data noted above. Here, the Court's position was clear. Section 7
reflected intense congressional concern over rising industrial concentration. This
concern, according to the Court:

*. . . warrants dispensing, in certain cases, with elaborate proof of market struc-
ture, market behavior, or probable anticompetitive effects. Specifically, we think
that a merger which produces a firm controlling an undue percentage share of the
relevant market, and results in a significant increase in the concentration of firms in
that market, is so inherently likely to lessen competition substantially that it must be
enjoined in the absence of evidence clearly showing that the merger is not likely to
have such anticompetitive effects.[33]*

The Court had, thus, established a two-part test: A horizontal merger violates the
law if it results in an "undue" market share for the emergent firm **and** a "significant" increase in concentration.[34] Although neither term was defined specifically,
the PNB–Girard merger met both criteria.

The merger was thus enjoined because of congressional concern over rising concentration, and the Court's position was one of unqualified hostility to such increases. Justice Brennan noted, in conclusion, that a merger that lessens competition "is not saved because on some ultimate reckoning of social or economic debits
and credits, it may be deemed beneficial."

Despite the strength and clarity of the *Philadelphia National Bank* decision, a
troublesome inconsistency must be noted. The Court held that Section 7 is designed
to bar anticompetitive mergers even where such mergers may have social and economic benefits. In Justice Brennan's words, "some price might have to be paid" for
denying certain mergers that threaten competition. The Court claimed that its
standard of judgment was faithful to economic theory, which holds that "competition is likely to be greatest when there are many sellers, none of which has any

---

[32] Ibid., p. 361.

[33] Ibid., p. 363.

[34] Notice that whether a given merger increases concentration significantly may depend upon what index of concentration is examined. At times, for example, a merger will have a large impact on the top-4 concentration ratio, but not on
the top-8 ratio.

significant market share.'' To restate the Court's position: Protection of competition requires the encouragement of atomistic or unconcentrated market structures, and this requirement holds even where the result may be the denial of benefits to consumers.

The economic inconsistency of this position should be obvious. It is true that competition, in a strict sense, is associated with powerlessness or atomistic structure. But the economic rationale for competition is not atomism itself; it is rather the **economic results** that competition implies. If competitively structured (atomistic) markets do not imply desirable economic results, then the economic rationale for such markets breaks down. The Court's position, however, seems to be that atomistic structures are desirable even where it is conceded that they may cause a deterioration in economic performance. One might wish to defend this position, but the defense cannot be based on economic arguments for competition. Indeed, in *Philadelphia National Bank* the Court had come close to equating competition with two specific structural measures, an approach considerably narrower than that suggested in *Brown Shoe*.

The Alcoa–Rome Case (1964)[35]   The acquisition of the Rome Cable Corporation by the Aluminum Company of America presented somewhat different issues than those raised by earlier cases. Alcoa, the nation's leading aluminum producer, was also the leader in production of aluminum conductor, a type of line used to transmit electric power from generating plants. Rome was one of the 10 largest producers of copper conductor wire and cable, as well as a ''substantial'' producer of aluminum conductor. Aluminum conductor and copper conductor were competitive in use, but in recent years aluminum had captured most of the conductor market.

A district court, in finding that the merger did not violate Section 7, held that insulated aluminum conductor and insulated copper conductor fall within the same market grouping. The Supreme Court, however, found that aluminum conductor—both insulated and noninsulated—was a submarket and a separate line of commerce. This definition ignored the fact that the two types of conductor are produced in very different ways and that firms dealing with insulated conductor could switch freely between aluminum and copper wire. The market as defined was thus something of an artifact created by the Court. Alcoa's share of this market was 27.8 percent; Rome accounted for 1.3 percent; and the nine largest producers jointly held 95.7 percent.

The Supreme Court held that Alcoa's acquisition of Rome violated Section 7. Any acquisition of a significant competitor by one of the dominant firms in a highly concentrated industry, said Justice Douglas, may lessen competition substantially. It was true, he noted, that Rome's share of the market seemed small. But here two points were relevant: Alcoa already controlled an ''undue'' percentage share of the market, and Rome was a significant competitor—an efficient, aggressive, innovative firm—in a highly concentrated market. Only a dozen companies had accounted

---

[35] *U.S.* v. *Aluminum Co. of America*, 377 U.S. 271 (1964).

for as much as 1 percent of the market in the past five years, and Rome posed the threat of effective competition to market leaders.

In *Brown Shoe,* the Court had expressed particular concer about merger in a fragmented market, arguing that it would be a step on the road to oligopoly. Here, the Court expressed equal concern about a small merger in an already concentrated market, stating: " . . . the more advanced the oligopoly, the more objectionable each step becomes."[36] Clearly, the evolving position on horizontal acquisitions was a stringent one. Read together, *Brown Shoe, Philadelphia National Bank,* and *Alcoa–Rome* indicate that mergers between rival firms will violate Section 7 if either company is a market leader.

The Continental Can Case (1964)[37]   The acquisition of Hazel-Atlas by the Continental Can Company posed a thorny problem of market definition, for the merger did not fit perfectly into the horizontal category. Continental was the nation's second largest manufacturer of metal containers, accounting for 33 percent of the market (the American Can Company had 38 percent, making the metal container industry something akin to a duopoly). Hazel-Atlas was the third largest producer of glass containers, with a 9.6 percent market share.

The difficulty in treating this merger arose from the fact that, although metal and glass containers serve in some similar uses, they are not really "the same" product. Even where they competed directly—for instance, in beer, soft drinks, and baby foods—customers might not readily switch back and forth in response to price or quality changes. In many areas, moreover, the characteristics of the two types of containers were sufficiently distinct to preclude competition.

The Supreme Court recognized the nature of the relationship, conceding that "interchangeability of use" between metal and glass containers is not as great as that normally found in **intra**industry mergers. Nevertheless, the Court contended, the **inter**industry competition between the two was sufficiently great to justify definition of a combined glass and metal container market as a separate line of commerce. Having established the combined market as relevant, the Court proceeded to consider the usual kinds of structural measures. Continental's share of the combined market was 21.9 percent, making it the second largest producer; Hazel-Atlas accounted for 3.1 percent; and the six largest manufacturers held a joint share of more than 70 percent.

The Supreme Court found that the merger violated Section 7. The joint market share of the emergent firm would have been about 25 percent—close to the presumptively anticompetitive 30 percent cited in *Philadelphia National Bank.* Moreover, the merger "reduced from five to four" the number of significant competitors who might challenge the position of the market leader. Having contrived a rather artificial definition of the market, the Court returned to its earlier tests of illegality in horizontal mergers.

[36] Notice that the second part of the Court's test of illegality in *Philadelphia National Bank*—a "significant" increase in concentration—was ignored here.

[37] *U.S. v. Continental Can Co.,* 378 U.S. 441 (1964).

The Court, however, did not rest its conclusion entirely on these conventional tests, perhaps because it recognized the precarious nature of the relevant market it had defined. Said Justice White:

Market shares are the primary indicia of market power, but a judgment under Section 7 is not to be made by any single qualititative or quantitative test.

Where a merger is of such a size as to be inherently suspect, elaborate proof of market structure, market behavior and probable anticompetitive effects may be dispensed with in view of Section 7's design to prevent undue concentration.[38]

The Court said, further, that Section 7 deals with "probable and imminent" competition, as well as with that competition existing at the moment. Glass and metal containers were becoming increasingly competitive in certain areas. Indeed, the nature of competition between the two was "long run." In this light, the merger would reduce potential future competition between Continental and Hazel-Atlas, even though the two companies might not compete much with each other at present.

The Supreme Court had, then, defined a relevant container market, but it had stopped short of tying its decision exclusively to projected changes in the concentration of that market. For the first time, the notion of "future" and "potential" competition was introduced, and, although the Court did not concede it explicitly, this turn toward a different concept was probably dictated by the novel circumstances of the merger and by the arguable nature of the relevant market as defined. Indeed, whereas the merger was treated in horizontal terms, *Continental Can* provided some harbingers for later product- and market-extension decisions.

The El Paso Natural Gas Case (1964)[39]   The El Paso Natural Gas Company's acquisition of Pacific Northwest Gas marked the first horizontal merger case in which market shares and concentration were not relevant to the final decision. At the time of the merger, El Paso was one of the largest gas pipeline companies in the country. The company had assets of almost $1 billion, and it was the sole out-of-state supplier to what the government called the "vast and still expanding California market." Pacific Northwest, with assets of $250 million, was termed "the only other important pipeline company west of the Rocky Mountains."

The Supreme Court defined California as the relevant section of the country, and the "production, transportation and sale of natural gas" as the relevant line of commerce. El Paso was an important supplier of natural gas in the California market; but Pacific Northwest, although attempting to make inroads, had no outlet to California and had not sold natural gas within the relevant section of the country. The merger, thus, had no immediately visible effect on the structure of the relevant market area as defined. If the Supreme Court had adhered strictly to its earlier tests of lessened competition, it might have had to conclude that no competitive impact was discernible, for Pacific Northwest had a zero share of production and sales in the relevant

[38] Ibid., p. 458.

[39] *U.S.* v. *El Paso Natural Gas co.*, 376 U.S. 651 (1964).

market. Whatever the implications of the merger might be, it would not immediately alter El Paso's existing market share or market concentration.

The Court, however, refused to be bound by its own past tests. Justice Douglas took careful note of Pacific Northwest as a competitive factor in the California market. The company had made efforts to sell natural gas in California and, despite its failure, was a "substantial factor" in the market. In one instance, Pacific had negotiated and reached tentative agreement to supply Southern California Edison, a major user of natural gas in California. Edison ultimately terminated the agreement and signed with El Paso; however, on the basis of its bargaining with Pacific, the company was able to obtain price discounts from El Paso. Thus, the Court concluded that even Pacific Northwest's unsuccessful efforts could exert a "powerful influence on El Paso." Said Justice Douglas:

Unsuccessful bidders are no less competitors than the successful one. The presence of two or more suppliers gives buyers a choice. Pacific Northwest was . . . one of two major interstate pipelines serving the trans-Rocky Mountain States . . . . It was so strong and militant that it was viewed with concern, and coveted, by El Paso. If El Paso can absorb Pacific Northwest without violating Section 7 of the Clayton Act, that section has no meaning in the natural gas field.[40]

The Penn-Olin Case (1964)[41]   The *Penn-Olin* case did not, strictly speaking, involve corporate merger or acquisition. It was rather a "joint venture" in which the Pennsalt Chemical Corporation and the Olin Mathieson Chemical Corporation formed a new company, the Penn-Olin Chemical Corporation. The purpose of the new company was to produce and sell sodium chlorate (an industrial chemical used primarily by the pulp and paper industry) in the southeastrn United States. There was no argument among the parties concerning the relevant line of commerce (sodium chlorate) or section of the country (southeastern United States). Rather the issues were: (1) whether Section 7 applies to joint ventures, and (2) if so, whether this joint venture violates either Section 7 or Section 1 of the Sherman Act.

The Supreme Court held that Section 7 does apply to joint ventures, although the language of the provision does not specifically extend to such situations. The test, said Justice Clark, is "the effect of the acquisition." Citing the Court's earlier language in *Philadelphia National Bank,* Justice Clark stated that to place joint ventures beyond the scope of Section 7 "would be illogical and disrespectful of the plain congressional purpose in amending" the law. Such ventures could threaten competition in much the same way as ordinary merger, and they were not to be treated differently.

An assessment of the competitive consequences of this "merger," however, was not directly made by the Court. Rather it confined its decision to the legitimacy of tests applied by the lower court, which found that the venture did not violate Section 7. The district court had noted that both Pennsalt and Olin possessed the resources to enter the southeastern market separately and that the forecasts of the companies

---

[40] Ibid., pp. 661–662.

[41] *U.S.* v. *Penn-Olin Chemical Co.,* 378 U.S. 158 (1964).

themselves indicated that plants could be operated profitably. However, the district court stated, these considerations were significant only insofar as they shed light on the probability that each company would enter individually. The lower court had thus held that the relevant test of the venture's impact on competition depended on the likelihood that **both** Pennsalt and Olin would move into the southeastern section as active rivals. Since the court found it "impossible to conclude that as a matter of reasonable probability **both** . . . would have plants in the southeast if Penn-Olin had not been created," it concluded that no violation of Section 7 was implied.

The Supreme Court held that the basis of the district court decision was incorrect. The probability of substantially lessened competition, said Justice Clark, could not be judged solely according to the likelihood of separate entry by both companies. One might have entered "while the other continued to ponder," and

There still remained for consideration the fact that Penn-Olin eliminated the potential competition of the corporation that might have remained at the edge of the market, continually threatening to enter. Just as a merger eliminates actual competition, this joint venture may well foreclose any prospect of competition between Olin and Pennsalt, in the relevant sodium chlorate market. The difference of course is that the merger's foreclosure is present while the joint venture's is prospective.[42]

The point made in this passage is important in the development of merger law. The notion of potential competition that the Court utilized in both *Continental Can* and *El Paso* seemed to refer to actual future competition between merging companies— that is, competition was expected to occur, and the merger would in each case have foreclosed it. Here, however, Justice Clark was going farther in asserting that the mere presence of a potential competitor—even one who may **never actually enter** the market—carries significant competitive implications.

In discussing the problem of proof of lessened competition, the Court seemed clearly to indicate its hostility to the Penn-Olin joint venture. The industry was a rapidly expanding one, and "each company had compelling reasons for entering the southeast market." Under the circumstances, the probability of diminished competition seemed high. The Supreme Court, however, confined its decision to an order that the case be reconsidered in view of the guidelines noted here. The case was to be retried in light of the competitive effect of entry by one firm while the other remained a potential entrant. Somewhat ironically, in view of the Court's expression of opinion, the Penn-Olin venture was again found by the lower court not to violate Section 7. On a second appeal, the Supreme Court upheld this decision by a tie (4 to 4) vote.[43]

The Von's Grocery Case (1966)[44]   The acquisition by Von's of Shopping Bag Food Stores produced a Supreme Court decision that approached a rule of *per se* illegality for horizontal mergers. The facts were not in dispute. Von's and Shopping

[42] Ibid., pp. 173–174.

[43] *U.S.* v. *Penn-Olin*, 389 U.S. 308 (1968).

[44] *U.S.* v. *Von's Grocery Co. et al.*, 384 U.S. 270 (1966).

Bag were the third and sixth largest competitors in a well-defined market: retail grocery sales in the metropolitan Los Angeles area. The market was unconcentrated (CR_4 = 24 percent), entry was easy, and competition was apparently intense. Von's and Shopping Bag accounted jointly for 7.5 percent of the market.

In finding the merger illegal, Justice Black for the majority placed heavy emphasis on a trend toward chain store operation in the relevant market. Since 1950 the number of owners of a single grocery store had declined substantially, while the number of chains grew apace—a change in the market effected partly through mergers. The Court saw in these facts a threat of increasing concentration, precisely what Section 7 was intended to prevent. Viewed against this background, a merger of two vigorous and growing competitors was not permissible.

The *Von's Grocery* decision was less an analysis of competitive impact than it was a lament for a changing world. The "Mom and Pop" grocery stores, once prominent in retailing, were being replaced by larger and more efficient enterprises. "Smaller businessmen" were being driven from the market. The stated purpose of Section 7 is to foster **competition.** As interpreted by the Supreme Court in *Von's*, however, its mandate was to maintain a market with the largest possible number of small competitors. In the words of Neale and Goyder:

The majority had apparently adopted the fallacy that competition is necessarily reduced when the number of competitors has declined[45]

A strong dissent from the majority opinion was lodged by Justice Stewart, who was joined by Justice Harlan. Justice Stewart pointed out that although the Court majority had spoken in terms of concentration of the market, it had cited only evidence bearing on the number of firms and mergers. Had the majority looked further, it would have seen considerable evidence that concentration was declining, even as the number of independent competitors declined as well.

The Court, in Justice Stewart's view, had made no effort to determine whether the merger would affect competition. It had, rather, engaged in "a simple exercise in sums," equated a decline in the number of firms in the market with a reduction in competition, and pronounced the merger illegal. The point made by the dissent is a real one. It is, of course, possible to argue cogently for protection of "small businessmen," but this argument taken alone has little or nothing to do with the competition that the antitrust laws are supposed to protect. It seems clear, moreover, that the Court's own test of anticompetitive impact relied less on actual market data than it did on a presumption that horizontal acquisition will harm competition.

The Citizen Publishing Case (1968)[46]   The *Citizen Publishing* decision was noteworthy for its treatment of the "failing company defense"—the doctrine that a merger that would otherwise violate Section 7 might be permissible if the acquired firm

---

[45] A. D. Neale and D. G. Goyder, *The Antitrust Laws of the U.S.A.*, 3rd ed. (Cambridge: Cambridge University Press, 1980), p. 192.

[46] *Citizen Publishing Co.* v. *U.S.*, 394 U.S. 131 (1968).

were about to be forced out of the market.[47] The only two daily newspapers in Tucson, Arizona—the *Citizen* and the *Star*—had negotiated an agreement under which their operations were to be closely integrated, although each would retain its separate identity. The government challenged the agreement as a violation of Section 7 as well as Sections 1 and 2 of the Sherman Act.

Terming the failing company argument the defendants' "only real defense," Justice Douglas found that Citizen Publishing was "not . . . on the verge of going out of business." A finding that the company was about to fail, however, would not have sufficed. It would also be necessary, said the Court, to show that the firm could not be successfully reorganized and that the acquiring company "is the only available purchaser" of the distressed enterprise. A successful failing company defense would thus have to meet stringent standards, and the applicability of this commonly cited doctrine is quite limited.

The General Dynamics Case (1974) The General Dynamics case arose as the result of a series of stock acquisitions beginning in the late 1950s. Material Services Corp. and its affiliate, Freeman Coal Mining, had acquired stock in United Electric Coal Companies. Shortly thereafter, Material Services was itself acquired by General Dynamics, a large and diversified company active in such areas as aircraft, communications, and marine products. By virtue of this merger, General Dynamics became the nation's fifth largest coal producer.

The government charged that the acquisition would lessen competition in coal sales, both in Illinois and the "Eastern Interior Coal Province Sales Area," which included Illinois, Indiana, and part of six other states. In support of its argument, the government introduced evidence that increased market shares in both areas would result from the merger. Production would become increasingly concentrated, precisely the sort of pattern that had served as the basis for earlier findings of illegality; indeed, the market share data presented by the government would have sufficed to prove a Section 7 violation under such precedents as *Philadelphia National Bank* and *Von's*.

By 1974, however, the composition and outlook of the Supreme Court had changed substantially since the 1960s. That the "Burger Court" might prove less sympathetic to government merger prosecutions than the "Warren Court" was a widely anticipated possibility. In *General Dynamics,* the Court found that evidence of **production** shares is of doubtful significance in the coal market.[48] Most coal, Justice Stewart observed, is produced and delivered under long-term requirements contract. Evidence of production and sales thus reflects only "the obligation to fulfill previously negotiated contracts at a previously fixed price." The "more significant indicator of a company's power to compete" is its "uncommitted reserves of recoverable coal," said Justice Stewart. But here the government's case was weak.

---

[47] The notion, implicit in the history of Section 7, has been invoked on rare occasions by courts as a justification for merger.

[48] *U.S.* v. *General Dynamics Corp.,* 415 U.S. 486 (1974).

United Electric had large current sales under previous contract but virtually no un-committed reserves; moreover, the company had only a "mere possibility" of ob-taining additional reserves. The government, said the Court, had presented evidence "insufficient" to establish a Section 7 violation.

The potential importance of this decision is plain. In earlier cases, the Supreme Court had accepted evidence of increased concentration and market shares as suffi-cient to prove a Section 7 violation. Although it had not explicitly asserted that ris-ing concentration and declining competition are the same thing, the inference was inescapable. Now the Court might be saying something different: that market share and concentration changes, although highly important in horizontal merger cases, are not necessarily conclusive.

Summary   The development of horizontal merger policy during the 1960s and 1970s was characterized by strict structural tests of competition. Mergers that would yield predictable increases in the shares of the emergent company and the concentra-tion of affected markets were subject to something close to a *per se* ban. Moreover, the Supreme Court was willing to act on such evidence even where structural data were based on somewhat artificial market definitions (*Continental Can, Alcoa-Rome*) and where the market shares and concentration levels were quite low (*Brown Shoe, Von's Grocery.*) Whether the *General Dynamics* decision signaled a change of direction toward a more permissive attitude is unclear because of the unusual facts surrounding the case.

Vertical Mergers

A merger between firms in a supplier–customer relationship raises issues similar to those suggested by vertical restrictions. Vertical integration, the result of mergers of this type, may produce real efficiencies. Certain processes are more economical when all stages are carried on at the same time and place by a single integrated producer. Integration will frequently provide some savings of transportation costs and transactions costs (the latter are the costs of dealing with outsiders, that is, of "using the market").

On the other hand, mergers yielding integrated firms may carry competitive im-plications. The business of a previously independent supplier (or customer) may as a result be foreclosed to other customers (or suppliers). And the existence of inte-grated firms may force new entrants to integrate also before coming into the market; if so, actual and potential entry may be discouraged. It is the balance of such consid-erations that confronts the courts in vertical merger cases.

The duPont–General Motors Case (1957)[49]   It was a vertical merger case that provided the impetus for Congress to amend Section 7.[50] Following the 1950

---

[49] *U.S.* v. *E. I. duPont de Nemours and Company et al.*, 353 U.S. 586 (1957).

[50] *Columbia Steel*, see footnote 6 above.

amendment, the first vertical situation to reach the Supreme Court turned out to be something of an oddity.

During the period 1917 to 1919, E. I. duPont de Nemours and Company had acquired a 23 percent stock interest in the General Motors Corporation. DuPont was a major supplier of automotive finishes and fabrics, and General Motors, at the time a relatively small automobile producer, was a user of these products. Further, the record showed that "duPont supplies the largest part of General Motors' requirements. . .''

The substantive question before the Court was reasonably straightforward: Did duPont's position as a major stockholder and supplier lessen competition substantially by foreclosing other suppliers from a portion of the market; that is, did duPont's "insulated" possession of the General Motors business in finishes and fabrics violate Section 7?

First, however, it was necessary for the Court to contend with two circumstances that lent the case its legal peculiarity.

1. The government had attacked the stock acquisition some 30 years after its consummation.
2. Although the case reached the Supreme Court after passage of the Celler-Kefauver amendment to Section 7, charges had been brought originally in 1949 under the old law.

The first issue caused the Court little difficulty. It was true, said Justice Brennan, that earlier Section 7 cases had been filed "at or near the time of acquisition"; but, he continued, nothing in these cases " . . . holds, or even suggests, that the Government is foreclosed from bringing the action at any time when the threat of the prohibited effects is evident." The question, in other words, was not when the merger took place, but rather when the possibility of a substantial lessening of competition became apparent.

The second issue, although disposed of quickly by the Court, presented greater difficulty. Legal action had been brought against duPont and General Motors under the old Section 7, which specifically proscribed mergers that might substantially lessen competition "between the corporation whose stock is . . . acquired and the corporation making the acquisition." Since duPont and General Motors did not compete with each other, the companies argued that they were not covered by the prohibition; that is, if the stock acquisition lessened competition, it did not do so by diminishing rivalry **between** the acquired and acquiring firms. This argument was rejected by the Court on the grounds that the intention of the original Section 7 was broader than its qualifying phrase would indicate. Said Justice Brennan:

. . . Section 7 . . . plainly is framed to reach not only the corporate acquisition of the stock of a competing corporation, where the effect may be substantially to lessen competition between them, but also the corporate acquisition of stock of any corporation, competitor or not, where the effect may be either (1) to restrain commerce in

any section or community, or (2) tend to create a monopoly of any line of commerce.[51]

On the basis of this interpretation, Justice Brennan held that:

. . . any acquisition by one corporation of all or any part of the stock of another corporation, competitor or not, is within the reach of the section whenenver the reasonable likelihood appears that the acquisition will result in a restraint of commerce or in the creation of a monopoly of any line of commerce.[52]

DuPont and General Motors contended that their relationship was based on objective business judgments and did not restrain commerce. General Motors' purchases of duPont products depended, said the companies, on the quality and price of those products—that is, on the same considerations that governed all purchases. The Court, however, refused to accept the suggestion that duPont's strong position as a supplier of General Motors was based simply on the excellence of its offerings. The Court did note that in later years competitors had obtained a larger proportion of the General Motors business, but went on to say:

The fact that sticks out . . . is that the bulk of duPont's production has always supplied the largest part of the requirements of the one customer in the automobile industry connected to duPont by a stock interest. The inference is overwhelming that duPont's commanding position was promoted by its stock interest and was not gained solely on competitive merit.[53]

The Court concluded:

The statutory policy of fostering free competition is obviously furthered when no supplier has an advantage over his competitors from an acquisition of his customer's stock likely to have the effects condemned by the statute . . . . The conclusion upon this record is inescapable that such likelihood was proved as to this acquisition.[54]

This decision, reached under the old Section 7, seemed consistent with the new law, perhaps more so than with the old. The Court had found that vertical foreclosure in a substantial share of a substantial market violated Section 7.

The Brown Shoe Case (1962) The *Brown Shoe* decision, which is discussed above, was the first expression of Supreme Court opinion on vertical mergers under amended Section 7.[55] At issue was the acquisition by Brown, the nation's fourth

---

[51]See footnote 49, pp. 590–591. The first paragraph of original Section 7 reads: "That no corporation engaged in commerce shall acquire, directly or indirectly, the whole or any part of the stock . . . of another corporation engaged also in commerce where the effect of such acquisition may be to substantially lessen competition between [the two] . . . or to restrain such commerce in any section or community or tend to create a monopoly of any line of commerce."

[52]Ibid., p. 592.

[53]Ibid., p. 605.

[54]Ibid., p. 607.

[55]See footnote 25 above.

largest shoe manufacturer and a retail chain as well, of the G. R. Kinney Company, the largest "family-style" retail shoe chain in the country and the twelfth largest shoe producer. The merger thus presented both vertical and horizontal considerations: Brown, as a manufacturer, was acquiring Kinney, as a retailer, and was thus integrating forward into the distribution of shoes. But Brown was also a retailer; hence acquisition of Kinney would add to Brown's existing market share at retail.

The Supreme Court based its decision largely on vertical grounds. The relevant product markets were defined as "men's," "women's," and "children's" shoes, and the relevant geographic area with respect to vertical impact was the nation as a whole. The companies had argued that the product lines should be more narrowly drawn according to differences in grade of material, quality of workmanship, price and end use; but the Court rejected such distinctions as "unrealistic."

Chief Justice Warren, writing for the Court, stressed the legislative history of Section 7. Congress' dominant motivation in revising the law, he stated, was to arrest "a rising tide of economic concentration in the American economy." The intention was to stop mergers at a time when this trend "was still in its incipiency." The history and language of the law, according to the Chief Justice, indicated congressional determination to have a strong merger policy, one that would place important legal obstacles in the way of further concentration increases. Thus, although Section 7 did not spell out specific tests for determining either relevant markets or diminutions of competition, its mandate was strong.

With this general outlook, the Court turned to the question of vertical effects on competition. Chief Justice Warren held that a lessening of competition in a vertical merger arises "primarily from a foreclosure." The question is: Does the acquisition of a customer by a supplier (or vice versa) foreclose other suppliers (customers) from a portion of the market? Although noting that such foreclosure is the main index of lessened competition, the Court stopped short of saying that any substantial foreclosure would automatically render a merger illegal. The size of the market share foreclosed, said the Chief Justice, is "seldom determinative"; it is necessary to look further into the historical and economic background of affected markets.

In the immediate case, the Court noted that the shoe industry was atomistic in structure. Brown's share of the national manufacturing market was on the order of 5 to 6 percent, whereas Kinney's retail sales accounted for less than 2 percent of the national market. Thus, although the merger involved leading firms, it would not have produced a company whose size would overwhelm the market. Nevertheless, the Court noted:

In this industry, no merger between a manufacturer and an independent retailer could involve a larger potential market foreclosure.[56]

Both past history and the testimony of Brown Shoe's president indicated that Brown would indeed "force" its shoes into Kinney stores by virtue of ownership—that is, the potential for foreclosure would be exploited. Further, said the Chief Justice, a

---

[56] Ibid., p. 331–332.

trend toward vertical integration in the industry was already apparent and made it increasingly difficult for nonintegrated shoe manufacturers to place their shoes in retail outlets. The Court did not quarrel with Brown Shoe's contention that the industry was highly competitive; however, it held that "remaining vigor" in competition cannot immunize a merger if "the trend in the industry is toward oligopoly."

The Court's position on the vertical aspect was clear. Congress had revised Section 7 to preserve competition and prevent the formation of "oligopolies" or industries of high concentration. Given this purpose, and considering the circumstances of the industry, the merger was suspect. The Court concluded:

> . . . the trend towards vertical integration in the shoe industry, when combined with Brown's avowed policy of forcing its own shoes upon its retail subsidiaries, may foreclose competition from a substantial share of the markets . . . without producing any countervailing competitive, economic or social advantages.[57]

Given the atomism of the market, the Court argued, the emergent Brown-Kinney retail chain would be in a strong position even though its national market share was low. Citing testimony that strong national chains "can insulate selected outlets from the vagaries of competition," Chief Justice Warren concluded:

> The retail outlets of integrated companies, by eliminating wholesalers and by increasing the volume of purchases from the manufacturing division of the enterprise, can market their own brands at prices below those of competing independent retailers. Of course, some of the results of large integrated or chain operations are beneficial to consumers. . . . But we cannot fail to recognize Congress' desire to promote competition through the protection of viable, small, locally owned businesses. Congress appreciated that occasional higher costs and prices might result from the maintenance of fragmented industries and markets. It resolved these competing considerations in favor of decentralization. We must give effect to that decision.[58]

Although the *Brown Shoe* decision makes several important points, none is farther reaching than that contained in this last passage. The Supreme Court in 1962 was searching for standards under which a lessening of competition could be inferred. Quite clearly, any tendency toward centralized or concentrated power would be a key, as would vertical extensions that either foreclose nonintegrated rivals or place them at some other "disadvantage." The emerging conception of competition was intimately tied to market structures, and especially to "viable, small . . . businesses."

Yet the Court appeared to go still further. A merger that contributes to the concentration of power diminishes "competition." It therefore violates the law without reference to other economic effects. Possible efficiencies, for example, that would

---

[57]Ibid., p. 334.

[58]Ibid., p. 344.

lead to lower costs and prices carry no weight. The competitive effect of merger lies solely in its structural implications for the relevant market. And a merger that is anticompetitive in this very specific sense cannot be saved from the Section 7 prohibition on any other ground.

The implications of this position are discussed further below, but it should be noted initially that the Court's viewpoint was an extreme one. Although undoubtedly based both in a careful reading of congressional intent and in the need for shorthand rules, *Brown Shoe* has generated controversy even to this day.

Congolomerate Mergers

The mergers that had come before the Supreme Court prior to 1965 were, for the most part, horizontal. *Brown Shoe* was a partial exception, decided on both vertical and horizontal grounds. *Continental Can* had conglomerate overtones, for the merging companies produced different products; however, competition between them was sufficiently strong for the Court to place an essentially horizontal context on its considerations. Beginning with *Consolidated Foods* (1965) and *Procter & Gamble* (1967), however, cases appeared that did not fit existing precedent. New approaches would have to be devised.

The Consolidated Foods Case (1965).[59] Consolidated Foods Corporation, a major foods processor selling at wholesale and retail, had acquired Gentry, Inc., a producer of dehydrated onion and garlic. Gentry's share of the market in dehydrated onion and garlic was 23 percent just prior to the merger. The market was a virtual duopoly, with Gentry and Basic Vegetable Products, Inc., accounting jointly for almost 90 percent of sales.

The Federal Trade Commission, finding a Section 7 violation, argued that the merger would enable the combined company to practice **reciprocity:** Consolidated could force its own suppliers to purchase onions and garlic from Gentry; the alternative, explicitly or implicitly, would be the loss of Consolidated's (substantial) business. And, said the commission, the practice would harm competition by foreclosing rival garlic and onion manufacturers from this portion of the market.

A circuit court had reversed the commission, citing evidence that in the decade that had elaspsed since the acqusition, Gentry had failed to expand its markets significantly (the company had gained 7 percent more of the onion market, but it had lost 12 percent in garlic).

The Supreme Court upheld the FTC. Reciprocity, said Justice Douglas, "is one of the congeries of anticompetitive practices at which the antitrust laws are aimed." Whereas the circuit court had given too much weight to postmerger evidence, careful inspection of this evidence tended to confirm the commission's concern: Gentry was able to do quite well in a rapidly expanding market depsite its own president's admission that Gentry's chief rival (Basic) supplied a "superior product."

[59]*FTC* v. *Consolidated Foods Corp.*, 380 U.S. 592 (1965).

Justice Douglas noted that the simple probability of reciprocity is not enough to condemn all mergers that carry it.[60] Here, however, the substantial market position of the acquired firm argued for support of the commission's finding.

The Procter & Gamble–Clorox Case (1967).[61]   As in *Consolidated Foods,* there was no way that Procter & Gamble's acquisition of the Clorox Chemical Company could be treated in horizontal terms. Procter was "a large, diversified manufacturer of low-price, high-turnover households products sold through grocery, drug and department stores." Its primary activity was the production of soaps and detergents, and it accounted for more than 54 percent of detergent sales. Clorox was the leading producer of household liquid bleach with 48.8 percent of the market; its largest competitor, Purex, accounted for only 15.7 percent. The soap and detergent products of Procter were not competitive with liquid bleach. In fact, the relationship, if any was complementary: Liquid bleach was used in conjuction with detergent products, and a greater demand for detergents, other things equal, would imply a greater demand for bleach. The relationship between the companies thus was not horizontal, but neither was it vertical, for Procter and Clorox were not in a supplier –customer relationship.

Neither the Fredral Trade Commission nor the Supreme Court called the merger "conglomerate," apparently preferring to reserve that term for purer cases in which the companies' activities bear no economic relationship to each other. Rather, the acquisition termed by the FTC a "product-extension" merger, since some product relationship was discernible.[62] Procter, the Commission said, had not diversified in the sense of expanding into an "unfamiliar market," but had instead entered an "adjoining" one.

Whatever the terminology, such mergers present the antitrust agencies and the courts with a formidable problem in determining competitive consequences. Since the acquiring and acquired firms are in different markets, the merger can have no immediately predictable impact on the structure of the market for the products of either firm. In a horizontal merger, initial structural effects are readily visible; it is necessary only to add up the market shares of the merging firms. Similarly, it is fairly easy to define the immediate degree of foreclosure of suppliers or customers that will likely result from vertical acquisitions. In the case of conglomerate mergers, however, there is no convenient guide. Procter's acquisition of Clorox would initially have no affect on market shares within either the soap and detergent or the liquid bleach markets.[63]

---

[60]Reciprocity by itself has not been attacked under the antitrust laws, and there is considerable uncertainty as to its economic effects. One can construct scenarios in which reciprocity will weaken competition, strengthen competition, or (perhaps more likely) have little effect in either direction. For pertinent discussions, see George W. Stocking and Willard F. Mueller, "Business Reciprocity and the Size of Firms," *Journal of Business,* **30** (April 1957), 73–95; and Joel Dean, "Economic Aspects of Reciprocity, Competition, and Mergers," *Antitrust Bulletin,* **8** (September–December 1963), 843–852.

[61]*FTC* v. *Procter & Gamble Co.,* 386 U.S. 568 (1967).

[62]Bleach and detergents, in addition to showing some complementarity, utilize the same retail distribution system.

[63]It may be recalled that the El Paso–Pacific Northwest merger presented a similar situation. The two companies had not sold in the same geographic market; thus, the merger had no effect on market shares or concentration.

Since the Supreme Court had relied so heavily on structural tests to demonstrate competitive consequences in earlier cases, the issue posed by Procter–Clorox was an important one. What are the appropriate tests of such an acquisition? Does the absence of changes in market shares imply that no competitive consequences will be found? Or, alternatively, if such a merger is found to threaten competition, does this imply that the market-share criterion is inappropriate or superfluous?[64]

The Procter–Clorox merger was subject initially to hearings and disposition by the Federal Trade Commission.[65] The FTC opinion, written by Commissioner Elman, noted that conglomerate mergers do not occupy a special legal category. They are subject to Section 7 despite the fact that the first 17 years of enforcement under the amended statute had largely ignored them. Congress and the courts had placed heavy emphasis on market concentration, but, said the Commission, "the concept of competition which underlies Section 7 has no simple or obvious meaning." The concept need not be **limited** to concentration, the Commission implied, and could logically extend to a second vital dimension of market structure: the condition of entry.

The effect of the immediate merger on market entry was found by Commissioner Elman to be potentially great. Procter was a huge company and the nation's largest advertiser. It could obtain quantity discounts in advertising. Further, the Commission argued, there is a variety of increasing returns to advertising. A company of Procter's size could purchase sponsorship of television programs, rather than being confined to less effective spot commercials; and, because of its diversification, it could advertise several products on one program, thus reducing per-product cost.

The Commission saw other important advantages to a company of Procter's size and resources in the liquid bleach market. It would have great bargaining power with retailers (primarily supermarkets) in an area in which shelf space and store displays are thought to have important effects on sales. Its tremendous financial depth would enable it to mount special promotional campaigns against new products of competitors and to focus its promotional efforts in specific sections of the country. Furthermore, the company would be so large vis-à-vis rival bleach producers that it might undertake predatory pricing policies if it so desired.

The thrust of these points was that the immediate impact of the Procter-Clorox merger would be to discourage entry of new firms into the liquid bleach market. Procter's imposing size—apart from its behavior after consummation of the merger—would scare potential competitors away and might also prevent existing rivals from competing too actively, lest they antagonize the dominant firm. It was primarily on this basis that the Commission concluded that the Procter–Clorox merger violated Section 7.

On appeal, the Supreme Court was responsive to virtually all arguments employed by the FTC. Justice Douglas, for the majority, reiterated earlier statements that Section 7 is intended to arrest monopolistic elements "in their incipiency" and

---

[64] Such questions might also have been pertinent in *Consolidated Foods*. However, the Federal Trade Commission tied its findings of illegality so closely to the practice of reciprocity that discussion of broader issues was diverted.

[65] *In the Matter of Procter & Gamble Co.*, Docket No. 6901 (1962).

that the law deals with the probability, not the certainty, of lessened competition. The substitution of the giant Procter for the already dominant Clorox, said Justice Douglas, could have several effects.

1. It "may substantially reduce the competitive structure of the industry by raising entry barriers and by dissuading smaller firms from aggressively competing."
2. It "eliminates the potential competition of the acquiring firm." Procter was not only large but was a growing and diversifying concern, which was regarded by both the Commission and the Court as the prime candidate for entry into the liquid bleach industry. The merger thus foreclosed the possibility that Procter would enter a competitor of Clorox.

As in *Brown Shoe* and *Philadephia National Bank,* the Court reiterated its position on the positive benefits that might accrue to mergers.

Possible economies cannot be used as a defense to illegality. Congress was aware that some mergers which lessen competition may also result in economies but it struck the balance in favor of protecting competition.[66]

The Court concluded that the Procter–Clorox merger presented a threat to competition in the liquid bleach industry, which could not be compensated by the fact that efficiencies might also accrue to the merged company.

Richard A. Posner has pointed out an inconsistency in the Supreme Court's view of Procter.[67] The decision treats the company as an omnipotent entity, one that could at any time enter the liquid bleach market and cause competition there to collapse. If that were the case, however, there would be little point in prohibiting the merger, for Procter's monopolistic proclivities would soon be reasserted.

Two facts suggest that Procter's threat as a potential entrant may have been less imposing than the Court believed. The first was the high price it was forced to pay for Clorox, $30 million (in stock) for a company that yielded net income of $2.6 million in the previous year. If Procter had been poised to enter the liquid bleach market with all the advantages the Court envisioned, it might well have negotiated a lower offer. Second, the fact that Procter has not gone into liquid bleach since 1967 suggests that the company did not view its prospects there as brightly as did the government.

The *Procter–Clorox* decision indicated that the Court will not be bound by the structural tests developed in horizontal and vertical merger cases. Where a merger does not permit structural predictions, attention turns elsewhere, toward such factors as effects on potential competition.

International Telephone and Telegraph Corp. Cases   International Telephone and Telegraph, the nation's eleventh largest industrial firm, engaged in a series of conglomerate acquisitions in the 1960s. The government attacked its acquisitions of

---

[66]*FTC* v. *Procter & Gamble Co.,* see footnote 61 above, p. 580.

[67]Richard A. Posner, *Antitrust Law* (Chicago: University of Chicago Press, 1976), pp. 218–220.

the Hartford Fire Insurance Company and Grinnell Corporation (a fire control and alarm producer) on the following grounds.

1. Opportunities for reciprocity, the same argument that had prevailed in *Consolidated Foods*.
2. Foreclosure of rivals of the acquired companies from ITT's business.
3. Increasing concentration.

The government's arguments failed uniformly. A district court, in separate but similar decisions, held that the market structures created by the mergers had not been established to be ''conducive'' to illegal reciprocity or to have otherwise anticompetitive implications.[68]

The court said, further, that although both mergers might contribute in a general way to increasing concentration, the government had failed to make any specific demonstration of lessened competition within a relevant product and geographic market.[68]

Neither case reached the Supreme Court. In 1971, ITT and the government entered a consent decree requiring the company to divest itself of some current interests and to limit future merger activity.[69] In retrospect, the primary importance of these cases seems to lie in the failure of the government's reciprocity arguments. Steiner, for example, points out that, had this objection succeeded, the ''view that Section 7 could readily embrace conglomerate acquisitions, would have been confirmed.''[70] The failure of the ITT cases has nurtured doubts that Section 7 is adequate to the task of treating conglomerate merger.

The Falstaff Case (1973).[71] Falstaff, the nation's fourth largest brewer in the 1960s, sought to acquire Narragansett, the leading seller of beer in New England, with a 20 percent share of that market. Although it was a national firm, active in 32 states, Falstaff did not sell in the northeastern section of the country.

In attacking the merger, the government argued that potential competition between the companies would be eliminated. Falstaff, not then in the relevant market (New England), might have entered either de novo (i.e., through internal expansion) or by means of a ''toehold'' acquisition of a small firm.

A district court dismissed the charges. Falstaff, it concluded, had no intention of entering the New England market except by acquiring Narragansett. Company executives had testified to this effect. Potential competition between the companies was thus not going to become actual competition in any event. And since the two companies were not at the time competing—their geographic markets did not overlap—no Section 7 effect could be seen.

---

[68] *U.S.* v. *International Telephone and Telegraph Corp., et al.,* (Grinnell) 306 F. Supp. 766 (1969); (Hartford) 324 F. Supp. 19 (1970).

[69] This was the controversial settlement (the ''Dita Beard case'') negotiated by the Justice Department under the Nixon administration.

[70] Peter O. Steiner, *Mergers: Motives, Effects, Policies,* see footnote 5 above, p. 162.

[71] *U.S.* v. *Falstaff Brewing Co.,* 410 U.S. 526 (1973).

The Supreme Court reversed this decision, remanding for retrial on the grounds that the district court had "erred as a matter of law." A company such as Falstaff, said Justice White, affects competition simply by its presence at "the edge" of the market. It constitutes a threat to those within, thus stimulating beneficial competitive behavior. To remove such a threat may affect competition; it is therefore, not necessary under Section 7 to conclude that, in the absence of the merger, the acquiring company—Falstaff—would actually enter the relevant market.[72]

The *Falstaff* decision advanced the "strong" potential competition doctrine. Elimination of a potential competitor through merger may reduce potential competition without the assumption that such potential would materialize—that is, become actual competition at some later date. The potential competitor is important not only as a future actual competitor but also as a present perceived threat.

The Marine Bancorporation Case (1974). The National Bank of Commerce (NBC), a subsidiary of Marine Bancorporation, was a large commercial bank based in Seattle. It proposed to acquire the Washington Trust Bank (WTB) a medium-sized state bank located at the opposite end of the state in Spokane. The two banks were not direct competitors, and the merger would have simply resulted in the substitution of NBC for WTB in the Spokane area.

The government argued that the merger would lessen competition on three grounds.

1. It would eliminate the prospect that NBC would enter the Spokane market either de novo or via acquisition of a smaller bank.
2. It would lessen NBC's "perceived presence on the fringe of the Spokane market," a potential competition point reminiscent of *Falstaff*.
3. It would end any probability that WTB might grow through merger with other medium-size banks.

The Supreme Court agreed with the district court definition of Spokane as the relevant geographic market, rejecting the government's claim that the state as a whole, although not a banking market, was a relevant "section of the country" for purposes of the case.[73] Justice Powell went on to note that under Washington state law, NBC could not move de novo into Spokane but could enter only by acquiring an existing bank. It was conceivable, if not probable, that NBC might enter in this fashion by acquiring a smaller bank in the future; but even if this happened, it was unlikely to produce "significant procompetitive benefits in the Spokane commercial banking market."

In sum, Justice Powell stated, the government "offered an unpersuasive case." It had argued that the merger would lessen potential competition, but it had failed to show "that NBC has alternative means of entry that offer a reasonable likelihood of producing procompetitive effects." The Court thus appears to have stated a broad

---

[72] The Court also noted that whereas it is not necesesary to disbelieve the testimony of company officials, such testimony may not be definitive as to what the company might do under hypothetical circumstances.

[73] *U.S.* v. *Marine Bancorporation, Inc., et al.*, 418 U.S. 602 (1974).

rule for judging such mergers: A merger violates Section 7 if the acquiring company has an opportunity for de novo entry (or a toehold acquisition and subsequent expansion) **and** if such entry would be likely to yield a procompetitive effect.

Did this decision signal a conservative retreat from *Falstaff*, in which the Court had emphasized the importance of a perceived threat of entry? Perhaps so, but the *Marine* opinion may only suggest the Court's view that the perceptions of market participants are grounded in reality, and that NBC could not have been viewed as a threat unless some reasonably promising entry routes were, in fact, available to it.

THE CURRENT LEGAL STATUS OF MERGERS

It is clear that antitrust policy under the Celler–Kefauver revision of Section 7 has had far-reaching effects. The acquisitions that have been found illegal by the courts and the Federal Trade Commission represent only the tip of the iceberg. Other cases have been settled by mutual consent, without full hearing or trial; and it is impossible to know how many prospective mergers have been abandoned because of the threat of antitrust prosecution.

Formidable legal lines have been drawn. Horizontal mergers where one or both firms are market leaders clearly violate Section 7 under current interpretation; and vertical mergers that involve significant foreclosure are similarly condemned. As we have seen, the stringent legal policy toward these traditional mergers is at least partially responsible for recent trends toward conglomerate acquisition (see Table 14.3). This is, in fact, one of the most clearly demonstrable results of American antitrust: not necessarily a slowdown of the merger "movement," but a dramatic change in its composition and character.

The status of conglomerates, as we have seen, is less well defined. Early Supreme Court opinions in *Consolidated Foods* (1965) and *Procter & Gamble* (1967) seemed to presage a "hard" standard in this area as well, but by the middle 1970s the issue was in doubt. A number of decisions adverse to the government— particularly *General Dynamics* and *Marine Bancorporation*—appeared, raising two obvious possibilities.[74] Either the Court itself was shifting ground, taking a more lenient view of mergers, or the cases themselves were somehow different from those decided earlier.

Robert H. Bork holds the latter view, concluding that the Court decisions have been narrowly drawn, rest on very specific peculiarities of the companies and industries involved, and thus "appear to have little general significance."[75] Roger D. Blair and Arnold A. Heggestad similarly believe that, although the Court has demonstrated "greater sophistication" in its later opinions, there has been no substantial break with earlier precedent.[76]

---

[74] See also *U.S.* v. *Connecticut National Bank*, 418 U.S. 656 (1974): and *U.S.* v. *Citizens Southern National Bank*, 422 U.S. 86 (1975).

[75] Robert H. Bork, *The Antitrust Paradox*, (New York: Basic Books, 1978), p. 218.

[76] "Some Remarks on Recent Merger Decisions," *Industrial Organization Review*, 5 (1977), 109–114.

F. M. Scherer, however, disagrees.[77] *General Dynamics* and *Marine Bancorporation,* in his view, demonstrate "the reluctance of a new and more conservative Supreme Court to continue to resolve the benefit of the doubt against sizable mergers."

Whether the Court is now more favorably disposed toward large mergers is, then, an arguable proposition. Some movement from its earlier positions seems apparent, but we may have to collect a few more decisions before deciding that a significant change has occurred. At the very least, however, we have passed the period when Justice Stewart could observe (in *Von's*) that ". . . under Section 7, the government always wins."

Regardless of future directions, the Supreme Court has established a structural view of competition in merger cases that is ulikely to erode very rapidly. The competitive effects of merger, in other words, are defined in terms of such magnitudes as concentration, market share, foreclosure, and, in a more general way, the number of alternatives that the market provides to sellers and consumers alike. At times this position has become so rigid that the Court has been accused of applying purely mechanical standards. If any criticism of the Court seems persuasive it is that in early merger cases, it seemed to expound the simplistic notion that an assessment of competition demands nothing more than a counting of the number of firms and their market shares. The Court, however, has demonstrated its ability to free itself from rigid structural doctrines. In cases as early as *El Paso* and *Penn-Olin,* the previous arithmetic tests were discarded; and more recent potential competition decisions contain some imaginative discussions of possible competitive implications. The Court's approach to merger has remained essentially structural, but it is evident that, where necessary, the Court will depart from the more confining manifestations of this approach.

In considering the "harshness" of Supreme Court merger policy, it must be recognized that the cases it has received are hardly typical of corporate acquisitions generally. The Court rules on mergers that are ordinarily "big," in terms of both the absolute size of the merging companies and their market positions. The cases that come before the Court result from a complex interaction between the Court and the antitrust enforcement agencies. The Court is influenced by the kinds of cases that the Department of Justice and Federal Trade Commission pursue; and the types of cases pursued by these agencies are influenced by what the Court has previoulsy said about mergers. Whatever the precise nature of this process, the Supreme Court considers only special subcategories of corporate acquisitions.

This is not to minimize, however, the strength of existing precedent. The Supreme Court has indeed been "hard" on the kinds of acquisitions that it has had to consider. Nowhere is this more evident than in its refusal to consider the likely effects of mergers on the future behavior of firms and industries (see especially *Brown Shoe*). If a merger fails those tests which have become accepted as indicators of

---

[77] F. M. Scherer, *Industrial Market Structure and Economic Performance,* 2nd ed. (New York: Rand McNally, 1980), p. 562.

lessened competition, it is not redeemed by other, positive benefits even if these are potentially important. This approach reflects not only the philosophy of the Court but the need for relatively simple legal decision rules. Whereas economists are inclined to argue that many factors ought to be considered in merger cases, such luxury might tie up the judicial processes in an unimaginable way. The Court's search for workable rules conflicts with the need for thorough economic investigation and has led some observers to propose that separate judicial bodies should be established for the disposition of antitrust matters.

The attitude of the Supreme Court toward mergers is, as we have seen, subject to change. But whatever route the Court may follow, the antitrust enforcement agencies bear a heavy burden of responsibility in shaping future policies. It is the Federal Trade Commission and the Antitrust Division of the Department of Justice that initiate the cases that ultimately reach the courts. Both of these agencies operate under the significant constraint of limited resources, and they must be selective in the cases they pursue. Until 1974, the government had a relatively easy time winning legal victories in merger cases. The social purpose of the agencies, however, is not to win victories but rather to obtain action on situations that could, if left untouched, damage competition. Ideally, of course, there is no distinction between these goals. In fact, howebver, they need not coincide. Some legal victories are trivial in economic terms, and some important situations may be neglected if the prospects of victory are higher in other areas. The courts can decide only on those situations that they have brought before them. And even the boldest judicial outlook may be thwarted by a timid approach in the executive agencies.[78]

THE ECONOMICS OF MERGER POLICY

The courts and, to a lesser extent, the Federal Trade Commission have been criticized for their interpretations of Section 7.[79] Although critics vary widely in their points of view, many charge that, in one way or another, "bad economics" is being applied to the legal disposition of corporate mergers.

As the cases above demonstrate, the legal view of competition under Section 7 is largely structural. That is, in attempting to estimate the effects that mergers have on competition, dimensions of market structure are taken to be the primary clues. A structural approach conforms generally to the basic precepts of economic analysis. Whatever we may mean by "competition," it is something that is strongly influenced by such factors as the number and size of firms in a market and the condition of entry for new firms. These elements influence the ways in which firms and industries behave. Criticisms of merger policy, then, do not often propose that market

---

[78] In 1981, for example, the Department of Justice cleared a proposed merger between duPont and Continental Oil Co. that almost surely would have been struck down by the Supreme Court in earlier years. What the 1981 Court would have done is uncertain.

[79] See, for example, M. A. Adelman, footnote 24 above; Robert H. Bork and Ward S. Bowman, Jr., "The Crisis in Antitrust," *Fortune,* **68** (December 1963), 138–140; Donald Dewey, "Mergers and Cartels: Some Reservations About Policy," *American Economic Review,* **51** (May 1961), 255–262; and Bork, see footnote 75 above.

structure be ignored; this would make little economic sense. Rather, the objections that have been lodged tend to cluster around two slightly different propositions.

1. The wrong structural approach is being utilized and ought to be replaced by different structural standards.
2. The structural approach is misguided because it dominates the consideration of mergers, to the exclusion of all other information bearing on competitive effects.

The first proposition has some appeal to those who believe that the courts are, in general, either "too hard" or "too easy" on mergers. At one extreme, a test of "quantitative substantiality" might be suggested under which any merger involving a "substantial" volume of commerce is automatically considered illegal. At the other extreme, it might be proposed that only mergers that involve a very high market share for the emergent firm be struck down. In between, compromises may be possible. Stigler, for example, has suggested that a legal presumption be made against mergers that yield the combined firm a market share of 20 percent or more, whereas a presumption be made in favor of mergers that result in a share of not more than 5 to 10 percent.[80] Between these limits , more extensive economic investigation is deemed desirable.

All proposals for new structural standards, however, encounter a common problem. The more general the proposal, the less useful it is likely to be. To tell the courts, for example, that automatic rules should be applied in extreme cases, whereas further analysis is in order for immediate cases, provides relatively little guidance. This is especially true if the preponderance of cases fall within the intermediate range. On the other hand, structural standards that are so specific as to be consistently applicable would result in the same rigidity for which the Court has been criticized. To tell the courts, for example, that they ought to approve all mergers that result in less than an X percent market share, while condemning mergers that result in X percent or more, would be highly objectionable. In the first place, there is no obvious basis for selecting the number X—should it be 5 percent? 15 percent? 40 percent? Second, and more important, however, no single "appropriate" number exists, because the meaning of any given number varies with other conditions in the industry. A merger between two firms, each of which has 5 percent of the market, is simply not the same event in the steel industry as it is in the book manufacturing industry.[81]

It is true that sensible structural rules would have to go farther than providing a single market-share number. But the more general problem is the arbitrary nature of any rules. This is the problem that plagues policymakers. The implication to be

---

[80]George J. Stigler, "Mergers and Preventive Antitrust Policy," *University of Pennsylvania Law Review,* **104** (November 1965), pp. 178–184.

[81]In 1968 the Department of Justice issued "guidelines" to mergers that it "probably" would challenge. In horizontal cases, for example, the probability of challenge would depend on the market share of both firms, and on the level and trend of market concentration. Acquisition of an "unusually competitive" firm would always be challenged, whereas that of a "failing" firm would not. In 1982 the Department issued revised guidelines that appear to relax the earlier standards in some instances. The new guidelines are also a good deal more complex. Whether a merger is challenged, e.g., may depend upon its effect on the Herfindahl index in the relevant market (refer to Chapter 7).

drawn is not that policy decisions ought to be avoided but that it is necessary to search further for appropriate standards. Wholly automatic structural criteria are inappropriate, for the ways in which a merger may affect competition are too complex to be reduced in this fashion. Moreover, some kinds of mergers—most notably conglomerates—cannot be easily assessed in quantitative structural terms.

The second kind of objection that is frequently lodged against legal merger criteria has to do with the tendency of the courts to rely solely on structural information, while ignoring other clues to competitive effects. This tendency was seen in decisions such as *Philadelphia National Bank* and *Von's Grocery*. The Supreme Court has stated clearly that mergers that lessen competition cannot be redeemed legally by the fact that they might, on balance, benefit society. But since the Court was willing to infer lessened competition from structural indicators, the doctrine amounted to one of structural exclusivity. Whether the present Court will change the rules cannot yet be known. To the extent that it continues to rely on a purely structural approach, however, potentially important kinds of information will be ignored.

A structural approach to mergers raises very basic questions not only about the courts' interpretation of the meaning of "competition", but also about the entire purpose of merger policy and perhaps of public antitrust policy generally. The notion of competition to which the courts have subscribed has been highly specific: It is, in effect, akin to the economist's definition of pure competition. Competition is seen as a market setting of many small firms, none holding a serious "competitive advantage." Virtually any movement toward fewer firms, higher shares, or competitive advantages is, thus, interpreted as a lessening of competition.

How valid an approach is this in economic terms? Certainly it is a very narrow view that at times seems to equate "competition" inversely with "concentration." Such an equation is quite crude; yet it might not be a poor working rule if qualified by other sorts of information. As Adelman has stated:

> . . . competition, or monopoly, is not a brute physical fact but rather a hypothesis confirmed by the available evidence. A high level of concentration, plus price behavior very different from competitive expectations, etc., indicates, let us say, chances of 9 to 1 of effective market control.[82]

The task of the courts under Section 7 is not to determine how much competition exists in a market, but what the direction of change will be when merger occurs. Nevertheless, Adelman's point is pertinent. The notion of competition is complex, if not actually elusive, and it is not amenable to extremely simplified measurement. The courts are in need of simple rules, but their pursuit of simplicity has unquestionably led to overly restrictive definitions of competition and competitive change in some instances.

Although economists may wish to quarrel with the ways in which judges define economic terms, this is not the primary issue. The significant question with regard

---

[82] See footnote 24 above, p. 237. For a pertinent discussion, see also Franklin M. Fisher, "Diagnosing Monopoly," *Quarterly Review of Economics and Business,* **19** (Summer, 1979), 7–35.

to mergers is rather one of results: that is, what kind of a policy have legal definitions of competition yielded? In order to describe merger policy more precisely, it
may be helpful to review briefly the kinds of change that growth in firm size may
imply. As we have seen earlier, increases in market concentration presumably occur
because they are profitable. This profitability, in turn, may reflect genuine economies, the ability to produce more efficiently in a larger or more integrated operation;
or it may reflect pecuniary economies that allow the larger firm to operate more
cheaply, but not more efficiently in a technical sense. At the same time, larger firm
size may be profitable for reasons related to the demand, rather than to the cost or
supply, side. The larger firm may possess greater market power and thus be better
able to exploit consumers' demand for its products.

From society's point of view, growth that is related purely to market power is
undesirable. Firm growth that is related to genuine economies, however, may be
socially desirable, since it permits the production of more goods at any given level
of resource employment. Growth for reasons of pecuniary economies might be considered undesirable as a rule if it implies more market power; but the question is
empirically complicated by the possibility that pecuniary economies may, in part,
reflect true efficiency. Merger is a method by which firms grow. Whether any particular merger is socially desirable depends on whether the positive benefits of increased efficiency outweigh the negative effects of increased market power. The
trade-off between efficiency and power is shown diagrammatically in Figure 14.1.

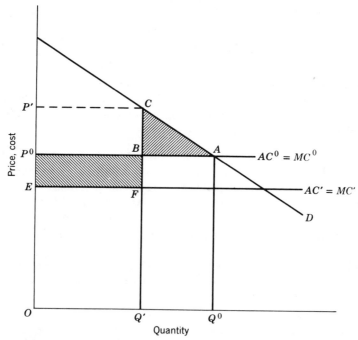

Figure 14.1 Possible price and efficiency effects of a merger.

Suppose that prior to merger, firms produce at point A (quantity Q^0, price P^0) and that after merger, market power is enhanced so that production shifts to point C (quantity Q', price P'). The welfare loss attributable to this increment in market power is represented by the shaded triangle ABC, the difference in society's position before and after merger. But suppose also that the merger introduces efficiencies into the production process, causing the average cost curve to shift down from AC^0 to AC'. The shaded rectangle P^0EFB represents the efficiency gain of the merger— the difference between the cost of producing quantity Q' before and after merger. The question is whether the efficiency gain of a merger is greater or less than the market power loss.

Oliver E. Williamson, who has stated the problem in these terms, has presented simple numerical examples showing that even a relatively small drop in average costs produces an efficiency gain that can be offset only by a much larger relative rise in price.[83] Even if the elasticity of demand is as high as 2, for example, a cost decrease of 1 percent produces gains that can be wiped out only if price rises by 10 percent; or, stated in reverse fashion, a merger that enables firms to raise price by 10 percent will not prove to be inefficient on balance, if average costs fall by only 1 percent. If demand elasticity were 1, costs would have to fall by only 0.5 percent to compensate a 10 percent price rise.

Williamson's examples appear to suggest a probability of mergers that are on balance "good," that is, the efficiency gains outweigh the market-power loss. There are, however, some very significant qualifications to such a likelihood.[84] For example:

1. If true efficiencies exist, the market may well exploit them without merger; the merger gain is therefore only a matter of timing, an may be short-lived.
2. The comparison is altered somewhat if the firm(s) prior to merger possess some market power; notice that in Figure 14.1, the premerger firms appear to price as pure competitors.
3. The analysis is partial (i.e., confined to the immediately affected industry) and thus ignores second-best implications.
4. It may be that society is concerned with the change in income distribution that results from merger; this suggests that the simple comparison between the deadweight loss and efficiency gain may not prove decisive, for we also care about who loses and gains.

The important question, however, is not whether one can generalize a priori about the "goodness" or "badness" of net merger effects; confident generaliza-

---

[83] Oliver E. Williamson, "Economies as an Antitrust Defense: The Welfare Tradeoffs," *American Economic Review*, **58** (March 1968), 18–36.

[84] A number of writers in addition to Williamson have pointed these out. See for discussion of various issues: M. E. DePrano and J. B. Nugent, "Comment," and Williamson, "Reply," *American Economic Review*, **69** (December 1969); Raymond Jackson, "The Consideration of Economies in Merger Cases," *Journal of Business*, **43** (October 1970); and Williamson, "Economies as an Antitrust Defense Revisited," *University of Pennsylvania Law Review*, **125** (April 1977), 699–736.

tions are most unlikely. Rather, the issue is whether the antitrust courts and enforcement agencies ought to be attempting such benefit-versus-cost comparisons. Clearly, they have not done so to the present time.

The obvious response is: Of course this should be done! All activities, including corporate merger, create both costs and benefits; and rational choices cannot be made without examining both sides of the ledger. In principle, any economist is likely to have a hard time disagreeing with this statement. But practical considerations also intrude.

Are cost-saving and market-power effects of mergers measurable with any real precision? And, if so, are the agencies and the courts equipped to do the job? Without generalizing too finely, some skepticism on both points can be justified. The potential costs and benefits of a merger may be identifiable, although even here arguments about potential magnitudes in particular cases will arise. The techniques for estimating the likely magnitudes are simply not well developed, and it is difficult to predict what use the legal system might make of them.

We are thus in a quandary. At least some mergers imply a trade-off between market power and efficiency. The courts have tended to focus on structural indices of power. They have furthermore stated that efficiencies, where they exist, are not relevant to the legality of mergers. Indeed, the courts have at certain times gone to the extreme by suggesting that efficiencies, because they create competitive advantages, may be anticompetitive! At this point it may seem that the economic justification of our legal approach to mergers is rather precarious.

There is, nevertheless, some rationale for the broad approach of the agencies and the courts. It is important to bear in mind that if bigness is efficient, firms are likely to grow big, whether by merger or internal expansion. Put differently, a legal prohibition on efficiency-creating mergers is not the same thing as a legal prohibition on increased efficiency. For this reason, the costs of the traditional policy—even if beneficial mergers are prevented with some frequency—may be limited.

The more general point, however, is that merger policy necessarily proceeds under considerable uncertainty. Whereas the true effects of many mergers cannot be known "for sure," the courts must make decisions. When stated in this way, the argument for a stringent antimerger policy becomes somewhat clearer. In fact, the most plausible defense of what the courts have done, has been stated by Richard B. Heflebower in terms of the ignorance surrounding corporate acquisition.[85]

According to Heflebower, no one is in a good position to predict the competitive effects of merger. Economic theory is "inconclusive" and empirical evidence is "paltry"; yet the courts are required to decide whether mergers may lessen competition. In Heflebower's view, the policies pursued by the Supreme Court could be interpreted as a strategy designed to make the least damaging kinds of mistakes. The Court has taken a hard position on mergers and, given its ignorance of future economic effects, it may well have prohibited some mergers that would not have

---

[85] Richard B. Heflebower, "Corporate Mergers: Policy and Economic Analysis," *Quarterly Journal of Economics*, **77** (November, 1963), 556–557.

harmed competition. Heflebower's argument is that this kind of error may be preferable to the mistakes that would be made by pursuing too easy a merger policy, that is, permitting some mergers that would reduce competition. Once mergers are permitted under an easy policy, the die is cast; however, a hard policy is always reversible. If the easy policy is pursued and found to be wrong, little can be done. The merged companies are a fact of life, and the courts are most reluctant to greak up going concerns. But if a hard policy is pursued and found to be wrong, the remedy is simple: Make the policy easier. Mergers that are prohitibed today can be allowed tomorrow, if we find that they are desirable.

This is not to suggest, however, that a stringent policy toward mergers is costless. One of the most useful functions of mergers is to eliminate inefficient managers of widely held corporations.[86] The owners of such firms may be impotent, for their influence is dispersed; and the major check on managerial wastefulness may thus be the "takeover" threat. A public policy that blocks acquisitions indiscriminately, loses this spur to efficiency.

An assessment of merger policy is not an easy task, and it is not the purpose of this discussion to grade the courts or the antitrust agencies on their performance. It is clear that Section 7 as amended has become a tremendously important antitrust tool. Large and medium-sized horizontal mergers appear to be all but illegal; large vertical acquisitions run a very substantial legal risk; and large conglomerates have, at times, proved vulnerable, although standards are still evolving. Even relatively small mergers may violate Section 7 if the history of the companies and trends in the industry are "undesirable." The main criticism of public merger policy through the early 1970s was that it had become a mindless weapon against corporate bigness, used to strike down large combinations without considering the possibility that large size may be economically justified. The Supreme Court's implicit answer to this criticism was that it was not concerned with economic justifications—nor with any benefit versus cost approach—but rather with "competition," defined in a particular structural fashion. Here, the economist will argue that the Court's definition of competition has been inadequate, but the Court's (again implicit) response is: that is what Congress intended. Whether the next few years will bring a sharp reassessment of this judicial outlook is a most important question.

---

[86] The classic reference is Henry C. Manne, "Mergers and the Market for Corporate Control," *Journal of Political Economy,* **73** (April 1965), 110–120.

CHAPTER 15

Price Discrimination

Price discrimination is a practice that is probably familiar even to those who are unaware of the term. For example, most people are aware that physicians may charge patients different fees for the same service, depending upon their ability to pay. Lawyers may make similar adjustments for clients, and in certain instances fees for a client vary with the outcome of the litigation. Shoppers will frequently find that the per-unit price of foods varies with the quantity purchased; for instance, soup may sell for 40 cents a can, or two cans for 79 cents. And even the telephone company charges different prices per unit; the long distance caller may be charged more for the first 3 minutes than for the second 3; thus the caller who speaks for 6 minutes pays a lower price per minute than the caller who speaks for 3 minutes.

THE DEFINITION ISSUE

Each of the above instances may constitute price discrimination. As economists use the term, however, discrimination refers not simply to the practice of charging different customers different prices for the same commodity or service; rather, it refers to the imposition of varying cost–price differentials upon different customers. A seller may be said to discriminate in price whenever the relationship between his costs and the price he charges varies among his customers, that is, when sales to some customers yield a higher net revenue or profit than sales to others. The examples cited above constitute price discrimination **only** if the different prices charged for the same goods or services do **not** reflect corresponding differences in the cost of production or distribution. If, for example, the cost of providing telephone service is the same, per minute, for 6-minute calls as for 3-minute calls, then the telephone company is discriminating against the 3-minute caller. If, however, the cost of the longer call is less per minute—and this is certainly possible—the lower charge for the second 3 minutes may only reflect this cost difference.

Section 2(a) of the Robinson–Patman Act, amending Section 2 of the original Clayton Act, makes it illegal:

. . . to discriminate in price between different purchasers of commodities of like grade and quality . . . where the effect of such discrimination may be substantially to lessen competition or tend to create a monopoly in any line of commerce.

Section 2(a) also provides that:

. . . . nothing herein contained shall prevent differentials which make only due al-lowance for differences in the cost of manufacture, sale, or delivery resulting from the differing methods or quantities in which such commodities are . . . sold or de-livered.

In other words, a seller accused of discrimination can justify his activities if he proves that price variations reflect different costs in selling to different customers.

The legal definition of price discrimination differs from the economic. By referring only to price differences, rather than to differences in the price–cost rela-tionship, the law takes a relatively narrow view. Under the Robinson–Patman Act, a seller can discriminate only by charging different prices for the same (or substan-tially similar) goods. In economic terms, however, the seller may discriminate also by charging the same price to all customers when different costs are incurred in sell-ing to some. So long as the price–cost differential is not the same for all customers, price discrimination in the economic sense exists.

Symbolically, price discrimination between customers A and B exists in an eco-nomic sense if:

$$\frac{P_A}{MC_A} \neq \frac{P_B}{MC_B}$$

It exists legally if

$$P_A \neq P_B$$

where P_A and P_B are the prices paid by A and B; and MC_A and MC_B are the mar-ginal costs of supplying A and B.

These discrepancies are illustrated in Table 15-1. Where the costs of serving dif-ferent submarkets and customers are similar, economic and legal notions of discrim-ination coincide; where costs vary, the definitions diverge. The Robinson–Patman Act thus focuses on one subset of all discrimination—that in which prices vary and costs do not; while ignoring another subset—that in which costs vary but prices do not. It also terms discriminatory, certain nondiscriminatory patterns (i.e., where prices and costs vary in tandem), but it does provide in principle a defense that would make such "discrimination" permissible. It is not possible to term one of these definitions "correct" and the other "incorrect" on logical grounds; but as we

Table 15.1 Price Discrimination: Legal and Economic Definitions

Cost of Selling Product in Submarkets A and B	Price of Product in Submarkets A and B	
	The Same	10 Percent Higher in A
The same	No discrimination	Economic and legal discrimination
10 percent higher in A	Economic but not legal discrimination	Legal but not economic discrimination

shall see, the legal notion of price discrimination makes for some economically dubious, and possibly harmful, public policy.

LEGAL AND ECONOMIC CONSIDERATIONS

A seller charged with price discrimination has several possible defenses. The first, noted above, is to show that the price differences made "only due allowance" for cost differences (i.e., discrimination in the economic sense did not exist). The second, sometimes called the "good faith" defense, is provided by Section 2(b) of the Robinson–Patman Act, which states:

> . . . *nothing herein contained shall prevent a seller from rebutting the prima facie case . . . by showing that his lower price or the furnishing of services or facilities to any purchaser . . . was made in good faith to meet the equally low price of a competitor. . . .*

A seller may thus argue that price differentials, although not cost justified were designed to meet competition. Both the "cost" and "good faith" defenses are absolute in the sense that, if proved, the seller's activities do not abridge the Act.

A third broad defense, commonly invoked along with the others, is that the seller's practices, even if found to be discriminatory, did not harm competition substantially. As in other Clayton Act areas, it is this contention that presents the most fundamental questions to the courts.

It is useful at this point to consider two questions suggested by the existence and public treatment of price discrimination.

1. Why and under what circumstances would firms be expected to discriminate?
2. Ought we to have legal sanctions against discrimination?

The first question may be answered in a reasonably unambiguous way. Any firm with some power over the price it charges[1] may find discrimination profitable if it has customers or submarkets with distinct demands.

Consider the example in Figure 15.1 of the company that sells a product such as canned fruit under its own nationally advertised brand name while also selling the identical fruit, unbranded, to supermarkets who resell it under their own private labels (e.g., Ann Page, Shop Rite). The demand curves for these two market segments, D_m and D_s, respectively, are distinct. This is not surprising since buyers of brand-name and private-label products are likely to have somewhat different characteristics. So as to keep the analysis simple, a common marginal cost curve (MC) is assumed.

What should this company do to maximize profits overall? It remains subject to the familiar maximization rule: optimal output occurs where $MR = MC$. But there is

---

[1] That is, the firm has some "monopoly" control. In a strictly competitive market, price would be forced to the level of marginal cost; thus, with some special-case exceptions, it would be impossible for a seller to impose two or more prices for the same product.

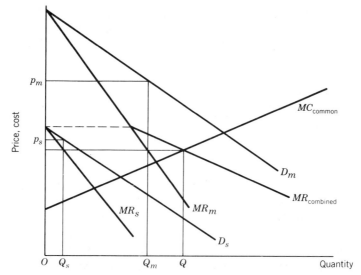

Figure 15.1 Price discrimination: the sale of canned fruit under brand name and private label.

an added consideration; how much of the firm's output should be sold in each market segment? The answer is intuitively reasonable. The firm should sell amounts such that marginal revenue in each segment is the same: $MR_m = MR_s$. After all, the cost of selling canned fruit in either market segment is, by assumption, the same. If the product returns more revenue at the margin in one segment, more cans ought to be sold there; so long as an inequality persists, the firm foregoes some revenue while incurring a given level of total costs.

Diagrammatically, optimal total output Q is determined by the intersection of MC and the combined MR curve. The combined MR, which is the horizontal addition of MR_m and MR_s, is a device that depicts the satisfaction of both marginal conditions. The output Q that occurs at the marginal-revenue–marginal-cost intersection ($MR = MC$) may be allocated such that marginal revenues in the individual submarkets are also equated. (This is accomplished by selling quantity Q_s in the private-label market and Q_m in the brand-name market.)[2]

The resulting prices in the two markets, P_m, and P_s, differ; thus profit maximization in this instance requires price discrimination (recall that costs of supplying the markets are the same). Indeed, we may make a more general observation. In cases of this type, price discrimination will be profitable so long as the separate market demand curves have differing price elasticities of demand at their profit-maximizing

---

[2]This discussion of diagrammatics is brief. For a fuller description see an intermediate price theory text, for example, Jack Hirshleifer, *Price Theory and Applications* (Englewood Cliffs, N.J.: Prentice-Hall, 2nd ed., 1980), pp. 350ff.

points.[3] One might suspect that this will ordinarily be true. After all, it would be sheer coincidence if two appropriate production points implied identical demand elasticities in two markets. The customer class with the less elastic demand pays the higher price.

It is not surprising to find that the price that maximizes canned fruit profits sold under brand name differs from the optimal price for the private label. Moreover, the nature of the products ensures that a two-price system is workable. Buyers of the lower-priced private brand could not very well relabel their cans and resell them in the higher-price market. If such a practice were possible, price differentials in the two segments could not persist. This type of discrimination requires that resale between markets be impractical, a condition that explains why discrimination is common in markets for services (try reselling your haircut or your appendectomy!).

Any time a seller offers his goods at a specified price, he is likely selling to some customers who would have been willing to pay more. Such a seller would benefit if he could find some way of extracting the higher prices from those with the greater willingness to pay. In the extreme, the seller may achieve **perfect** (or **first-degree) discrimination;** here every consumer pays the maximum he is willing to offer for every unit. Each unit receives its demand price, and all consumers' surplus is "captured" by the seller. Such a result is unusual and would require, among other conditions, an individually negotiated sale for every unit. The market segmentation example above, known as **third-degree** discrimination, is more common and presents the bulk of antitrust policy issues.[4]

If price discrimination can be profitable, it may not yet be obvious why such a practice is undesirable and ought to be subject to legal restriction. Indeed, price discrimination is not inevitably undesirable from society's point of view.[5] The law, however, takes aim only at those discriminatory practices that may substantially lessen competition. Such cases often involve buyers with sufficient market power to extract price concessions from sellers. As noted in Chapter 11, pressure for enactment of a strong price-discrimination law came from relatively small wholesalers and retailers who complained that larger rivals were obtaining preferential treatment from suppliers. It is precisely this kind of situation at which the Robinson–Patman Act is directed. If a large firm can purchase supplies at more favorable terms than its smaller rivals, it holds a competitive advantage. Indeed, one of the more troublesome aspects of discrimination is that favored companies may be able to establish prices that are profitable for them but unprofitable for smaller firms that must pay more for inputs.

---

[3] This conclusion follows quickly if one is aware that marginal revenue may be devined as: $MR = P(1 + 1/e^d)$, where e^d is elasticity of demand. For the profit maximizing condition $MR_m = MR_s$, then requires $P_m = P_s$ **only** if elasticities in both markets are equal. To turn the point around, if demand elasticities in the markets differ, equality of marginal revenues will require different, discriminatory prices in those markets.

[4] **Second**-degree discrimination is an intermediate case involving finer distinctions than third degree, but falling short of first-degree perfection.

[5] See Joan Robinson, *The Economics of Imperfect Competition* (London: Macmillan, 1938), p. 206; and Lucile Sheppard Keyes, "Price Discrimination in Law and Economics," *Southern Economic Journal,* **27,** (April 1961) 320–328.

DELIVERED PRICING SYSTEMS

Sellers and buyers in a line of commerce are often geographically dispersed. When this is the case, costs of transporting the product may be relatively important, especially if it is heavy or bulky and has a relatively low price (sugar, steel, and cement are pertinent examples). Sellers in this situation must choose among pricing procedures with respect to customers at different locations. The initial decision is whether to quote price at the point of origin (seller's location)—often termed the "f.o.b." (free on board) price—or at the point of destination (customer's location)—a "delivered price."

Perhaps the most obvious possibility is that every seller will quote prices f.o.b. and have each customer pay the cost of transporation. Assuming similar or identical products, each seller will have an advantage with nearby customers, who pay little freight, but may be strongly disadvantaged with respect to distant customers. Conceivably, each seller will have a sheltered market and a market that he cannot penetrate.[6] Whether such a pricing system proves to be workable is a complex problem that depends upon the geographic distribution of the market, among other factors. It is possible that certain sellers will find that they sell too little under such conditions; they may thus attempt to penetrate more distant segments of the market by absorbing part or all of the freight charges for customers so located.

A second possibility is that sellers may quote the same delivered price to all customers. Such a price would include an average freight charge, that is, a charge for transportation of goods that, imposed uniformly on all customers, would cover total transportation costs. Such a pricing system implies that nearby customers will pay more than the actual cost of transporting to them; this extra charge is known as phantom freight. Distant customers pay less than the actual cost of transportation; they are the beneficiaries of freight absorption by the seller. Clearly, this delivered pricing system is economically discriminatory. The seller, in charging a uniform delivered price, has failed to take account of cost differences among customers; he discriminates against nearby customers who must pay for transportation that they do not require, and in favor of distant customers who do not pay the full cost of transporting to them. In effect, the close customer subsidizes the distant one.

Under a variation of this delivered pricing system, a seller will establish geographic zones and charge a uniform delivered price within each zone. Here the price charged in any zone presumably includes the average cost of transporting to customers in that zone. Once again, the seller undertakes freight absorption for those customers within a zone who are relatively far away and charges phantom freight to customers within the zone who are relatively near.

A wide variety of delivered pricing systems has appeared at various times in American industry. Primary policy attention has been given to **basing point systems,** a category of delivered pricing in which selling firms act in a generally concerted way. The usual effect of such systems—and perhaps the primary purpose—is

---

[6] See the discussion of the Hotelling duopoly model in Chapter 3.

to modify or eliminate the delivered-price differentials that might occur were each seller to pursue an independent pricing policy. As Fritz Machlup has pointed out:

The basing-point technique of pricing makes it possible for any number of sellers, no matter where they are located and without any communication with each other, to quote identical delivered prices for any quantity of the product in standardized qualities and specifications, going to any of the 60,000 or more possible destinations in the United States.[7]

The Single Basing-Point System

Under a single basing-point system, every seller uses the same point of origin in calculating the freight charge to be added to his base, or f.o.b., prices. If the base prices are the same, every seller's price at any given destination will be identical, although the price will vary among destinations.

Consider, for example, the old "Pittsburgh plus" system once utilized by steel producers. Under this system, Pittsburgh was the single basing point; thus every steel producer in calculating his delivered price to a customer, acted as if he were shipping steel from Pittsburgh to the customer's location, regardless of where the shipment actually originated. The system is illustrated in Figure 15.2 and Table 15.2. Every producer has a uniform base price, specified arbitrarily as $100 per unit[8]; costs of shipping a unit between various cities are specified, also arbitrarily for purposes of illustration. Table 15.2, part A illustrates the workings of the pricing scheme in sales to a Pittsburgh customer, that is, to a customer located at the basing point. Here the uniform freight charge dictated by the system is zero, since the customer is located at the basing point. All shippers—whether in Pittsburgh, Chicago, New York, Los Angeles, or elsewhere—charge nothing for transportation to the Pittsburgh customer. Thus all charge a delivered price of $100. In this situation, every seller not located in Pittsburgh must absorb freight, that is, charge the Pittsburgh customer less than the actual cost of shipping the goods.

In Table 15.2, part B, sales to a Los Angeles customer are considered. Once again every seller determines his delivered price to this customer by adding to the base price the cost of shipping from Pittsburgh to the customer. Every seller charges the Los Angeles customer $160; the base price of $100 plus the shipping cost from Pittsburgh of $60. Shippers who are farther away from the customer than Pittsburgh is from the customer will absorb freight; the New York producer, for instance, incurs shipping costs of $65 but charges only the $60 that it would cost to ship from Pittsburgh to Los Angeles.[9] Shippers who are closer to the customer than Pittsburgh

---

[7] *The Basing-Point System* (Philadelphia: Blakiston, 1949), p. 7.

[8] It is interesting to contemplate how uniform base prices, common in such systems, are established. One possibility is collusion, and the courts have at times decided that basing-point systems were simply one facet of broader conspiracies.

[9] This is not as unprofitable as it sounds, for the system is likely to permit f.o.b. price to be raised above the level that would hold under more competitive circumstances.

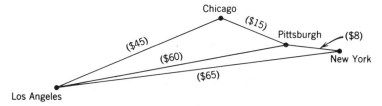

Figure 15.2 Transportation costs. The numbers in parentheses indicate the actual unit cost of transportation between cities.

is to the customer, will charge phantom freight; the Chicago producer charges $60, although his actual freight cost is $45; and the Los Angeles producer, whose actual shipping cost is zero, also charges $60.

Producers at the basing point never discriminate, since the freight they charge to customers is calculated from the point at which they are located. Their delivered price to varying locations differs by precisely the difference in their actual freight to those locations; in other words, the price variation makes "only due allowance" for cost differentials. Sellers not located at the basing point, however, invariably discriminate, since their price differentials do not reflect actual differences in their shipping costs. Whenever a non-basing point producer makes a sale, he either charges phantom freight (if the customer is closer to him than to the basing point) or absorbs freight (if the customer is farther from him than from the basing point).

Table 15.2 A Pittsburgh-Plus System: Basing-Point Pricing with Pittsburgh as the Single Basing Point

	Location of Producer			
	Pittsburgh	Chicago	New York	Los Angeles
A. Sales to a Pittsburgh Customer				
Base price	$100	100	100	100
Freight cost from Pittsburgh to customer	0	0	0	0
Delivered price quoted by producer	100	100	100	100
Actual freight cost from producer to customer	0	10	8	60
Phantom freight				
Freight absorption		10	8	60
Discrimination	No	Yes	Yes	Yes
B. Sales to a Los Angeles Customer				
Base price	$100	100	100	100
Freight cost from Pittsburgh to customer	60	60	60	60
Delivered price quoted by producer	160	160	160	160
Actual freight cost from producer to customer	60	45	65	0
Phantom freight		15		60
Freight absorption			5	
Discrimination	No	Yes	Yes	Yes

The single basing-point system produces two consistent results. The price paid by any buyer increases with the distance of the buyer from the basing point; and the buyer pays the same price regardless of which supplier makes the sale.

Multiple Basing-Point Systems

A number of systems may arise in which two or more basing points are used. Generally, the controlling basing point will be the one that is closer to the customer. Suppose that in the example of figure 15.2, both Pittsburgh and Chicago were used as basing points. Chicago would be the relevant point for sales to Chicago and Los Angeles, as well as all other locations closer to Chicago than to Pittsburgh; while Pittsburgh would be the controlling point for sales to Pittsburgh and New York, as well as any other location closer to Pittsburgh than Chicago.

In the extreme case of a multiple basing-point system, every production location is a basing point governing sales to the closest customers. The delivered price to any customer is therefore the base price charged by all producers plus freight from the closest producer to the customer.[10]

A Review of Relevant Cases

Basing-point systems have been attacked in three distinct ways under the antitrust laws. They have been prosecuted under the Sherman Act as unreasonable restraints of trade or attempts to monopolize; here the government's contention is likely to be that the establishment and maintenance of the system reflects a conspiracy among participating producers. Basing points have also been attacked as violations of Section 5 of the Federal Trade Commission Act; the common argument here is that pricing is unfair to customers who happen to be located near some producers but a greater distance from the nearest basing point. Finally, and of primary interest to the immediate discussion, basing-point pricing has been prosecuted under the Robinson–Patman Act as price discrimination.

The Corn Products Refining Case (1945)[11] *The Corn Products Refining* case represents the first Supreme Court decision on the status of basing-point systems under the Robinson–Patman Act. Earlier in both the *Maple Flooring*[12] and *Cement Manufacturers*[13] cases, the Court had considered the legality of behavior involving basing-point systems; but in neither case was price discrimination an issue.

The immediate case concerned a manufacturer of glucose (a candy ingredient) and its subsidiary. Although located in Kansas City, the companies used Chicago as a basing point, charging glucose buyers a base price plus transportation from

---

[10]The charging of identical base (f.o.b.) prices by all producers is an assumption that does not always apply in such systems. If producers do not charge the same base price, analysis of the system may become more complicated.

[11]*Corn Products Refining Co.* v. *Federal Trade Commission*, 324 U.S. 726 (1945).

[12]*Maple Flooring Manufacturers Association* v. *United States*, 268 United States, 563 (1925).

[13]*Cement Mfrs. Protective Association* v. *United States*, 268 U.S. 588 (1925).

Chicago to each buyer's location. The Federal Trade Commission found that this pricing system resulted in systematic price discrimination. The appeal of the FTC decision to the Supreme Court raised two issues. First, did the basing-point system constitute price discrimination? Second, it if did, was the effect of the system damaging to competition?

On the first point, the companies argued that their practices were not discriminatory under the Robinson–Patman Act. The Act, they contended, was aimed only at discrimination between buyers at the same delivery points and covered only discrimination in price itself. Since the basing-point system did not discriminate among buyers at the same location, and since the discrimination that existed involved different conditions of sale rather than different prices,[14] the companies argued that their pricing policies did not fall within Section 2(a). These arguments were rejected by the Court. Chief Justice Stone found no basis in law for distinguishing between discrimination at a single location and discrimination among different locations. Further, the Court held, any sales practice that results in effective price discrimination falls within the Robinson–Patman provisions, even though price itself may not be the manipulated variable.

The question remained whether the effect of the system on competition was such as to make it illegal under Section 2(a). On this issue, the Court noted that the law:

. . . does not require a finding that the discriminations in price have in fact had an adverse effect on competition. The statute is designed to reach such discriminations "in their incipiency," before the harm to competition is affected. It is enough that they 'may' have the prescribed effect.[15]

It was thus not necessary to demonstrate that the basing-point system has actually damaged competition; it would suffice to show that the system might, with some unspecified probability, be expected to have such an effect. Here the court noted that:

Since petitioners' basing point system results in a Chicago delivered price which is always lower than any other, including that at Kansas City, a natural effect of the system is the creation of a favored price zone for the purchasers of glucose in Chicago and vicinity. . . . Since the cost of glucose, a principal ingredient of low-priced candy, is less at Chicago, candy manufacturers there are in a better position to compete for business. . .[16]

The competitive advantage conferred on Chicago-area producers of candy was found to support a conclusion of illegality. The advantage was significant enough in th eyes of the Court to justify the Commission's inference of a "reasonable probability" that competition might be lessened substantially.

---

[14] This contention is the result of hairsplitting. The argument was in effect: "We charged all customers the same price but provided some with more extensive shipping services."

[15] *Corn Products Refining Co.* v. *F.T.C.,* op. cit., p. 738.

[16] Ibid.

The Staley Case (1945).[17]   The *Staley* case concerned another facet of the basing-point system employed in *Corn Products Refining*. The A. E. Staley Company and its sales subsidiary utilized the "Chicago-plus" basing-point system in selling glucose, although the glucose itself was produced in Decatur, Illinois. The defendant companies mounted a "good faith" defense, arguing that their adoption of a discriminary pricing system was made purely to meet the equally low prices of competitors.

The facts presented to the Court indicated that in 1920, when Staley entered the glucose manufacturing business, a Chicago-plus pricing system was already established. The company thus went along, "by first quoting the same prices as were quoted by competitors and then making whatever reduction in price . . . was necessary to obtain business."[18] This, then, was the companies' "good faith" defense: they had entered the market at a time when existing firms were already pursuing a system of uniform prices at any delivery point; in order to sell, the companies had to adopt the same prices as their competitors, which in this instance meant the adoption of a discriminatory pricing system.

The Supreme Court rejected this defense. If the companies' argument were sound, said Chief Justice Stone, it would mean that any firm could legitimately adopt discriminatory pricing practices so long as the practices had first been employed by others. The good faith provision, he said, "places emphasis on individual competitive situations, rather than upon a general system of competition." Thus, while a company might argue the need to match competitors' prices on particular occasions, it could not justify adoption of a rival's pricing system. Beyond this, said the Court, the Robinson–Patman Act permits only the matching of a competitor's lower price or additional services. In the case at issue, the Staley company had adopted a system under which it charged phantom freight to those customers who were farther from Chicago than from Decatur; it had, in these instances, raised its price to conform to the system.

The *Staley* and *Corn Products* decisions together struck a hard blow against geographic price discrimination of the basing-point variety. If such a system results in major cost advantages for sellers near the point, it is not only discriminatory but is also likely to lessen competition substantially within the meaning of the law. Furthermore, there appears to be no way in which a company adopting a discriminatory pricing system can maintain successfully that it has done so in "good faith."

The Cement Institute Case (1948).[19]   The Cement Institute, consisting of 74 companies and 21 associated individuals, employed a multiple basing-point system in the sale of cement. The practice was attacked as a violation of both Section 5 of the Federal Trade Commission Act and of the Robinson–Patman Act. The Supreme Court found that the existence of the system amounted to a concerted effort to suppress competition, and was illegal under Section 5.

---

[17] *Federal Trade Commission v. A. E. Staley Mfg. Co.*, 324 U.S. 746 (1945).

[18] Ibid., p. 751.

[19] *Federal Trade Commission v. Cement Institute*, 333 U.S. 683 (1948).

Indeed, the significance of the *Cement Institute* decision lies less in its direct implications for Robinson–Patman issues than its suggestions about the Supreme Court's attitude toward collusion. The Court was willing to infer an unlawful agreement from adherence by firms to a basing-point system that assured that every buyer of cement saw only one price; and in which enforcement measures were taken against price-cutting members. Prices quoted by cement suppliers on government bids were in some cases identical to the 6th decimal place, a striking fact that further suggested to the Court that the companies were not acting independently.

In the *Rigid Steel Conduit* case,[20] defendants argued that their adherence to a multiple basing-point system reflected only independent decisions by individual firms to join the prevailing pattern of market conduct. An appellate court rejected this contention. Individual utilization of the system with the knowledge that competitors are doing likewise, the court held, violates Section 5 of the Federal Trade Commission Act when it produces price uniformity among the sellers.

OTHER ISSUES IN PRICE DISCRIMINATION

The kind of geographic price discrimination implied by most basing-point systems was not the primary target of framers of the Robinson–Patman Act. Rather, the Act was aimed at major buyers who could gain competitive advantages by extracting concessions from their suppliers. Discrimination in such cases is based on the size and market power of the customer, rather than upon his location.

Discrimination in Favor of Large Buyers: A Review of Relevant Cases

The Morton Salt Case (1948).[21]   The Morton Salt Company was a major salt producer that sold to both wholesalers (or jobbers) and to retailers, including large food chains. The company offered the following price schedule for its high-grade salt.

Less-than-carload purchases	$1.60 per case
Carload purchases	1.50 per case
5,000-case purchase in any 12 consecutive months	1.40 per case
50,000-case purchase in any 12 consecutive months	1.35 per case

This schedule represents a combination of quantity discounts and volume discounts, the latter referring to discounts given for cumulative quantities purchased over time. Such a discount system favors larger buyers, and only five companies—major retail food chains—had ever bought enough salt to obtain the minimum ($1.35) price.

The first question confronting the Supreme Court was whether such a volume or quantity discount schedule is discriminatory within the meaning of Section 2(a).

---

[20] *Triangle Conduit and Cable Co.* v. *Federal Trade Commission*, 168 F. 2d 175 (1948).

[21] *Federal Trade Commission* v. *Morton Salt Co.*, 334 U.S. 37 (1948).

The company argued that since its discounts were "available to all on equal terms," they were not discriminatory. The Supreme Court disagreed, stating that the discounts were available to all only in a theoretical sense. In practical terms, large customers received larger discounts, and smaller independents sometimes bought salt from Morton in quantities that did not qualify them for any discount. It was precisely this kind of advantage for large buyers that the Robinson–Patman Act sought to prevent, said the Court.

Having found the discount system to be discriminatory, the Court considered the question of whether it had also had the proscribed effect upon competition. The company maintained that no harm to competition had been demonstrated by the Federal Trade Commission, and argued specifically that the salt that it sold in low volume was an insignificant portion of its customers' business. Morton claimed, in other words, that its discriminations in price were not important; salt was, after all, only one of many items that its retail grocery buyers carried. This contention was rejected by the Court, which stated:

There are many articles in a grocery store that, considered separately, are comparatively small. . . . Congress intended to protect a merchant from competitive injury attributable to discriminatory prices on any or all goods . . . whether the particular good constitutes a major or minor portion of its stock. Since a grocery store consists of many comparatively small articles, there is no way to protect a grocer . . . except by applying the prohibitions of the Act to each individual article. . . .[22]

The Court noted further that the Robinson–Patman Act was specifically "concerned with protecting small businesses which were unable to buy in quantities, such as the merchants here who purchased in less-than-carload lots. . . ."[23] The nature of the discounts and the purpose of the law thus justified the conclusion that competition might have been injured, said the Court. This injury to competition was tied directly to the injury done to the position of small competitors who were forced to pay higher prices for salt.

A question remained as to whether the discounts might yet be justified on a cost basis. If it were more economical for the company to sell in large lots, the price discrepancies might make "only due allowance" for cost differences. Here again the company argued that the FTC had failed to demonstrate illegality. But, said the Court, the burden of proof was on the company to show that its price differences were justified; it was not up to the Commission to show that they were not.

The Supreme Court found the price schedule to be in violation of Section 2(a) and restored a sweeping FTC order against future discounts.

The *Morton Salt* decision indicates that the existence of "substantial" price differentials among customers may well be sufficient to establish a violation of law. Such differentials, the Court reasoned, harm the position of companies that buy at

[22] Ibid, p. 49.
[23] Ibid.

higher prices, and thus harm competition. Any extensive inquiry into the actual competitive mechanism was apparently considered unnecessary. The decision also makes it clear that the burden of proving a cost justification of discriminatory prices falls wholly on the defendant. As we shall see, it often proves impossible to amass convincing evidence on this point. The cost defense therefore may be unavailable, as a practical matter, to most firms charged with price discrimination.

The First Standard Oil Case (1951).[24]   The first *Standard Oil* case raised the issue of the "good faith" defense under the Robinson–Patman Act. Standard had been selling gasoline to large "jobbers" at 1½ cents less per gallon than it sold to retail service stations, and it was ordered to cease and desist this practice by the Federal Trade Commission. In appealing the Commission's order, the company argued that its lower prices had been offered in good faith to meet the equally low prices of competitors.

The Commission had found that Standard's price discounts to jobbers damaged competition. Two of the jobbers to whom it sold had lowered retail prices in their own service stations and had also lowered their wholesale price to other retail stations. This result, according to the Commission, had disadvantaged those retail service stations that could not purchase gasoline at the lower price. Standard argued that its lower prices had been granted under competitive pressure in order to retain the jobbers as customers; that is, had the discounts not been granted, the jobbers would have gone elsewhere. But the Commission held in effect that this defense was irrelevant, stating:

> . . . *even though the lower prices in question may have been made . . . in good faith to meet the lower prices of competitors, this does not constitute a defense in the face of affirmative proof that the effect of the discrimination was to injure, destroy and prevent competition. . . .*[25]

The Commission had thus asserted that good faith is not an absolute defense to a charge of price discrimination.

It was on this point that the Supreme Court took exception to the Commission's findings. Said the Court:

> . . . *there has been widespread understanding that, under the Robinson–Patman Act, it is a complete defense . . . for the seller to show that its price differential has been made in good faith to meet a lawful and equally low price of a competitor. . . . We see no reason to depart now from that interpretation.*[26]

The Court noted that the wording of the Robinson–Patman Act was identical with respect to both the cost justification and good faith defenses. There was, said the Court, no basis for treating the two differently, as the Commission had done. The

---

[24] *Standard Oil Co.* v. *Federal Trade Commission,* 340 U.S. 231 (1951).

[25] Cited in footnote 24, p. 239 (41 F.T.C. 263, 281–282).

[26] Ibid, p. 246–247.

Court refrained from deciding on the merits of the case; that is, it did not judge the validity of Standard's good faith argument. Rather, it held that the company's argument should be considered, and ordered the case remanded to the FTC for rehearing.

The Second Standard Oil Case (1958).[27]   Upon rehearing, the Federal Trade Commission again ruled that Standard's discounts to jobbers violated the Robinson–Patman Act. The Commission considered the good faith defense, but held that although Standard's price discounts had, in fact, been made to meet the equally low prices of competitors, they were not made in good faith. This conclusion, which the Supreme Court termed "not altogether clear," had been overruled by an appeals court.

The Supreme Court upheld the appeals court on narrow grounds. The case, said the Court, turned on a factual issue. The appeals court had made a fair assessment of the record; thus there was no basis for overturning its decision. The Court did go on to note briefly that Ned's—the only jobber to have its price discount instituted after passage of the Robinson–Patman Act—had indeed "pressured" Standard with information about "more attractive price offers. . . ." Ned's had given Standard ultimatums, after which it had received price discounts. It was upon this kind of information, said the Court, that the court of appeals had legitimately found the discounts to be a response to specific competitive pressures.

The Court's decision, in a 5 to 4 vote, was sharply criticized in a dissenting opinion by Justice Douglas. Standard's definition of a "jobber," said Justice Douglas, was entirely arbitrary; a jobber was simply a big customer, thus the discount system was discriminatory. A discriminatory system, he went on, cannot be protected under Section 2(b) simply because it succeeds in holding customers against competitive offers.

The effect of the second *Standard Oil* decision was to reaffirm the status of good faith as an absolute defense to a charge of price discrimination. If a seller discriminates within the meaning of Section 2(a) in good faith to meet the equally low price of a competitor, he is protected even if the effect of his discrimination had been to harm competition.

The Borden Case (1962).[28]   Borden, a leading seller of fluid milk products, had established a pricing system under which two categories of customer were defined. The first group consisted of two major food chains, A&P and Jewel; the second embraced 1322 independent stores, varying in size, but all smaller than the chains.

The company charged lower prices to the first group and attempted to show that the differentials were cost justified. Average cost of sales to the chains, Borden contended, was lower, in part because drivers, clerical, and sales employees were required to spend less time thereon relative to the value of deliveries. A district court concluded that Borden had met its burden of proving a cost justification. On appeal,

---

[27] *Federal Trade Commission* v. *Standard Oil Co.*, 355 U.S. 396 (1958).

[28] *United States* v. *Borden Co.*, 350 U.S. 460 (1962).

the Supreme Court defined the "only question" as "how accurate this showing must be in relation to each particular purchaser."

The Court found against Borden on the ground that its classification of customers was not "of sufficient homogeneity." Whereas there might well be economies in supplying the large chains, these economies applied also to some of the less-favored independents who bought in large volume. The independents were a diverse group whom Borden had lumped together as if they were homogeneous.

The *Borden* decision is a significant indicator of the difficulty firms would face in mounting a cost defense. Comparing average costs between groups of customers will not suffice if there are variations within the groups. It appears that a successful defense must establish cost differences among customers on an individual basis (although customers may be grouped if they are homogeneous). This, in turn, implies that very precise cost differences must be shown in order to justify "discriminatory" prices.

The Sun Oil Case (1963).[29]   The issue raised in *Sun Oil* is whether a seller can discriminate in price to meet the lower price of a buyer's competitor; that is, can the seller lower price to one customer in order to enable that customer to meet **his** competition?

Sunoco had sold gasoline at a discount to McLean, an independent service station dealer in Jacksonville, Florida, for precisely this purpose. The Federal Trade Commission found that this discrimination in price damaged other Sunoco service stations and thus violated Section 2(a). The company argued that McLean was simply a "conduit" of Sunoco, and the the price cut was thus a good faith meeting of competition. The Supreme Court held that the good faith defense cannot be extended to include the meeting of competition by the discriminating seller's customers.

The Court might well have decided differently had Sunoco owned McLean. (Courts are not in the habit of policing the terms at which companies sell "to themselves.") It is interesting to consider whether the distinction between treatment of an owned subsidiary and an independent agent is justified by any meaningful difference in the economic functions served by each.

"Like Grade and Quality"

Price discrimination presupposes a defined product, or, in the words of the law, commodities of "like grade and quality." Occasionally, sellers respond to charges of discrimination by arguing that the goods they sold to different customers were, in some sense, not "the same," and thus beyond the reach of the Robinson–Patman Act.

Where physical differences in the products can be demonstrated, this is a substantial defense. But what if physically standardized goods are "differentiated" in some other way? This issue reached the Supreme Court in *Federal Trade Commission* v.

---

[29] *Sun Oil Co.* v. *Federal Trade Commission,* 371 U.S. 505 (1963).

Borden Co. (1966).[30] Borden sold evaporated milk under its own nationally advertised name. At the same time, it supplied "physically and chemically identical"
milk to supermarket customers to be resold under the various private-brand labels of
those markets. The private-label milks were supplied and sold at lower prices than
Borden's, and the FTC charged the Company with price discrimination.

Borden's response, upheld by an appeals court, was that the two types of milk,
although physically the same, were not "of like grade and quality." The labels differentiated the products, and the fact that buyers were willing to pay more for
"Borden" milk confirmed the commercial distinction between the two.

The Supreme Court restored the Commission ruling on narrow grounds, stating:

*The Commission's view is that labels do not differentiate products for the purpose
of determining grade and quality, even though the one label may . . . command a
higher price in the marketplace. . . . [T]his is the Commission's long-standing
interpretation. . . . These views of the agency are entitled to respect . . . and represent a more reasonable construction. . . .[31]*

Most economists would, of course, object to the view that product differentiation is
purely a matter of physical characteristics (recall that in the Chamberlin model of
monopolistic competition, it does not matter whether product differences are "real
or fancied"). Distinctions are often in the mind of the beholder—here consumer—
and may not be eradicated by "objective" observations about product similarities.
The reasonableness of the Commission's view is thus debatable, but the Court was
willing to permit it, apparently because it did not wish to be drawn into the job of
determining when similar goods are of "like grade and quality."

Competitive Discrimination and "Predatory" Intent

A variety of practices, although not so consistent and highly structured as basing-
point systems or discount schedules, may result in price discrimination. Suppose,
for example, that a retailer offers a special price on some item "this Saturday
only." It might be said that the seller has discriminated against shoppers who do not
buy on Saturday. Similarly, a seller may price his product differently in one city or
region than in another. Although no one is discriminated against within each area, it
could be argued that discrimination across areas exists. Or, to take yet another example, a seller might try out a new price "selectively" rather than "across-the-
board," to determine at relatively low cost whether the change seems promising.

So long as price discrimination is temporary or sporadic, legal problems for the
seller are relatively unlikely. But a dilemma remains. Price competition itself may
dictate discriminatory patterns. The company that prices differently in one area than
another, may not only be acting rationally but in some sense more competitively
than it would if forced into a single-price policy. A firm may be willing to cut prices
in one area but not another, or at one time but not another. Such a firm may simply

[30] 383 U.S. 637 (1966).
[31] Ibid, p. 640.

be responding to competitive pressures that vary in place and time, yet under legal constructions it may also be discriminating illegally.[32]

In a similar vein, concessions to individuals may be an important means by which prices are eroded; to the extent that they are prevented, prices may not be cut. Prohibitions on price discrimination might thus result in more rigid pricing structures, a possibility that poses a potentially strong economic argument against the Robinson–Patman Act.

Some thorny issues of competitive discrimination were raised in an important private case, *Utah Pie Co.* v. *Continental Baking Co.* (1967).[33] Utah Pie, a relatively small regional producer of frozen dessert pies, charged three large companies—Continental, Carnation, and Pet Milk—with discriminatory pricing.

The defendant companies had dominated the Salt Lake City pie market until 1957. At that time Utal Pie entered, offered consumers sharply reduced prices, and captured about two thirds of the market in short order. In response to this assault, Continental, Carnation, and Pet Milk cut their pie prices in Salt Lake City but not elsewhere. Active price-cutting continued during the period 1958 to 1961, and the prices of all pie manufacturers fell significantly. Utah Pie's market share in 1961 stood at 45 percent, its sales grew dramatically, and it remained profitable throughout the price-cutting period.

It was the defendants' sales of pies in Salt Lake City ''at prices lower than it sold pies of like grade and quality in other markets considerably closer to its plants'' that formed the basis of Utah Pie's complaint. Specifically, the Supreme Court Observed:

1. Pet Milk sold pies to Safeway supermarkets to be resold under the ''Bel-air'' label at prices significantly lower than its own comparable ''Pet-Ritz'' pies.
2. Pet Milk had also sold ''Pet-Ritz'' in the Salt Lake City market at prices lower than in California or other Western markets.
3. Continental had in 1961 sold pies at prices ''substantially'' below those it charged elsewhere; such prices had at times failed to cover the company's ''direct cost plus an allocation for overhead. . . .''
4. Carnation cut prices for its ''Simple Simon'' pies in Salt Lake City, ''to a level admittedly well below its costs. . . .''

Said Justice White:

Section 2(a) does not forbid price competition which will probably injure or lessen competition by eliminating competitors, discouraging entry . . . or enhancing the market shares of the dominant sellers. But Congress has established some ground rules for the game. Sellers may not sell like goods to different purchasers at different prices if the result may be to injure competition. . . .[34]

---

[32] See *United States* v. *The New York Great A&P Tea Company,* 67 F. Supp. 626 (E.D. Ill., 1946).

[33] 386 U.S. 685 (1967).

[34] Ibid, p. 702.

The Court found that the three major producers had violated Robinson–Patman in a number of ways: by selling their own brand-name pies at lower prices in Salt Lake City than elsewhere, while lacking a cost justification; by selling private-label pies in Salt Lake City at lower than brand-name prices, where differentials ''could not be cost justified in their entirety''; and by selling at prices that at times appeared to be ''below cost.'' There was, said the Court, ''evidence of predatory intent'' on the part of the three.

The *Utah Pie* decision has, unsurprisingly, been a subject of much controversy. Three pie producers had responded to a price-cutter by reducing their own prices in the Salt Lake City market. The Supreme Court failed to discern a competitive element in this behavior and ignored the fact that price reductions as a rule yield consumer benefits—precisely those benefits that competition is expected to provide. Instead, the Court found alleged damage to a competitor, Utah Pie, not simply the decisive element, but the only element worthy of discussion.

The Robinson–Patman Act, Justice White observed, ''reaches price discrimination that erodes competition.'' In this case, evidence of a ''drastically declining price structure'' could be attributed to ''continuing or sporadic price discrimination.'' And a trial jury was entitled to conclude that the effect of such discrimination may have been substantially to lessen competition. The Court thus asserted that an illegal ''erosion'' of competition may be proved by a pattern of declining prices associated with merely ''sporadic'' price discrimination.

This is a remarkable legal rule that, some economists believe, turns economic analysis on its head.[35] Active price rivalry, a hallmark of competition, is taken as a sign of anticompetitive ''erosion'' if accompanied even by nonsystematic instances of discrimination. It is apparent that behavior in the Salt Lake City pie market during the late 1950s and early 1960s was intensely competitive. Under the doctrine of *Utal Pie,* it was also illegal.

The question of what constitutes a proper public policy toward price discrimination, where discrimination is part of the competitive process, is not a simple one. Legal precedent is not voluminous, but we see again indications that the courts will demand policies that tend to hurt no one.

Section 3 of the Robinson–Patman Act, a criminal provision, bars sales ''at unreasonably low prices for the purpose of destroying competition or eliminating a competitor.'' At what point does a desirable competitive price become ''unreasonably low'' or ''predatory''? When does a low price cease to be ''good'' and become ''bad''?

As one might suspect, this question has no simple answer. The notion of a predatory pricing strategy is associated with some form of long-run profit seeking. The predator sets a low price that sacrifices immediate profits and drives rivals from the market; at that point the firm enjoys monopoly power and may recoup profits at higher prices.

---

[35] See Ward S. Bowman, ''Restraint of Trade by the Supreme Court: The Utah Pie Case,'' *Yale Law Journal,* **77** (Novermber 1967), 70–85.

In an important article some years ago, John S. McGee argued that such a scenario is implausible.[36] Price-cutting in McGee's view is invariably inferior to merger as a means of monopolizing the market; better to buy one's rivals than force them out, for the latter course is more costly. This argument assumed that merger is legally permissible. Rules developed under Section 7 of the Clayton Act during the 1960s and 1970s, however, suggest that acquisition of rivals by a large and aggressive firm will be prohibited in most instances (refer to Chapter 14).

McGee's position, however, remains influential. Even if the merger route is blocked, predation is a costly form of conduct[37]; its prospects for success may well be uncertain, and one might thus wonder whether it is more than an occasional aberration in corporate behavior. Once the possibility of predatory pricing is conceded, however, practical questions of law become relevant. How can a predatory price be identified? What evidence should the courts seek?

These questions are the subject of a relatively recent, quite voluminous—but highly equivocal—literature.[38] Richard A. Posner defines a predatory price as one "calculated to exclude *from the market an equally or more efficient competitor.*"[39] Such a definition suggests a price–cost comparison: to exclude the efficient competitor, one must price below one's own (as well as the competitor's) cost. But what cost? Average? Marginal? Or something else?

Areeda and Turner argue that pricing below marginal cost is the signal of a predatory strategy; but that because marginal cost is exceptionally difficult to measure, average variable cost should serve ordinarily as the practical proxy.[40] Other writers have proposed somewhat different cost rules, or have suggested that output behavior rather than price–cost comparisons, may be more useful.[41]

Although the Supreme Court has long taken the position that "unreasonably" low prices refer to "selling below cost," the issue of appropriate cost measurement is not yet well developed in the law.[42] Some recent lower court decisions have attempted to follow the Areeda–Turner suggestion, but it will likely be a number of years before the shape of authoritative legal rules begins to emerge clearly.[43]

---

[36] "Predatory Price Cutting: The Standard Oil (N.J.) Case," *Journal of Law and Economics,* **1** (October 1958), 137–169.

[37] See John S. McGee, "Predatory Pricing Revisted," *Journal of Law and Economics,* **23** (October 1980), 289–330.

[38] For an early important discussion, see Phillip Areeda and Donald F. Turner, "Predatory Pricing and Related Practices under Section 2 of the Sherman Act," *Harvard Law Review,* **88** (February 1975), 697–733. A later useful treatment with references to the intervening literature is William J. Baumol, "Quasi-Permanence of Price Reductions: A Policy for Prevention of Predatory Pricing," *Yale Law Journal,* **89** (November 1979), 1–26.

[39] *Antitrust Law* (Chicago: University of Chicago Press, 1976), p. 188.

[40] See footnote 38. The reasoning is that pricing below average total cost is, at least occasionally, profitable; whereas pricing below marginal cost is seldom profitable **except** as part of a strategy to drive rivals from the market.

[41] See, for instance, Oliver E. Willliamson, "Predatory Pricing: A Stragetic and Welfare Analysis," *Yale Law Journal,* **87** (December 1977), 284–339.

[42] See *U.S.* v. *National Dairy Products Corp.,* 372 U.S. 29 (1963).

[43] See, for instance, *Janich Bros., Inc.* v. *American Distilling Co.,* 570 F. 2d 848 (9th Cir., 1977).

Inducing Discrimination

Section 2(f) of the Robinson–Patman Act prohibits the knowing inducement or receipt of a discriminatory price. Precisely what this may mean was addressed by the Supreme Court in a 1979 case involving the A&P Company.[44] Borden Company had supplied A&P's private-label milk in the Chicago area for many years, and sought to renew its contract. After some negotiations, A&P informed Borden that it had a better offer, and that Borden's bid was "so far out of line it is not even funny. You are not even in the ball park." Borden responded with a substantially improved bid, which A&P accepted. Thereupon the FTC sued, charging A&P with inducing a discriminatory price from Borden.

A&P's defense was straightforward: Borden's milk price had been cut in good faith to meet competition and retain the A&P account. Borden therefore had not violated Robinson–Patman, and A&P could not be guilty of inducing an illegal discrimination.

This defense was successful. Justice Stewart for the Court noted that Section 2(f) refers only to the inducement or receipt of prices prohibited by the law; a buyer thus violates 2(f) **only** if the seller has violated 2(a) or 2(b).[45] Here, however, Borden "acted in a reasonable and good-faith effort to meet its competition." Since Borden had a valid defense for its price, A&P could not be liable.

THE LEGAL AND ECONOMIC STATUS OF PRICE DISCRIMINATION

Price discrimination encompasses such a wide variety of business practices that it is difficult to summarize its legal or economic status precisely. We have seen, however, important inconsistencies between legal doctrine and economic analysis. Price differentials that consistently favor certain customers (especially large ones) are likely to violate the Robinson–Patman Act. Yet the difficulty of proving a cost justification is so great[46] that this illegality may **either prevent or require** price discrimination. If the costs of serving all customers are similar, then price differences are indeed discriminatory. If costs differ, nondiscriminatory treatment requires prices to differ as well; but if the cost differences are not amenable to precise proof, then a company that reflects such differences (imperfectly) in price leaves itself open to prosecution.

A second, and perhaps even more basic, inconsistency is seen in judicial attitudes toward "competition," as the issue arises in price-discrimination cases. What is it that the courts are trying to accomplish in their treatment of discriminatory practices?

---

[44]*Great Atlantic & Pacific Tea Co., Inc.,* v. *Federal Trade Commission,* 440 U.S. 69 (1978).

[45]This was previously recognized by the Court in *Automatic Canteen Co. of America* v. *F.T.C.,* 346 U.S. 61 (1953).

[46]This difficulty has been noted by the Supreme Court itself, which has referred to the "elusiveness of cost data," and at one point observed: "proof of cost justification being what it is, too often *no one can ascertain whether a price is cost-justified.*" (Emphasis added.) *Automatic Canteen Co.* v. *Federal Trade Commission,* 346, U.S. 61 (1953).

The Robinson–Patman Act prohibits discrimination only where the effect may be substantially to lessen competition. Yet it seems fair to observe that the courts have made little inquiry into the competitive implications of price discrimination or nondiscriminatory price differences. In place of inquiry and analysis, the courts have, rather, substituted an assumption: if differentials in price give some competitors an advantage over others, harm to competition is implied. In other words, a price difference that hurts one or more **competitors** is interpreted as hurting **competition.**[47] This is the fundamental premise of basing-point decisions such as *Corn Products Refining* and *Staley,* in which the disadvantage incurred by customers distant from the basing point was presumed to harm competition; of *Morton Salt,* in which competition was assumed to be lessened by a higher charge to smaller buyers; and of *Utah Pie,* in which the Supreme Court focused on the effects of a price struggle on a single competitor.

It is interesting to note that this view of competition is in close accord with the position taken by the courts in merger and tying cases. In each situation, hardship to competitors is equated with damage to competition. The economic difficulty with such an outlook should be quite obvious. Competition as a process is inevitably hard on competitors. Its rationale is precisely that it drives competitors to their best efforts and penalizes those who do not perform well. Certainly the economist's defense of a private market system would be unimpressive if inefficient firms within the system were to be protected. The *raison d'être* of the system is its efficiency, and the maintenance of inefficient competitors in order to ''protect competition'' is a contradition in terms.

To be sure, the courts have not deliberately set out to promote inefficiency. The emphasis placed on protection of competitors, however, is such as to raise questions about the priorities that are operative. Such questions are broader than the treatment of price discrimination and extend into virtually all areas of antitrust enforcement. Presumably, we do not want competitors to be hurt without economic justification. But the difficult policy question is what to do when competitors are hurt with economic justification. In the area of price discrimination, the apparent answer of the courts is that competitors are to be protected without extensive analysis of economic cause.

---

[47]For a still-pertinent discussion, see Morris A. Adelman, *The A & P Case—A Study in Applied Economic Theory* (Cambridge, Mass.: Harvard University Press, 1949).

CHAPTER 16

Vertical Restrictions: Price Fixing, Refusals to Deal, Tying, Exclusive Dealing, and Territorial Limitations

Vertical restrictions involve companies in a customer–supplier relationship. A manufacturer, for example, may agree to supply a wholesale or retail distributor only if the distributor agrees to a prescribed pattern of behavior. This might mean agreement to charge a particular price, to buy other items from the manufacturer in question, not to deal with other manufacturers, or to sell the manufacturer's goods only within a defined area—price fixing, tying, exclusive dealing, and territorial restriction, respectively.

Such restrictions raise antitrust issues because, quite plainly, they may impinge on competition. If a retail seller, for example, is under exclusive contract to one supplier, other suppliers are foreclosed from that outlet; notice that such foreclosure is closely analogous to the foreclosure created by vertical merger. In fact, public policies toward vertical restrictions imply a position on vertical integration. For any company that is prevented from imposing conditions on its distributors could, as an alternative, integrate forward, that is, become a distributor itself.

VERTICAL PRICE FIXING

Efforts by manufacturers to control the prices at which distributors may resell their goods have a long record in American history. Typically, suppliers have specified **minimum** resale prices, although maximum prices also have been imposed at certain times.

Economic Issues

Vertical price fixing may reduce or eliminate **intrabrand** competition, that is, competition among dealers in the product of a particular manufacturer. If, for example, General Electric sets the resale price of its refrigerators, wholesalers and retailers of those refrigerators cannot compete with one another in terms of price. Should all

320

refrigerator manufacturers follow suit, specifying similar or identical resale prices, **interbrand** price competition (among sellers of different brands) also will be affected. In the extreme, a series of vertical pricing requirements by competing suppliers could have the effect of eliminating horizontal price competition at the retail level. This possibility provides some policy presumption against vertical price fixing.

The issue, however, is not entirely simple. It is easy enough to see why a small retailer, for example, would like the supplier of his product to specify a minimum resale price. The dealer is then freed from price competition by other dealers in the same good; he need not worry, for example, that "discount houses" will undercut his price and take customers away. This argument, however—which amounts to a simple preference to avoid competing—does not explain why the supplier would wish to impose a pricing restriction on dealers.[1]

Suppose, for example, that a manufacturer of headache remedies knows that his retail drug outlets will charge customers a "low" price for his product if no minimum resale price is specified. The manufacturer would like druggists to sell as much of his product as possible. From the manufacturer's point of view, then, competition at retail may be desirable. The price of his product will be lowered, and (if demand curves look the way economists think they do) more will be sold. The druggist, who receives a lower profit margin, would be happier with a specified minimum price, but the manufacturer need not be.

In this simplest case, its appears that a manufacturer would not want to set a minimum resale price. There are, however, some further considerations. The headache remedies produced by the manufacturer may well be less attractive to druggists if they must be sold under conditions of active price competition. If prices and profit margins are driven down substantially, druggists may demand less of the product from the manufacturer than they otherwise would. For this reason, retail price competition could ultimately reduce the manufacturer's sales, especially if competing manufacturers offer druggists alternative headache remedies at fixed retail prices. A major consideration for the manufacturer, then, may be retailers' treatment of his products. Even if retailers continue to carry his headache remedies, they are likely to "push" those fixed-price products that offer them the higher net return.

Another frequently cited motivation for manufacturers to establish minimum resale prices is the fear that "low" prices reduce the value of products in the eyes of consumers. Producers may believe that the market judges quality by price. If so, reduced prices could harm a product's reputation and future marketability. This concern may be particularly strong if the product supplied might be used by dealers as a loss leader, that is, sold at a price that fails to cover the dealer's full cost as a "come on" to consumers. The difficulty with this argument is its essentially speculative nature. There is not much evidence, for example, to suggest that manufacturers believe markets judge quality by price; or that fear that a product will be used as a loss leader is at all widespread.

---

[1] For a thorough discussion, see Lester G. Telser, "Why Should Manufacturers Want Fair Trade?" *Journal of Law and Economics*, **3** (October 1960), 86–105.

A final argument as to why a manufacturer might want to specify minimum prices applies to products that require extensive dealer services, for example, automobiles, appliances, and other complex (often durable) goods. In such cases, it is possible that dealers who cut price will also choose to economize by providing fewer services. ("We will sell to you at the lowest possible price, but you'll have to go elsewhere for maintenance or repairs.") If services are reduced, products may not perform as well, and the manufacturer's reputation is likely to suffer.[2] Quite possibly the manufacturer will wish to impose a minimum resale price rather than confront such a prospect.

Legal Status

Vertical price fixing has an unusual legal history. The courts have been generally hostile to this practice, yet for almost 40 years (1937–1976) certain resale price agreements, known commonly as **fair trade,** were exempt from antitrust prosecution.

In *Dr. Miles Medical Co.* v. *John D. Park & Sons, Inc.,*[3] Miles, a manufacturer of proprietary medicines (produced under "secret formulas"), pursued a comprehensive system controlling both wholesale and retail prices of its products. Park, a drug wholesaler, had refused to enter into Miles' required contracts, allegedly inducing others to supply it at "cut prices," in violation of their agreements with Miles; upon which Miles sued.

The Supreme Court struck down Miles's vertical restrictions. Justice Hughes provided a two-part rationale: (1) once a manufacturer parts with title to his goods, he has no interest in their subsequent disposition; (2) specification of minimum resale price—a vertical restriction—is the equivalent of horizontal price fixing at the resale level. Although both arguments rest on shaky economic grounds, they laid the basis for a hostile attitude by the courts toward various vertical restrictions.

In *United States* v. *Colgate & Co.,*[4] the Court established an exception to the rule of *Dr. Miles.* A company may simply announce the conditions under which it will deal (or refuse to deal) with others, and follow those conditions. The company may go no further, however. Any agreement with distributors to adhere jointly to specified terms, or effort to punish distributors who deal with noncomplying sellers, will abridge the Sherman Act. As Bork notes, the Colgate exception is of limited practical importance, since "the fatal element of agreement" could be created very easily, perhaps by a manufacturer's discussion of price conditions with a retailer, or by a retailer's unsolicited statement that he would adhere to the supplier's conditions.[5]

---

[2]There is, in effect, a "free rider" problem: consumers will have an incentive to buy from discounters but obtain "free" services from higher-priced dealers. See Richard A. Posner, *Antitrust Policy* (Chicago: University of Chicago Press, 1976), pp. 149ff.

[3]220 U.S. 373 (1911).

[4]250 U.S. 300 (1919).

[5]Robert H. Bork, *The Antitrust Paradox* (New York: Basic Books, 1978), pp. 280–281.

During the 1930s a series of fair trade laws was passed by most states. These laws permitted manufacturers of branded products to specify minimum resale prices and usually provided that all distributors within a state were bound to minimum price agreements so long as one seller had signed a contract to this effect. In 1937 Congress passed the Miller–Tydings Act, exempting fair trade contracts from antitrust prosecution where the states permitted them. And in 1952 the McGuire–Keough Act, permitting enforcement of fair trde contracts against nonsigning resellers, was enacted. These federal enabling laws were passed under strong lobbying by retail trade associations.

Between 1937 and the 1960s, fair trade laws had a substantial impact on some markets, as manufacturers took advantage of the antitrust exemption to impose minimum resale prices. By the 1970s, however, state support for fair trade had eroded quite substantially; and in 1976 Congress repealed the federal enabling statutes. Although this action formally eliminated fair trade, many manufacturers have continued to issue ''suggested'' resale prices for their products. They now lack the legal means to enforce such suggestions, but there no doubt remain some ways to ensure that the suggestions are taken seriously in certain instances.

In *Kiefer-Stewart Co.* v. *Joseph E. Seagram & Sons,*[6] the Supreme Court refused to allow an agreement by liquor manufacturers to impose a **maximum** resale price on a wholesale distributor. Seagram and Calvert, two jointly owned suppliers, sold liquor only to distributors who would not resell above specified maximum prices. The companies argued that their scheme was an effort to counteract a price-fixing conspiracy among liquor wholesalers. The Court, however, held simply that any agreement ''to stop selling to particular customers'' violates the Sherman Act.

In *Albrecht* v. *Herald Co.,*[7] the Supreme Court again struck down a supplier's attempt to impose a maximum price on distributors. Herald, the publisher of the *Globe–Democrat,* a St. Louis newspaper, advertised suggested retail prices. It granted exclusive territories to its carriers, but canceled those carriers who refused to comply with the suggested maximum price. One may well ask whether decisions such as *Kiefer-Stewart* and *Albrecht* serve the interests of consumers, who might be thought to benefit from maximum price restrictions. The Court has been quite consistent in its reasoning, however. Agreements or combinations to restrict price are illegal, whether it is maximum or minimum limits that are involved; the ''perhaps erroneous judgment of a seller,'' said Justice White in *Albrecht,* cannot substitute for ''the forces of the competitive market.''

REFUSALS TO DEAL

Vertical refusals to deal are intimately related to vertical price fixing. Indeed, under the rule of *Colgate,*[8] refusal to deal is the only lawful weapon a supplier may use to induce distributors to follow suggested prices.

[6] 340 U.S. 211 (1951).

[7] 390 U.S. 145 (1968).

[8] See footnote 4.

This type of practice creates something of a quandary for public policy. On the one hand, the right of a manufacturer—or any business enterprise—to deal or not deal with whomever it pleases is both well established and reasonable. If a corporation manager decides that it is not advantageous to deal with a particular firm, why should government ever interfere with this judgment? Is it not precisely the job of the manager to make such decisions?

On the other hand, however, there are circumstances in which vertical refusals to deal with price-cutting distributors can achieve resale price maintenance almost as effectively as an unlawful contract to fix resale prices. Since vertical price fixing may restrict competition, there *is* a rationale for government to prevent not only price fixing itself but other practices that produce similar results. How then is such conflict to be resolved?

The general answer of the courts has been a strict interpretation of the *Colgate* principle. In *Federal Trade Commission* v. *Beechnut Packing·Co.*,[9] the company had refused to deal with wholesalers or retailers who did not adhere to its resale price schedules. It also had instituted an elaborate policing system and refused to supply wholesalers who dealt with violating retailers. The company contended that since it did not have contracts binding resellers to specified prices, its conduct should be found lawful. The Supreme Court, however, rejected the contention, stating "the Beech-Nut system goes far beyond the simple refusal to sell." The company's methods of securing compliance, the Court held, were "as effectual as agreements," and could not be excused by the "nonexistence of contracts."

This narrow reading of the *Colgate* rule was reinforced by the Court's decision in *United States* v. *Parke Davis & Co.*[10] Parke Davis, a drug manufacturer, issued catalogs containing suggested minimum prices for both wholesalers and retailers; the company announced in the same catalogs that it would deal only with those distributors who adhered to its suggestions. Wholesalers generally complied, but a number of retailers sold Parke Davis vitamin products at prices substantially below the suggested levels. The company responded by informing wholesalers that not only would it refuse to deal with them unless they followed the price suggestions; but it would not deal with them if they supplied violating retailers.

This program, said the Supreme Court, "plainly exceeded the limitations of the *Colgate* doctrine. . . ." Parke Davis was not content to announce price suggestions and follow them with "a simple refusal" to deal with noncompliers; it went further, involving its wholesalers "in a combination . . . to maintain retail prices." It was this additional element, more than a "simple refusal to deal," that violated the Sherman Act.

We see, then, that the right of a manufacturer to refuse to deal with a wholesale or retail distributor has been upheld by the courts, but only in the narrowest of circumstances. I may lawfully refuse to supply you with my goods if you fail to observe my resale suggestions. But I may not enter an agreement with you to observe these suggestions, nor may I involve others in an effort designed to secure your observance.

[9] 257 U.S. 441 (1922).
[10] 362 U.S. 29 (1960).

TYING AND EXCLUSIVE DEALING

Section 3 of the Clayton Act makes it illegal to lease or sell commodities,

. . . on the condition, agreement or understanding that the lessee or purchaser thereof shall not use or deal in the goods . . . of a competitor or competitors of the lessor or seller, where the effect . . . may be to substantially lessen competition or tend to create a monopoly in any line of commerce.

This provision is commonly directed against tying and exclusive dealing practices, as are sections 1 and 2 of the Sherman Act.

Tying

The typical tying arrangement provides that the buyer can purchase one product, the **tying good,** from the seller only if he agrees to purchase something else, the **tied good,** as well. The seller states in effect: "I will sell you my tying good only if you also buy the tied good from me."

Why should such an arrangement be desirable from the viewpoint of a rational firm? The company in question sells (at least) two products. If it wishes to maximize profits, could it not simply follow the usual maximization rules in both (all) of its markets?[11] Tying the sale of two of its products would then prove superfluous, and might even reduce profits overall.

It turns out that tying arrangements may be desirable for a number of different reasons. One possibility, which the courts term **leverage,** is that the tie will enable the firm to extend its power from one market to another.[12] In this scenario, the tying good has a "strong" demand; the firm exercises some monopoly power in the tying market, perhaps even pure monopoly, as in the case of a patented machine. The tied good, in contrast, is sold in more competitive circumstances: there are close substitutes, and the demand for it is thus "weak." When sale of the two goods is tied together, customers who want the desirable tying good are "forced" to buy the less desirable tied item as well. In this way the company bolsters the demand for its tied product. Conceivably, demand for the tying product may suffer, but if its position is strong enough, any reduction may be relatively small. Increased profits in the tied market are therefore expected to outweigh any likely reduction in the tying market.

This view of why tie-ins pay, however, is oversimplified and may be misleading. For it seems to imply that the firm can achieve something by tying that could not ha ve been achieved in some other way, say, by manipulating the individual prices of the two goods. While this might be the case, it is not inevitably so.

---

[11] If the firm's products are related either in supply or demand (i.e., have interdependent cost or revenue functions), "simple" profit-maximizing policies in each market are **not** likely to maximize profits overall. See Martin J. Bailey, "Price and Output Determination by a Firm Selling Related Products," *American Economic Review,* **44** (March 1954), 82–93.

[12] As we see below, this is virtually the only explanation of tying that has been accepted by the Supreme Court.

At this point an example may be helpful. Suppose that a company produces a very popular brand of shoes and a very ordinary kind of shoelaces, and decides to tie the two items in the following way: instead of selling the shoes for $30 and the laces for 50 cents, it will now sell a package consisting of one pair of shoes and two "extra" pairs of laces for $31. The firm hopes to expand its sales of laces while maintaining its sales of shoes. Every shoe customer now buys two extra pairs of laces. And it seems unlikely that many prospective shoe buyers will be discouraged from purchasing because of the tie-in; after all, the extra laces will be needed eventually, and the laces produced by this company are presumably just as good as anyone else's.

Consider, however, the implications of the company's expectation. More laces will be purchased, but this result could also have been obtained by lowering the price of the laces. A few less shoes may be sold, but this result could have been obtained by raising the price of the shoes. Indeed, if it is more profitable to sell the $31 package, then perhaps $30 and 50 cents were not the optimal prices to begin with; and the company thus could have expanded profits by changing the separate prices of shoes and laces rather than by tying their sale.

It is important to realize that there is no magical transformation when prices are quoted in combination. Anyone willing to pay $31 for the shoes-and-laces package must rationally be prepared to purchase the two goods individually at some prices that add up to $31.

We are thus left with the initial question: why do tie-ins pay? One reason is that tying facilitates **price discrimination,** which might otherwise be impossible. Consider a simple case of two goods, A and B, and two consumers, 1 and 2. The willingness of each to pay for each item is shown in Table 16.1. Note that if the seller of A and B offers these items as a tied package for $10, both consumers will buy it, and the seller receives $20 in revenue. But there is no nondiscriminatory set of prices at which separate sales of A and B will yield as much revenue (the maximum attainable with separate prices is $18—$10 for two units of A priced at $5 each plus $8 for two units of B priced at $4 each). Tying may thus permit a seller to take advantage of different demands (willingness to pay) by individual customers. Whereas price discrimination would also achieve this result, discrimination may be costly or impossible.[13]

A slightly different form of price discrimination sometimes motivates tying arrangements. When IBM tied computer cards to use of its computers, and when Xerox tied copying paper to its copying machines, the complementary tied good served a metering function. Each company was able to exploit varying intensities of demand for its tying good (computers, copiers), charging heavier users more, in toto, for the tied good.

---

[13] This is an exceedingly simple example (a type known as "block booking") that constitutes only one of many possible variations on a similar theme. The seller need not force customers to purchase the two items in fixed proportions. Rather, he might require that in order to maintain their access to A (the tying good), customers fill any and all requirements for B (the tied good) from him. This sort of requirements provision has been used, for example, by IBM (computers and tabulating cards) and Xerox (copying machines and paper).

Table 16.1

	Maximum Price Consumer Will Pay for	
	Item A	*Item B*
Consumer 1	$5	$5
Consumer 2	$6	$4

It is important to note that this sort of arrangement may well increase output and sales above the level that would be supplied by a nondiscriminating firm with the market power of an IBM or Xerox. In the extreme case, the monopolistic seller is able to discriminate so perfectly that total output approximates that of the competitive market. This observation is significant because it suggests that at least some kind of tying arrangements may have a positive implication for economic welfare.[14]

Alternative tying rationales also exist. It may be, for example, that the tie-in represents an acceptable form of competition for some markets in which direct price change is considered unacceptable.Tacit price agreements might not be considered to be violated if the product in question is tied to some other good; but a direct price reduction would be considered a violation and might precipitate price warfare. Perhaps more important, tie-ins may at times act as an effective long-run barrier to entry. When IBM, for example, tied service contracts to its computers, one result was to forestall entry of competing service organizations. Initially, IBM might have done just as well by lowering service prices and raising the prices on its machines; but it could not have been sure that someone—for example, its customers—would not have found out enough about the machines to enter the service market. Tie-in arrangements are sometimes profitable for longer-run reasons of this type.

Still other rationales for tying surface occasionally. One infrequent use of the tie-in is as a means of evading government price controls. During the 1974 gasoline shortage, for example, one enterprising service station owner required customers filling their tanks to purchase a last will and testament form along with the gasoline! This was the alternative to raising the price of gas, which would have been illegal under the controls then in existence.

It should be emphasized that many tie-ins are trivial and have no plausible effect on competition. Indeed, the definition of a tie-in may prove difficult: should we consider the Sunday newspaper a tie-in of news, sports, and comics sections? Or a restaurant meal a tie-in of meat, vegetables, and a beverage? Arguably, the sale of any product with separable components is a tie-in sale of those components. Obviously these sorts of examples have no antitrust implications. They do, however, suggest the need to define both the "product" in question and the importance of the tying arrangement before legal prosecution is undertaken.

---

[14] See Ward S. Bowman, "Tying arrangements and the Leverage Problem," *Yale Law Journal,* **67** (1957), especially pp. 23–24.

A Review of Relevant Cases

The International Salt Case (1947).[15]   The International Salt Company, the nation's largest producer of salt for industrial uses, held patents on two salt dispensing machines. The company leased these machines under provisions that required the lessees "to purchase from it all unpatented salt and salt tablets consumed. . . ." That is, customers could lease the machines from International Salt only if they used the company's products to fulfill their requirements of salt. The government charged violations of Section 1 of the Sherman Act as well as Section 3.

The Supreme Court held that although patents conferred a limited monopoly on the salt processing machines, they "confer no right to restrain use of, or trade in, unpatented salt." The company argued that the trial court had precluded consideration of the reasonableness of the practices (under Section 1) and of the probability of lessened competition (under Section 3). The Supreme Court held, however, that it is "unreasonable *per se*" to foreclose competitors from any market; and found that the leasing provision had this effect by precluding rival salt producers from selling to users of International Salt Machines. The practice thus violated Section 1. Further, said the Court, Section 3 bars agreements that tend to create a monopoly, whether "the tendency is a creeping one rather than one that proceeds at full gallop; nor does the law await arrival at the goal before condemning the direction of the movement. . . ."[16]

The company lodged one further argument that might have impressed the Court under different circumstances. It contended that since, under the leasing arrangements, it was required to repair and maintain its machines, "it was reasonable to confine their use to its own salt because its high quality assured satisfactory functioning and low maintenance cost." The Court stated that "a lessor may impose . . . reasonable restrictions designed in good faith to minimize maintenance burdens," but noted also that no one had argued "that the machine is allergic to salt of equal quality" produced by other companies. Presumably the tie-in might have been permissible if it had been shown that salt produced by anyone other than International would have damaged the machines.

The Northern Pacific Railway Case (1958).[17]   The Northern Pacific Railway Company had large land holdings that it leased and sold for various uses. The Company included in its agreements "preferential routing" provisions that required lessees or buyers to ship on Northern Pacific lines all commodities produced on that land so long as the Company offered rates and services equal to those of competing transporters. The practice was challenged by the government as a violation of Section 1 of the Sherman Act.

The Supreme Court noted that the Sherman Act had not been read literally by the courts to prohibit **every** restraint on trade. However, said Justice Black:

[15]*International Salt Co.* v. *United States,* 332 U.S. 392 (1947).

[16]International's progress toward a monopoly in salt was far from impressive. The company managed to capture only 4 percent of the market with its tie-in. See John L. Peterman, "The *International Salt* Case," *Journal of Law and Economics,* **22** (October 1979), 351–364.

[17]*Northern Pacific Railway Co.* v. *United States,* 356 U.S. 1 (1958).

. . . there are certain agreements or practices which because of their pernicious effect on competition and lack of any redeeming virtue are conclusively presumed to be unreasonable and therefore illegal without elaborate inquiry as to the precise harm they have caused or the business excuse for their use. This principle of per se unreasonableness not only makes the type of restraints which are proscribed by the Sherman Act more certain but it also avoids the necessity for an incredibly complicated and prolonged economic investigation. . . .[18]

Among the practices deemed *per se* illegal in past cases were price fixing, division of markets, group boycotts, and tying arrangements. The present circumstances amounted to a tie-in according to Justice Black. He found no question "that the defendant possessed substantial economic power by virtue of its extensive landholdings," and that the volume of commerce affected was substantial. Accordingly, the Court held that the preferential routing clauses violated Section 1.

The *Northern Pacific* decision created a stringent rule with respect to tying arrangements. Tying is *per se* illegal whenever the defendant possesses sufficient power in the tying good market to restrain competition appreciably in the market for the tied good; and when the amount of commerce affected in the tied market is "not insubstantial." The notion of "sufficient" economic power in the tying market may be inferred without precise quantitative tests (such as the company's market share). Here the inference of sufficient power was drawn from the railway's extensive landholdings, which induced its customers to accept the tie ins.

The Jerrold Electronics Case (1960).[19] In *Jerrold,* a district court followed the suggestion of *International Salt* that tying might be permissible where necessary to protect the performance of a manufacturer's product. Jerrold, a pioneer in sales of community antenna television systems, tied service contracts to its equipment. As the court noted, the equipment tended to be "sensitive and unstable," and presented in each location "different problems giving rise to different equipment needs." This was, furthermore, "a new business with a highly uncertain future." If the systems failed to function consistently, not only Jerrold's reputation but that of the entire industry would be jeopardized.

A need for servicing by qualified persons familiar with the equipment was thus demonstrated; and, said the court, Jerrold could not have met this need except by tying service to equipment. The tie-in was thus found to be permissible for a limited period.

The *Jerrold* decision provides an important qualification to the rule of *Northern Pacific.* A tie-in may be justified under certain circumstances, here to protect the goodwill of a company in a new and uncertain business where no alternative means of protection was available. The broad implication is that despite the *per se* language of the courts, tying arrangements may be judged in practice on their reasonableness.

---

[18] Ibid., p. 5.

[19] *United States* v. *Jerrold Electronics Corp.,* 187 F. Supp. 545 (E.D. Pa. 1960); affirmed *per curiam* 365 U.S. 567 (1961).

The Loew's Case (1962).[20] At issue in the Loew's case was the practice of block booking of copyrighted motion pictures. Six major distributors were charged with violating Section 1 of the Sherman Act by making the sale of one or more feature films to television stations conditional on the purchase of other films. The practice had forced buyers to purchase undesirable films in order to obtain those features that they wanted. For example, to get *Treasure of Sierra Madre, Casablanca, Sergeant York, Johnny Belinda,* and *The Man Who Came to Dinner,* WTOP (a Washington television station) also had to purchase such films as *Nancy Drew Troubleshooter, Tugboat Annie Sails Again, Kid Nightingale, Gorilla Man,* and *Tear Gas Squad.*[21]

The Loew's case combined several lower court cases that raised identical issues and were considered together. The first issue considered by the Supreme Court was whether tying arrangements violate Section 1. Justice Goldberg reasserted the Court's earlier contention that tie-ins have no real justification and are viewed with concern because they may "force buyers into giving up the purchase of substitutes for the tied product . . . and they may destroy the free access of competing suppliers of the tied product to the consuming market." These effects, said the Court, may occur when the seller, "by virtue of his position in the market for the tying product, has economic leverage sufficient to induce his customers to take the tied product along with the tying item." The test of illegality thus rests upon an assessment of the market power held by the seller.

In the immediate case, the Court held that a patent or copyright on the tying good creates the presumption of the requisite market power. Here Loew's and the other distributors held copyrights on films desired by the stations, and this was taken to imply sufficient leverage. The defendants argued that the relevant line of commerce was television programming, of which motion pictures (at that time) comprised only 8 percent. The Supreme Court, however, agreed with the district judge that each copyrighted film block "was in itself a unique product." There was no question that block booking had adverse effects upon competition, said Justice Goldberg. Those stations that were forced to buy unwanted films were denied access to films marketed by other distributors; and the other distributors were, in turn, foreclosed from selling to the stations. The Court thus concluded that the practice violates Section 1. The motion picture distributors henceforth were required to quote prices for individual films upon request, although they could continue to offer blocks for purchase.

The Fortner I and II Cases (1969, 1977). The *Fortner* cases involve a treble-damage suit by Fortner Enterprises against U.S. Steel and its subsidiary, United States Steel Homes Credit Corporation. Fortner charged that in order to obtain loans from Credit Corp., it was required to purchase prefabricated houses from U.S. Steel—specifically, one house for each lot purchased with the loan proceeds.

---

[20] *United States* v. *Loew's Inc.,* 371 U.S. 45 (1962).

[21] As George J. Stigler has noted, block booking may be inspired by the desire to price discriminate, as in the example cited earlier. ["A Note on Block Booking," in Stigler, *The Organization of Industry* (Homewood, Ill.: R. D. Irwin, 1968), pp. 165–170.]

Fortner alleged that the houses were sold at "artifically high prices," and that the arrangement constituted an illegal tie-in.

In *Fortner I,* a district court granted summary judgment for the defendants, finding that neither "sufficient market power over the tying product" nor "foreclosure of a substantial volume of commerce" had been established. The Supreme Court reversed and remanded for trial on the ground that the district court had applied the wrong tests.[22] "Sufficient economic power," said Justice Black, does not, as the lower court believed, require "that the defendant have a monopoly or even a dominant position" in the tying market. In fact, power "far short of dominance" may suffice. Tying arrangements are illegal whenever they produce an "appreciable restraint on competition," a result that occurs if the seller "can exert some power over some of the buyers . . . even if his power is not complete." Further, the requirement that a "not insubstantial" volume of commerce be affected by foreclosure means only that dollar volume must be more than "merely *de minimus.*" The requirement makes no reference to market shares or the scope of the market itself.

Upon trial, a district court concluded that U.S. Steel was liable because it did have the requisite economic power. This judgment was upheld on appeal, but reversed by the Supreme Court in *Fortner II.*[23] The question in tying cases, said the Court, is whether the seller can force buyers to accept "burdensome terms." In this instance, Justice Stevens observed, Credit Corp. had not done so. Rather, it had given Fortner a good credit bargain that was unavailable from other credit companies. "Appreciable economic power" therefore had not been demonstrated.

Taken together, *Fortner I* and *II* establish significant precedent. In *Fortner I* the Supreme Court majority accepted the contention that a sale in which the seller extends credit may be prosecuted as a tie-in. Furthermore, as dissenting Justices White and Harlan pointed out, the Court was willing to admit the possibility of sufficient economic power even though the record omitted "any offer of proof that the seller has any market power in the credit market. . . ."

The latter point, something of an anomaly, was modified in *Fortner II* when the attempt to demonstrate sufficient power in the credit market failed. Yet, said the Court, such a demonstration will not generally require that the seller hold a "monopoly" or even a "dominant position." Although Fortner lost the battle, these decisions may point to an increase in the legal vulnerability of some future tying arrangements.

An Appraisal of Tying Policy. The legal status of tying arrangments is subject to some linguistic ambiguity. Because the courts claim to see no potential social benefits in tying, they apply a relatively stringent standard sometimes described as "*per se*" illegality. Yet the actual treatment of the arrangements does not conform to a *per se* standard as the term has been understood with respect to other kinds of violations. As Baldwin and McFarland have observed:

[22] *Fortner Enterprises, Inc.* v. *United States Steel Corp.*, 394 U.S. 495 (1969).

[23] *Fortner Enterprises, Inc.* v. *United States Steel Corp.*, 429 U.S. 610 (1977).

[per se] . . . *means that* . . . *the Court need only be shown that the act itself was committed. If tying arrangments are illegal per se the plantiff need only prove that the act itself was committed.*[24]

Despite judicial assertions of *per se* illegality, this is not the standard that has been employed. The courts have found tie-ins to be illegal only where "economic power" in the market for the tying good and a "not insubstantial" market foreclosure in the tied good exist. In addition, tying arrangments have been permitted in at least one instance (*Jerrold Electronics*) in which both market power in the tying good and substantial commerce in the tied good were present.

As Eugene Singer has put it:

A rose may be a rose, but it is quite clear that one per se violation is not equivalent to another. Four market practices are generally listed as per se violations of the antitrust laws; price fixing, division of markets, group boycotts, and tying arrangements. But the standard of proof associated with each of these market practices is quite distinct.[25]

In short, whether tying arrangements are *per se* illegal depends upon what one may wish to call "*per se* illegal"; but the *per se* doctrine of tie-in sales is not the same thing as the *per se* doctrine of price fixing. As Singer goes on to point out, however, the argument over what should or should not be called *per se* is irrelevant to substantive antitrust questions. The important issue is what kinds of proof the courts require in different sorts of cases.

The fundamental question before the courts in tying cases is: Under what circumstances are such arrangements likely to damage competition? As we have seen, the courts contend that tie-ins serve no purpose beyond economic leverage, the extension of monopoly power from one market to another. This contention is a dubious one that does not fully describe the motivations of the arrangements in the cases discussed above. As Ward S. Bowman, Jr., showed some time ago, a rational monopolist is unlikely to extend his monopoly to another market by means of tying arrangements.[26] Bowman points out that many of the tying cases that have come before the courts indicate a purpose other than leverage.[27] IBM, as we have seen, tied its computer cards to its computing machine leases until this practice was found to violate Section 3.[28] As noted above, such a tie-in forces customers to pay in

[24]W. L. Baldwin and David McFarland, "Some Observations on 'Per se' and Tying Arrangements," *Antitrust Bulletin,* 6 (July–December, 1963), 433–439; quotation at 435.

[25]Eugene Singer, "Market Power and Tying Arrangements," *Antitrust Bulletin,* 8 (July–August, 1963), 653.

[26]See footnote 14.

[27]Richard A. Posner makes the same point, stating: "One striking deficiency of the traditional 'leverage' theory of tie-ins, as the courts have applied it, is the failure to require any proof that a monopoly of the tied product is even a remotely plausible consequence of the tie-in." *Antitrust Law* (Chicago; University of Chicago Press, 1976), p. 172. And Kenneth G. Elzinga observes in a similar vein: "The successful transfer of a monopoly position from one market to another by tying arrangements would be a remarkable achievement." "The Goals of Antitrust: Other Than Competition and Efficiency, What Else Counts?" *University of Pennsylvania Law Review,* , 125 (June 1977), 1191–1213; quotation at 1204–1205.

[28]*International Business Machines Corp.* v. *United States,* 298 U.S. 131 (1936).

proportion to their use of the leased equipment—heavier users of the IBM machines had to purchase more cards and thus pay more. The tie-in served the same function as a meter recording the use of the equipment.

Aside from this purpose, tying may actually serve as a means of price competition. In some circumstances, direct price cuts may be regarded as undesirable (perhaps a needlessly provocative policy). Sellers may, rather, adopt tying arrangments in which the tied good is akin to a bonus. For example: "If you buy my new razor, I will 'throw in' an extra supply of blades at especially favorable terms." Viewed in this context, it is clear that tie-ins need not serve the detrimental ends that the courts have envisioned.

What is more disquieting, however, is the courts' implicit view of the way tie-in contracts work. This view holds that tie-in sales generally permit a seller with some market power over the tying good to extend this power to the market for the tied good. Although such a possibility cannot be precluded, the effects of tying arrangements are varied, and no such generalization is easily defended. A pertinent question is whether tying permits the seller to accomplish something that could not be accomplished by more usual means such as price change. Bowman has shown that a monopolist may be able to extend his position if the tied good is complementary and is used in variable proportions with the tying good.[29] M. L. Burstein has argued more generally that tie-ins of the requirements contract variety—that is, those in which the buyer must fulfill his requirements through the seller, but no quantities are specified—may be profitable even if the goods are unrelated.[30] In these instances it appears that the tie-in may be an effective device for extracting profits from a tied market in which direct price discrimination is impossible.

Exclusive Dealing

Analytically, exclusive dealing arrangements are distinct from tie-ins, although some similarities may be noted. Suppose, for example, that a shoe manufacturer decides to sell to retailers on an exclusive basis. It tells the retailers: "You can purchase our shoes only if you do not carry the shoes produced by our competitors." Such a condition has two contradictory effects upon the demand for the manufacturer's shoes. To the extent that retailers accept the condition, demand will tend to rise, for these stores must now fill their entire requirement from one producer; but to the extent that retailers refuse to accept the condition, they will cease purchasing from this producer, and demand will tend to fall. The desirability of the arrangement from the producer's viewpoint depends at least partially upon the **net** effect of these tendencies.

Exclusive dealing may also be desirable for reasons of efficiency. A manufacturer may find it less costly to deal with a relatively small number of large distributors;

[29] See footnote 14.

[30] "The Economics of Tie-in Sales," *Review of Economics and Statistics*, **32** (February 1960), 68–73.

and any given distributor may enjoy savings as the result of an exclusive relationship with one supplier.[31]

The potential anticompetitive element in exclusive dealing is market foreclosure. Exclusivity removes distribution outlets (or, possibly supply sources) from use by other suppliers (or distributors). The preemption of many favorable outlets or sources may affect the fortunes of rivals and conceivably act as an entry barrier to new firms.

A Review of Relevant Cases.

The Standard Fashion–Magrane Case (1922).[32] One of the earliest cases brought under Section 3 of the Clayton Act concerned an exclusive dealing arrangement imposed by a manufacturer of paper dress patterns. Standard Fashion and Magrane-Houston entered into a contract that provided that Magrane would sell Standard's dress patterns under the condition that the patterns of other companies would not be sold on its premises.

The question before the Supreme Court was whether the contract would tend to lessen competition or create a monopoly, and thus fall within the prohibition of Section 3. The Court agreed with the circuit court observation that:

The restriction of each merchant to one pattern manufacturer must in hundreds, perhaps in thousands, of small communities amount to giving each single pattern manufacturer a monopoly of the business in such community. Even in larger cities . . . [the practice] may tend to facilitate further combinations. . . .[33]

The exclusive dealing requirement was thus found by the Court to violate Section 3.

The Standard Stations Case (1949).[34] The Standard Oil Company of California and its subsidiary, Standard Stations, had entered into exclusive supply contracts with 5937 independent service stations in the "Western area" of the United States. Under the contracts, service stations that were supplied by Standard were bound to fill their entire requirement for one or more products from the company. The provisions varied somewhat in product coverage, but the common effect of the agreement was that the stations served by Standard could not purchase some or all of the products they offered to consumers from any rival petroleum company.

The service stations involved in the exclusive contracts comprised 16 percent of total area outlets, and Standard was the largest seller of petroleum products in the area. There was thus little question of the substantiality of the commerce affected. Moreover, Standard's competitors practiced a similar kind of exclusive dealing; only 1.6 percent of the area service stations were "split-pump," that is, suppliers of

---

[31] Efficiencies could result in a number of ways. If, for example, it is desirable for a retailer also to service the equipment he sells, and if the equipment is complex, it may well "pay" both parties to have the retailer specialize and become expert in the goods of a single manufacturer.

[32] *Standard Fashion Co.* v. *Magrane-Houston Co.*, 258 U.S. 346 (1922).

[33] 259 Fed. 793, 170 C.C.A., 593.

[34] *Standard Oil of California and Standard Stations, Inc.* v. *United States*, 337 U.S. 293 (1949).

more than one company's gasoline. The Supreme Court concluded that the exclusive requirements contracts created a "potential clog on competition," and were in violation of Section 3; but Justice Frankfurter's discussion of the issues was perhaps more significant than the actual decision.

The first substantive question considered by the Court was whether a showing that competition actually has been impaired is necessary under Section 3. The district court had held that the substantiality of commerce affected implied a substantial lessening of competition, but Justice Frankfurter noted that there was no real precedent for such an implication. In some cases, he stated, an examination of the actual economic consequences of an agreement may be necessary; in others (such as *International Salt*), examination of actual consequences was not necessary once it was established that the volume of business affected was significant.

Justice Frankfurter distinguished between tying agreements, which, he stated, serve no purpose beyond the suppression of competition; and requirements contracts, which "may well be of some advantage to buyers as well as sellers, and thus . . . to the consuming public." The advantage of such arrangements, according to the Court, lies in the assurance of a steady source of supply to buyers and a steady demand for sellers. Long-term planning is facilitated, and selling expenses may be lowered accordingly. The implication of this argument seems to be that tying ought to be illegal *per se* because it can have no positive justification; while exclusive dealing ought to be judged under some rule of reason, since positive benefits are possible. Interestingly, however, Justice Frankfurter refrained from applying a rule of reason in *Standard Stations*. It was true, he noted, that Standard's competitive position had not improved during the period covered by the exclusive requirements contracts, but it was impossible to say what would have happened to its position in the absence of the contracts. Said the Court:

> . . . to demand evidence as to what would have happened but for the adoption of the practice that was in fact adopted or to require firm prediction of an increase in competition as a probable result of ordering the abandonment of the practice, would be a standard or proof if not virtually impossible to meet, at least most ill-suited for ascertainment by courts. . . .[35]

The *Standard Stations* decision is thus something of an oddity. The Court said that exclusive requirements contracts, unlike tying arrangements, might be shown to be desirable. Yet because of the "serious difficulties" that would attend any effort to apply the necessary tests, a presumption was made against contracts involving a substantial volume of business. The Court seemed to argue for a rule of reason approach, while actually applying a *per se* test modified by the significance of commerce affected.

The Tampa Electric Case (1961).[36] The Tampa Electric Company and the Nashville Coal Company had entered into a contract in which Tampa agreed to fill

---

[35] Ibid, pp. 309–310.

[36] *Tampa Electric Co.* v. *Nashville Coal Co.*, 365 U.S. 310 (1961).

its entire coal requirements from Nashville for a period of 20 years. Nashville later advised Tampa that the agreement was illegal under Section 3 of the Clayton Act and refused to supply the coal. (Presumably Nashville believed that it could more profitably sell to others). Tampa thereupon sued for a judgment declaring the agreement to be legal.

The Supreme Court disagreed with district and appellate court decisions that the requirements contract violated Section 3. The Court assumed (without actually ruling) that the contract amounted to exclusive dealing. But whereas such prolonged contracts are suspect, said Justice Clark, they are not illegal *per se*. The amount of commerce involved in this contract, $128 million, was hardly trivial, but, said the Court, "the dollar volume by itself is not the test. . . ." The Court found that this sum amounted to less than 1 percent of the relevant market, and was not sufficient to imply a Section 3 violation. Once again the Court took the position that exclusive dealing arrangements may have positive benefits and are to be judged under a rule of reason approach.

The Brown Shoe Case (1966).   In *F.T.C.* v. *Brown Shoe Co.,*[37] the Commission challenged as an unfair practice (under Section 5 of the Federal Trade Commission Act) Brown's efforts to induce retailers to deal primarily in its own shoes. The Company offered distributors such "special services" as assistance with promotion and store design. Agreements, which were not mandatory, were obtained from about 650 retailers, representing roughly 1 percent of the nation's shoe stores. In finding the arrangement unlawful, the Commission cited an "incipient attempt" to reduce competition in shoe retailing and to "further the dominant position of Brown in the shoe industry. . . ."

The Commission was reversed by an appeals court but was ultimately upheld by the Supreme Court on narrow grounds. Under Section 5, the Court held, the Commission has the authority to define as unfair a practice that "conflicts" with antitrust principles; and it need not demonstrate that the practice is an "outright violation" of either the Sherman or Clayton acts. The Court has thus permitted the FTC to act against practices such as exclusive dealing without the burden of proving an anticompetitive effect.[38]

An Appraisal.   If an exclusive dealing arrangement diminishes competition, it does so by foreclosing suppliers from distribution outlets (or vice versa). In other words, it makes it difficult for some suppliers to offer their commodities to the market, thereby hurting not only the suppliers themselves, but also the consuming public whose alternatives are reduced. The anticompetitive tendencies of exclusive dealing can be viewed in *reductio ad absurdum* fashion by noting that any sale by a supplier to a distributor forecloses other suppliers from that portion of the market. If an agent purchases something from me, he cannot buy it from you; you are thus

---

[37] 384 U.S. 316 (1966).

[38] For a critical analysis, see John L. Peterman, "The Federal Trade Commission v. Brown Shoe Company," *Journal of Law and Economics,* **18** (October 1975), 361–419.

foreclosed from making that sale. Gordon Shillinglaw, in a discussion of this point, notes that the restrictive effect is limited.

Among a group of sellers competing for a particular sale, one must be successful, the others unsuccessful. The essence of the competitive system lies in competition before each sale. The fact of the sale does not remove this competition but is its direct result.[39]

One effect of an exclusive dealing arrangement is to enlarge the units of sale, thereby reducing the number of "sales" that occur. If, for example, a shoe store is bound to a manufacturer by an exclusivity clause, competition has not necessarily disappeared. The manufacturer presumably won his contract—exclusivity provision and all—in competition with other manufacturers; he will have to win it again upon expiration. But the interval between sales has been lengthened; that is, the unit of sale is enlarged. Rather than competing for every lot of shoes that the store requires, manufacturers now compete for every contract; contracts come up with relative infrequency. The "amount" of competition might be said to diminish in the sense that fewer competitive confrontations occur, but it is not clear that such a reduction will imply inferior performance.

The courts have stated that competitive diminution is to be weighed against the possibility that exclusive dealing will permit greater efficiency. Although efficiency gains can be hard to quantify, they are likely to be important in some instances. Improved planning, scale-type economies, and more attentive promotion and service by distributors are among the benefits. Where exclusive dealing provisions affect only a minor portion of a market in which entry barriers are minimal, "monopoly" is not a plausible outcome. In such cases there is some presumption that the arrangement is efficiency oriented.

TERRITORIAL LIMITATIONS

Manufacturers specify with some frequency the geographic areas within which each of their distributors may sell. Such limitations are commonly part of "franchise" agreements in which dealers are granted exclusive rights to their "own" areas; if one is to have an exclusive area, others must obviously be kept out of that area. The territorial restriction thus serves both a "carrot" and "stick" function; it keeps others out of one's own backyard, but prevents one from attempting to penetrate elsewhere.

The economic effects of territorial restriction are ambiguous. The immediate impact is likely to be a reduction of *intrabrand* competition; if, for example, Schwinn bicycle dealers are given exclusive territories, there is likely to be less competition among sellers of the Schwinn brand than there would be otherwise. But the implica-

---

[39]Gordon Shillinglaw, "The Effects of Requirements Contracts on Competition," *Journal of Industrial Economics,* **2** (April 1954), pp. 147–163; quotation at pp. 148–149.

tion for interbrand competition—between Schwinn and other manufacturers' bicycles—is less clear.

One possibility is that Schwinn dealers will focus on promotion and servicing, perhaps enhancing their ability to compete with sellers of rival brands. Territorial restrictions may also permit a relatively small manufacturer to enter the market and establish a reputation for good quality supported by reliable dealer service.

Alternatively, widespread territorial restriction in combination with exclusive dealing may make market entry more difficult. A commonly cited example is automobiles, an industry in which leading manufacturers may "tie up" the most favorable distribution outlets; entry into the manufacturing stage of the industry is then hindered by the difficulty of establishing a strong dealership network.[40]

Legal Status

Territorial limitations have been challenged infrequently in the courts, and legal doctrine is not especially well developed. For this reason, only a brief line of cases need be examined.

The White Motor Case (1963).[41] White Motor, a manufacturer of trucks and truck parts, supplied dealers on the condition that they sell only to customers located within assigned areas. A district court granted summary judgment in favor of the government under Section 1 of the Sherman Act. This court held that the (*per se* illegal) nature of the practice made a trial unnecessary.

On appeal, the Supreme Court reversed. Justice Douglas noted that vertical territorial limitations "may or may not" have the purpose or effect of stifling competition. Further, he stated:

We do not know enough of the economic and business stuff out of which these arrangements emerge to be certain. They may be too dangerous to sanction or they may be allowable protections. . . ."[42]

For several years the *White Motor* opinion was widely interpreted as a statement that territorial restrictions would be judged under a rule of reason. Read literally, however, the Court may have been saying only that it could not yet tell whether a rule of reason or a *per se* standard was appropriate; and that, given such uncertainty, the defendant was entitled to a trial.

The Schwinn Case (1967).[43] Arnold, Schwinn, a bicycle manufacturer, had supplied dealers under the so-called Schwinn Plan since 1952. The plan provided, among other things, that Schwinn distributors could only sell to retailers within des-

---

[40] See B. Peter Pashigian, *The Distribution of Automobiles: An Economic Analysis of the Franchise System* (Englewood Cliffs., N.J.: Prentice-hall, 1961).

[41] *White Motor Co.* v. *United States* 372 U.S. 253 (1963).

[42] Ibid., p. 263.

[43] *United States* v. *Arnold, Schwinn & Co.*, 388 U.S. 365 (1967).

ignated (and exclusive) territories; and that Schwinn retailers could sell only to consumers or to each other—that is, they could not supply other retailers who did not hold Schwinn franchises.

The Supreme Court distinguished between instances in which Schwinn retained title to its bicycles, with dealers acting as agents or salesmen, and instances in which the company actually sold the bikes to its dealers. In the former case, said Justice Fortas, a territorial restriction violates Section 1 only it if constitutes an unreasonable restraint of trade; that was not the case here. Where Schwinn had relinquished title to the bicycles; however, any attempt to restrict resale was a *per se* violation of law.

The economic difficulty with this reasoning should be apparent. Territorial restrictions on bicycle dealers may or may not have an adverse impact on market competition, but the outcome does not depend on the technicality of who holds title to the bikes at the time of sale. The distinction drawn by the Court was thus irrelevant in an economic sense. If Schwinn's restrictions on consignments to agents did not harm competition, as the Court found, then similar restrictions where bicycle titles passed to Schwinn dealers could not have done so either.

The *Schwinn* outcome was surprising, particularly to those who had read *White Motor* as a rule-of-reason statement. The Court noted that franchising itself is permissible (a company may designate certain dealers "to whom, alone he will sell . . ."); but having sold bicycles to a dealer, Schwinn could no longer tell that dealer where or how to resell.

The Sylvania Case (1977).[44]   GTE Sylvania, a television manufacturer, utilized a system of franchised retailers. Television sets were sold to retailers, and Sylvania required that the retailers resell only from designated franchise locations. Dealers were not assured of exclusive territories.

Continental T.V., a Sylvania dealer, advised Sylvania that it wished to open a new store in Sacramento. Sylvania denied the request, but Continental advised that it was nevertheless "moving Sylvania merchandise . . . to a new retail location." Sylvania's response was to terminate Continental's franchise. Continental then filed suit under Section 1 of the Sherman Act.

The Supreme Court, in an unusual move, reversed its own *Schwinn* doctrine. Justice Powell pointed out that the *per se* rule of *Schwinn* had itself been "an abrupt and largely unexplained departure" from earlier precedent. Terming the impact of vertical restrictions "complex," Justice Powell stated that they simultaneously reduce intrabrand competition (among Sylvania televisions) and increase interbrand competition (e.g., between Sylvania and R.C.A.).

The Court thus found that territorial limitations may have both good and bad implications. Such restrictions are lawful where they promote interbrand competition sufficiently to outweigh any loss in intrabrand competition. The implied comparison may require extensive analysis embracing the nature and extent of the restrictions themselves and their impact on both types of competition. It is interesting to observe

---

[44]*Continental T.V., Inc.* v. *GTE Sylvania*, 433 U.S. 36 (1977).

that the *Sylvania* reversal of the *Schwinn* rule coincided with a change in the composition of the Supreme Court, and might thus presage further departures in the future from the antitrust criteria of the earlier Warren Court. Such departures are not a certainty, however. The facts surrounding *Sylvania* were distinctive, and it is conceivable that the Court that decided *Schwinn* would have come to a similar conclusion here.

An Appraisal

The law governing territorial limitations has not yet been developed in great detail. Few economists are likely to quarrel with the Supreme Court's latest, rule-of-reason position as a matter of principle. But the main question, still quite open, is how the rules will be defined. It is interesting to note parenthetically that while the Court recognizes the "mixed" impact of vertical territorial restrictions, it has taken a much harder view toward horizontal restrictions of this sort. If competing sellers divide a manufacturer's market geographically, the practice is viewed as a straightforward Section 1 conspiracy, subject to *per se* prohibition.[45]

SUMMARY

The courts' treatment of vertical restrictions could be termed "balanced" or "ambiguous" depending on one's viewpoint. The presence of potential costs and benefits has generally been recognized. Even in the tying area, where a *per se* standard has been asserted, decisions have not gone "automatically" against challenged practices.

The costs of vertical restrictions are usually defined by the courts as market foreclosure or some tendency to exclude certain competitors from (a portion of) the market. Benefits are viewed in terms of "efficiencies" that are, as a rule, not spelled out in much detail. Where both costs and gains are present, the outcome of a case is in doubt; but, as in other areas, the courts are more likely to prohibit a practice if harm to some competitors is apparent.

Some writers suggest that by limiting vertical restrictions, the courts attack vertical integration itself. And, as noted above, the need for restrictions could be circumvented if the practitioner would integrate into the affected market.[46] A careful reading of legal opinion, however, suggests not so much a broad intention to prohibit integrated operations as it does uncertainty and some confusion about the effects of integration.

---

[45] See *United States* v. *Sealy, Inc.*, 388 U.S. 350 (1967); and *United States* v. *Topco Associates*, 405 U.S. 596 (1972).

[46] Whether such integration is legal might depend on how it occurs. As we have seen, vertical mergers may be challenged under Section 7. And in one instance, now quite old, a firm was convicted of conspiring with its own vertically related "affiliates." *United States* v. *Yellow Cab Co.*, 332 U.S. 218 (1947).

CHAPTER 17

Some Exceptions to Competition in Antitrust Policy

As we have noted at several points, antitrust enforcement does not extend equally to all segments of the economy. It would seem logical that policies designed to encourage competition would be restricted largely to those areas in which the market mechanism is thought to be workable. This would exclude most notably the "natural monopoly" or "public utility" type industries. In fact, however, the application of the antitrust laws is not so consistent as a simple dichotomy between "competitive" and "noncompetitive" sectors might suggest. Regulation of monopoly has not been fully substituted for encouragement of competition in many of the latter industries; there are also a number of significant exemptions and exceptions to the search for competition within the former sector.

Both these "inconsistencies" have been quite controversial. Some observers suggest the the government ought to fish or cut bait, that is, decide where competition will work and where it will not, and pursue appropriate and consistent policies within each area. This is an appealing suggestion, but it does not provide an easily implemented approach to public policy; for, as we shall see, the question of whether competition is in principle workable within particular industries often has no precise answer. Competition is not a simple yes-or-no, on-or-off condition. It succeeds or fails by degrees, and our notion of the proper mixture of market and regulatory forces in any industry may change quite rapidly.

THE REGULATORY ALTERNATIVE TO ANTITRUST POLICY

We have thoroughly described the virtues of competition. Yet virtually every American corporation and industry is publicly regulated to some degree; and in certain instances we have departed sharply from the market, turning instead to government agencies for important economic decisions. The most notable cases are public utilities (electricity, natural gas and water suppliers, transportation, and communications industries) and financial institutions. Why have we done so? Some of the main reasons, which we have alluded to earlier, now bear fuller attention.

The Public Utilities

Several industries are usually considered to fall within the public utilities framework: electric power and gas; communications (excluding the print media); and
some forms of transportation. Regulation in this area represents one of our more
severe forms of government control. Not only prices, but the quantity and nature of
services supplied, may be subject to regulatory agency approval. Government thus
intervenes in the ordinary, day-to-day decisions of the affected businesses.

Natural Monopoly.   This is a frequently cited reason for public utility regulation.
Recall the potential importance of scale economies. In some activities, large-scale
enterprises are inherently more efficient for technical reasons. Figure 17.1 portrays
the extreme case of such economies, known as natural monopoly. Each short-run
average cost (*SAC*) curve is associated with a different scale of operation or plant
size. If market demand is *D*, it turns out that a single large-scale plant (*SAC**) is
most efficient. It is capable of supplying the market (output level *Q**) at a cost per
unit of *P**. Were the market to contain instead more numerous smaller plants—for
example, *SAC*$_1$, each producing Q_1—production costs would soar to P_1.

Two observations about such an industry are important. First, the most efficient
form of organization is a single, large producer, in effect a monopolist. To maintain
a regime of smaller, more numerous producers would waste resources. Second,
even if we wished to maintain several smaller units, it would prove difficult to do
so. Since production costs are decreasing throughout the range of output that the
market demands, every firm has an incentive to expand and take over the market.
The ultimate outcome might thus be a kind of chaotic competition, with the market
finally monpolized by the last survivor; or a series of defensive consolidations by
firms, with the end result again akin to monopoly.

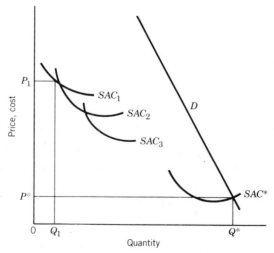

Figure 17.1   Natural monopoly.

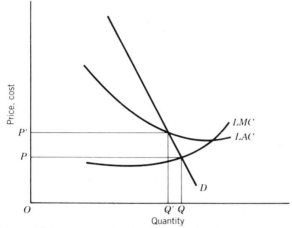

Figure 17.2   The regulated pricing choice in natural monopoly.

The rationale for public regulation of such an industry is quite clear. The industry, if left alone, will inevitably (naturally) become a monopoly, and may impose heavy costs on consumers. Government thus enters, licenses the monopoly (which is going to exist in any event), and regulates its behavior so as to prevent exploitation of consumers. This is a pertinent argument for the regulation of some public utilities industries.

Whereas the rationale may be plausible, however, the nature of appropriate regulation has long been a topic of debate. Presumably we want our public agencies to compel behavior that will maximize "social welfare" or "the public interest," but what does this mean? Traditional welfare economics suggests that price should be equal to marginal cost (recall the optimality conditions of Chapter 1), but in a decreasing cost industry, that is, natural monopoly, $P = MC$ creates a well-known dilemma. Figure 17.2 shows demand (D) and long-run average cost (LAC) curves that are essentially the same as those of Figure 17.1 (LAC in 17.1 would simply be the lower envelope of the SAC curves.)

It is the long-run marginal cost curve (LMC) that shows the problem. If price is set at marginal cost in Figure 17.2, the regulated firm will not cover its total costs. Price P lies below the average unit cost of producing the associated quantity Q.[1] Were the firm forced to price at this point, it would therefore require some sort of subsidy to survive the long run.

The obvious alternative to a policy of marginal cost pricing is average or full-cost pricing: (P', Q') in Figure 17.2. Here the regulatory agency permits the firm to cover all costs, including some rate of return that is "drawn into" the LAC curve; but not to extract an excessive price from consumers.

---

[1]This diagrammatically obvious point is frequently noted in introductory economics courses. If an average quantity (such as (LAC) is falling, the associated marginal quantity (here LMC) must be less than the average. In the immediate case, then, $P = LMC$ implies $P < LAC$.

In a broad sense, this is what public regulatory commissions usually do. Notice, however, that in order to specify a permissible price, the commission must define an appropriate rate of return. Moreover, since the rate of return is tied to the company's capital assets, the commission must also decide how the assets, known as the rate base, are to be valued. An ostensibly simply principle thus leaves room for much conjecture and debate.

Peak Load Demands   The demands for many goods and services vary a good deal over time. Sales of everything from pretzels to bed space in hospitals depend to some extent upon the time of year, week, or even day that one examines. In some circumstances, such variability does not raise a significant issue. But where the demand changes are sizable, the item sold is not readily storable, and supplying firms have large fixed investments, peak-load problems arise. These conditions are again typical of some regulated industries (e.g., electricity and natural gas).

Since the good in question cannot be stored, peak demands can be satisfied only by building additional supply capacity; and the cost of the capital investment needed to do so is likely to be substantial. This condition raises two questions: (1) how much capacity should be built? (2) how should the cost of building capacity be apportioned among users of the good produced?

The traditional analysis of these questions is shown in Figure 17.3, in which D_1 is the demand for the good—say, electricity—by off-peak users; D_2 is the demand by peak users; and C is the unit cost of building capacity, assumed constant. One might think of peak users as those who demand electricity during normal business hours—roughly 9 A.M. to 5 P.M.—when demand is "high"; while the off-peak users demand electricity at "odd" hours when demand in toto is "low."

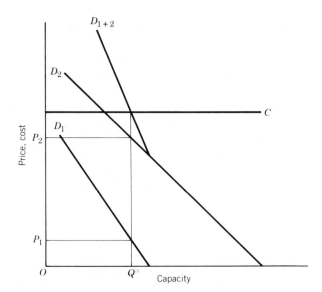

Figure 17.3 Peak load pricing.

The question: how much capacity should be built? finds its answer in the usual marginal principle. Add capacity to the point at which its marginal cost and marginal value are equal. The marginal cost of capacity in Figure 17.3 is given by C. Marginal value is D_{1+2}, the "total" demand by peak and off-peak users. This curve is obtained by summing D_1 and D_2 vertically. It answers the question: what is the value placed by the two groups of users on any specified level of capacity?[2] Diagrammatically, the optimal capacity level is Q^*, the intersection of D_{1+2} with C.

The peak-load problem now is to apportion the costs of Q^* between the two user groups. The usual analysis suggests that each group should pay its marginal valuation of that capacity level: off-peak users will be charged P_1 and peak users P_2 if we follow this principle. Notice that we are discussing only the cost of building capacity. Electricity users will also be charged for such variable costs as the fuel used to generate the power that they consume.

The analysis of Figure 17.3 is oversimplified, in part because of the assumption that electricity generation is subject to constant costs.[3] More "realistic" assumptions will complicate the analysis a bit, and point to somewhat different optimal results. The basic lesson of the traditional analysis, however, remains both valid and important. Peak-load problems generally suggest the desirability of differential pricing; that is, peak and off-peak users should not be charged the same amounts. Peak users should, as a rule, pay more; it may be appropriate for them to bear the lion's share—and in certain circumstances all—of the costs of adding production capacity.

One purpose of public regulation, then, is to deal with peak demand pricing in a reasonable way. Historically, the record of the regulatory agencies has not been very impressive. One difficulty (seen in a slightly different context in Chapter 15) is the inclination of some public officials to regard all price differentials as discriminatory. This attitude limits the use of differentials in cases in which they would be economically appropriate.

Where the regulatory agencies have permitted different groups to be charged different prices, the results have been mixed. Varying electricity rates to categories of users—residential versus commercial or industrial—is a crude device that does little to assign consumers the true costs they impose on suppliers. In contrast, variations in long-distance telephone rates or airline ticket prices, when based on time of use rather than user category, approach more sensible solutions; and experimentation with electricity price differentials by time of day are becoming more common.

---

[2] Notice that D_{1+2} is not the same as the usual market demand curve. The latter is obtained by summing individual demand curves horizontally, and answers the question: how much will consumers demand at any specified price?

[3] For a good traditional exposition, see Alfred E. Kahn, *The Economics of Regulation* (New York: Wiley, 1970), Chapter 4. The implications of altering some traditional assumptions are shown by John C. Panzar, "A Neoclassical Approach to Peak Load Pricing," *Bell Journal of Economics*, **7** (Autumn 1976), 521–530. A helpful discussion of Panzar's rather technical presentation is provided by H. Craig Peterson, *Business and Government*, (New York: Harper & Row, 1981), pp. 264ff.

The "Public Interest."   The legal notion that an industry may be publicly regulated if it is "clothed with a public interest" is traced to a Supreme Court decision in *Munn* v. *Illinois*.[4] Munn, an operator of grain elevators and warehouses, had violated a state law regulating rates and services. Illinois sued, and Munn responded in part that the state law deprived him of property without due process. On appeal, the Supreme Court approved the state regulation, citing both the critical importance of elevators and warehouses in the Midwest and the fact that the market was a "virtual monopoly."

The notion of a special group of industries "clothed" or "affected" with "a public interest" has been used to justify virtually every area of public regulation. At times the courts have refused to extend this category, for example, to gasoline stations, theater ticket brokers, and employment agencies. At first glance, the public interest test appears plausible. It is expensive to set up a regulatory apparatus, and the apparatus, once in place, generates ongoing costs. Why bother to do this unless our interest in the affected industry is compelling?

Unfortunately, the idea of industries that are sufficiently "important" to be worth regulating does not imply useful decision criteria. How are we to measure the importance of an industry, and what level of importance implies the need for direct public controls? The answers are not obvious, and decisions to regulate are not fully explicable in terms of this criterion.

Forms of Regulation.   Still other reasons for regulation may be cited. In at least one case, radio and television broadcasting, there exist purely technical restraints on the number of market participants.[5] Demands for some utility services are highly inelastic within certain price ranges, and consumers experience varying degrees of immobility in switching among competing suppliers (for example, switching sources of home heating is likely to be more difficult than switching modes of transportation). These conditions suggest particular consumer vulnerability to a monopoly supplier.

The reasons for public regulation are, then, diverse, and, by similar token, so are the forms of public control that we adopt. A rather typical example of traditional regulation is the case of electric power and gas. Here the Federal Power Commission (now the Federal Energy Regulatory Commission) historically has had broad jurisdiction over interstate transmission and sales.[6] Its specific responsibility has been to ensure rates that are "just and reasonable" and "nondiscriminatory."

Much important regulation of electricity and gas, however, takes place at more localized levels. State utilities commissions typically rule on company requests for rate and service changes. The criteria for pricing public utility services are the sub-

---

[4] 94 U.S. 113 (1877).

[5] Innovation has loosened the restraints substantially, however. Dramatic increases in the number of television broadcasters, via both UHF and cable, have already occurred.

[6] Its role has eroded, however, with recent moves toward "deregulation." Under the Natural Gas Policy Act of 1978, price regulation at the wellhead will be fully phased out no later than the mid-1980s.

ject of a vast literature that we shall not attempt to survey.[7] A few of the important aspects of pricing decisions, however, deserve some attention.

A landmark Supreme Court decision, *Smyth* v. *Ames,*[8] set forth the general principle upon which utilities rates were to be set. Regulated companies are entitled to a "fair return" on a "fair value" of their property (capital assets, commonly termed the **rate base**). The problems that this rather vague language posed for public agencies should not be difficult to imagine. The meaning of a fair return is in the eye of the beholder; the buyer and the seller of a service are unlikely to define it the same way. Yet the regulatory commission must decide, without much objective guidance from the Court.

Valuation of the rate base, company assets, is equally troublesome. The Supreme Court directed that among the factors to be considered are "the original cost of construction, the amount expended in permanent improvements, the amount and market value of its bonds and stock, the present as compared with the original cost of construction, the probable earning capacity of the property . . . and the sum required to meet operating expenses. . . ."[9] In practice, rate base valuation has narrowed this menu, focusing mainly on original cost of assets (including improvements) and on current value or reproduction cost. Plainly, however, the commissions have substantial leeway; and consideration of appropriate valuation methods can easily become a morass.

The Court's rather ill-defined suggestions for rate base valuation were in a sense simplified by a 1944 decision, *Federal Power Commission* v. *Hope Natural Gas Co.*[10] The Commission had ordered Hope to reduce its rates on interstate shipments of gas so as to cut its operating revenues by about $3.6 million annually. Hope won reversal of the order in a circuit court, by arguing in part that the Commission's calculation of its rate base was faulty. The FPC had estimated an "actual legitimate cost" base of $33.7 million, whereas Hope contended that a properly calculated estimate (based on "fair value") would have been about $66 million.

The Supreme Court, restoring the Commission's order, held that rate making is not tied to "any single formula or combination of formulae." Under the law, "it is the result reached, not the method employed which is controlling." Regulatory agencies therefore need not agonize too much over methods of asset valuation. The test of an order is whether, taken as a whole, it implies a "just and reasonable" impact on the market. This decision served to shift somewhat the focus of regulatory considerations from definition of the rate base—most state agencies now use original cost estimates—to analysis of the appropriate rate of return.

---

[7]For extended discussions and evalaution, see William G. Shepherd and Clair Wilcox, *Public Policies Toward Business* (Homewood, Ill.: R. D. Irwin, 6th ed., 1979); and Paul W. MacAvoy, *The Regulated Industries and the Economy* (New York: W. W. Norton, 1979).

[8]169 U.S. 466 (1898).

[9]Ibid., pp. 546–547.

[10]320 U.S. 591 (1944).

The task of public utilities commissions may be viewed as finding values for the following equations:

$$ROR = \frac{TR - TC}{K} \tag{1}$$

or

$$TR = TC + ROR(K) \tag{2}$$

where ROR is the (regulated) rate of return, TR is the total revenue of the regulated company ($=\Sigma p_i q_i$ for a company suppling i services), TC is the total costs of the company (including costs of inputs, depreciation, and taxes), and K is the value of company assets, the rate base, usually defined as original cost minus accrued depreciation.

In reaching a decision, the agency must define both K (the rate base) and the appropriate ROR on that base. TC data are provided by the regulated company and are scrutinized by the agency. Once these values are determined, the commission must set the rates, that is, the p_i, that yield the ''correct'' TR. The correct TR is simply the revenue that satisfies the equations by permitting return ROR to be earned on base K.[11]

Once a method of defining K is adopted, the key question becomes: what is the appropriate ROR? In principle, the answer is straightforward. It is whatever rate permits the regulated firm to attract the efficient level of new capital investment for its activities. The company confronts some cost of capital. It must, in other words, provide a return sufficient to induce investors to buy the company's stocks and bonds, that is, to supply the funds necessary to the firm's investment activities. In a real sense, the job of the regulatory commission is to define the rate of return that permits a company to meet its cost of capital.[12]

In practice, this ROR can be empirically difficult to define. Some commissions attempt to measure the cost of capital directly, but there are elusive elements. It is new investors, not old ones, who define the pertinent ROR; what they may require as an inducement to invest in the future cannot be known with precision. The cost of raising capital via equity (common stock) sales also poses a problem for regulators. Purchasers of shares in effect buy a gamble. Neither the future price of the stock nor the dividends it will receive are assured. As a result, the ''cost'', or necessary return, associated with this component of capital is difficult to pin down.[13]

---

[11] Notice that a particular value of TR can result from different combinations of ROR and K.

[12] If ROR is much *above* this level, the firm will perform as a monopolist—it will price too high, and underinvestment will occur. If, on the other hand, ROR is too low, we encounter the opposite problem: low prices will swell demand for the company's services, and excessive investment will be necessary to meet these demands (the company, however, may have considerable trouble financing such investment).

[13] Nor can the problem really be finessed by looking at the returns to comparable investments elsewhere. Which investments are in fact comparable to the one in question is itself subject to debate; historic data are, once again, not a certain guide to the future.

Arguments about the correct *ROR* are thus virtually inevitable. Yet the stakes are high. An apparently small variation in the regulated return can have a very substantial impact on the fortunes of affected companies and their customers.

As if the practical problems were not enough, there is also some conceptual difficulty confronting the regulatory agencies. This is sometimes described in terms of "circularities." In broad terms, the agency is attempting to discover the *ROR* that is appropriate or efficient in light of a regulated firm's environment. Yet that environment is heavily influenced by the policies of the agency. A utilities regulator might thus find himself in the following sort of conundrum.

I must define the ROR *that will permit a company to raise necessary capital in view of its risk characteristics, as perceived by investors. But the perception of risk characteristics will be determined in part by what I permit the company to do, including perhaps the* ROR *that I define!*

While the situation is not hopeless, there is some element of chasing one's own tail in the rate of return problem.

The Deregulation Trend.   Public regulatory activities have long received mixed reviews (or worse). Part of the reason is implicit in the discussion above. The task of regulation is difficult. Few clear guideposts exist, and almost any decision contains an arbitrary element. When we attempt to substitute the judgment of a committee for the forces of market competition, failures are simply unavoidable (even if our committed members are superbly qualified for their jobs!).

In recent years, dissatisfaction with regulatory efforts has grown. As early as the mid-1970s there was something of a political consensus that direct government regulation had gone too far; some serious deregulation policies took shape in the Ford administration.

The dissatisfaction was in part political, but was aided substantially by economic arguments. Some observers have for many years believed in a "capture theory" of regulation, which contends that regulated firms and industries typically control the regulatory apparatus. They may, in fact, seek regulation as a means of suppressing competition. The textbook principles of the system are thereby turned on their head. The "regulated" enterprises call the tune, while the "regulators" (in effect captured) act to protect the interests of those they are supposed to restrain.[14]

This "theory" is not very precise and has numerous variants; yet casual observation suggests some claim to validity. A common version of the theory focuses on the type of person appointed to the regulatory commissions. If we wish to regulate industry X, we need experts to serve as commissioners. Where will we find them? The answer is obvious: most of the experts work in industry X. Such people may be highly qualified, but their sympathies might well be inconsistent with tough regulation of their former colleagues. Furthermore, regulatory appointments do not last

---

[14]For a relevant discussion, see George J. Stigler, "The Theory of Economic Regulation," *Bell Journal of Economics and Management Science,* **2** (Spring 1971), 3–21.

forever. At least some commissioners may hope to return to the industry when their days in public service end. Stepping on the toes of industry executives while one attempts to regulate them is unlikely to be the best reentry strategy!

Another source of dissatisfaction with public regulation concerns the incentives that the regulatory system creates for its constituent firms. One particular problem, known as the Averch–Johnson effect, traces to the fact that the earnings of regulated firms are tied to their capital asset base.[15] If the permitted rate of return is above the cost of capital but below the monopoly level, a reasonable supposition, this aspect of rate setting creates a wasteful bias in favor of capital expansion.

The argument, in rough form, is straightforward. The regulated firm uses various inputs to produce its services: labor, materials such as fuel, and capital equipment. Every dollar of labor and materials purchased by the company costs a full dollar. But when the firm buys another dollar of capital, this input enters the rate base. If the firm is permitted to earn 10 percent on its rate base, a dollar's worth of capital will boost profits by 10 cents; the capital in a sense costs the firm only 90 cents. What the rate making system does, then, is artificially to lower the price of capital vis-à-vis other factors of production. The result is likely to be an expansion of capital by the firm, not because such expansion is technically efficient, but because of this price distortion. The Averch–Johnson effect is thus a source of inefficiency in regulated firms, although its quantitative impact may not be consistently large.[16]

A more general problem of incentives originates in the "cost-plus" nature of public utility pricing. As seen in equation (2) above, regulated pricing permits the firm to earn a return to capital above and beyond all operating expenses; prices are set so as to cover all costs including the "fair" rate of return. In principle, one might argue that the regulated *ROR* should be a maximum, or ceiling, rate; in practice, however, it may well be regarded by both the firm and the commission as a guarantee—a fair rate to which the firm is entitled.

If this is the case, the incentives of company management to operate efficiently may be greatly weakened. Suppose the firm acts wastefully, thereby raising its costs. The company's profit rate is now likely to fall, but at this point the firm may make the following argument to its regulatory agency.

Our profits have fallen below the fair rate of return that you have defined; you should therefore permit us to raise prices (rates) until we get back to the ROR *we are entitled to enjoy.*

If the agency agrees—as it is likely to do unless it monitors company costs with great vigilance—the regulated company may escape much of the cost of its own inefficiency. The waste is real, but the burden is borne largely by consumers of the firm's services.

---

[15] Harvey Averch and Leland L. Johnson, "Behavior of the Firm Under Regulatory Constraint," *American Economic Review*, **52** (December 1962), 1052–1069.

[16] See William J. Baumol and Alvin K. Klevorick, "Input Choices and Rate-of-Return Regulation: An Overview of the Discussion," *Bell Journal of Economics and Management Science*, **1** (Autumn 1970), 162–190.

The arguments for reducing government regulation are both plausible and abundant, but whether the trend toward deregulation will produce major economic benefits is not yet known. In at least one instance, airlines, in which significant deregulation began in 1978, there is some positive evidence. Theodore E. Keeler reports that air fares for major routes were considerably lower in 1980 than they would have been had strict regulation continued.[17] This salutory effect, moreover, did not appear to be accompanied by any general deterioration in service to low-density routes (those that serve small, sometimes out-of-the-way areas).

Antitrust Issues. In the public utilities sector, the regulatory system is intended to substitute for the competition that is foregone when government sanctions the monopolistic position of utility companies. In these circumstances certain kinds of antitrust issues common to other industries tend not to arise. We would not expect, for example, that a power company holding a regulated monopoly would be challenged under the Sherman Act for monpolizing its market. Such a challenge would be inconsistent with the very purpose of regulation, and would in effect use one governmental policy to attack another.

Similarly, it would not be expected that the rates charged by regulated companies would come under close antitrust scrutiny, although their reasonableness can be questioned within the regulatory apparatus itself. The pricing decisions of the companies are controlled by the system in the form of the appropriate commission. When controls are ineffective, there exist a number of avenues of remedy; but, again, it would make little sense to attack regulated companies for pricing in ways that the system of regulation sanctions.

Public utility regulation thus serves to limit somewhat the range of antitrust challenges likely to arise in affected industries. But it does not eliminate them entirely. One issue that has received substantial attention throughout the regulated sector for many years is merger. The regulatory commissions typically have the responsibility to pass on merger proposals. When an application for merger is disapproved, that is generally the end of the matter; but not infrequently, applications that have been approved by a commission are challenged in the courts.[18] Such challenges may arise on the rather technical point that a particular commission did not have jurisdiction over the merger in question; this is sometimes the case, for example, if the merger is effected through stock acquisition. A more basic question is raised, however, when the courts are asked to consider a merger on its merits. The question then is: what are the proper criteria—and particularly, what weight is to be given to competition—in passing on a merger that involves regulated companies?

We have already seen a major acquisition, that of Pacific Northwest by the El Paso Natural Gas Company, struck down by the Supreme Court. This merger had

---

[17]"The Revolution in Airline Regulation," in Leonard W. Weiss and Michael W. Class (Eds.), *Case Studies in Regulation: Revolution and Reform* (Boston: Little, Brown, 1981), pp. 53–83.

[18]Public utilities rates also have been challenged by private groups in the courts. Here the question ordinarily concerns a commission's judgment in defining a "fair" rate of return or an appropriate rate base, not an antitrust issue.

previously been approved by the Federal Power Commission, but the Court ruled in 1962 that the Commission had no authority to pass on acquisitions currently being challenged under the antitrust laws.[19] In considering the merger on its merits, however, the Supreme Court applied the standards of Section 7 of the Clayton Act,[20] and stated in effect that the consolidation of two regulated natural gas companies was to be judged by its probable impact on competition; that is, the test of the merger was to be no different than the test of any other corporate merger under the antitrust laws.

The Court has not always gone so far. In *McLean Trucking Co.* v. *United States,*[21] a case involving a merger of motor carriers, the Court held that the Interstate Commerce Commission has the power to approve a merger that might otherwise violate the antitrust laws. According to the Court, the Commission could not ignore antitrust considerations in its decisions, but neither could it be required to apply antitrust standards to mergers of common carriers. The Commission's task is to further the goals of national transporation policy, such as an adequate and efficient system that imposes reasonable and nondiscriminatory charges. The attainment of these goals, the Court noted, is related to competitive factors. For this reason, the ICC must take such factors into account in judging the desirability of mergers. The special aspect of the transportation industries, however, is the public interest in something more than "competition." It would be unsatisfactory to have an inefficient system of transportation, for example, even if the industry were highly "competitive" under some accepted definitions. Therefore, the Commission must consider other factors as well; and it may decide that a merger that reduces competition is, on balance, permissible.

The *McLean* doctrine was more recently reaffirmed by the Supreme Court in *Seaboard Air Line R. Co.* v. *United States,*[22] albeit in a somewhat different context. Here a merger of two railroad lines was approved by the ICC despite apparent anticompetitive implications. The Court, in remanding the case, insisted that the Commission demonstrate rigorously the public benefit of a merger that reduces competition. However, the Court held, an adequate demonstration could insulate the merger despite the competitive problem.

The issues raised in these cases suggest some problems that commonly arise in attempting to reconcile antitrust and regulatory objectives. As we shall see, the Supreme Court has held consistently that immunity from the antitrust laws is not to be lightly implied. The fact that a company's activities are publicly regulated may protect it from certain kinds of attack under the antitrust laws, but will not ordinarily provide a broad shield against all manner of prosecution.

---

[19]*California* v. *Federal Power Commission,* 369 U.S. 482 (1962).

[20]*United States* v. *El Paso Natural Gas Co.,* 376 U.S. 651 (1964).

[21]321 U.S. 67 (1944).

[22]382 U.S. 154 (1965).

Financial Institutions

Public regulation extends to areas in which the traditional utilities rationales for controls are absent. In commercial banking, insurance, and the securities markets, two broad reasons for regulation are of major historic importance.

1. Many consumers are ignorant about the nature of the commodities they purchase in these markets, and are therefore vulnerable to fraudulent, manipulative, or simply unsound practices. A need for consumer protection thus exists.
2. The consequences of poor market performance are potentially severe in these markets, and raise implications for the national economy as well.

Although the need for financial market regulation may be "as strong" as it is in, say, electric power, the type of regulation that has evolved is rather different. It is directed primarily toward the prevention of business practices that would mislead the consuming public or endanger the solvency of established firms, thereby threatening the stability of the markets.

Banking.   Nowhere have the consequences of widespread business failure been so dramatically demonstrated as in the commercial banking industry. During the 1920s and early 1930s some 8000 banks failed, inflicting tremendous financial losses on depositors. The traumatic effects of these failures led directly to a system of rigorous and continuous scrutiny of banking operations. Three federal agencies—the Federal Reserve System, the Comptroller of the Currency, and the Federal Deposit Insurance Corporation—exert broad controls over many banks; those that do not fall within the purview of these agencies are subject to regulation by the states in which they are chartered.

Although some moves toward more lenient banking regulation have occurred in recent years, there is no question as to the thoroughness of the regulatory system. Minimum bank reserves are specified, loan quantities are indirectly controlled, maximum interest rates on deposits are prescribed, and the banks are subject to independent audit and to unannounced examination. In addition, the structure of the industry is regulated by restrictions on branch banking and the necessity for approval of merger applications. Few persons would doubt that current conditions and safety differ vastly from those that prevailed in 1933.

As was the case with public utilities industries, antitrust issues in banking have arisen within limited areas. Although controls over the rates and services provided by banks is not so pervasive as that exercised by some utilities commissions, there has been little antitrust challenge to the day-to-day operations of the industry. Many of the major questions have, rather, arisen in connection with mergers. As we saw earlier, it was not until the Supreme Court decision in *Philadelphia National Bank*[23] that bank mergers were known to be vulnerable to Section 7 of the Clayton Act.

[23] *United States* v. *Philadelphia National Bank,* 374, U.S. 321 (1963).

In this case the merging banks argued that bank acquisitions fell within the scope of the Bank Merger Act of 1960 rather than Section 7. Under this Act, the bank regulatory agencies were required to consider competitive factors in passing on merger applications. The defense position was that this requirement effectively immunized bank mergers from antitrust prosecution; and that the agencies could approve mergers that might otherwise violate Section 7, much as the ICC had done in *McLean*.

The Supreme Court rejected this argument, citing its earlier statement that "immunity from the antitrust laws is not lightly implied." There was nothing in the language or history of Section 7, said the Court, that indicated congressional desire to exempt the banking industry from its provisions. Further, the Bank Merger Act conferred no "express immunity." Said the Court:

Repeals of the antitrust laws by implication from a regulatory statute are strongly disfavored, and have only been found in cases of plain repugnancy between the antitrust and regulatory provisions. . . .[24]

If the Court was unwilling to find an implied exemption in existing law, it might yet have concluded that there was a "repugnant" relationship between antitrust and regulation in banking, and gone on to reconcile the conflict in favor of the regulatory agencies. Here, however, the Court stated:

The fact that the banking agencies maintain a close surveillance of the industry with a view toward preventing unsound practices that might impair liquidity or lead to insolvency does not make federal banking regulation all-pervasive, although it does minimize the hazards of intense competition.[25]

At this point the Supreme Court was touching upon the primary question in many similar cases: is the regulatory apparatus of an industry so complete that competition has literally no role to play? The Court's negative answer in this instance was unambiguous.

After the *Philadelphia National Bank* decision, Congress passed the 1966 Bank Merger Act, providing explicitly that the regulatory agencies may approve a merger if it can be shown that adverse competitive effects are outweighed by the "convenience and needs" of the community affected.[26] The Supreme Court, however, has continued to hold that bank mergers fall within the antitrust laws, and has interpreted the 1966 Act to mean that the banking commissions are to make findings tha may then become subject to independent judicial review. This position is plausible. The authority granted to the Justice Department to challenge mergers suggests that independent review was intended by Congress.

---

[24] Ibid., pp. 350–351.

[25] Ibid., p. 352

[26] Section 5(B) of the Act states that an agency shall not approve any merger "unless it finds that the anticompetitive effects are clearly outweighed in the public interest by the probable effect of the transaction in meeting the convenience and needs of the community to be served." The Act also provides that the Department of Justice may challenge any approved acquisition within 30 days of its approval.

The dilemma in banking, as in other industries, is that competition is at once desirable and feared. Competitive conditions will encourage efficient performance, yet "too much" competition raises the specter of bank failure, an event still viewed with great public unease. In these circumstances, the appropriate policy balance is difficult to define and is still evolving.

Securities. The stock market collapse of 1929 disclosed the remarkable extent of unsound and deceptive practices common in securities trading. It became clear that the investing public was in need of comprehensive protection, and the behavior of securities dealers and companies seeking to market their shares has been closely regulated in the period since the great crash. Public concern over the operation of the market is related to the possibility of severe financial damage to those who lose their savings; however, this concern goes beyond sympathy for specific individuals. The securities markets serve a vital capital-raising function for private corporations, which could be impaired if public confidence in the markets were dissipated. Moreover, brokerage houses act in a fashion somewhat akin to commercial banks and savings institutions. They often hold the portfolios of investors, much as the banks hold the deposits of their customers. Accordingly, concern for the failure of investment houses is acute.

Unlike some other regulated industries, the antitrust issues in securities trading have not focused mainly on mergers. This may be because of the relatively atomistic structure of the industry, although some recent mergers could significantly alter the concentration of market shares. The issues that have been raised recently concern, rather, the rules and behavior of organizations such as the New York Stock Exchange.[27] The major exchanges are subject to control by the Securities and Exchange Commission. If the Commission finds that an exchange does not have rules that are "just and adequate to insure fair dealing and to protect investors," it may revoke the registration of that exchange.

The broad task of the SEC is to protect securities purchasers, not only through regulation of trading but via requirements for detailed disclosure of financial information by firms seeking to raise money capital. The commission has by most standards succeeded quite well, but it has not acted as a pervasive regulator of day-to-day activities in securities markets.

Conflicts between securities regulation and antitrust parallel those in commercial banking. Intense competition raises the specter of business failure, which is in turn regarded as a socially costly event. Some limitations to competition are therefore accepted, but the difficult question is how far to go. Reducing the risk of corporate failure may be a sound public policy in certain industries, but it does not follow that all vestiges of competition must be sacrificed in order to achieve a reasonable level of safety.

---

[27]The Department of Justice did bring suit in 1947 against 17 investment banking firms, charging that the common practice of syndicating (joint underwriting) new issues violated the Sherman Act. These charges were dismissed in *United States* v. *Morgan*, 11B F Supp. 621 (S.D. N.Y., 1953), and no similar challenges have occurred since then.

The conflict in securities is also tied to the heavy reliance on voluntary self-regulation that has characterized the markets since the 1930s. It would be virtually impossible for an agency such as the SEC to regulate the behavior of all firms and their employees in a completely effective way. Accordingly, much of the responsibility for regulating behavior has been undertaken by private organizations such as the stock exchanges and associations of securities dealers. This type of control may be effective, but it implies, in the words of the SEC itself, " 'private' formulation of restrictive standards of business conduct and their enforcement by, at the very least, exclusionary practices."[28] It is much as if an industry trade association were given unlimited power to determine and enforce comprehensive rules of behavior for members. This may be an effective way of securing adherence to the desired code; but it will, almost inevitably, imply the kind of concerted behavior that would normally violate the antitrust laws. The key question—as yet unanswered—is when and to what extent such behavior is truly necessary to ensure safe and stable markets.

Insurance.   The insurance industry is regulated at the state level to perhaps a greater degree than any other area within the government "controlled" sector. Like banking, a primary purpose of regulation is to ensure the financial soundness of companies; like securities, another significant purpose is to prevent fraudulent and misleading practices. The insurance industry had long been thought to be exempt from the antitrtust laws because of an 1869 court decision that insurance is intrastate rather than interstate commerce.[29] This view was overturned in 1944,[30] and the industry responded in 1945 by securing passage of the McCarren–Ferguson Act, exempting rate-making agreements in insurance from antitrust prosecution for 3 years. Following this period, the antitrust laws would again apply; yet the insurance industry has been relatively free from conflict between public regulation and competition policies.

The reasons for this freedom are curious. Although the formalities of state regulation exist everywhere, actual regulation of insurance firms tends to be less than severe (and is in some states close to nonexistent). Insurance markets are often structurally competitive, with large numbers of rivals and low barriers to entry. In this setting, the regulatory mechanism, which permits concerted rate making, may be little more than a device by which companies limit price competition. Some writers in fact suggest that the insurance industry is a prime candidate for deregulation.[31]

---

[28] *Report of Special Study of Securities Markets of the Securities Exchange Commission* (Washington, D.C.: U.S. Government Printing Office, 1963), Part 4, p. 502.

[29] *Paul* v. *Virginia*, 8 Wall 168 (1869).

[30] *U.S.* v. *South-Eastern Underwritiers Assn.*, 322 U.S. 533 (1944).

[31] For pertinent arguments and evidence, see Paul L. Joskow, "Cartels, Competition, and Regulation in the Property-Liability Insurance Industry," *Bell Journal of Economics and Management Science,* **4** (Autumn 1973), 375–427; Richard A. Ippolito, "The Effect of Price Regulation in the Automobile Insurance Industry," *Journal of Law and Economics,* **22** (April 1979), 55–89; and H. E. Frech III and Joseph C. Samprone, Jr., "The Welfare Loss of Excessive Nonprice Competition: The Case of Property-Liability Insurance Regulation," *Journal of Law and Economics,* **23** (October 1980), 429–440.

The Learned Professions

The notion of a "profesional," as opposed to someone who merely holds a job, is not entirely clear-cut. Yet the so-called learned professions—medicine, law, accounting, social work, teaching—do have two common elements: (1) practitioners are licensed by the state following tests of qualifications; and (2) there is a public service aspect to their work; many professionals act as agents whose job is presumably to maximize the welfare of others: patients, clients, students.[32]

The status of the learned professions is a genuine curiosity in modern antitrust law. Not surprisingly, professional associations have argued that they are exempt from antitrust prosecution, usually on the grounds that a profession is not part of "trade or commerce," and is therefore beyond the scope of the Sherman Act. This position is plausible in some instances. For example, the associations typically adopt codes of ethics governing their practices that might, in a different setting, be attacked as collusive agreements.

As we shall see, the courts have recently adopted a more stringent view of what professional groups are permitted to do. Some codes of ethics are now being challenged, and agreements that suggest price (or fee) fixing are highly suspect.

THE REGULATED SECTOR: ANTITRUST STATUS

The antitrust status of regulated industries is difficult to characterize, in part because developments move rapidly. The issues are increasingly important, however, and bear some attention.

In *Parker* v. *Brown*[33] the Supreme Court was obliged to determine the legality of a raisin marketing program mandated by the State of California (Parker was the state's agriculture director). Brown, a packer of raisins, sought to enjoin Parker from enforcing the program, which was clearly anticompetitive (it included price fixing among other restrictions). The Court upheld the program on narrow grounds. The Sherman Act, said Chief Justice Stone, regulates private practices but "makes no mention of the state. . . ." At issue here was action undertaken at the "legislative command" of California. The state "adopts the program and enforces it. . . ." Thus an exemption was created for "state action" whose anticompetitive character would have rendered it illegal if undertaken privately.

In *California Retail Liquor Dealers Ass'n.* v. *Midcal Aluminum, Inc.,*[34] the Supreme Court placed limits on this exemption. A California statutory plan permitted wine producers to "fair trade" their products, that is, to specify minimum resale prices. Midcal, a wholesaler, sold wine for less than a producer's specified price, and also sold wines for which no fair trade schedule had been filed. Both actions allegedly violated the California plan. The legal issue raised was whether the plan,

---

[32]This is plainly a different definition of professional than that applied to, say, the "professional ballplayer." A professional in the latter sense is simply one who is paid rather than who works out of love for the job (the amateur).

[33]338 U.S. 341 (1943).

[34]445 U.S. 97 (1980).

clearly a Sherman Act violation if created privately, was protected by the "state action" exemption.

The Supreme Court held that the exemption did not apply. Justice Powell distinguished the situation from that of *Parker*. In the earlier case, he noted, the state established, adopted and enforced the program, exerting "extensive official oversight." Here, however, the state did not actively supervise the fair trade plan; it neither established prices nor reviewed the reasonableness of prices set by producers. The plan simply authorized producers to fix prices vertically in any way they might choose. In the absence of active supervision by the state, the plan could not enjoy a "state action" exemption.

The issue of antitrust immunity for an electric utility company was raised in *Otter Tail Power Co.* v. *United States*[35]. Otter Tail served communities in the upper Midwest. Upon expiration of their franchise agreements, several communities tried to establish their own municipal distribution systems rather than renewing with Otter Tail. The company refused to sell them power at wholesale or to "wheel" (transfer) power to such systems, making it impossible for the municipal efforts to succeed.

Responding to charges under Section 2 of the Sherman Act, Otter Tail claimed that the Federal Power Act, under which the company was regulated, immunized it from antitrust attack. The Supreme Court disagreed. Nothing in the legislative history of the Act, said Justice Douglas, "reveals a purpose to insulate the electric power companies from . . . antitrust." And it was ". . . abundantly clear that Otter Tail used its monopoly power in the towns in its service area to foreclose competition" in violation of the law.

The Supreme Court again rejected a utilities company argument for antitrust immunity in *Cantor* v. *Detroit Edison*.[36] The company had long followed a program of distributing light bulbs to many of its electricity customers without extra charge. This practice had been approved by the state Public Service Commission, and could not have been discontinued without that Commission's permission. Quite clearly, this program was in the nature of a tie-in sale that would likely have run afoul of the Sherman Act in a purely private setting. Detroit Edison was using a monopoly position in electricity to establish itself as a supplier of light bulbs.

The company's argument was simple and reminiscent of most earlier cases: it was a "pervasively" regulated utility, and was here following a practice explicitly approved by its regulatory agency; indeed, the company could not legally discontinue the light-bulb program without PSC action. Therefore, it should be exempt from antitrust attack. The Supreme Court agreed that Detroit Edison was subject to pervasive regulation, but refused to conclude that antitrust exemption is implied in such circumstances. Justice Stevens cited three counterarguments.

[35] 410 U.S. 366 (1973).

[36] 428 U.S. 579 (1976).

1. Private conduct, even if regulated by the state, need not be inconsistent with antitrust standards.
2. Where such conduct **is** inconsistent, the conflict must not inevitably be resolved against the antitrust interest.
3. Even if Congress wanted the antitrust interest subordinated in a regulated industry, such subordination would not extend to an unregulated industry such as light bulbs.

Regulation might provide a shield against the Sherman Act, but only where a strong and specific showing of need could be made. In some instances, said Justice Stevens, "the very purpose of . . . government control is to avoid the consequences of unrestrained competition. . . ." But where that is not the case, the Court will not find that regulation implies antitrust immunity. The Detroit Edison program, although publicly sanctioned, was not "necessary to make the regulatory act work," and was therfore not permissible.

In *Goldfarb et ux.* v. *Virginia State Bar et al.*,[37] the central issue was the antitrust status of a learned profession—the law. The Fairfax County Bar Association published a list of minimum fees for common legal services. The list was apparently an effective price-fixing device, for when a couple (the Goldfarbs) sought a title search, 19 county lawyers quoted them prices at or above the published minimum. The Virginia State Bar, although claiming that the list was only "advisory," acted as an informal enforcer of its terms.

A district court concluded that the fee schedule violated the Sherman Act, but was reversed on appeal. The circuit court agreed that the fee schedule was anticompetitive, but held that the profession of law is not "trade or commerce," and therefore is not vulnerable to Sherman Act prosecution.

The Supreme Court reinstated the district court judgment, citing its repeated "heavy presumption" against implied immunity from antitrust. Chief Justice Burger noted that a state might decide that ordinary forms of competition are "inappropriate" for a particular profession. But it had not done so here. Nothing in Virginia law or legislative history suggested that the state had intended to immunize the legal profession from antitrust enforcement. The authority of the state to regulate its professions stands undiminished, said the Chief Justice. But such authority does not permit price fixing in the absence of any intention or need by the state to do so.

The present antitrust status of the regulated sector thus appears to be reasonably clear. Exemptions will be implied at times, but a strong and specific showing of need is required. To argue that the existence of "public regulation" implies broad permission for anticompetitive practices, will not suffice; only where a particular practice is necessary for the regulation to work, will it likely be immunized. The impact of this doctrine may be felt most heavily in professions such as law, medicine, and accounting, where antitrust enforcement until very recently has been almost nonexistent.

[37] 421 U.S. 773 (1975).

SPECIAL CASES OF EXEMPTION

Labor Unions

One of the clearest departures from the procompetitive orientation of the antitrust laws occurs in the treatment of labor unions. Section 6 of the Clayton Act provides the following specific exemption.

. . . *Nothing contained in the antitrust laws shall be construed to forbid the existence and operation of labor, agricultural, or horticultural organizations, instituted for the purposes of mutual help . . . or to forbid or restrain individual members of such organizations from carrying out the legitimate objects thereof; nor shall such organizations, or members thereof, be held or construed to be illegal combinations or conspiracies in restraint of trade under the antitrust laws.*

Yet, as E.S. Mason has put it,

Whether labor unions are monopolies is a question hardly worth considering. Whatever else a union is, it is certainly an agreement among workers not to compete for jobs.[38]

Labor unions are, in Clayton Act terminology, "mutual help" organizations designed to secure desirable and improved working conditions for members. The monopoly aspect of the union lies in the agreement of members to bargain as a single group rather than as individuals. Members do not compete with each other for jobs, but band together to secure the best available terms for all. If a union sets a $10.00-per-hour wage for its members, those workers who might be willing to take less are foreclosed from offering their services at the lower rate. Union members are thus enabled to engage in a form of price fixing without running afoul of antitrust prohibitions. Certainly such cooperative efforts alter the competive situation of labor markets. Employers must negotiate with large groups of employees who often possess, in the aggregate, the power to shut down the employing company by means of a strike.

The rationale for the union exemption may never have had much to do with the Clayton Act assertion "that the labor of a human being is not a commodity or article of commerce." Indeed, the early motivation for allowing such organizations seems to have sprung from the belief that large employers could inevitably exploit their workers. The bargaining situation prior to unions was seen as a highly uneven one in which large business firms could offer terms to workers on a take-it-or-leave-it basis. Actually, the uneven bargaining problem does not arise unless firms are large relative to their labor market (i.e., they possess monopsony power). In competitive circumstances employers would compete for labor, and workers would gravitate toward firms making the best offers. The more general problem, however, is that labor mobility is limited; there are costs to switching jobs, and a switch that involves a geographic change may be especially difficult. Accordingly, workers might be

[38] "Labor Monopoly and All That," *Economic Concentration and the Monopoly Problem* (Cambridge: Harvard University Press, 1957), p. 196.

exploited not because their employers were somehow "bigger" than they were, but rather because they could not take full advantage of the variety of offers that might be available.

Whatever the original merits of the exploitation argument, labor market conditions today are vastly different from what they were 60 or 70 years ago. The labor force is now protected by a network of legislation encompassing health and safety conditions, restrictions on child labor, and minimum wage levels. One might surmise that unions are no longer needed to protect workers, but it should be noted that while the area of possible exploitation has been reduced, it may not have been eliminated completely.

Although the Clayton Act exemption for labor does not permit the unions to engage legally in any activity, the courts have interpreted it to imply considerable latitude for union behavior. In *Apex Hosiery Co.* v. *Leader,* [39] for example, the Supreme Court ruled that a striking union could seize a company's plant and stop outgoing hosiery shipments without violating the Sherman Act. The Court permitted this clear restraint of trade on the grounds that the restraint was only incidental to the union's legitimate purpose of advancing its own interests. In *United States* v. *Hutcheson,* [40] the Supreme Court upheld the right of a carpenters union to boycott the products of a brewing company that had contracted with machinists for certain dismantling jobs. Once again, the reasoning was that the union was acting in pursuit of a legitimate interest, whatever the attendant restraints upon commerce may have been.

An important limitation to union behavior under the antitrust laws was established by the Court in a 1945 case, *Allen Bradley* v. *Local 3, International Brotherhood of Electrical Workers.* [41] The union, which operated in New York City, had waged "aggressive campaigns" to obtain closed-shop agreements with employing manufacturers. The union then entered agreements with contracting firms that limited these firms to purchase only from manufacturers with whom the union had closed-shop arrangements. The evident purpose of this agreement was to bolster the business of those firms that employed members of Local 3 and had agreed to the closed-shop demands. The Supreme Court noted that the actions in question would violate Sections 1 and 2 of the Sherman Act unless immunized by the participation of the union. Such immunization, however, was not found. Said the Court:

> . . .*we think Congress never intended that unions could, consistently with the Sherman Act, aid non-labor groups to create business monopolies and to control the marketing of goods and services.* [42]

The principle that labor groups may not conspire with non-labor groups to restrain trade was thus clearly established. This is, however, one of the few limits to labor union immunity to antitrust prosecution.

---

[39] 310 U.S. 469 (1940).
[40] 312 U.S. 219 (1941).
[41] 325 U.S. 797 (1945).
[42] Ibid., p. 408.

The exemption for labor unions is highly controversial, and some advocate application of the antitrust laws in this area.[43] Application of the laws could mean many things, however. The Sherman Act might, for example, be invoked against certain restrictive practices that now are protected by the exemption. Alternatively, the Act could be used as a basis of attacking the monopoly power of the unions rather than specific kinds of union behavior.

One's view of the appropriate way of dealing with the unions depends upon whether such organizations are seen to be good or bad. Many economists undoubtedly believe that some curbing of union practices is in order. At the same time, however, there are arguments about the merits of collective bargaining which suggest that the labor union *qua* union ought to be allowed to function. If the view is accepted (and it need not be) that union operations should be restricted, but not in ways that would cripple union effectiveness, a line between legitimate and illegitimate activity must be defined. Union effectiveness often implies restraint of trade, and the identification of those restraints that might be disallowed without doing damage to union interests is not obvious.

Our ability to formulate reasonable antitrust policies toward labor unions is handicapped by an absence of relevant empirical evidence. Despite the great interest economists have taken in these organizations, relatively little is known of their economic effects. It appears, for example, that wage-rate behavior in unionized and nonunionized areas does not differ as much as might be expected; yet we have little idea of what wage rates generally would look like had there never been a trade union movement.[44] Similarly we do not really know what the effects of restricting union activities or power might be. Any effort to apply the antitrust laws more fully implies a trade-off: there would be some gain in restricting restraints of trade and monopolistic pricing practices, but some loss in a weakening of the collective bargaining process. Conceivably the gain would be, great and the loss negligible. But until we have some objective idea of relevant magnitudes, the debate over proper treatment of the unions will proceed on a frequently emotional level.

Professional Sports

Owners of professional sports teams have frequently claimed that they ought to be exempt from antitrust prosecution. Although these claims have not been generally successful—only baseball enjoys true immunity—most major sports have managed to pursue anticompetitive practices that would be astounding in another setting. Primary among these are:

---

[43] For a general discussion of opposition to labor unions, see Neil W. Chamberlain, Donald E. Cullen, and David Lewin, *The Labor Sector* (New York: McGraw-Hill, 3rd ed., 1980), Chapter 3.

[44] For evidence on the wage effects of unions, see H. Gregg Lewis, *Unionism and Relative Wages in the United States* (Chicago: University of Chicago Press, 1963); and Orley Ashenfelter, "Union Relative Wage Effects: New Evidence and a Survey of their Implications for Wage Inflation," in Richard Stone and William Peterson, *Econometric Contributions to Public Policy* (New York: Macmillan, 1978).

1. **The draft system,** under which negotiating rights to free-agent players are assigned to specific teams.
2. **The free agency system,** under which an established player may first "play out his option"[45] in order to become a free agent; and may then find that his current team has the right of first refusal on his services or is entitled to "compensation" if he moves to another team.

Consider just how unusual these practices are. Let us suppose that you are about to graduate from law school, and receive the following letter from the firm of Gander and Ford in Green Bay, Wisconsin:

Congratulations!

Gander and Ford have obtained exclusive negotiating rights to your services in this year's law school draft. We shall send an agent shortly to offer you a contract.

What if you do not care for Gander and Ford, or simply do not like the idea of living in Green Bay, Wisconsin? You do not, of course, have to sign with G&F (it is still a free country!). But if you do not, no other law firm in G&F's "league" will offer you a job. Thus, if the league is an effective monopoly, you will not be able to practice law as a member of an established firm. It may be that by "sitting out" a year (during which you do not practice), you will be able to reenter the draft and hope that you are chosen by a more desirable firm.

Should you, on the other hand, go to work for G&F, you will no doubt join a professional lawyer's union or association. Your union will probably have negotiated an arrangement with the league that permits you to (again) become a free agent after staying with G&F for a specified number of years. At that point, several firms may claim negotiating rights to your services simultaneously; or you may even be free to negotiate with anyone.

If you wish to leave G&F, however, you may still have some problems. G&F may have the (first-refusal) right to retain your services by matching any alternative offer you would like to accept. Moreover, if you go to another firm, your new employer may be forced to compensate G&F by sending them a lawyer of proven ability from their own staff. If this is the case, you may well find that other firms are not so anxious to sign you as they might otherwise be.

Such practices would be ludicrous not only in law, but in virtually any occupation. How then can they exist in professional sports? Consider one reasonably straightforward rationale. A sports league is unlike an ordinary business market in one essential respect: it depends upon a degree of "competitive balance" for success. That is, the league's constituent firms (teams) may prosper *provided* that they are *all* reasonably competent (competitive) in their sport. A team owner or player wants his team to win, just as any business executive or employer wants his company to do well; but the owner or player does not want rival teams to do so poorly

---

[45] Typically by playing one year beyond his contract expiration date, at terms that vary with the sport in question.

that fans (customers) lose interest and stop buying the league's services. The scope of competition is therefore subject to a most unusual limitation.

The argument has been used by professional sports leagues and franchises to justify a draft system in which weaker teams are favored (the common method is that teams draft in reverse order of past season performance—worst goes first, and so forth). Such a procedure presumably works to promote the balance that is needed.[46] It has also been used as a rationale for broad removal of players' bargaining rights, on the empirically weak ground that a free labor market in sports will result in monopolization of talent by the richest teams, that is, destruction of the competitive balance once again.[47]

Interestingly, the bargaining practices unique to professional sports are only partially related to their antitrust status. A complete antitrust exemption for baseball was asserted by the Supreme Court in *Federal Baseball Club of Baltimore* v. *National League*.[48] Baltimore claimed that its (Federal) league had been driven out of existence by the combined efforts of the established National and American leagues, and it sued for damages. The Court, however, held that baseball games are not interstate commerce and thus are not covered by federal antitrust laws. This position has been widely criticized, even ridiculed, in recent years, but the courts have refused to overturn it. They have instead argued narrowly that it is up to Congress to decide whether a long-standing antitrust exemption shall or shall not continue.[49]

The issue of player compensation was addressed by an appellate court in *Mackey* v. *National Football League*.[50] Mackey, a player, challenged the so-called Rozelle Rule under which the League Commissioner ("Pete" Rozelle) was assigned broad compensation powers. A player could "play out his option" as described above, and then negotiate with any other team. The player's original team was entitled to compensation from his new team. If the two could not agree on that compensation, Commissioner Rozelle was authorized to award one or more players or draft picks of the acquiring club to the original club. This authority was not agreed to by the players, but was granted "unilaterally" by the league; and under league rules, a Rozelle compensation decision could not be appealed.

The appellate court agreed with a district court finding that the Rozelle Rule inhibited movement of players, suppressed their salaries, and amounted to a boycott. Judge Lay held for the court that: (1) professional football is subject to the antitrust laws; and (2) the Rozelle Rule is illegal as an unreasonable restraint of trade rather than as a *per se* offense. Having won the legal battle, however, the NFL players

---

[46] Whether it is effective, however, is unclear. See Leonard Koppett *A Thinking Man's Guide to Baseball* (New York: Dutton, 1967). Koppett has argued persuasively here and in his newspaper columns that the draft does little to promote competitive balance in baseball or football.

[47] It also has been suggested that free bargaining will produce more rapid "turnover" of players, thereby weakening fan "loyalties" and interest in sports. The available evidence does not support this view.

[48] 259 U.S. 200 (1922).

[49] The most recent decision is *Flood* v. *Kuhn et al.*, 407 U.S. 258 (1971).

[50] 543 F. 2d 606 (Eighth Cir., 1976).

association later agreed to a system of compensation and first-refusal rights under which movement of free agents has been minimal.

Although the antitrust issue remains controversial, current bargaining practices in professional sports are themselves the subject of negotiation between the leagues and the players associations. Even a "complete" antitrust exemption would not imply that a league can permanently remove all bargaining rights from its players. To attempt to do so—as baseball did under its old "reserve clause"—might escape antitrust prosecution but run afoul of public policies bearing on labor contracts.[51]

THE PATENT EXEMPTION

Certain economic activities are exempt from antitrust prosecution. Strickly speaking, the number of these activities is quite large; it would include, for example, price discrimination undertaken in good faith and tying sales that do not impair competition. Our interest at this point, however, centers on one important area—patents—that might well violate the antitrust laws were it not for the specific circumstances that have motivated exemption.

A patent is in effect a temporary monpooly granted by the government to an inventor. The inventor of an original and significant process, product, or improvement may obtain exclusive rights to his invention for a period of 17 years under present law.[52] During this period the inventor is under no compulsion to utilize his invention in any way. He may put the invention to work or do nothing with it; or he may license others who wish to use the invention, on his terms. The essence of the patent is its exclusivity, for no other person or company may make, use, or sell the patented invention during the period covered, except on terms agreed to by the patent holder.

The patent system may appear inconsistent with the antitrust objective of promoting competition, since one of its effects is to free the patent holder from competitive pressures. However, the two primary reasons for this procedure are actually procompetitive. The first harkens back to the basic economic idea that all activity, invention and innovation included, responds to the prospect of financial gain. Presumably the monopoly reward induces individuals[53] to greater inventive effort, and society is the ultimate beneficiary of improved products and processes. The second reason is to assure that the developers of original inventions will disclose their ideas.

---

[51] Under the reserve clause, baseball claimed that a player's club retained exclusive negotiating rights to him for his full professional career, regardless of when his contract expired. This claim ended in 1975 when Andy Messersmith, a pitcher, played 1 year beyond the expiration of his contract and was declared a free agent by a labor arbitrator. The arbitrator found that the reserve clause in the collective bargaining agreement allows only the 1-year option on a player's services.

[52] Standards of patentability, including an assessment of what is original and significant, are determined by the United States Patent Office.

[53] Patents are granted only to individuals, but are widely utilized by business firms. Commonly, employees work for companies under contracts that require them to transfer to the employing company the right to all inventions patented as a result of their work during the contract.

The patent holder need not do anything with his invention, and this may be a drawback of the system; but in order to obtain the patent he must provide all pertinent information. Society in effect strikes a bargain. In return for exclusive rights it receives information; possibly this information will not be put to use during the term of the patent, but it becomes common property thereafter.

A host of legal problems are associated with the patent system. The Patent Office is understaffed, and standrads of patentability suffer accordingly. Patents may be granted to different individuals for essentially the same product or process simply because the Office cannot adequately check the originality of every application. Patent infringement suits in such instances are common. Additionally, the possibilities for legal harassment are abundant. Patent infringement suits, whether justified or not, are easy to file and expensive to defend. The inventor who is small in terms of financial resources may therefore present a tempting target for an infringement action. For even if the merits of the suit are weak, the inventor might find it desirable to settle ''out of court.''

Apart from this type of problem, patents may be part of broader attempts to establish monopoly positions. Here conflicts with the antitrust laws arise. We have already discussed one case in which a company holding patent rights to salt dispensers attempted to tie in sales of nonpatented salt to its inventions.[54] The Supreme Court refused to allow this practice, but in other instances the rights of the patent holder have been found to be extensive. In a landmark decision, *United States* v. *General Electric Co.*,[55] The Supreme Court ruled that a patent holder may specify the price at which a licensee sells his invention. In fact, the patentor may restrict the terms of a license in virtually any way he desires, specifying not only price but the quantity to be produced.

Very commonly, one company may hold a basic patent on a product or process while another company patents some improvement on the original. In such instances, the basic patent holder may not use the improvement, and the improvement patent holder may not use the basic product or process. Such companies often will engage in **cross licensing,** whereby each is granted the right to utilize the other's patented invention. Frequently, a particular product or process will be covered by a large number of patents held by various companies. Here it is likely that the companies will pool their patents. Each company contributes its invention to the pool and receives the right to utilize the entire pool. Under these more complicated circumstancess, the *General Electric* precedent might seem to permit a comprehensive system of price fixing to exist. The courts, however, have not extended the doctrine in such instances. In *United States* v. *Line Material Co.*,[56] two firms adopted restrictive cross-licensing agreements pertaining to patents on electrical equipment devices. The specific sale price to be charged by sublicensees were fixed in the agreement. The Supreme Court held that such agreements go beyond the

[54]*International Salt Co.* v. *United States,* 332 U.S. 392 (1947).

[55]272 U.S. 476 (1926).

[56]333 U.S. 287 (1947).

rights conferred by patent. A clear conflict between competition and patent rights was thus resolved in favor of competition.

The use of patents and licenses to form a cartel also has been restricted by the Court. In a 1945 case, *Hartford Empire Co. v. United States,* [57] a group of glassware manufacturers had established a pool of several hundred patents pertaining to glassware manufacturing machinery. The group had formulated extensive cross-licensing agreements that had the effect of allocating particular portions of glassware manufacturing activities to particular companies. As the Supreme Court observed,

> . . . *control was exercised to allot production in Corning's field to Corning, and that in other restricted classes within the general container field of Owens, Hazel, Thatcher, Ball, and such other smaller manufacturers as the group agreed should be licensed. The result was that 94% of the glass containers manufactured in this country on feeders and formers were made on machinery licensed under the pooled patents.*[58]

The Court held that the formation of the patent pool and elaborate cross licensing agreements had been employed to discourage invention of glass-making machinery and to suppress competition in the manufacture of unpatented glassware. The arrangement had effectively divided the market and set the prices of various glass containers. In so doing, it had established powers that were beyond those conferred by the patents themselves.

A difficult and persistent problem arises when an individual company attempts to establish a monopoly market position by accumulating patents. In *Kobe, Inc., v. Dempsey Pump Co.,*[59] a circuit court held that a company cannot buy up all the patents in an area as a means of monpolizing the industry. At the same time, however, mere possession of many patents has never been found to violate the law.[60] The company that develops numerous inventions and as a result monpolizes an industry presents a thorny problem. To limit the company's monopoly position would seem to abridge patent rights; but to uphold the position is to pay a potentially large competitive price for new inventions.

Important problems in patent policy remain unresolved. In part, these problems relate to the fact that there is an anticompetitive element in the patent grant. The accumulation of patents by an initially powerful firm or group may imply great market control; and whereas the courts have said that accumulation alone does not violate the law, there is a question as to whether society may not be giving up more than is necessary in such instances, to induce invention and innovation.

Significant problems also are raised by the behavior of patent holders. Patentees may license their inventions, and there is little question that they have a right to

---

[57] 323 U.S. 386 (1945).

[58] Ibid., p. 400.

[59] 198 F. 2d 416 (1952).

[60] See, specifically, *Automatic Radio Mfg. Co. v. Hazeltine Research Inc.,* 339 U.S. 827 (1950).

impose restrictions that could have been accomplished by refusing to license in the first place. The difficulty is that licensing restrictions may go beyond this reasonable right. Cross-licensing arrangements present particular problems, for whereas they may serve a socially useful purpose—to permit the use of complementary inventions in conjunction with one another—they may also be employed as a vehicle for cartelization. In extreme instances such as *Hartford Empire,* it may be apparent that patent holders have used their rights to monpolize a market. But, absent such an elaborate scheme, it is often hard to determine when an arrangement goes beyond those rights that patents are intended to confer.

Perhaps the primary problem with the present patent system is its rigidity. All patents have the same legal status, whether they are trivial or significant. Accordingly, all may be used with equal force to impose restrictions through licensing provisions. The use of a trivial patent to impose important restrictions is not uncommon, and this aspect of the system demands reform.

Numerous reform of the patent system have been suggested, and it would take a rash person to claim that the system cannot be improved. Most observers agree that upgrading standards of patentability and eliminating duplication would be desirable, provided, of course, that this can be done at reasonable cost. Some have argued that the duration of the patent grant is excessive, and ought to be shortened, either across-the-board or selectively (with less important patents receiving shorter protection). It also has been proposed that since one purpose of patents is to improve actual technology, the protection be tied to use of the invention—an appealing notion, but one likely to encounter significant implementation difficulties.

As is frequently the case with public policy, evaluation of the patent system is no simple matter. Economic analysis clearly identifies the benefits and costs of the system, but tells us nothing about their relative magnitudes, either in toto or at the margin. The essential difficulty is that we cannot know how much invention and innovation would have occurred without the system, but with all other things the same; thus we cannot be sure how much progress the system "buys" us. Some experienced observers voice skepticism about the probable net benefits, but hard and precise measures are lacking.[61]

SUMMARY

This discussion has not attempted to survey all exceptions to a procompetitive policy in the United States.[62] Even within the relatively small group of significant exceptions that have been discussed, there is little homogeneity. The reasons for exempting particular groups or activities vary widely, as do the exemptions themselves. But if the situations differ, the questions that need to be asked about each do not. Any exemption from antitrust prosecution implies the possibility of a

[61] See, for example, F. M. Scherer, *Industrial Market Structure and Economic Performance* (Chicago: Rand McNally, 1980), Chapter 16.

[62] For a fuller discussion of the issues in some regulated sectors, see Almarin Phillips (Ed.), *Promoting Competition in Regulated Markets* (Washington, D.C: Bookings Institution, 1975).

reduction in competitive vigor. A sensible policy must proceed to grant exception only where such a possibility can be justified.

If there is a generally applicable criticism that may be made of antitrust exemptions, it is that the justification for a competitive loss is often vague. In the case of fair trade, for example, this was because the purely intuitive arguments for exemption are unconvincing. In the case of patents, the intuitive arguments are plausible, but the magnitude of gain and loss that we reap from the system is unknown. The justification for exempted industries and unions tends to be unclear on both counts; that is, the arguments that regulation of some sort ought to supersede competition are conceptually shaky, and evidence on the magnitudes of gain and loss is lacking.

There have been some changes in attitudes toward antitrust exemption in recent decades that are, on balance, likely desirable. The courts view claims of antitrust immunity with consistent skepticism. Not only is regulated status *per se* a weak reed upon which to rest a claim for exemption, but the value of regulation itself has been widely reassessed. Arguments for the regulation of industries such as airlines, trucking, and television simply are not the same today as they were when the regulatory systems were instituted. This does not necessarily mean that we have ''too much'' regulation, but may well indicate that the type of regulation we have has become anachronistic.

In order to grant any type of antitrust immunity, sensibly it is necessary to make two showings: first, that there exist identifiable benefits associated with such a move (i.e., we do not grant immunity without reasons); and second, that the benefits are expected to outweigh any anticipated costs of decreased competition. The latter showing, which is necessarily empirical, has not been attempted regularly, in large part because relevant magnitudes are difficult to measure.

The pertinent question at this point concerns the kinds of decisions that we ought to make, given existing uncertainty. Suppose that we grant antitrust exemptions and then discover that we have made a mistake. Is this preferable to not granting exemptions and finding out that we were wrong? At the very least, this is the kind of question that might usefully be asked. For if it is not, we may give up on competition in areas where its merits are in fact substantial.

CHAPTER 18

Some Evaluations of Antitrust Policies

Although simple characterizations of antitrust are impossible, it would be inappropriate to conclude without some assessments. Do the current "rules of the game," developed largely by the courts, make economic sense? Is the effect of enforcement on the economy salutary or deleterious? Or is it perhaps imperceptible? Such questions are important and demand attention even if satisfactory answers are difficult to find.

THE MEANINGS OF COMPETITION IN ANTITRUST POLICY

We have noted at many points that the ostensible purpose of antitrust policy is to enourage a system of competitive markets. Indeed, if one accepts the statements of judges and other public officials, there has been little deviation in policy from this noble objective. The difficulty, as we have also noted, is that the term **competition** carries different meanings, and a wide variety of policies can be justified in its name.

We have now had close to a century of experience under the Sherman Act, and almost three quarters of a century with the Clayton Act. It might be thought that in this time some definitions of competition and monopoly would have won broad acceptance. In fact, however, this is not the case. The points of disagreement over these terms are perhaps better clarified now than they were a few decades ago, but the disagreements themselves persist.

Legal–Economic Dichotomies

In a classic article written many years ago, Edward S. Mason pointed out that lawyers and economists use the word **monopoly** (and therefore the word **competition**) in very different ways.[1] The term monopoly as used in the law, Mason noted, is "a standard of evaluation." It is used simply to designate situations that are not in the public interest; competition, the antithesis of monopoly, designates situations that are in the public interest. In economics, on the other hand, monopoly and competi-

---

[1] "Monopoly in Law and Economics," *Yale Law Journal*, **47** (1937), 34–49.

tion are used as tools of analysis, rather than simply as labels for "bad" or "good" market situations.

It would be inaccurate to state that lawyers and economists are homogeneous groups, each holding identical views of competition and monopoly. Mason's dichotomy between "legal" and "economic" concepts, was thus an oversimplification of sorts; yet it retains relevance today. Under the legal approach, monopoly consists of restriction—some limitation on the freedom of business units to engage in legitimate economic activity. The economic definition of monopoly, on the other hand, is related to control—the power of business units to influence the terms at which they sell goods and services.

The difference between these views is evident, yet neither implies an obviously correct basis for public policy. If we ask what each view contributes to policy formulation, it appears that the legal outlook carries at least two important virtues: certainty and simplicity. Few persons doubt that the elimination of restrictive practices is beneficial, both on economic and other grounds. Furthermore, restrictive practices frequently are easy to identify and thus to act against. The kind of policy that follows from the legal standard, then, is straightforward and, in an important sense, workable.

The economic view of monopoly carries neither of these virtues. Market power or control in the broadest sense may be easy to identify; indeed, there exists some control whenever the conditions of pure competition are absent, although specifying its degree may be difficult.[2] But within rather broad limits, the mere existence of control carries no certain policy implications. When a powerful firm or group is observed, the relevant question for policy becomes: what is the source of that power? As we have seen, this question can be extraordinarily difficult to answer; yet without an answer, the nature of an appropriate public response is unclear. It is for this reason, as Mason pointed out, that economic contributions to antitrust policy have been largely negative. The analysis casts considerable doubt on the adequacy of the purely legal approach, but fails to provide a complete alternative.

Competition as a Good Conduct Phenomenon: The Sherman Act Approach

What Mason termed the legal view of monopoly has won substantial acceptance in the enforcement of sections 1 and 2 of the Sherman Act. Under current judicial interpretation, restraints of trade and attempts to monopolize are defined to mean particular restrictive practices. Even the fait accompli of illegal monopolization, as we have seen, has been viewed by the courts as something necessarily attributable to past business conduct. In very extreme cases of market dominance, a company may be found to violate the law even though it was relatively well behaved; yet even here the courts have found it nesessary to show the existence of some kind of restrictive action in the company's history.

---

[2] Franklin M. Fisher's discussion of the problem is worth reading. "Diagnosing Monopoly," *Quarterly Review of Economics and Business*, **19** (April 1979), 7–33.

Present Sherman Act standards thus parallel Mason's legal definition of monopoly, although some attention has of course been devoted to the economic aspect as well. If, for example, a company is charged with monopolization, a court will seek to determine whether its market position justifies the accusation. But market position, while sometimes necessary to sustain a monopolization charge, has in no case been sufficient grounds for establishment of a violation. There is apparently no way in which market power, taken alone, can breach the law.

The strongest challenge to this conduct-oriented approach is represented by the conscious parallelism reasoning of the late 1940s. Under a strict parallelism doctrine, a violation of law would continue to depend upon observed conduct; but the point at which conduct would imply illegality would be quite different from what it is today. Coordinated behavior still has a place in the law, but its role has diminished. The courts may one day turn back in the direction of the stricter parallelism approach, but we have come a long way from the days when writers believed that parallel behavior among competitors was, by itself, virtually illegal.

Economic criticisms of Sherman Act interpretation properly focus not so much on what the law does as on what it neglects to do. There is wide, although not universal,[3] agreement that a *per se* approach toward conspiratorial conduct is justified. To the extent that conspiracy is effective, the chance for vigorous price competition is reduced. There is some evidence which suggests that price fixing is often ineffective, yet even if this were inevitably the case, the effort is so flagrantly anticompetitive that *per se* prohibitions might still be justified.

In addition, *per se* is a quite certain and easily administered rule, and its effectiveness in barring formal and overt conspiracy is seen by some economists as the major achievement of American antitrust policy.[4] Reservations about Sherman Act policy therefore tend to focus not so much on what the law does as on what it may fail to do. The Act makes monopoly illegal only if firms behave in "restrictive" or othewise anticompetitive ways. Yet we have seen as early as Chapter 1 that some of the probems posed by monopoly are independent of the particular stratagems adopted by the monopolist.

Since the law focuses primarily on the stratagems, it is not surprising to find that some economists are critical of Sherman Act enforcement.[5] There are, however, two qualifications that serve somewhat to mitigate criticism. The first is that legal standards are not rigid or constant over time. As both Judge Hand and Judge Wyzanski have shown, the Sherman Act can be interpreted in ways more consistent with economic notions of competition and monopoly, and nothing that the courts

---

[3] See Donald Dewey, "Information, Entry and Welfare: the Case for Collusion," *American Economic Review,* 69 (September 1979), 587–594.

[4] See Donald Dewey, *Monopoly in Economics and Law* (Chicago: Rand McNally, 1959), p. 305; and Richard A. Posner, *Antitrust Policy* (Chicago: University of Chicago Pres, 1976), p. 39.

[5] Indeed, an economist could hardly find the Sherman Act approach fully satisfactory unless it is believed that monopoly in the economic sense can arise **only** through illegal behavior. If this were the case, then economic monopoly could not exist unless a company engaged in practices that violate the Sherman Act; in which case it would be prosecuted. Unfortunately, it is difficult to place full confidence in such a doctrine.

have said recently precludes future movement in this direction. If judges have failed to embrace economic concepts in monopolization proceedings, they have not yet made it impossible for this to occur.

The second, and perhaps more compelling, qualification follows from the observation that economic analysis does not provide a ready-made alternative to present policy. If we were to use the Sherman Act to curtail monopoly in a strict economic sense, the results would be difficult to imagine. Under a literal interpretation, for example, the law might be invoked against any firm with a perceptible degree of market power—not a course that any sensible economist would recommend.

Competition as a Structural Condition: The Section 7 (Clayton Act) Approach

If competition has been defined in a legalistic fashion under the Sherman Act, its fate in merger cases has been substantially different. Horizontal mergers have been judged on a largely structural basis and usually have been found illegal when an increase in the centralization of market power is a possible result. The test for vertical mergers has been the degree to which customers or suppliers would be foreclosed from the part of the market represented by one of the merging firms. Our limited experience with conglomerates provides no sharp expectation. Early legal decisions such as *Procter & Gamble*[6] suggested that anticompetitive implications might be found in the overall size of the emergent firm; but more recent cases make it appear that the Supreme Court will not likely move in this direction, at least in the foreseeable future.[7]

Although the tendency of the courts to emphasize the structural effects of merger is in accord with economic notions of competition and monopoly, we have already noted some difficulties with this approach. Two particular problems (discussed in Chapter 9) are pertinent.

1. Simple structural tests may become overly rigid as the courts search for broadly applicable rules of thumb. The underlying problem is that structure alone is not a precise predictor of market behavior.
2. An emphasis on structure may be used to preclude other relevant information about merger effects. Efficiencies are the prime example. As we have seen, the Supreme Court at one time went so far as to suggest that efficiency-creating mergers might be undesirable because the merged firm would gain ''competitive advantages'' over rivals.[8]

---

[6]*Procter & Gamble Co. versus Federal Trade Commission*, 386 U.S. 568 (1967).

[7] A question of equal practical importance is whether the executive branch of government will prosecute large conglomerate mergers. In 1981 the Department of Justice ''cleared'' du Pont's acquisition of Conoco, that is, informed the companies that it would not be challenged under the antitrust laws. A merger of this size clearly would have been suspect—and quite possibly would have been found to violate Section 7—under the standards applied by the Supreme Court during the 1960s.

[8]*Brown Shoe Co. v. U.S.*, 370 U.S. 294 (1962).

The validity of these criticisms will be assessed differently by different individuals. The Supreme Court has very likely denied some mergers that would not have lessened competition perceptibly. Yet the Court must consider not only the immediate effects of its decisions but also their implications as future precedent. It is possible, for example, that 1 merger will not affect competition in an industry, but that 20 similar mergers would do so adversely. The dilemma of a court in this situation is a real one. To prohibit the merger is to act against an occurrence that is benign, and therefore by all logic legal; but to approve the merger may open the gates to future acquisitions which, in toto, damage competition substantially.

The nature of an "appropriate" public merger policy remains controversial and uncertain. Some observers believe that only horizontal acquisitions present a threat to competition;[9] and that vertical and conglomerate marriages therefore ought to be left alone. Others contend that all large mergers, by increasing the aggregate concentration of corporate wealth in the nation, may do great social damage—even if their purely economic effects are not easily defined.[10] Proponents of both viewpoints stress their concern with the protection of "competition." On this basis alone, it is apparent that no consensus about the meaning or measurement of competition yet exists.

Protection of Competition Versus Protection of Competitors

As we have noted earlier, some observers of antitrust have accused the courts of acting to protect the interests of competitors rather than competition. This issue arises largely in connection with the Clayton Act prohibitions that apply to certain actions only if their effect may be substantially to lessen competition. The courts are therefore required to consider not only the nature of the behavior in question, but also its competitive impact.

It is clear that the courts have frequently considered competitive effects in terms of the fortunes of affected competitors. In price-discrimination cases, a primary question is whether the behavior at issue has made it more difficult for discriminated-against firms to operate successfully . Similarly, a major consideration in tying and exclusive dealing litigation has been the "competitive disadvantage" incurred by those firms that are excluded from some portion of the market. Even in merger cases the courts have been concerned with the prospects of companies that would remain in competition with the merged firm. In general, the imposition of competitive disadvantages on specific firms has been taken by the courts as a strong indication that competition may be lessened.

This sort of approach is not especially controversial so long as harm to firms flows from behavior of an anticompetitive nature. Actions that in fact restrict competition by doing damage to competitors are not uncommon. Controversy arises when firms are harmed by practices that are not obviously anticompetitive; and it is

---

[9]For example, Robert H. Bork, *The Antitrust Paradox* (New York: Basic Books, 1978).

[10]See, generally, Mark J. Green, "The High Cost of Monopoly," *The Progressive*, **36** (March 1972), 15–19.

heightened when damage to firms is inflicted by behavior that itself reflects competition. A classic example of conflict occurs whenever a company achieves efficiencies that its rivals cannot match. Increased efficiency implies social benefits; but it must also hurt those firms that have not become more efficient.

Competition at times hurts competitors. Anticompetitive behavior also can hurt competitors. In Clayton Act cases, the courts have at times failed to inquire carefully into the origins of harm to competitors. Rather, they have tended to assume implicitly that such damage, **whatever its cause,** is a uniformly unhealthy event.

Have the courts, then, been acting in an unwise and unsound way? Some will conclude that the answer is yes, but the issue is not a simple one. We must again return to the question of society's priorities. Perhaps the community wishes to protect competitors, even if they are inefficient. There is nothing in economics that condemns this objective, although the objective ought not to be confused with protection of **competition.** The problem with our legal treatment is not that a necessarily "bad" goal has been pursued; but, rather, that the pursuit of a goal proceeds without much explicit effort to assess its economic cost.

Summary

That "competition" has no single, well-defined meaning in antitrust is perhaps more a symptom than a cause of policy confusion. Competition and monopoly are treated primarily as phenomena of conduct under the Sherman Act and of structure under the Clayton Act. The mere fact that treatments of the terms differ is not surprising, for the purposes of the laws are not identical. The Sherman Act tends to deal with flagrantly anticompetitive practices, often promulgated by firms holding substantial market power; the Clayton Act, on the other hand, addresses borderline practices that may not be inevitably anticompetitive, and mergers, whose effect may be to create market power where it did not previously exist.

In light of this simplified dichotomy it is not necessarily appropriate that both laws view competition and monopoly in the same way. The existence of different definitions is less troublesome than the shortcomings of each definition taken alone. Under present construction of the Sherman Act, an effectively monopolized industry need not violate the law; while under the Clayton Act, events that reflect competition may be said to lessen competition if they damage the interests of some firms. This does not imply that the laws in general work poorly, but it does indicate that our legal system has not yet come to grips with some rather basic questions.

THE EFFECTIVENESS OF ANTITRUST POLICY

The effectiveness of American antitrust policy is, of course, related to judicial interpretations of law, but also depends heavily upon other factors. The vigor with which federal agencies, especially the Department of Justice and Federal Trade Commission, enforce the laws is highly significant, as is the receptiveness of the courts to the agencies' arguments and proposed remedies. Moreover, the magnitude of resources devoted to the program is important, for even the most stringent interpretation of law would mean little without broad enforcement.

Clues to Effectiveness

A common problem besets efforts to measure the effects of any economic policy. Since so many variables are changing at once, it is difficult to isolate that portion of the behavior of relevant factors which is attributable to policy actions. In the case of antitrust policy, the measurement problem is compounded, for the variables that reflect the impact of policy are themselves hard to define. Assessments of monetary or fiscal policies, for example, can proceed by examining the behavior of income and price levels, the elements that those policies seek to affect. But the element that antitrust policy seeks to affect—the competitiveness of the economy—is not subject to precise measurement.

The subject thus appears inhospitable to direct empirical evaluation, yet a few interesting investigations have been undertaken. George J. Stigler, in what remains the most comprehensive effort to date, was able to report only "meagre and undogmatic" conclusions[11]: (1) the Sherman Act has had "only a very modest effect" in holding down concentration; (2) the Celler–Kefauver amendment has had a "strongly adverse effect" on horizontal mergers, a pattern seen clearly in Chapter 14; and (3) Sherman Act enforcement has "reduced the amount and effects of collusion."

Examinations by Feinberg[12] and by Block, Nold, and Sidak,[13] have found some antitrust impact on the behavior of affected industries; and also an indication of deterrent effects, whereby policy action in one area may discourage would-be violators elsewhere. Direct measurement of the magnitudes of antitrust impact on the American economy, however, remains an undeveloped art.

Since direct estimates are difficult, some investigators have tried instead to draw inferences about likely policy results from the nature of enforcement efforts. This is hardly an ideal procedure—in effect it examines inputs in order to say something about outputs—yet some interesting observations have been made.

If one looks, for example, at the "quantity" of federal enforcement, the numbers are unimpressive. Total budgets for the major agencies were under $80 million in the late 1970s, a rather paltry sum for a national law enforcement effort. Furthermore, the number of cases filed is small. Richard A. Posner has reported that during the 1960s, for example, the Department of Justice instituted an average of 41 antitrust cases annually, and the Federal Trade Commission another 13 or 14 (exclusive of Robinson-Patman Act filings).[14] Even a staunch believer in the deterrent effects

[11] "The Economic Effects of the Antitrust Laws," *Journal of Law and Economics,* **9** (October 1956), 225–258.

[12] Robert M. Feinberg, "Antitrust Enforcement and Subsequent Price Behavior," *Review of Economics and Statistics,* **62** (November 1980).

[13] Michael Kent Block, Frederick Carl Nold, and Joseph Gregory Sidak, "The Deterrent Effects of Antitrust Enforcement," *Journal of Political Economy,* **89** (June 1981), 429–445.

[14] "A Statistical Study of Antitrust Enforcement," *Journal of Law & Economics,* **13** (October 1970), 365–419.

of policy will have some difficulty arguing that such a program has a large impact on the shape of the economy. Indeed, it is private rather than public actions that have increasingly come to dominate the antitrust scene.

When one attempts to look at the quality, as opposed to the quantity, of enforcement, no clear picture emerges. Posner concludes his painstaking statistical study by stating that the agencies "are ignoring the prerequisites . . . of serious planning."[15] There are suspicions, perhaps quite widespread, that government antitrust officials act haphazardly from an economic standpoint, more concerned with the "won–lost record" than with effects on economic welfare; and that the government is consistently overmatched in its confrontations with affluent corporate defendants. While these suspicions may be both strong and plausible, it must be pointed out that they are difficult to document in an objective fashion.[16]

Quantitative evidence on patterns of antitrust enforcement tends to be inconclusive. Long, Schramm, and Tolison have found, for example, that industry welfare losses—estimates of the "deadweight" triangle—do a poor job of explaining case-bringing activity by the Department of Justice.[17] Cases, in other words, do not center in those industries whose characteristics suggest heavy monopoly costs, although more cases are filed in larger industries (measured by dollar sales). John Siegfried has concluded after extending the Long–Schramm–Tollison analysis that "economic variables have little influence" on Depatment case-selection policies,"[18] but there are difficult problems in attempting to move from broad statistical evidence to definitive statements about the nature of policy criteria.[19]

Among policymakers it is an article of faith that the unseen (deterrent) effects of antitrust are extremely important, comparable in magnitude to the underside of an iceberg whose size can only be imperfectly imagined from above the surface. They could be correct, but the proposition simply is not yet a demonstrable one.

The Problem of Remedies

A distinctive aspect of antitrust effectiveness has to do with the sanctions that are imposed once a violation of law is found to exist; and with the terms on which "out of court" settlements are reached by mutual consent of the parties to a legal proceeding. Obviously a determination that the law has been breached is likely to mean

---

[15]Ibid., p. 418.

[16]For pertinent discussions, see William G. Shepherd and Clair Wilcox, *Public Policies Toward Business* (Homewood, Ill.: R. D. Irwin, 6th Ed., 1979), Chapters 4 and 9; and Suzanne Weaver, *The Decision to Prosecute* (Cambridge, Mass.: Massachusettts Institute of Technology Press, 1977).

[17]William F. Long, Richard Schramm, and Robert Tollison, "The Economic Determinants of Antitrust Activity," *Journal of Law & Economics,* **16** (October 1973), 351–364.

[18]John J. Siegfried, "The Determinants of Antitrust Activity," *Journal of Law & Economics,* **18** (October 1975), 559–574.

[19]See, for instance, Peter Asch, "The Determinants and Effects of Antitrust Activity," *Journal of Law & Economics,* **18** (October 1975), 575–581.

little if no effective action follows.[20] It is necesary to find a remedy that, ideally, will ensure that repetition of the violation does not occur.

Several kinds of remedies are commonly employed in antitrust proceedings. In criminal cases, often involving conspiracy, fines are typically imposed upon those found guilty of Sherman Act violations. The maximum fine was increased in 1974 from $50,000 to $1 million per violation for corporations, and from $50,000 to $100,000 for individuals. Actual fines, however, tend to be much smaller. The most important potential penalty in many cases is provided by the private treble-damage action, which may be invoked by anyone who suffers economic loss as a result of the illegal act. Although the determination of damages is an uncertain art, the sums that may be recovered from defendants are frequently much greater than the fines levied under the law. Sherman Act violations are now treated as felonies, with maximum prison sentences of three years; but the use of imprisonment as an antitrust tool is rare.

Another category of remedy deals directly with the behavior of offending companies and, less frequently, with the structural environment in which violations have occurred. Illegal action frequently results in an injunction to discontinue the practice in question. At times, however, it is doubtful whether such a restriction, even if it is combined with other, positive conduct requirements, is sufficient. The nature of an appropriate remedy obviously depends upon the violation that has occurred. In cases of patent abuse, the courts may impose compulsory licensing requirements. The obvious remedy in cases of illegal merger is prohibition of the merger, or divestiture if it has already been consummated. And where illegal conduct such as price discrimination or tying arrangements is the issue, conduct prohibitions may be appropriate.

Many economists have long regarded remedies as the weakest link in antitrust enforcement,[21] and some useful analyses and suggestions for improvement have appeared in recent years.[22] One approach is to treat an antitrust violation much like any other crime. It is a socially costly act that can in principle be deterred by making it sufficiently expensive to would-be violators. The policy task is then to define the socially correct level of deterrence, and to establish the penalty structure that will bring it about.

Some writers argue that a system of fines is the efficient course of action; that is, an antitrust conviction would be followed by monetary penalties (possibly to the exclusion of any other punishment) geared to the social cost of the violation in question. Readers familiar with issues of environmental policy will note that this is somewhat akin to levying a tax on pollution. The immensely difficult task would be

---

[20]Determination that a violation exists may itself be significant if the action or situation in question was not previously known to be illegal. In general, however, the fact that a court defines something as illegal probably is not a sufficient remedy.

[21]Mark S. Massel, for example, has spoken of legal decrees written on the basis of "hunches" and without provision for review of their effects. *Competition and Monopoly* (Washington, D.C.: Brookings Institution, 1962), pp. 97ff.

[22]See, especially, Kenneth G. Elzinga and William Breit, *The Antitrust Penalties* (New Haven: Yale University Press, 1976).

to determine the appropriate size of fines[23]; yet it may be that even if the optimal set eluded us, we could devise a system that would improve on present arrangements.

One difficulty that a system of fines might not solve involves violations of law that relate to the market power of defendant firms. Fines will deter acts, that is, specific manifestations of conduct. But as we have argued earlier, certain competitive problems may inhere in the structure of a market. If this is the situation, it may do us little good to tinker with conduct, for conduct itself is not the problem.

A prime case in point is the *American Tobacco* decision of 1946.[24] Although the Big Three cigarette manufacturers were found guilty of monopolizing trade, the only sanctions imposed were a series of fines that left the closely coordinated group intact. The size of the fines may have been "wrong," that is, inappropriate to the social cost of the violation; but no set of fines would have disturbed the structural interdependence that produced noncompetitive behavior in this market.

What the appropriate remedy would have been is unclear. To break up the convicted companies—an obvious possibility whenever concentrated power is at the root of the problem—might not have worked well. Physical facilities would have been easy to duplicate, and the companies' power was not a function of their physical size. Rather, it appeared, the position of the Big Three was tied to public loyalty to the existing brands of cigarettes. Conceivably the power concentration could have been reduced by requiring divestiture of brand names, or perhaps by placing future limits on advertising, the primary source of the brand loyalty. Such potentially useful procedures were not adopted, however, and a landmark legal victory for the government produced virtually no meaningful change in the condition of the affected industry.

The *Tobacco* case was unusual in that the ordinary kinds of remedies would have been ineffective. In many instances, however, the obvious remedy of dissolution is passed over in favor of pure conduct requirements. A notable example is the 1956 consent decree agreed to in *United States versus Western Electric Co. and American Telephone and Telegraph Co.*[25] The Department of Justice, acting under a recent Supreme Court ruling,[26] sought to require A.T.&T. To divest itself of Western Electric, the telephone company's equipment-producing subsidiary. The government's hope was that Western could be split into three companies that would then compete in selling to A.T.&T. At the time of the proceedings, Western was the only significant supplier of telephone equipment. The actual decree effected none of these basic structural changes. Instead, strict constraints were placed upon the companies' future behavior.

More recently, however (in January 1982), the Department of Justice and A.T.&T. entered into a settlement of a government monopolization case that will

---

[23]For informative discussions, see Elzinga and Breit, ibid., Chapter 7; and Richard A. Posner, footnote 4, pp. 221–226. The difficulty, as Posner points out, is greater than that of defining appropriate taxes on pollution.

[24]*American Tobacco Co. v. U.S.*, 328 U.S. 781 (1946). For discussion of this case, refer to Chapter 12.

[25]Civil Action No. 17-49 (D. Ct. N.J., 1956).

[26]*U.S. v. Pullman Co.*, 330 U.S. 806 (1947).

produce structrual change. A.T.&T. agreed to divest itself of local operating companies that controlled about two thirds of the corporation's assets. The ultimate effects of this agreement on competition in telephone communication and other markets are uncertain, but important shifts in both structure and behavior may well occur.

The courts have occasionally imposed conduct-oriented remedies that provide for later review of structural conditions. This was done in the *United Shoe* case, and the effects of Judge Wyzanski's 1953 order were the subject of a hearing in 1964. At the hearing, the government requested that United be broken into two companies; while the company asked for modification of certain conduct provisions in the earlier order. Judge Wyzansky denied both requests, finding that competitive conditions in the shoe machinery industry had improved substantially; but was reversed by the Supreme Court, which held that the government was entitled to structural relief.[27]

In two notable cases, *United States v. Eastman Kodak Co.*[28] and *United States v. International Business Machines Corp.*,[29] consent decrees were entered requiring specific conduct; but providing explicitly that divestiture would be required in the future if satisfactory structural conditions were not attained. The *Eastman* decree required that company to split the tie-in between its color film and color film-processing activites. Eastman would be required to divest itself 7 years hence of any processing facilities in excess of 50 percent of national capacity; but divestiture would not be required if in 6 years it were shown that purchasers of Eastman color film had easy access to processors other than Eastman.[30] Divestiture was not required; in 1961 both the government and the company agreed that independent processors had captured more than 50 percent of the market.

The *IBM* consent decree was in some ways similar to *Eastman*. IBM had been alleged to hold about 90 percent of the tabulating-card market for computing machines in 1952. A consent decree required that the company follow specified conditions of conduct: machines were to be offered for sale or lease; IBM was not to purchase used machines; its lease periods were limited to 1 year for a period of 10 years; and its patents were to be licensed at reasonable terms to new competitors. The decree provided, however, that IBM would divest itself of any card manufacturing capacity in excess of 50 percent of national capacity, unless it could show, 7 years hence, that "substantial competitive conditions exist. . . ." In 1963, IBM was required to divest itself of 16 card printing presses. According to at least one observer, however, the original decree had already resulted in "an impressive improvement in structure and in economic performance. . . ."[31]

---

[27] *U.S. v. United Shoe Machinery Corp.*, 391 U.S. 244 (1968).

[28] Trade Cas. Par. 67,920 (W.D.N.Y., 1954).

[29] Trade Cas. Par. 68,245 (S.D.N.Y., 1956).

[30] In addition to splitting the tie-in, Eastman was required to license its processing patents at "reasonable" and "nondiscriminatory" royalty rates, thereby hopefully encouraging new entrants.

[31] William Lee Baldwin, "The Feedback Effects of Business Conduct on Industry Structure," *Journal of Law & Economics,* **12** (April 1969), 123–154.

How serious is the problem of inadequate remedies in antitrust cases involving substantial market power? Economists divide on this issue, as we have seen at several points. Some contend that power or structure by itself is seldom (if ever) the problem; if so, then remedies designed to restrict abusive conduct, while leaving structure untouched, may well suffice. Others assert that concentrated power is itself the problem in some instances; if so, conduct limitations are an exercise in futility.

Observers such as Baldwin, however, present a somewhat more optimistic scenario.[32] Conduct remedies may have beneficial ("feedback") effects on market structure. Where this is the case, problems related to market power may be eased by remedies that do not attack that power directly. The strict "structuralists" who argue for dissolution of monopolistic firms have ignored or underestimated such effects and are thus prone to depict the remedy situation as worse than it is.

Whatever one's view, the devising of appropriate remedies in power-related cases involves practical as well as conceptual problems. Even if dissolution is in principle the "proper" remedy in some cases, firms are often difficult to break up. The government has at times requested the dissolution remedy, yet been unable to produce a "workable" scheme that would clearly reduce a company's power, yet clearly not harm its efficiency. When this sort of difficulty is combined with the typical reluctance of the courts to tamper with existing concerns, the general lack of "strong" structural remedies is not hard to understand.

The identification of an antitrust violation and the formulation of a remedy for that violation are separate problems, but in reality they are not always considered independently. In some instances, poor prospects for remedying a situation may influence the findings with respect to legality. This is a natural interaction since a finding of illegality may be insignificant (and courts may be reluctant to reach it) if the possibilities for a useful remedy are poor.

PROPOSALS FOR ANTITRUST REFORM

Despite the uncertainties surrounding American antitrust policy, condemnation and calls for substantive reform have been commonplace for several decades. Suggestions for major change have tended to cluster around two rather extreme positions that are worthy of brief attention.

At one end are those who view most antitrust activity as an unwarranted intrusion in the marketplace. The reform commonly proposed by this group is a severe curtailment of public policy enforcement. Some suggest that antitrust challenges be confined to only two types of business conduct: explicit collusion and flagrant predatory conduct.

---

[32] Ibid. See also Don E. Waldman, *Antitrust Action and Market Structure* (Lexington Books, 1978). Waldman presents case studies that suggest that antitrust action frequently affects market structure and performance indirectly, and thus is independent of the remedy employed. Indirect effects might even appear where the government loses an action and no remedy is imposed.

The reasoning behind such proposals is not uniform. Some individuals argue simply that "the market" is the ideal mechanism for economic decision making, and ought to be left free to work its will.[33] The possibility that the market will fail in one way or another may be conceded in principle, but the strong presumption is that things work correctly. In this view, which we have seen in earlier discussions, business managers pursue efficient types of behavior (and know far more about what is efficient than any public official). For government to restrict these efforts, except for the isolated instances in which the behavior becomes clearly anticompetitive, is thus to interfere with efficiency and to harm economic performance.

Others who suggest curtailment of antitrust policy argue on different grounds. Some believe, for example, that antitrust policy is totally ineffective and thus a sham; better, then, to do away with it rather than continue the pretense that we exercise real control over the power and conduct of our major corporations. Still others would admit that antitrust policy produces some benefits and conclude, nevertheless, that in a period of severe economic difficulty—inflation, slow growth, stagnant productivity, potential energy disruptions, and so on—corporate managements must be left as free as possible to devise new "solutions."

At the other end of the debate are those who contend that antitrust policy has failed by doing too little. The laws, in other words, have not "worked," because they have not been pushed far enough to produce a truly competitive market system. The central problem in this view is that existing power is untouched by antitrust policy, which operates to curb only certain abuses of that power.[34]

This position, frequently associated with the "structuralists," has produced several similar reform proposals during the past 40 years. In 1973, for example, the late Senator Philip Hart introduced the "Industrial Reorganization Act."[35] This bill, like its earlier counterparts, would have made the "possession of monopoly power" by a corporation illegal. Such power could be inferred from high profits (a post-tax return on net worth of more than 15 percent in 5 of the 7 previous years); from high market concentration (a top-four concentration ratio of 50 percent or more "in any line of commerce in any section of the country"); or from an absence of "substantial price competition" in any defined market. Companies found to possess "monopoly power" would be required to divest themselves of such power unless they could show either that valid patents were the sole source of their strength, or that divestiture would imply the loss of "substantial economies."

This type of proposal, which would clearly change existing law dramatically, has never made much headway in Congress, and its future prospects seem dim. It has,

---

[33] This position is sometimes identified with the "Chicago School" in economics. Representative writings by some leading advocates include John S. McGee, *In Defense of Industrial Concentration* (New York: Praeger, 1971); Harold Demsetz, "Two Systems of Belief About Monopoly," in Harvey J. Goldschmid, H. Michael Mann, and J. Fred Weston (Eds.), *Industrial Concentration: The New Learning* (Boston: Little, Brown, 1974); Robert H. Bork, footnote 9; and Yale Brozen, "The Concentration–Collusion Doctrine," in Eleanor M. Fox (Ed.), *Industrial Concentration and the Market System* (Section of Antitrust Law, American Bar Association, 1979).

[34] See, for example, Walter Adams, "Corporate Power and Economic Apologetics," in Goldschmid, Mann, and Weston, ibid.; and Mark J. Green, footnote 10.

[35] S. 1167, March 12, 1973.

however, demonstrated remarkable persistence, and we may well see it again in somewhat varied forms.[36]

Do economic analysis and existing evidence provide a clear choice between these positions? It is tempting to observe that both positions are extreme, and the wise course probably lies "in between." But while this observation is accurate, it is not terribly useful: since the two schools of thought are diametrically opposed, the ground "in between" is vast, and there is no obvious point of compromise.

One view holds that almost all business conduct—and any concentration of power—should be presumed "good" and left intact, except perhaps in unusual circumstances. The other view simply reverses the presumption: power is "bad" and will be tolerated only in unusual circumstances. If economic analysis and evidence tell us anything, however, it is that few activities or situations can usefully be termed "good" or "bad." Most events are mixed. We seldom see only benefits or only costs.

The policy question remains, however, and it is a critical one: which way should we tilt? Where should the burden of proof lie? Should we presume that power, where we observe it, is justified unless compelling evidence to the contrary can be produced? In a private enterprise economy, this is a plausible position that places the burden of proof on those who seek change. Yet one can also argue that in a democratic society some justification should be required for extensive and persistent concentrations of economic power. This would shift the burden of proof to defenders of the status quo.

The dilemma is not an easy one. And the answer, if one exists, may have to drawn from our values rather than from "objective" analysis.

SOME PLAUSIBLE INTERPRETATION OF ANTITRUST POLICY

Why has antitrust policy evolved to its present state? Is modern antitrust policy something that has come about through design or through blunder? Does it reflect values that society holds to be important, or does it reflect an incompetent search for those values? Such questions cannot be answered categorically, but some alternative suggestions may be offered.

As a Commitment to the Status Quo

American antitrust policy can be interpreted partially as a commitment to the status quo. A survey of the various branches of antitrust policy indicates that, whatever its positive acccomplishments may be, it has not often been a vehicle for sharp change. Indeed, it may be said to resist change quite effectively. That portion of the policy that is directed toward business conduct may have had the effect of reducing the

---

[36]The most recent versions have been termed "no fault" monopoly proposals. The basis suggestion, however, goes back at least to 1959, when Carl Kaysen and Donald F. Turner proposed legal limits on "unreasonable" power. *Antitrust Policy* (Harvard University Press, 1959).

frequency of conspiracy and other restrictive practices; however, it has stopped short of doing anything about the market conditions that make such practices possible. This may be a rational policy, for it is conceivable that the necessary alteration in market structures might do more harm than good. The thrust of policy, however, does not seem to have been based upon this kind of calculation. Rather, it appears that the courts and the federal agencies have been reluctant to tamper with existing firms and markets almost as a matter of ethical principle.

Even merger policy, perhaps the most significant area of antitrust policy in recent years, may be viewed as a commitment to resist change. If we are unwilling to attack established market positions under the Sherman Act, we seem also unwilling to permit the establishment or extension of new positions through merger. There are obvious inconsistencies implied by this dual standard. The dominant firm that attained its monopoly power long ago will not have its position challenged; but even a modest increment in power that would accrue to a nondominant firm through merger may not be permitted.

The Sherman and Clayton Act approaches may be reconciled partially when viewed as part of a broader program to retard major changes in the structure of markets. Despite this, the status quo interpretation of antitrust policy cannot be carried too far. The policies have not been designed to freeze existing market structures, and they have proven to be amenable to changes that come about in certain ways. What can be said is that the posture of antitrust with respect to structural change has been strongly conservative, so much so that the status quo seems to be valued to some extent for its own sake.

As the Product of an Inconclusive Economics

A second interpretation of antitrust policy is that it has sought primarily economic objectives but has been handicapped by a lack of economic guidelines. It is not unreasonable to suggest that the ultimate general goal of public competition policy has been good economic performance, subject to social and political constraints on the centralization of economic power.

If this be so, then the policymaker has received relatively little help from the economist. Traditional economic analysis suggests that optimal performance can be secured by establishing a regime of truly competitive markets, populated by relatively small and impotent firms. Once the impossibility of such a regime is conceded, however, the analysis does not provide clear choices among a large array of imperfect alternatives. The prime question is: to improve economic performance, should we rely upon competition among as many as possible (and as small as possible) business units in each industry; or should we rely upon the efficiency of fewer, larger firms?

Such a question cannot be answered on the basis of a priori reasoning. Rather, the answer lies in empirical analyses of what actually happens in different markets. As we have seen, a great deal of relevant information has been gathered, and some useful clues have emerged. Despite these clues, however, the evidence is still fragmentary and inconclusive; and it may be hypothesized that the absence of clear empirical distinctions has prevented policymakers from adopting a strong and consistent position on such basic matters as the treatment of industry concentration.

This interpretation of antitrust is not acceptable as a full explanation of policy evolution. It presupposes that our objectives are well defined and that policy is hindered only by an inability to predict which actions will best secure those objectives. Certainly this involves some overstatement of the clarity of policy priorities. It is true, nevertheless, that better notions of the economic implications of alternative policy actions would facilitate more rational choices.

As the Product of Conflicting and Ill-defined Goals

A third view of antitrust policy might stress the confusion in defining policy objectives rather than lack of economic information. Policy problems may not be a matter of knowing what we want to do but not having the information to do it; but, more simply, of *not* knowing what we want to do. This view has been touched upon in earlier chapters. The objectives of antitrust are clear only so long as they are stated in a general way. Once it is recognized that various objectives are competitive, some specification of priorities is necessary, and it is at this point that the clarity in defining goals breaks down. It is easy to support economic progress, optimal allocation of resources, equitable distribution of income, and economic freedom; and difficult to stipulate precisely the order and degree of preference among them.

One common conflict is our desire for both economic efficiency and narrow limits to the extent of market power. Another policy complication is imposed by a strong social emphasis on fairness that runs through antitrust enforcement. To some, the pursuit of fairness parallels the restriction of power; for it is the large and powerful who are seen to place "unfair" limits on the opportunities of rivals.

This consideration complicates further the definition of a consistent set of antitrust goals. Certainly we all want to be "fair." Who could possibly challenge the legitimacy of such a public policy objective? The issue, however, is not whether we should be fair, but rather what the word means and how far other objectives ought to be subordinated to this one.

A competitive market system is not inherently fair, if by fair we mean assuring all participants of success. Quite the contrary, it is the essence of the market that those who do not perform efficiently will be penalized by failure. The system is harsh, and we do many things publicly to mitigate its effects. But those who equate "competition" with "fairness" may need to redefine their terms.

As the Product of Ultimate Wisdom

Lest the preceding paragraphs appear too uniformly critical of antitrust policy, it must be noted that the policy can be, and perhaps ought to be, interpreted in a favorable way. If antimonopolization policies have been "weak," this may simply reflect society's view that we ought to proceed cautiously in treating established firms;

in light of our limited knowledge of the efficiency effects of dissolution, such caution may be justified. Similarly, if merger policy has been "strong," this may only follow from the view that the growth of firm size and power ought to be subject to certain market tests that mergers may avoid. Finally, stringent antitrust treatment of restrictive practices can be rationalized on the grounds that the practices may reduce the vigor of competition without being likely to aid efficiency.

A full defense of antitrust policy suggests that the policies, in fact, represent the wishes of society; and that the wishes themselves reflect a desirable reconciliation of objectives. Such arguments cannot be easily treated within the framework of an economic approach to public policy. The proposition that antitrust policy does what we, collectively, want it to do, cannot be proved or disproved; and there is no objective basis for analyzing the suggestion that what the policy does is, on various grounds, "good."

CONCLUSIONS

What then, is the sum and substance of antitrust policy? Many answers have been proposed. Some persons see modern antitrust as an unwarranted attack on bigness, an effort to protect small and inefficient firms from the rigors of the competitive wars. Others see a protectionist quality, but in reverse: antitrust policy simply protects existing market power from the aggressive growth of smaller competitors. Still others regard the modern corporation as virtually a public institution that long ago succeeded in liberating itself from the constraints of the marketplace, and thus from policies designed to alter the market.

The thrust of these diverse views is much the same: antitrust policy is a monumental irrelevancy. At best, it does nothing but squander a few million dollars of resources annually. At worst, it has the capacity for considerably more mischief.

It is easy, but not especially illuminating, to point out that these opinions are oversimplified. It is perhaps more pertinent to note that the world—our part of it, at least—has changed in ways that call into question the appropriateness of traditional policies. This is one factor that the authors above have in mind. Firms are not only bigger than they once were, they are more diversified. Such changes are fundamental. From the economist's standpoint, they not only make relevant information harder to obtain, but also greatly complicate the conceptualization and explanation of firms' behavior.

The economist's job is thus more difficult. In order to contribute usefully to policy, it is necessary to delineate the consequences of alternative public actions. But our older theories, based implicitly on the idea of single-product, profit-maximizing business units, may not prove adequate. If this is the case, a radical redirection of our thinking may be required before the contribution can be expanded much beyond its present bounds.

As we have noted at many points, ideal economic information is a necessary, but not sufficient, condition for rational public decision making. It will also be necessary to decide what kinds of economic results, and ultimately what kind of a society, we wish to have.

Name Index

Subject Index

Index of Legal Cases